BIOPHYSICS

Concepts and Mechanisms

REINHOLD BOOKS IN THE BIOLOGICAL SCIENCES

Consulting Editor

PROFESSOR PETER GRAY

Department of Biological Sciences
University of Pittsburgh
Pittsburgh, Pennsylvania

CONSULTING EDITOR'S STATEMENT

It is unfortunate that many students of biology regard biophysics as an esoteric and "difficult" subject. The introduction of Professor Casey's "Biophysics: Concepts and Mechanisms" to the REINHOLD BOOKS IN THE BIOLOGICAL SCIENCES should do much to dispel this view. Certainly, if every premedical student had a course in biophysics—and certainly no better book than Casey's exists for that purpose today—he would find his subsequent struggles with physiology enormously simplified. This is not to suggest that Professor Casey either dilutes or oversimplifies his subject. The simplicity of this book lies in the transcendent clarity and utter logic of the presentation. A brief introduction to the necessary mathematics starts the book. This leads to a discussion of the physical forces exemplified in man, of matter waves, electromagnetic radiations, and radioactivity as they apply to biological research. The author then passes to big molecules, and through them to an introduction to bioenergetics and the speed of biological processes. The chapter on biophysical studies on nerve and muscle that follows draws point to all that has come before. The chapters on ionizing radiations and biophysical control excellently round out the broad scope of the book. All this, it must again be emphasized, is couched in language intelligible to any interested science major. I feel confident that the physicist, clinician, and biologist will find this book an ideal synthesis of an exciting interdisciplinary science.

PETER GRAY

Pittsburgh, Pennsylvania
October, 1962

BIOPHYSICS

Concepts and Mechanisms

E. J. CASEY

University of Ottawa

Head, Power Sources Section
Defence Research Chemical Laboratories
Ottawa, Canada

REINHOLD PUBLISHING CORPORATION, NEW YORK

Chapman & Hall, Ltd., London

TO
MY WIFE, MARY
MY PARENTS
and
MY CHILDREN

Preface

This book is primarily intended to provide the student of biological sciences or of medicine with a substantial introduction into Biophysics. The subject matter, discussed in the Introduction, has been carefully chosen during ten years of teaching the subject. During this time the author has watched, in the literature, the subject begin to crystallize out from a rather nebulous mass of ideas and practices; and at the same time he has been able to observe what the students of this discipline require. Therefore, the book has been written with the needs of both student and teacher in mind, with the hope that this presentation of the choice of subject matter and the method of presenting it will be useful to others.

Three objectives have been kept in mind in the presentation: (1) to build up from the easy to the difficult; (2) to make the presentation interesting; and (3) to unify it. Accordingly, the book generally increases in difficulty from an oriented review with pertinent examples in the first part, through more difficult material in the middle and later parts. Occasional relaxations, which reduce the information rate and afford occasions for exemplification with biological material, are included. A rather vigorous insistence on dimensional analysis has been hidden in the presentation, in the attempt to make the concepts and definitions precise. Following early definition, different units and methods of expressing them are used, so that the reader will not be awed by them when he studies further elsewhere. Wherever possible, recent work is introduced.

Since the name "Biophysics" means so many different things to so many different people, the big difficulty has been to decide what *not* to write. In the interests of a unified presentation within a two-semester book, the limits chosen were concepts and mechanisms, with a minimizing of the methodology which has already been treated in elegant fashion by others.

There are some novel features about this book. The author has found them useful in his classes and would be pleased to receive the reader's opinions. Although bioenergetics in the broad sense of the term permeates the major part of the book from Chapter 2 through Chapter 9, it reaches its peak of interest in Chapter 7 in a conceptual presentation where the rigor of thermodynamics is sacrificed in favor of the development of a useful impression containing the necessary relationships: and these are illustrated. The electromagnetic spectrum (Chapter 4) and the matter wave spectrum (Chapter 3) are both surveyed, and stress is placed on those fractions which interact with (exchange energy with) biological material. The treatment of the effects of ionizing radiations (Chapter 9) surveys the hierarchy of structures, from effects on simple molecules right up the scale to man. The unified treatment of speeds (Chapter 8) attempts to show similarities and differences of mechanisms among all rate processes: chemical reactions (catalyzed), fluid flow, diffusions, and electrical and heat conductance. The apparatus of physical control is described in Chapter 10; and in Chapter 11 the bases of control biophysics are introduced in terms which attempt to span the bridge between computer technology and brain mechanisms. The author has not hesitated to introduce a difficult concept if it would later serve a useful purpose, but has tried to get the reader through it in a simple manner.

Because the scope is so broad, depth in every part of the subject could not be achieved in a book of this size. However, the bibliography is substantial, and further reading is explicitly suggested in those cases where the proper direction is not obvious.

The chief inspiration for this work was the late Dr. Jean Ettori, Associate Professor at the Sorbonne and Professor of Biochemistry at the University of Ottawa. Known to his students as "the man who always had time," he died a hapless victim of cancer in 1961, at the age of 56. This man, who had gifts of vision in the biosciences as well as deep humility and love for his students, introduced the author to this subject and emphasized the need for what he called a "psychological presentation."

The following colleagues, all specialists in their own right—in chemistry, physics, or the biosciences—read parts of early drafts of the manuscript and made many helpful suggestions: Dr. C. E. Hubley, Prof. A. W. Lawson, Prof. L. L. Langley, Dr. J. F. Scaife, Prof. M. F. Ryan, Dr. S. T. Bayley, Mr. G. D. Kaye, Mr. G. T. Lake, and Dr. G. W. Mainwood. Several other close colleagues helped by catching flaws in the proof.

Mrs. Lydia (Mion) Labelle and Miss Nadine Sears struggled through the typing of a hand-written manuscript, Miss Sears in the important middle and late stages, and produced something which Mrs. Dorothy Donath of Reinhold could further mold into a finished text. The perceptive Miss Rosemary Maxwell turned out the best of the line drawings, and these in turn illustrate her talent.

The author has had the encouragement of Dr. J. J. Lussier, Dean of the Faculty of Medicine, University of Ottawa, and of Dr. H. Sheffer, Chief

Superintendent of the Defence Research Chemical Laboratories, Ottawa, where the author carries on a research program in the interests of National Defence.

E. J. CASEY

Ottawa, Canada
October, 1962

Contents

Introduction

Biophysics is today the youngest daughter of General Physiology, a sister to Biochemistry and Pharmacology. The subject matter is not yet very well defined, as the introduction to almost any of the recent essays on the subject quickly attests. Although the basic skeleton is clear enough—it being the engineering physicist's concept of a "system" suitably molded to describe the living thing—it may be many years before the dust has settled on discussions of what appendages are proper to the skeletal framework of the subject.

Consider some of the pertinent disciplines in terms of Table 1. Biochemistry and biophysics attempt to describe and interpret the chemical and physical processes of biological materials in terms of the principles of organic chemistry, physical chemistry, and physics. Biophysics is concerned with questions about the physics of biological systems. It has the advantages of less complexity and more certainty than the biological subjects, but has the disadvantage of being limited to only specific aspects of the whole living system. For the human being, biophysics can be thought of as providing a description of his whole physical system from the particular view of physics. For medical research, for the highest forms of medical specialization, and for the general medical practitioner of the years to come, the requirement seems inevitably to be a strong background and experience in the medical arts, coupled with a thorough grounding in the scientific knowledge of medicine and the scientific approach to it. The same is true of the biosciences.

The scope of biophysics today is rather broad, if judged by the attitudes of authors of papers in several of the current journals, and in various essays. Yet the master, A. V. Hill, a Nobel prize winner who published his first paper in 1910 and is still active in research and physiology, has cautioned that the use of physical techniques or ideas alone for investigation of biological problems does not of itself make biophysics. He defines the subject as: "the study of biological function, organization, and structure by physical and physiochemical ideas and methods," and then hastens to emphasize that he has put *ideas* first. He further expands* and drives home the key point as follows:

---

*From "Lectures on the Scientific Basis of Medicine," Vol. 4, Athlone Press, London, 1954–1955; reprinted in *Science*, **124**, 1233 (1956).

There are people to whom physical intuitions come naturally, who can state a problem in physical terms, who can recognize physical relations when they turn up, who can express results in physical terms. These intellectual qualities more than any special facility with physical instruments and methods, are essential . . . . Equally essential, however, are the corresponding qualities, intuitions and experience of the biologist . . . . The chief concern in the development of biophysics is that those [experimental] skills should be acquired by people who start with the right intellectual approach, both physical and biological.

On the question of *scope* of medical biophysics, Hill says:

. . . If biophysics is to make its contribution to medicine, it is necessary that *most* physicians should have some idea at least of what it is about, while *some* physicians should have a pretty good idea. The ideas and methods of physics and physical chemistry are being applied today and will increasingly be applied, not only directly to physical medicine and radiology, but to neurology, to the study of circulation, of respiration and excretion, and of the adjustment of the body to abnormal conditions of life and work. At longer range, moreover, they will be aimed at the fundamental problems of minute structure and organization, of the physical basis of growth and inheritance, of the ordered and organized sequence of chemical reactions in vital processes, of the means by which energy is supplied and directed to vital ends.

TABLE 1.   Disciplines Surrounding Biophysics

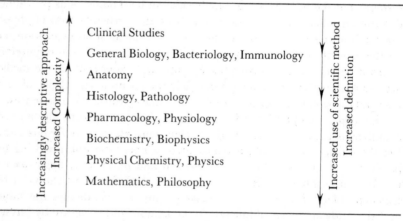

Today, by the very nature of its origin, biophysics reaches into general physiology to some extent. Today, what subject matter is proper to biophysics, and even more so to medical biophysics, is not unequivocally defined. Further, just as did biochemistry, it will probably take 25 to 50 years for the scope of biophysics to evolve into general acceptance.

SUBJECT MATTER

From recent and current literature, and within the scope discussed, it has been possible to arrive at a fair idea of the topics which are termed "Biophysics."

Table 2, aided by Figure 1, is an attempt to classify the subject matter in a form which lends itself to an integrated presentation. One must realize, of course, that clear-cut distinctions cannot be made, and that each of these subjects must overlap the other to a greater or lesser extent—for all are parts of a system; and these parts interact.

TABLE 2. A Classification of Biophysics

	Chapter
I. Physical Biophysics ("True" Biophysics)	
(a) Classical:	
Mechanics, hydrostatics and hydrodynamics, optics and sound in man	2, 3
(b) Modern:	
Radiological physics, both electromagnetic and matter waves; absorption; scatter; radioactive tracers	4, 5, 9
II. Physicochemical Biophysics (Biophysical Chemistry)	
(a) Structure of large molecules, colloids, and gels	6
(b) Energetics or thermodynamics:	
Energy balance and energy transfer; temperature; food values; electrochemical control of and by redox systems	7
(c) Kinetics and mechanisms of physical biological processes:	
Osmotic flow and water balance; incompressible flow in circulatory systems; membrane differentiation	8
III. Physiological Biophysics (Physical Physiology)	
(a) Classical:	
Bioelectricity; brain and heart measurements; volume conduction; membrane potentials	7, 8, 10
(b) Modern:	
Effects of high energy radiations; effect of physical and thermal shocks (radiation therapy, modern space medicine); system control; bioenergetics	9, 7
IV. Mathematical Biophysics	
Biostatistics; computers; cybernetics; growth rates and cycles; the systems concept	11

METHOD OF PRESENTATION

After a review of useful and necessary mathematics, which the author has found to be a pragmatic need and a valuable teaching aid, two chapters have been devoted to Topic I (a) (see Table 2). These are followed by two chapters which introduce Topic I (b). Then after one chapter on Topic II (a), three chapters deal with Topics II (*b*), II(*c*), and III(*a*), in an attempt to carry the important basic concepts through to useful applications. Systematic organization, so necessary in this era of specialization, demands a proper appreciation of the rather simple concepts which exist under the rather terrifying names!

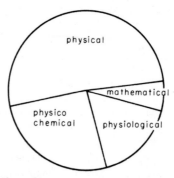

The subject matter of biophysics (expressed as an "Area" of biological science).

Figure 1

Then the ninth chapter deals with biological effects of ionizing radiations, Topic III(*b*), and the tenth with more complicated biophysical subjects which have arisen out of physiology and for which the biophysical approach provides a useful method of organization and investigation.

Of special interest may be Chapter 11, on concepts and mechanisms of control, in which an introduction is given to some of the important consequences of the use of the systems concept, principles of control, and information theory.

Although the purpose of the book is to give physicians, medical students, and students of the biosciences a readable introduction to the concepts of biophysics rather than to make biophysicists out of them, students and practitioners of pure science and engineering may relish the zest of a human biological flavor in the presentation.

Some simple, pertinent problems or exercises have been given at the end of each chapter.

References to introductory and time-proven texts, and to some late reviews, have been carefully selected with emphasis on clarity and imagination in presentation; others have been selected for factual content only.

If the principles to follow are pondered at length, and reillustrated by the reader in other examples of his choice, the clarity of thought, and the true power and scope of the basic principle will become evident.

Conversely, it seems axiomatic, but it is often forgotten, that the serious reader should seek and expect to find in a book such as this a continuous thread of purpose in all the material contained between its covers.

CHAPTER 1

The Systems Concept, and Ten Useful Pillars of Mathematical Expression

In scientific thought we adopt the simplest theory which will explain all the facts under consideration and enable us to explain new facts of the same kind.

The catch in this criterion lies in the word "simplest." It is really an aesthetic canon such as we find implicit in our criticisms of poetry or painting.

The layman finds such a law as

$$\partial x/\partial t = k\partial^2 x/\partial y^2$$

much less simple than "It oozes," (or "It diffuses," or "It flows"), of which it is the mathematical statement.

The physicist reverses this judgement, and his statement is certainly the more fruitful of the two so far as prediction is concerned.

(J. B. S. Haldane.)

THE "SYSTEMS" CONCEPT

In modern science and engineering an almost unbelievably broad and comprehensive use is made of the term "systems" and its various connotations. Chemists have long used the term to indicate the collection of chemicals—the chemical system—on which an experimenter was working. Biologists have long used the term to indicate the group of materials and events within the containing walls of the living thing: the biological system, or the living system. It was in the military campaign of ancient times that the idea or concept of control, within the military system, began to creep in. In modern military systems, in educational, government, and business systems, the idea of organization and control by the central authority of the system has been developed. The concept has reached its highest state of definition and description in military defense systems—based principally on the extension of the use of electronic circuitry to other tasks than those performed by the simple oscillators of thirty years ago. Nevertheless, in those days a one-tube affair had all the elements of a modern *system*: a detector or source of information fed a voltage signal into the grid of the vacuum tube; the signal modified the plate current by exercising a control over the direction of flow of electrons in the tube; the modified plate current passed through an external load of resistors, the voltage drop across one of which was fed back into the input grid and exerted instantaneous control of the plate current; while the voltage drop across the rest of the load was used to perform the task assigned—in this case to feed the stable oscillating voltage into further circuitry.

The elements of this system are simple enough: a *detector or source* of information (grid input), the *transmission* to a central authority (the grid), the *control* by the authority of *expenditure of energy* (in the plate circuit), and feedback of part of the expended energy into the central authority so that the latter can know whether or not the energy is being expended in the desired manner and make corrections if necessary. One other element which the simple tube circuit does not have is the facility of being able to *store information* for use when required. A modern computer has this facility.

The living thing, and man especially, if a *self-contained system* (Figure 1-1) in this sense, having all the essential elements, with *versatility* and *adaptability* as well. The sensory organs (which enable one to see, touch, taste, smell, and hear) are the detectors of relevant information. Nerve is the transmission line to the central authority, the brain, which stores information, analyzes and abstracts the relevant part, decides what to do, and then dispatches the necessary commands (electrochemical signals) to the nerve for transmission to the muscles (say) which expend energy in response to the command. Both a part of the muscle's expenditure and a continuous observation by the sensory organs feed back information to the brain so that the central authority can know if the commands are being carried out. If not, corrective commands can be dispatched.

Each of the ten chapters to follow is concerned with some aspect of man's operation as a system. He is the most complex system we know, to be sure, and it is not always immediately obvious what is the relation between the detail which we must describe and the over-all systems concept. However,

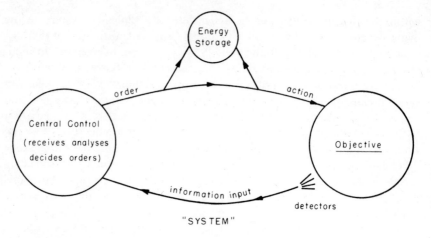

Figure 1-1. The Parts of a System.

the reader should always have this organization in the back of his mind during study of the following pages.

Some of systems engineering can be reduced to mathematical description.
Many details of medical physics can be reduced to simple arithmetical or
algebraic expression. Hence, in this subject of biophysics, mathematical
terminology is very useful, and in fact in some special cases quite necessary,
if the length of the description of the subject matter is to be kept within
reasonable limits.

INTRODUCTION TO THE TEN PILLARS

Mathematics has been defined as the concise, quantitative expression and
development of ideas. It is in this sense that we shall use the material to
follow.

Concise, quantitative description of natural phenomena is the goal of the
physical scientists. Indeed, Lord Kelvin (1883) has written: "I often say
that when you can measure what you are speaking about, and express it in
numbers, you know something about it; but when you cannot measure it,
when you cannot express it in numbers, your knowledge is of a meager and
unsatisfactory kind; it may be the beginning of knowledge, but you have
scarcely in your thoughts advanced to the stage of science." The approach
made in this book introducing biophysics is to use the mathematical method
of concise expression wherever possible without allowing the elegance to
cloud the facts or ideas being discussed. Cumbersome manipulations have
been omitted, and the methods have been used only when they serve in a
simple manner to display clearly the material being discussed.

For subsequent use in the introductory phases of biophysics we now define ten conveniently grouped concepts. Since most of this is review, the presentation is cryptic. Since only the language and the logic, and not the operations, are necessary for future use in this book, we follow the principle so aptly stated by Lord Dunsany: "Logic, like whiskey, loses its beneficial effect when taken in too large quantities."

THE TEN PILLARS

1. The Variable

If sóme entity—it may be a physical property or some other combination of length, mass and time—changes under the influence of a force, that entity is called a *variable*. There are *dependent* and *independent* variables in nature. The value of the independent can be chosen at random, but any variable dependent upon that choice is thereby fixed in value.

The ideal gas law, $PV = nRT$, illustrates this. In a closed vessel of volume V, containing n moles of gas, the independent variable (on the right-hand side of the equation by convention) is the temperature, T. The temperature can be chosen at will. However, once T has been fixed, the pressure, P, dependent upon T in this case for its value, has also been fixed.

2. The Function

Further, it can be said that P is *proportional to* T, or *varies directly* as T, or $P \propto T$; that P *varies inversely* as V, or is proportional to $1/V$, or $P \propto 1/V$. The constant number, R, which serves to equalize the dimensions or units on the two sides, never varies with experimental conditions, contains all our further ignorance of this relationship expressing the equivalence of thermal and mechanical energy, and is one of the *universal constants* of nature, (π, the value of the quotient of the circumference of a circle and its diameter is another example). There are constants other than the universal ones—they are simply variables held constant over the course of a particular changing situation. V in the preceding paragraph is an example. They are called "constants of the system."

A relationship between two variables, such that a choice of a value for one fixes the value of the other, is called a *functional relationship*. In general terms, if we do not know the exact relationship between two variables, y and x say, but we know that one exists, we can say y *varies with* x, or y *is a function of* x, or in shorthand form $y = f(x)$.

Now $y = f(x)$ is so general that it could describe any functional relationship between y and x. In nature we find both rational and transcendental functions. Rationals can be expressed as a sum of simple terms, transcendentals cannot. Three examples of the former functions are: (a) linear,

(b) parabolic, and (c) exponential. The periodic functions are transcendental (see Figure 1-2).

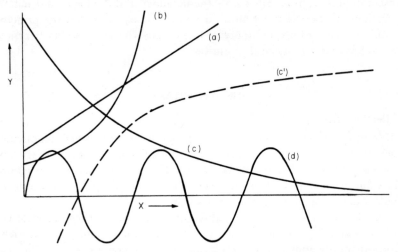

Figure 1-2. The Graphical Shape of Some Important Functional Relationships Defined in the Text.

(a) $y = kx$ is a *linear* rational function, and y plotted against x is a straight line of the form $y = mx + b$, with $b = 0$. The ideal gas law, $PV = nRT$, again can be used as a pertinent example.

(b) $y = mx^2 + b$ is a *parabolic* rational function. In the case of the area of a spherical cell, the value, A, increases faster than that of the radius, r, so that the plot of $A(\equiv y)$ vs $r(\equiv x)$ sweeps up rapidly in a curve toward higher values of A, as r is increased.

(c) $N/N_0 = e^{-kt}$ is an *exponential* rational function, in this case a decay (minus sign) or lessening, as time t increases, of the fraction N/N_0, where N_0 is the value of N when $t = 0$; and k is a proportionality constant. This function has less curvature than the parabolic. Radioactive decay is an example. The constant, k, can itself be negative. The weight of a growing baby is an example.

(c') $y = \log x$ is a cousin of (c), called the logarithmic function. It has the same curvature as (c) but a different node. An example is the voltage across the living cell's wall, a voltage which is dependent upon ratio of salt concentrations inside and outside the cell.

(d) $y = k \sin t$ is a *periodic* function. The familiar sine wave of alternating current, the volume of the lungs as a function of time, and the pressure in the auricle of the heart as a function of time, are all examples.

Figure 1-2 illustrates the four functional relationships.

These functions are all *continuous*; that is, at no point does the slope change suddenly from one value to another. It is probable that there are no discontinuous functions in nature, although the change in slope may be so sharp as to seem discontinuous in the first and cursory observation. Thus, phenomena involving the interface or juncture of two phases, as for example at the cell wall, are examples of rapidly changing continuous functions which at first sight appear to be discontinuous.

3. Limits

If a variable, changing in accordance with some assigned law, can be made to approach a fixed constant value as nearly as we wish without ever actually becoming equal to it, the constant is called the *limiting value* or *limit* of the variable under these circumstances.

A circus abounds with examples in which exceeding a limit in either distance or time would mean a severe penalty. Consider the "hell drivers" who ride motorcycles inside a 40-ft cylinder, approaching the top—the limiting height—as closely as they dare, yet never suffering the disaster of actually reaching it. In other words, if $y = f(x)$, and if, as x approaches a, y approaches some value, b, then b is said to be the limit of $f(x)$ when x equals a. In shorthand, for the functional relationship $y = f(x)$, if $x \rightarrow a$ as $y \rightarrow b$, then

$$\operatorname*{Lim}_{x \to a} f(x) = b$$

It is often useful to approach a limiting value and study its properties without having to suffer the embarassment sometimes associated with the limit itself. This concept was introduced by Leibnitz 300 years ago.

4. Increments

A small fraction of any quantity under observation is called an *increment*. Increment is thus exactly translated as "a little bit of." It is given a symbol, the Greek letter delta, Δ.

As the variable, x, increases (Figure 1-3) from zero to high values, that amount of x between A and B (i.e., $x_2 - x_1$) is "a little bit of" x, and is written in shorthand: Δx.

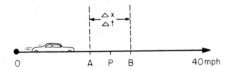

Figure 1-3. Increments of Distance and Time, Δx and Δt, used in defining velocity, $\Delta x/\Delta t$, about point P, or dx/dt at point P.

Increments may be as large or as small as we like. If we reduce the distance between A and B, the value of Δx is reduced; this can continue until Δx is infinitesimally small (so small that we cannot think of anything smaller). Infinitely small increments are called *infinitesimals*, and are written in shorthand with the Arabic letter "d", i.e., dx.

Combining the ideas of Sections 3 and 4, it is seen that as A and B approach P, Δx gets smaller and smaller until, *at the limit*, $\Delta x \rightarrow dx$, and it can be made infinitely small. This means that if we view the point, P, from B, we can move B in on P as closely as we please—in fact to an infinitely small distance away—and observe P from as closely as we please. At the limit we observe P from an infinitely small distance away, i.e., as $\Delta x \rightarrow 0$.

With the concepts of increments and limits we have implicitly introduced the concept of *continuous number*, as opposed to the discrete number which is familiar to us in our unitary, decimal, and fraction systems. Continuous number admits of the possibility of continuous variation of x between A and B; the number of steps can be infinite. Continuous number is involved when a car accelerates from 0 to 40 mph: the car passes through *every conceivable* velocity between 0 and 40, and not in the discrete jumps which our decimal and/or fraction systems would describe. At best, these latter are but very useful approximations, and can be considered as convenient, regular stop-off points, or stations, along the path of continuously increasing number.

5. Instantaneous Rate of Change

Any living being is a complex system of interrelated physical and chemical processes. Each of these processes in the "well" being is characterized by a particularly critical rate (speed or velocity) which enables it to fit into the complex system without either being too slow and holding all the other subsequent processes back, or too fast and allowing a runaway of certain subsequent processes. The study of the factors affecting the rates of processes is called "kinetics," and is discussed in detail for some biological processes, in Chapter 8.

Average rate or speed, over some time interval, is often useful; but it is the instantaneous rate, or the speed at any instant, that is most useful for an understanding of these complex, interrelated reactions.

If $y = f(x)$ and the function is continuous, we may be interested in how fast y changes *at* any value of x. In a diffusion process, for example, y would be a concentration and x the time. The question is: How much is the concentration in some particular volume changing per second at some particular second in time? The following three examples, one experimental, one graphical, and one analytical, illustrate the use of limits and increments to describe this situation.

(1) *Experimental:* To measure the instantaneous velocity of an automobile (refer again to Figure 1-3) requires measurements of distance and time between two stations, A and B. Two observers with stop watches and a tape measure can easily do this. They measure a value of $\Delta x/\Delta t$, which is the increment of distance covered in an increment of time. But the car is accelerating between A and B, and hence $\Delta x/\Delta t$ is only an average value between A and B, and may be quite different from the velocity as the car passes P. Better values can be obtained the closer the observers are to P, but of course no value can be obtained if both observers are *at* P because $\Delta x = 0$ and $\Delta t = 0$, and $0/0$ is indeterminate, or can have any value from $-\infty$ to $+\infty$. The best value is obtained by taking observations at several values of A and B, at smaller and smaller values of Δx, until a good extrapolation to $\Delta x = 0$ can be made. Hence the limit of $\Delta x/\Delta t$ as Δt approaches zero is the instantaneous velocity at the point, P. In shorthand notation, the instantaneous velocity at P is $\lim_{\Delta t \to 0} \Delta x/\Delta t$.

This symbolic description is further simplified by use of the infinitesimal symbols: $\lim_{\Delta t \to 0} \Delta x/\Delta t = dx/dt$. Conversely the previous statement is actually the definition of dx/dt. In other words, dx/dt is the instantaneous rate of change of x as t changes. A very simple experimental check on the method is to ride in a car and note the speedometer reading at point P.

Both of these methods of determining instantaneous rate are exemplified in biological processes.

(2) *Graphical:* A graph of the function which expresses the volume of the spherical cell, $V = 4/3\pi r^3$, is shown in Figure 1-4. The question arises: How fast does the volume of the cell change with change in radius at a particular value of the radius, r_1? In other words, how "steep" is the slope of the curve, V vs r, at the point, r_1?

Slope or gradient is defined by surveyors as "rise"/"run," where "rise" is the vertical height from the base to the top and "run" is the level, or horizontal distance from the foot of the hill to the top. The ratio "rise/run" defines the value (trigonometric function) of the *tangent* of the angle enclosed by the level direction and the direction toward the top.

The same is true in analytic geometry, the slope of the straight line joining P and P' being given by the ratio of the distances between P and P' as measured along the ordinate and along the abscissa. For example, slope

$$\frac{V_2 - V_1}{r_2 - r_1} = \Delta V/\Delta r.$$

What we want to know is the value of the slope of the straight line which cuts the curve, V vs r, only once and at point P, that is, the slope of the tangent (geometrical figure) at P. This will give the instantaneous rate of change of V as r changes, at P, or dV/dr at r_1.

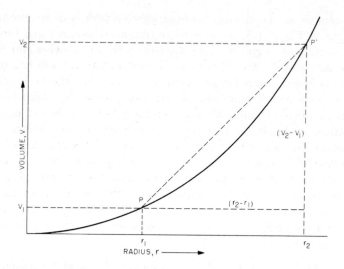

Figure 1-4. Volume of a Spherical Cell as a Function of its Radius. Determination of rate of change of V as r changes, i.e., dV/dr.

This case is now similar to (1) and need not be discussed in detail. A point, P', is chosen; a straight line joining P and P' is drawn, and the value of $\Delta V/\Delta r$ determined from the graph. At successive points closer and closer to P the same thing is done, until it is more or less evident what will be the limiting value of $\Delta V/\Delta r$ as Δr approaches zero. Once again, $\lim\limits_{\Delta r \to 0} \Delta V/\Delta r = dV/dr$, the slope *at P*. It turns out that for this case $dV/dr = 4\pi r^2$.

(3) *Analytical:* A simple example* will illustrate one way in which this can be done algebraically.

The law established by Galileo at Padua governing the free fall of a body (Figure 1-5) toward earth, is expressed as $S = 1/2\ gt^2$, where S is the distance fallen, t is the time of fall, and g is the value of acceleration due to gravity (32 ft per sec per sec.) This example is chosen not because of its specific relation to medical physics but because of its simplicity as an illustration of the algebraic determination of instantaneous rate of change by means of the method of increments. The experimental and graphical examples, (1) and (2), are limited in that an extrapolation of incremental proportions is always necessary. In the algebraic method this is not necessary, but the limit still can be examined from as close in as it is possible to imagine.

---

*As an alternative one could have considered a child blowing up a balloon, and asked the question: How fast does the *area* of the balloon change as the radius changes? The area is given by $A = 4\pi r^2$, also a parabolic function. Less easily conceived examples appear later.

The question is: What is the velocity of the falling body at the instant it passes the point, S?

At S, $S = 1/2\ gt^2$ $- -$ (1-1)

At $S + \Delta S$, $S + \Delta S = 1/2\ g(t + \Delta t)^2$.

Multiplying out the square,

$S + \Delta S = 1/2\ gt^2 + gt\Delta t + 1/2\ g\Delta t^2$ $- - - - - - - - - - - - - - - - -$ (1-2)

Between the two points, then, the value for ΔS is given by Eq. (1-2)–Eq. (1-1):

$$\Delta S = gt\Delta t + 1/2\ g\Delta t^2$$

The average rate, over a small increment of time is:

$$\Delta S/\Delta t = gt + 1/2\ g\Delta t$$

Hence, the instantaneous rate is:

$$dS/dt = \underset{\Delta t \to 0}{\text{Lim}}\ \Delta S/\Delta t = gt + 1/2\ g \times 0 = gt$$

That is, the instantaneous rate of change of distance with time (or velocity) at the point, S, is:

$$dS/dt = gt \quad - (1\text{-}3)$$

For example, 5 sec after free fall starts, Eq. (1-1) says that the distance fallen is 400 ft; and Eq. (1-3) says that the velocity as it passes the 400-ft mark is 160 ft per sec.

Maximum and minimum values of functions with changing slope and curvature must be given by the values of the function for which the instantaneous rate of change, or slope, is zero. This can be visualized in the periodic function of Figure 1-2, for example.

6. The Differential and Integral Calculus

It has been seen that, given the explicit form of the "mother" function, it is possible by the method of increments to determine the explicit form of the

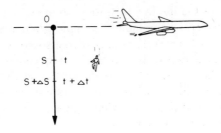

Figure 1-5. The Falling Body.

expression which describes the instantaneous rate of change—the "daughter," or derived, function. A system of "operations" has also been developed by which the same thing is accomplished. In this sense d/dx is an "operator," operating on y in a specific manner which accomplishes the same result as the method of increments gave us in Example (3).

Conversely, if the rate of change is given (most often directly from the experiment), it is possible from the daughter equation to reverse the method of increments, and establish and examine the mother equation (Figure 1-6). The process is simply to sum the increments, under special conditions, when they are infinitesimally small. A system of operations has also been worked out for this process. The operator is symbolized as an elongated "S", called the "integral sign," $\int$, contrasted against the operator, "d", for the inverse process.

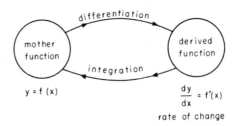

Figure 1-6. Definition of Differentiation and of
Integration.

Described in the previous Sections 1 to 5 are the basic ideas of the calculus. The process of finding from the mother function, $F(x)$, the daughter function, $F'(x)$, which expresses rate of change, is called *differentiation*, or *obtaining the derivative* or derived function; the reverse process of summation of an infinite number of values of the derived function, $F'(x)$, to give the mother function, $F(x)$, is called *integration* or obtaining the *integral*.

Two more definitions in shorthand will prove to be useful, the *second order derivative* and the *partial derivative*. Both are actually quite simple concepts. We often run into a situation in which we wish to express how fast the *speed* is changing. (Consider the automobile example, given in Section 4, in which we are now interested in acceleration.) Since speed is dS/dt, the rate of change of speed is $d/dt(dS/dt)$, which is abbreviated d^2S/dt^2 with the operator, "d," in the numerator squared and the whole differential in the denominator squared. It is obvious that the rate of change of acceleration would be expressed as d^3S/dt^3, and that higher orders exist, although they are not of common interest to us here.

Sometimes one or more independent variables (y, z) are kept as constants of the system while another (x) is varied. The rate of change of the dependent variable, ϕ, as x changes, is expressed as an incomplete or partial derivative. To emphasize the partial character, a rounded operator, ∂, is used; and the constants of the system are stated as subscripts outside parentheses which enclose the partial derivative. Thus:

$$(\partial \phi / \partial x)_{y,z}$$

expresses the rate at which ϕ changes as x is changed, when y and z are kept constant.

The second-order partial derivative, the "acceleration," is expressed as before:

$$(\partial^2 \phi / \partial x^2)_{y,z}$$

This notation is used in all heat and mass transfer-considerations. For instance, note the Haldane quotation which introduced this chapter.

At this stage of development of biophysics (1962), the terminology of the calculus is being used in published work, hence the need for introduction to the bases and terminology of the subject. But explicit descriptions of most biophysical phenomena are very rare; hence there seems to be no need to introduce the operational calculus into an introductory book on biophysics at this time. Therefore no attempt has been made to display the actual operations by which either differentiation or integration is accomplished. Operational calculus is treated in detail in many standard textbooks.

7. Distribution of Observations

A great many biological phenomena lend themselves to statistical methods of expression, i.e., age, height, weight, bloodcount, sugar analysis, etc. This is so true that the "average value" over a large number is considered the "normal" value, describing the "normal man." Hence it is instructive to examine some of the methods of statistical expression, and to discuss their reliability.

Statistics has come a long way since the publication in 1662 of John Graunt's "Natural and Political Observations Made upon the Bills of Mortality," a study based on the records kept during the Black Plague in London; and since Sir Edmund Halley (of "Comet" fame) wrote his basic paper on life insurance, which appeared 30 years later. In the 20th century statistical methods have penetrated nearly every field of learning in which numerical measurement is possible. Moroney's book[4] gives a delightful introduction to the subject.

First of all, there are two factors which will result in a distribution in a number of observations. One is errors in measurement; the other is a real distribution in what is being measured. Measuring the length of a room with a 12-in. ruler will result in a fairly wide error, and although the mean value of a number of observations should be close to fact, there may be a large uncertainty in an individual measurement. Besides such *random* errors, there may exist also *constant* errors which are sometimes very important but too rarely recognized. Suppose the ruler has been made 1/16 in. too short at the factory. If the room were 32 ft long, in addition to the random errors, every measurement would have been 2 in. short: even the mean value cannot be trusted in the presence of a constant error! It is revealing to read the temperatures on several of the thermometers in the laboratory thermometer drawer! Constant errors and the need for calibration become quite obvious. Even under the most carefully controlled experimental conditions, unknown constant errors creep in. In addition, *personal bias* is always with us, in reality if not in principle.

The variation in the quantity being measured is often called "biological variance." Consider the height of 80 people at a lecture—it usually has a distribution from about 5 ft, 0 in. to 6 ft, 3 in., with the average approximately 5 ft, 7 in. Deviations from 5 ft, 7 in., however, could hardly be considered as errors or abnormalities!

Constant errors are deadly and can result in gross misinterpretations. Analytical chemistry done without proper calibrations is an example. It has been shown to be prevalent even in routine analyses done day in and day out in the hospitals, with large variations in mean values being reported between them—each hospital apparently having its own constant errors! This is embarrassing, but it is a fact. Under these conditions, diagnoses made with reference to some published work from another hospital could easily be wrong. It is necessary continually to be on the alert against constant errors, or "biased [not personal] observations," as they are sometimes called.

Random errors and natural distribution in the variable measured can both be treated with statistical methods. The most reliable methods, and in fact the only reliable method in constant use, presuppose that the observations distribute themselves about a mean or average value such that the density of points is greatest at the mean and progressively less and less as the deviation from the mean becomes larger. That is, it presumes a "normal" distribution in the observations. Figure 1-7 shows the normal distribution curve. It can be interpreted two ways:

(1) P represents the number of observations, N, which are Δx units less than the mean;
(2) P represents the probability that any measurement now being made will have a deviation less than Δx from the mean.

It is axiomatic that any expression of confidence made in terms of normal distribution, presupposes normal distribution; and that any such expression concerning a distribution which is not normal is not only unwarranted, but also useless, and may be quite misleading. There are statistical methods for handling non-normal data, but they are not simple and are seldom used correctly. Mainland's book[3] goes into some of these, using examples of medical interest.

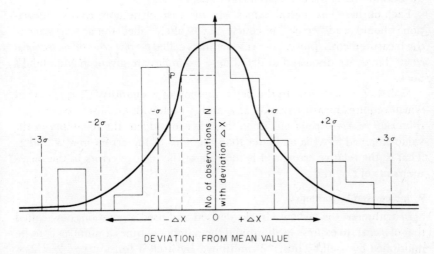

DEVIATION FROM MEAN VALUE

Figure 1-7. Normal Distribution of Observations. *Solid Curve:* Area under curve between $-\sigma$ and $+\sigma$ includes 68 per cent of observations; between -2σ and $+2\sigma$, 94 per cent; and between -3σ and $+3\sigma$, greater than 99 per cent. *Blocks:* Typical Observations of Heights of Thirty People at a Lecture.

8. Expressions of Deviations

The most common method of expressing a number of observations, x, of the same phenomenon is by the common *average*, or *arithmetic mean*, $\bar{x}$. There are others, such as the median and the mode, which have some use in nearly normal distributions, but only the mean will be considered. Deviations Δx from the mean can easily be computed by subtraction, and then averaged, the result being expressed as the *mean deviation* $\overline{\Delta x}$ from the mean $\bar{x}$.

A very common method of expressing the distribution is by the *standard deviation*, σ, defined as the square root of the average of the deviations squared:

$$\sigma = \sqrt{\overline{\Delta x^2}}, \quad \text{or} \quad \sigma = \sqrt{\sum \Delta x^2 / n}$$

Bessel's correction is introduced if the number, n, of samples is small (< 30); then

$$\sigma = \sqrt{\sum \Delta x^2/(n - 1)}$$

The *most probable deviation*, r, is that value of the deviation such that one-half the observations lies between the limits $\pm r$.

The *relative deviation*, usually expressed as a per cent, is the fraction which the deviation is of the observed mean value, i.e., $\Delta x/\bar{x}$.

Each of these has several names. In the case of random errors, "deviation" should read "error," of course; Δx is often called the *absolute error* of the measurement. *Relative error* is sometimes called *per cent error* or *proportional error*. These are discussed in detail, and examples are given, in Mainland's book.

Superposition of Errors. In the determination of a quantity, A, a $f(x, y, z)$ which requires measurement of x, y, and z, each with an absolute error, *the errors must be superimposed* one upon the other, or added; the reliability of the value obtained for A is no better than the sum of the errors in x, y and z. That is, the relative error in A is the sum of the relative errors in the measurements of x, y, and z.

9. Indices and Logarithms

In arithmetic the ancient Greeks devised and used a notation, now called that of *indices*, to express in shorthand the number of times a number is to be multiplied by itself. Thus, "2 multiplied by itself 5 times" (i.e., $2 \times 2 \times 2 \times 2 \times 2$) $= 32$. This is written in shorthand as $2^5 = 32$. The index, 5, is placed as a superscript to the base number 2.

A number of *laws of indices* can be shown to exist for the manipulation of such numbers. These laws were observed for cases in which the indices are whole numbers.

Now there is no reason to suppose that the rules would be different for fractional indices, although to multiply 2 by itself 5 1/2 times would really be tricky! Nevertheless, the rules are assumed to apply to fractional indices, as well as to whole-number ones, and further also to algebraic, unknown indices. In general, the laws of indices are as follows:

(1) $a^m = a \times a \times a \times a \times a \ldots \ldots \ldots \ldots \ldots \ldots \ldots \ldots m$ times

(2) $a^m a^n = a^{m+n}$

(3) $a^m/a^n = a^{m-n}$ if $m > n$

or $a^m/a^n = \dfrac{1}{a^{n-m}}$ if $n > m$

(4) $(a^m)^n = a^{mn}$

(5) $(ab)^m = a^m b^m$

(6) $(a/b)^m = a^m/b^m$

Fractional indices are called *roots*. Thus, $a^{\frac{1}{2}} = \sqrt{a}$, the square root of a; and in general $a^{1/m} = \sqrt[m]{a}$, the mth root of a.

(7) $a^0 = 1$

(8) $a^{-n} = 1/a^n$

(9) $a^\infty = \infty$

(10) $a^{-\infty} = 1/a^\infty = 0$

Logarithms

Let $A = a^x$. *The index x*, which tells how many times the base number a must be multiplied by itself to give A, *is defined as the logarithm of A to the base a*. In shorthand this statement is given by $x = \log_a A$, where "to the base a" appears as a subscript to the abbreviated "logarithm."

Logarithms are indices and must obey the ten Laws of Indices, just as any other. For example:

$\log AB = \log A + \log B$

$\log A/B = \log A - \log B$

$\log A^m = m \log A$

A change of base from base a to base b turns out to be analogous simply to a change of variable. In other words the logarithm to the base, a, is related to the logarithm to the base, b, by a constant, $\log_b a$. One is a linear function of the other.

This can be shown as follows. Suppose $A = a^x$ and $A = b^y$, so that $a^x = b^y$. Then $\log_a A = \log_a b^y$, or $x = y \log_a b$.

There are two systems of logarithms in daily use in biophysics, as in all other science and technology:

(a) *Common logarithms*, to the base $10 (y = 10^x$ for example), used to simplify the manipulations of multiplication and division, based on rules (2) and (3). The abbreviation is *log*, or log_{10}.

(b) *Natural logarithms*, to the base e ($y = e^x$ for example), where $e = 2.71828 \ldots$. The base, e, and the functional relationship, $y = e^x$, occur over and over again in man's description of nature, and therefore will be illustrated further. The abbreviation is *ln*, or log_e.

Conversion, as described above, is accomplished as follows:

$$\log A = \frac{1}{2.303} \ln A$$

where $2.303 = \log_e 10$.

10. Infinite Series; $y = y_0 e^{-ax}$

A series is any group of numbers, arithmetically related, which differ from each other in some regular and explicit manner. Thus

$$1 + 2 + 3 + 4 + 5 \ldots \ldots \ldots \ldots \ldots \ldots \ldots \ldots \ldots \ldots \ldots \ldots + n$$

is a series. This particular series is *divergent*, since the larger the n chosen, the greater the sum becomes. There are other series which are *convergent*, whose value approaches a limit as the number of terms is increased toward infinity. One such convergent series is

$$1 + \frac{x}{1} + \frac{x^2}{2 \times 1} + \frac{x^3}{3 \times 2 \times 1} + \frac{x^4}{4 \times 3 \times 2 \times 1} + \cdots$$

This series, for a value of $x = 1$, simplifies to

$$1 + \frac{1}{1} + \frac{1^2}{2 \times 1} + \frac{1^3}{3 \times 2 \times 1} + \frac{1^4}{4 \times 3 \times 2 \times 1} + \cdots$$

which converges to the numerical value $2.71828\ldots$ as more and more higher index terms are added. In shorthand e^x is written for the first, and e^1 or e for the second series. Thus

$$e^x = 1 + \frac{x}{1} + \frac{x^2}{2 \times 1} + \frac{x^3}{3 \times 2 \times 1} + \frac{x^4}{4 \times 3 \times 2 \times 1} + \cdots$$

and

$$e = 1 + \frac{1}{1} + \frac{1^2}{2 \times 1} + \frac{1^3}{3 \times 2 \times 1} + \cdots = 2.71828\ldots$$

More generally, when x is preceded by a constant, k, kx is substituted for x:

$$e^{kx} = 1 + \frac{kx}{1} + \frac{(kx)^2}{2 \times 1} + \frac{(kx)^3}{3 \times 2 \times 1} + \frac{(kx)^4}{4 \times 3 \times 2 \times 1} + \cdots$$

The constant, k, simply tells *how slowly* the series converges for any particular value of x: the greater the value of k the greater the number of terms which will be necessary to define e^{kx} to a chosen number of significant figures.

Now, when x is the variable, and k constant, we can call its evaluation proportional to y and write

$$\text{or } y \propto e^{kx} \mathrel{-}\mathrel{-}\mathrel{-}\mathrel{-}\mathrel{-}\mathrel{-}\mathrel{-}\mathrel{-}\mathrel{-}\mathrel{-}\mathrel{-}\mathrel{-}\mathrel{-}\mathrel{-}\mathrel{-}\mathrel{-}\mathrel{-} (1\text{-}4)$$

The series typified by e^{kx} is the only functional relationship in all of mathematics for which its instantaneous rate of change at a value of x is exactly proportional to itself. That is, it is the only function for which both

$$y \propto e^{kx} \hspace{4cm} (1\text{-}4)$$

and

$$dy/dx \propto e^{kx} \; (\text{or} \propto y) \hspace{3cm} (1\text{-}5)$$

are true.

For completeness, if the proportionality constant in Eq. (1-4) is introduced,

$$y = y_0 e^{kx} \hspace{4cm} (1\text{-}4')$$

and

$$dy/dx = ky_0 e^{kx} \hspace{3.5cm} (1\text{-}5')$$

or

$$dy/dx = ky$$

This, however, explains the importance of e^x in mathematics. The importance in biophysics is that a great many naturally occurring phenomena *are observed* to behave according to Eq. (1-5'): many chemical reactions, growth, diffusion processes, radioactive decay, radiation absorption phenomena, etc. (Figure 1-8).

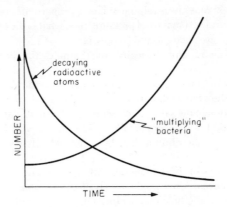

Figure 1-8. Two Exponential Relationships:
Growth (positive k), and Decay (negative k).

For example, let y be the number of atoms of a given sample which give out a radioactive emanation (alpha, beta, or gamma ray), and x be the time. Eq. (1-4') says that the rate of emanation is *always* proportional to the number of atoms which are left and are capable of disintegrating, a statement which, if reflected upon, will become quite obvious because it is not only a "natural" law, an observed law of Nature, but also a logical deduction.

In our examples, most commonly a decay is involved, in this case the decay of a concentration. Thus k is a negative number. If the minus sign is taken out of the k and k replaced by $-\lambda$, the expression becomes $N = N_0 e^{-\lambda t}$, sometimes written $N = N_0 \exp(-\lambda t)$, for radioactive decay, where N_0 is the number of particles present when $t = 0$.

Figure 1-8 shows the shape of the exponential curve for positive k values (growth), and for negative k values (decay). Note that the former increases to infinity, unless checked by the onset of some other law; and that the latter decays toward zero, reaching zero only after an infinitely long time, although it may be below the lowest measureable value within a very short time. The larger the value of k, the faster the growth curve sweeps upwards, and the sooner the decay curve approaches zero.

PROBLEMS

1-1: (a) If a student must pass biochemistry, and John is a student, then . . . ?

    (b) If $y = 2x$ and $z = y$, then what functional relationship exists between z and x?

    (c) If $y = f_1(x)$ and $z = f_2(x)$; and $f_2(x) = f_1(x) \cdot f_3(x)$, then what is the relationship between x and y?

    (d) If $A \propto B$, and $B \propto C$, what is the relationship between A and C?

    (e) If the weight of a given volume of gas is proportional to density, and if the density is proportional to its pressure, then what is the relationship between weight of a given volume and its pressure?

1-2: Choose at random, alphabetically for example, the heights in inches of 25 students.

    (a) Is the distribution normal? Was the sample biased?

    (b) What are the average deviation, $\overline{\Delta x}$, and the standard deviation, σ?

    (c) What fraction of the sample falls within the mean deviation from the mean?

    (d) What fraction of the sample falls within one standard deviation from the mean? If the distribution had been normal, what would have been the fraction?

    (e) What fractions of the sample fall with $\pm 2\sigma$ and $\pm 3\sigma$? If the distribution had been normal, what would have been the fractions?

1-3: Make a table showing how the distance fallen, the speed, and the acceleration of a parachutist change in the first 5 sec before the chute opens. (Make the calculations for each second.)

    Suppose he hits the earth at a velocity of 120 ft per sec without the chute opening. From what height did he jump?

1-4: The decay of Sr^{90} follows the exponential law $N = N_0 e^{-\lambda t}$, where N is the concentration of radiating material at any time, t; N_0 is the concentration at some arbitrary zero of time; and λ is the decay constant of Sr^{90}, namely 0.028 years^{-1} (i.e., 0.028 is the fraction lost per year).

(a) Make a table showing values of $-\lambda t$, $e^{-\lambda t}$, and $N_0 e^{-\lambda t}$ for various values of t (years), assuming that $N_0 = 100\%$ at $t = 0$.

(b) From the results, make a plot of N vs t, and estimate the half-life (the time, τ, in years, when $N = 50\%$ of N_0).

(c) Sketch decay curves for P^{32} ($\tau = 14.3$ days), I^{131} (8 days), C^{14} (5100 years), Co^{60} (5.3 years), Po^{210} (138 days), and Ra^{226} (1620 years), all on the same graph. Compare them.

REFERENCES

1. Petrie, P. A., *et al.*, "Algebra—a Senior Course (for High Schools)," The Copp Clark Publishing Co. Ltd., Toronto, 1960. (See p. 314 *ff* for discussion on increments.)

2. Thompson, Silvanus P., "Calculus Made Easy (Being a Very Simplest Introduction to Those Beautiful Methods of Reconing which are Generally called by the Terrifying Names of the Differential and Integral Calculus)," 3rd ed., MacMillan & Co. Ltd., London, 1948.

3. Mainland, D., "Elementary Medical Statistics," W. B. Saunders Co., Philadelphia, Pa., 1952.

4. Moroney, M. J., "Facts from Figures," 3rd ed., Penguin Books Ltd., Toronto, 1956.

CHAPTER 2

Some Physical Forces Exemplified in Man

(Mechanical; Osmotic; Electrical)

All physical reality is a manifestation of what force does. *On the question of what force* is, *science can do no better than to call it by other names.* (*Truth is a virtue, however inconvenient.*)

INTRODUCTION

Force and energy, along with optics and acoustics, are the concerns of classical medical physics, and some of the principles have been understood for well over a hundred years. In this chapter the nature and the units of force are reviewed, and the relationship between force and energy discussed. The transfer of energy is reserved for Chapter 7.

The living system is in a state of continual exchange of force and energy with the environment. What is force? According to Newton (1687), it is *vis impressa*, an influence, measurable in both intensity and direction, operating on a body in such a manner as to produce an alteration of its state of rest or motion. Generically, force is the cause of a physical phenomenon. It is measured by its effect. Further penetration of the nature of force seems destined to remain a philosophical question, because the range of experiment stops at measurement of the effects.

By experiment it is possible to measure the effect of different forces on the same object, and devise a system of interconversion factors by which one kind of force is related to another (for example, mechanical to osmotic). Efforts to penetrate the generic nature of the "force field"—to develop a unified theory—received much impetus, without much success, during the life of Albert Einstein, but one notices now that efforts at unification are falling off as theorists drift into other problems. Hence the question most fundamental to all science, biophysics included, viz: "What is force?", seems destined to remain unanswered for a long time yet. It is a more fundamental question even than "What is life?", for life is only one manifestation of force!

MECHANICAL FORCES

Newton's Three Laws of Motion

These three laws are the basic description of mechanical systems. From the simple statements can be inferred many properties of mass and inertia.

First Law: A body at rest tends to stay at rest, and a body in motion tends to continue moving in a straight line unless the body is acted upon by some unbalanced force (F). The property of the body by virtue of which this is true is given the name *inertia*. The measure of amount of inertia is called the *mass* (m).

Second Law: A body acted on by an unbalanced force will accelerate in the direction of the force; the acceleration (a) is directly proportional to the unbalanced force and inversely proportional to the mass of the body.

This second law describes the familiar experimentally derived relationship $F \propto ma$, or $F = kma$. If the dimensions of F are suitably defined, this becomes $F = ma$. The need to choose the dimensions in this manner results from the fact, discussed earlier, that we really do not know what the nature of force is, but rather do we know only its effects. This is certainly true of the common forces of gravitation, electrostatics, and magnetism. Yet frictional force we are able to relate to physical interference of microroughnesses and physical attraction of two surfaces—and thus have some idea of what this force is. The force exerted by the finger to push the pencil, or the force exerted by the thumb on a hypodermic needle drive home to us a meaning of mechanical force based on its effects.

Third Law: For every physical action there exists an equal and opposite reaction. The recoil of a rifle as the bullet is ejected, and the swinging arms which help man to maintain his balance while walking briskly, are examples.

Careful consideration of the statements themselves will enable the reader to appreciate the far-reaching consequences of these laws, consequences which range from suspension bridges to the molecular interactions of biochemistry, from the effects of high centrifugal forces on the pilot of a high-speed aircraft to the simple levers of which the human body in motion is a remarkably complex, though well coordinated, example.

Units and Dimensions

It is useful now to introduce definitions of certain quantities in mechanics. By the first law, a force is defined as anything which changes the state of rest or of motion in matter. The basic unit of force, in the centimeter-gram-second system, is called the *dyne*. This is the force which will produce an acceleration of 1 cm per sec each sec (1 cm sec^{-2}) on a mass of 1 gram (1 g). All other forces (electrical, etc.) can be related by suitable experiments to this fundamental quantity of motion.

Force gives to mass an *energy*, a capability of doing work. In the system of mechanics, the amount of energy acquired by a mass under the influence of a force depends upon how long or over what distance the force acts. The energy imparted to 1 g of mass by a force sufficient to give the mass an acceleration of 1 cm sec^{-2} within the distance 1 cm, is called 1 *erg*. One erg = 1 dyne cm. This is an inconveniently small unit of energy, and a quantity of ten million (10^7) ergs has been defined as 1 *joule* (1 jou).

By contrast with this definition of energy units in the mechanical system, the unit of heat energy, the small calorie, has been defined as the amount of energy which it takes to raise the temperature of 1 g of water 1° C, between 4.5 and 5.5°C, where water is the most dense.* (As the temperature is lowered, water molecules begin to line up in "anticipation" of freezing, and the volume increases; as the temperature is raised, increased thermal energy tends to drive the molecules apart, and the volume also increases). Experimentally, by transformation of mechanical motion into heat in a water calorimeter, 1 cal has been found to equal 4.18 jou. One thousand cal, or 1 kilocalorie (1 kcal), has been defined 1 Cal, or large calorie. This is the unit used to describe the energy available from different foods.

Power is the rate at which energy is expended; that is, energy expended per unit time. The basic unit of power is the joule per second, called the *watt* (w). One-thousand watts is 1 kilowatt (1 kw). One horsepower (1 hp) is equivalent to 746 w or 3/4 kw.

Energy exists in two general forms, kinetic and potential. *Kinetic energy* is that possessed by mass in motion. In mechanics *potential energy* is that possessed by a mass because of its position. In other disciplines potential energy assumes different forms: the energy stored in chemicals, or that stored in extended muscle, or in an electrostatic charge separation across a cell membrane, could be released to do useful work or provide heat.

Heat energy is all kinetic energy. It is the total energy of motion of all the molecules in the body under consideration. Temperature is an indicator of the amount of heat in a body, and can be considered to be the "force-like"

---

*The amount of heat required to raise 1 g of a substance 1°C is called the *specific heat, c*. It can be measured under constant pressure (c_p) or under constant volume (c_V).

factor of heat energy. The accompanying capacitive factor in effect sums up the energies which can go into all the vibrations, rotations, and translations of each molecule. This capacitive factor is called *entropy*, S. Heat energy is therefore given as the product TS, and S must have the units calories per degree, since the product must be simply calories.

Heat energy was chosen over electrical, mechanical, or other forms for no other reason than that it is so common. *All* forms of energy can be factored into two parts, a potential part and a capacitative part: thus in addition to heat energy, we have force times distance for mechanical energy; voltage times charge for electrical energy; pressure times volume for the mechanical energy contained by a compressed gas; chemical potential times number of moles for chemical energy. Energy and its factors will be considered more fully in Chapter 7.

Kinetic energy of mass in motion is given by force × distance, which has the dimensions (g cm/sec^2) cm, or g cm^2/sec^2. Kinetic energy of motion is also given by the familiar $1/2\ mv^2$, with the same dimensions. Another familiar property of mass in motion is the *momentum*, M, defined as mv. Hence $KE = 1/2\ Mv$.

Some of these quantities can be illustrated by the example of a 200-lb** football player running at full speed with the ball. His potential energy in the form of food has been reprocessed into glycogen, etc., and stored as potential energy. That part ready for rapid conversion is available in the form of the mobile chemical adenosine triphosphate (ATP), whose role as a mobile power supply is wondrously general throughout the living system. During the motion this chemical energy is being transformed, at least in part, to the mechanical kinetic energy of motion. His KE amounts (speed 100 yds in 12 sec; 1 lb = 454 g) to about 26,000,000,000 (or 26 × 10^9) ergs, or 2600 jou, about 550 small calories. If he is stopped completely within 1 sec by collision, he will have transferred energy at an average rate during that second of 2600 jou per sec, 2600 w, or just over 3 hp. If that energy all went into heat, it could vaporize about 1 g of water. On the other hand this energy could have been transformed into electricity, and the power delivered could have lighted twenty-four 100-w light bulbs to full brilliance for a second! A further insight into the power expended in such collisions can be gained if it is remembered that the bulk of the energy is transferred in about 1/10 sec of contact, during which time the power is about 30 hp! It is obvious that, in spite of the delights attached to such athletic pursuits, from the point of view of pure physics alone, they are sheer waste of energy and power which could be used more efficiently to do other tasks. In fact even

---

**Weight, a force. Since $F = ma$: 1 lb force = 1 lb mass × 32 ft/sec^2, and 980 dynes force = 1 g force = 1 g mass × 980 cm/sec^2. (1 lb force is the force of attraction between the earth and 454 g mass.)

at its slowest, when no work is being done, basal metabolism amounts to about 0.1 hp. The human machine needs a minimum of 0.1 hp to keep it alive, and can put out continuously a maximum of about 0.01 hp of useful mechanical work, with occasional surges to several horsepower.

The football player's momentum just before collision was $(200/32) \times (300/12) = 154$ lb sec. If this were transferred in 0.1 sec during collision, the impressed force, defined as rate of change of momentum, dM/dt, was $154/0.1 = 1540$ lbs. This can be expressed as a "shock" (force per unit mass) of about 7.7 g, where g is the acceleration of all bodies due to gravitational attraction to the earth (32 ft/sec², or 980 cm/sec²). The value 7.7 g is obtained directly from the second law, viz

$$a = F/m = \frac{1540}{200/g} = 7.7\,g$$

By contrast, and as further illustration, the passengers on a modern commercial jet line experience about 2 g during take-off. The jet pilots for fighter aircraft and the astronauts have been tested up to 18 g. The famous right hand of boxer Joe Louis was said to impart up to 40 g to a stationary and nonelastic target. A laboratory centrifuge will provide a centrifugal acceleration of some thousands of g; and the ultracentrifuge used in sedimentation experiments in which molecular weights of large molecules are obtained, develops up to 100,000 g. Centrifugal motion is convenient for varying at will the inertial mass of a body: e.g., in the human centrifuges in space-research laboratories.

As a machine, man is very versatile. However, he is quite inefficient because of the continuous power being expended to keep him alive when he is not "in use." His highest purely physical role is that of a computer.

Two forces will now be considered: a mechanical force as applied to a lever, and the mechanical force of a compressed gas.

The Lever

A lever is one of a great number of machines—devices for doing work. This particular device permits mechanical energy to be factored into such values of force and distance that some desired mechanical result can be accomplished. The lever does not create energy, of course, but simply makes the energy more available to do the particular job at hand. The familiar example of the crowbar to dislodge a large stone, using a log as a pry, is an example. In this case a relatively small force applied over a relatively large distance at the hands is transformed into a relatively large force applied over a relatively small distance at the stone. The mechanical advantage is the ratio of the two forces; it is inversely proportional to the ratio of the two distances since $F_1 d_1$ must equal $F_2 d_2$.

The three classes of levers, expressed in terms of the relative positions of applied force, F_a, resultant force, F_r, and fulcrum, with directions denoted by the arrows, are given in a classical example in Figure 2-1.

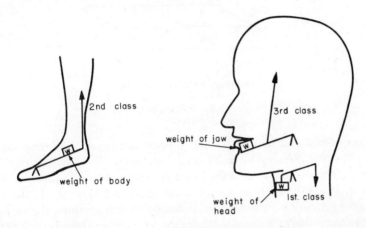

2nd class

weight of body

weight of jaw

3rd class

weight of head

1st. class

Figure 2-1.   First-, Second-, and Third-Class Levers.

The muscular-skeletal system of the human body is a complex system of levers. The majority of these are third-class levers. A runner on tiptoe has a second-class lever in his foot: the ball is the fulcrum, F_a is at the heel, applied by Achilles' tendon and the calf muscle, and F_r is exerted near the instep. The jaw, the forearm, and the fingers of the hand are all third-class levers. However Jiu-jitsu is a study in first-class levers, and the arm and leg locks used in wrestling are almost invariably first-class levers. While doing push-ups the body is operating as a second-class lever. The pump of an old-fashioned well and a wheelbarrow are second-class levers, and there are countless other examples of each among man's tools. Simple levers were man's first machines.

Compressed Gas

Pressure is mechanical force per unit area (Figure 2-2). Atmospheric pressure is simply the weight force of a column of air 1 cm^2 in area and of a height, h, equal to the effective height of air above the earth. From basic definitions $P = \rho g h$, where ρ is the average density over the height, h. The units of pressure are dynes cm^{-2}, and of g, cm sec^{-2}.

However, it is common practice, where differences or ratios of pressure are involved, to ignore the factor, g, which is constant at any particular spot on the earth's surface. The weight of the column of air is about 1,050 g or 15 lb above 1 in.^{2} The common unit is 15 lb (force) per sq in. (15 psi) = 1 atmosphere (1 atm) at sea level.

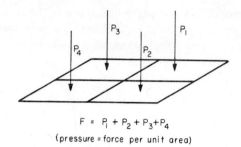

$$F = P_1 + P_2 + P_3 + P_4$$
(pressure = force per unit area)

Figure 2–2. Pressure and Force.

It has been found that 15 psi can support a column of mercury about 30 in. (76 cm or 760 mm) high. That is, if a glass tube of any diameter (the larger the cross-sectional area the larger the force, since the pressure is 15 psi) is mounted vertically in a pool of mercury, and if the air in the tube above the mercury is exhausted substantially to zero pressure, the air pressure on the outside of the pool will force the mercury up the tube to a height of about 30 in. above the level in the pool. If the supporting pressure (difference between air pressure on the mercury in the pool, open to air, and on the mercury in the column) is less than 15 psi, the height of the column is correspondingly less. Atmospheric pressure varies with the weather, from about 29 to 31 in. of mercury between very stormy, low-pressure weather and fine, high-pressure weather.

Living systems operate under this continuous pressure of 15 psi, but do not collapse for two reasons. Firstly tissue is about 80 per cent water by weight, and water is nearly incompressible. Secondly, air can pass fairly freely into those interior parts which are not solid or liquid, and the internal gas pressure is about the same as the external. A large reduction in pressure (e.g., 12 psi) over a small area of the skin surface can be tolerated for some minutes without ill effects. On the other hand, pressure-increases up to 327 psi at a new record depth in water of 726 ft were recently tolerated. The current skin-diving record is 378 ft, where the total pressure, P, is of the order of 12 atm!

The total pressure (psi) is given by:

$$P = P_{atm} + 0.43 D$$

where P_{atm} = 14.8 psi, D is the depth in feet, and 0.43 is the weight, in pounds, of a column of water 1 in.^{2} in area and 1 ft high. At the record skin-diving depth, the total force on the body (20 sq ft) is about 270 tons!

The troubles start when pressure changes occur rapidly, such as during collisions or impact. Consider the skin diver equilibrated 200 ft below the surface of the water. An extra amount of nitrogen will be dissolved in all the body fluids, including the blood stream. Henry's law describes how the amount of gas dissolved, w, increases linearly as pressure increases: i.e., $w = HP$, where H is the proportionality (Henry's) constant. This expresses the condition of the diver at equilibrium with his environment. If now, suddenly, he rises to the surface, the nitrogen which has diffused into the blood stream is not able to diffuse out fast enough, and will come out of solution in the form of small gas bubbles, which rapidly coalesce to form larger ones. Under the conditions described, the bubbles so formed would be easily large enough to form "air locks" and prevent the flow through the blood capillaries. This illustration simply shows the physical facts of the condition known as "bends": circulation ceases, waste products of muscle activity accumulate, muscles cannot be reactivated; excruciating pain, paralysis, and death can result. The only treatment is to increase the pressure in a pressure tank in the hope that the nitrogen bubbles will redissolve.

A second problem, and often a more important one, illustrates another physical point. It is a fact that sometimes during fear the individual will hold his breath tightly as he pops to the surface from a considerable depth: since the opening at the epiglottis is small, only a small force by the muscles is necessary to apply the considerable pressure needed to keep this valve closed. Up from even 25 ft, for instance, the external pressure has dropped from 30 psi to 15, and if the extra gas is not exhaled, the excess pressure is a full atmosphere on the delicate walls of the lungs. Punctures, called air embolism, can occur, and cause a condition not unlike pneumonia, in which air-CO_2 exchange on the lung walls is retarded.

The results are similar in the case of a high-flying airman if he is ejected from the aircraft and is unprotected by a pressurized flying suit; or in the case of a space traveller whose pressurizing equipment fails. In these cases, in which the pressure is suddenly reduced from about 1 atm to (say) 0.01 atm, a second, more serious factor is introduced in addition to the first: the body fluids boil at pressures below about 25 mm Hg at 37°C.

Facts which the anesthetist should know about gases are expounded and illustrated beautifully by MacIntosh et al.[5]; and aside from the ideal gas law, Henry's law, and recollections about thermal conductivity and resistance to flow through tubes—properties which are discussed briefly later—no further discussions on gases are presented in this book. The reader will have erred if he fails to consult MacIntosh at this level of study.

Some Important Mechanical Properties

If a mechanical pressure (dynes cm^{-2}) produces deformation, the pressure is called a *stress*. The amount of deformation, e.g., deformed length divided by the original, unstressed length, is called the *strain*.

Elasticity is the property by virtue of which a body resists and recovers from deformation produced by a force. If the elongation, s, is produced by a weight of mass, m, in a sample with cross-sectional area, A, and length, l, the modulus (Young's) for stretching is given by

$$m = \frac{\text{stress}}{\text{strain}} = \frac{mg}{A} \Big/ \frac{s}{l} = \frac{mgl}{As}$$

which has dimensions of a pressure. m is high for materials difficult to stretch.

The smallest value of the stress which produces a permanent alteration is called the *elastic limit.* Concussions, fractures, torn ligaments, and even bruises are examples of tissues having been forced beyond their elastic limit, usually during impact.

Impact resistance, or hardness, can only be measured relatively. It usually is done by dropping a hard steel sphere, or pointed instrument, on the material, then reading either the diameter of the deformation caused by the sphere, or the depth of penetration of the pointed instrument. Bone, teeth, and nail have yielded useful values for impact resistance.

Impulse is the product of pressure (stress) and time of application (consideration of the second law will show that impulse is also equal to momentum transferred per unit area). This is the physical description of the impact. Impulse measurements during impact applied directly to the brains of animals show that impulses composed of pressures of 30 to 90 psi acting for 1 millisecond (1 msec) or more cause physiological concussion (defined here as an immediate posttraumatic unconsciousness). Further, the impulse necessary to cause such damage increases rapidly with decreasing stress or pressure. There is a minimum time of application, of course, below which no damage is done.

Analysis of stress-strain patterns in the human being has been going on for many years, especially studies on bones in relation to how bones are formed, grow, and are broken; and on lumbar intervertebral discs. Strain in a bone is most accurately measured by an electric wire strain gauge; the electrical resistance of the wire changes with stress. By transverse loading of a femur, for instance, with stresses of ~ 1 ton/in.^{2}, strains of the order of only 0.0001 in./in. are found. The bone is remarkably rigid. On the other hand, the discs are relatively easily strained, as they must be if they are to do their job during spinal maneuvers. Strains per disc are of the order of 0.02 in.

On Hydro- (or Hemo-) Statics

It was indicated on page 30 that the gravitational force of attraction of a body to the earth is given by $m\,g$, where m is the mass in grams, and g is the acceleration (cm/sec^2) or the force by which 1 gram mass is attracted to the earth at sea level (980 dynes/g). Our goal now will be to show what problem is introduced by the simple facts that man's head is 6 ft away from his feet and he walks upright.

Two fluids circulate independently through the body: blood and lymph. Both move via a canal system. The former is a closed system driven by a pump; the latter is driven by muscle movement along the canals.

Because a column of air 6 ft high, of 1 in.^{2} cross-section, has negligible weight, there is no difference in the weight force of air at the head and feet. However, the weight of a column of water (or blood) of the same dimensions is 2.8 lb, quite an appreciable fraction (12 per cent) of 14.8 psi of atmospheric pressure. In terms of the mercury manometer (1 atm, 14.8 psi, supports a column of mercury 30 in., or 760 mm high, remember?) this extra pressure at the feet due to the weight of the blood is 120 mm over 760. Hence the pump must force blood along against a 120-mm back-pressure. Add to this a small resistance to flow, mostly in the large arteries and veins in which the total area of flow is relatively small and the flow rate high.

The heart is a pulse pump. It distends, collecting a volume of blood freshly oxygenated in the lungs, closes its inlet valves, and contracts, forcing the blood out through the aorta. The aorta, like the rest of the circulating system, has elastic walls, which, in turn, distend under the hydraulic force impressed by the contracting heart muscles. The pressure-rise in the aorta, for a rather typical stroke-volume of 30 cc, may vary from 30 to 150 mm Hg pressure depending upon the reaction of the walls of the arterial system to the pulse and the physical position of the person. In the highly elastic walls of the young and healthy the value will be small; as the tissues become harder with age, or disease, it will rise.

The maximum value is called the *systolic* pressure, and is due directly to the factors outlined. It is usually of the order of 120 mm. The minimum value—reached after the walls of the aorta, distended by the stroke from the heart, have relaxed to the original diameter, having forced the blood along the artery-capillary system—is called the *diastolic* pressure. Typically in a healthy, adult male it is ~80 mm Hg. The mean value is about 100. The pulse period is about 1 sec. Because the veins in the legs are more easily distended than the arteries, most of the venous blood is stored there and recalled when needed. The center of gravity is thus lowered, and storage requires less work.

THE OSMOTIC FORCE

What Is It?

One of the most important forces at work in the living system is the osmotic (literally, Greek: "impulse") one. It is the force which drives the diffusion of water, nothing more, and is a property of a solution just as are freezing point, vapor pressure, and boiling point. All of these properties have a value which depends only upon the number of solute particles present in the solution. Thus, pure water has no osmotic pressure; and the greater the concentration (c) of alcohol, for instance, dissolved in water, the greater the osmotic pressure. In fact the osmotic pressure, π, varies directly as the concentration (number of moles, n, per volume, V):

$$\pi = \frac{n}{V} RT = cRT$$

where R is the universal constant and T the absolute temperature. Note the analogy with the ideal gas law:

$$PV = nRT$$

Hence the former could be considered to be an ideal solution law.

Naturally, the higher the concentration, c, of solute the faster will such a solution diffuse into pure water. However, conversely, the lower the solute concentration the higher is the water concentration, until in the limit, the solution is pure water. Since the laws of diffusion are just the same for water as for any solute, water will diffuse from the solution of higher water concentration to that of lower water concentration; that is, it will diffuse from the solution of lower salt concentration to the solution of higher salt concentration, or, in other words, from the solution of low osmotic pressure to that with high osmotic pressure (see Figure 2-3(a)). It will diffuse from pure water into any solution. The diffusion of water is called *osmosis*. The direc-

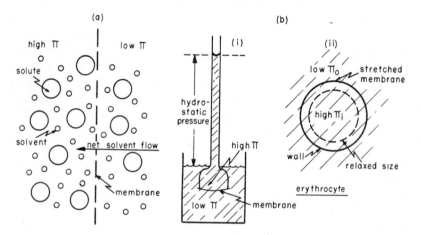

Figure 2-3. Water Balance. (a) High and low osmotic pressures; (b) osmotic pressure difference balanced by applied mechanical pressure; (i) hydrostatic, (ii) elastic, restoring pressures.

tion of osmosis is determined by the osmotic pressure difference between the two solutions in contact, but otherwise there is no relationship between osmosis and osmotic pressure.

The osmotic pressure can be measured by determining the mechanical pressure which must be applied to the solution of high osmotic pressure so that osmosis ceases. The mechanical pressure might be a hydrostatic one (Figure 2-3 (b) i), an elastic restoring force per unit area (Figure 2-3 (b) ii), or some other.

Water Balance

In the body (mostly water) the balance among tissues is maintained by a curious assortment of mechanical and osmotic forces, dictated in large part by the physical characteristics of membranes which separate the fluids. All living membranes pass water with ease. It is the solute content which determines the osmotic pressure difference between the two solutions separated by the membrane, and this is determined in part by the membrane itself. Some membranes pass everything—water, salts, molecules—excluding colloids and larger particles; the large intestine is an example. Membranes in the kidney pass water, salts, and many small molecules readily and rapidly. The membrane which forms the cell wall of the red blood cell passes water and salts, and some small molecules readily. Nerve cell membrane passes water and Cl^- readily, but balks at most molecules (its metabolic rate is low), and lets K^+ and Na^+ through only with difficulty.

Since those species which can pass freely equalize their concentrations on opposite sides, only those which are restricted from passage can give rise to a difference in osmotic pressure. In the erythrocytes, water balance is thus controlled by the difference in soluble protein content between the cellular fluid and the plasma. Since the concentration is slightly greater inside than outside the cell, water runs in. As the cell walls become stretched, the restoring pressure (the wall is elastic, like a balloon) applies a mechanical pressure on the liquid. An equilibrium is reached at which

$$\pi_i = \pi_0 + P_R$$

where the π's are osmotic pressures inside and outside the cell, and P_R is the restoring pressure of the walls of the distended cell. Table 2-1 gives a quantitative illustration of this important point.

When membranes are ill-formed and cannot discriminate as they should, or when metabolic processes produce impenetrable species such as a protein whose concentration is different from the normal, the osmotic pressure difference, $\pi_i - \pi_0$, is not the same, and the powerful osmotic force differs from what it should be. The small mechanical compensation mechanisms (such as the restoring force in the erythrocyte wall) become strained, and edema may result. These facts are the physical basis of the salt-free diets and other chemical attempts to control water balance.

TABLE 2-1.   The Balance Between Osmotic Pressure Difference and Restoring Pressure in Cell Walls.

Ion content of blood plasma (meq/l):				
Na^+	138	Cl^-	105	
K^+	4.5	HCO_3^-	25	
Ca^{++}	5.2	protein	16	Total: 149.7
Mg^{++}	2.0	PO_4^{-3}	2.2	$\therefore \pi_0 = 7.4$ atm
		$SO_4^=$	0.5	
		remainder	1.0	

Ion content of red blood cells (meq/l):				
Na^+	16	Cl^-	55	
K^+	96	HCO_3^-	15	Total: 117
Ca^{++}	0.5	other ions	47	$\therefore \pi_i = 5.7$ atm
Mg^{++}	4.6			

$P_R = \pi_0 - \pi_i = 1.7$ atm (25.5 psi) exerted by stretched walls of cell.

If cell radius is 10μ (10^{-3} cm), total force exerted by stretched cell wall is only 0.00005 lb.

ELECTRICAL FORCES

Electrostatic Force

Like the gravitational and osmotic forces, we know little about the nature of electrical and magnetic forces either, but we can go a long way by studying and applying their effects.

The basic concept of electrostatics is that of the *potential*, Ψ (psi), at a point. The potential is defined as the work required (hence it is an energy) to bring one positive charge from an infinite distance and place it at the point or position in question. The unit of potential is, therefore, joules/coulomb.

Potential itself is impossible to measure, but *differences* in potential can be measured very accurately by the work they can do in the field or volume of space in which they exist—work of repulsion of pith balls, for example, or the work involved in deflecting the needle of a voltmeter or driving electric charges through some closed circuit. The potential difference, $\Psi_2 - \Psi_1$, between two points is usually called "V jou/cou, or volts."

The term "charge" should be amplified. It is the quantity or amount of electricity in a bundle—whatever electricity is. We know there are, formally, two kinds of electrical charge; they are called positive and negative.

Positives repel; negatives repel; but positive attracts negative. Coulomb observed that the force of repulsion of like charges increases as the size of each, and decreases as the square of the distance. Thus

$$F = \frac{q_1 q_2}{\epsilon d^2}$$

where F is the force in dynes, q_1 and q_2 are the charges in coulombs, d is the distance in centimeters, and ϵ is the proportionality constant, called the dielectric constant (Figure 2-4). Unit charge is formally defined through Coulomb's facts: when two like charges are 1 cm apart and repel each other with a force of 1 dyne, each carries unit charge.

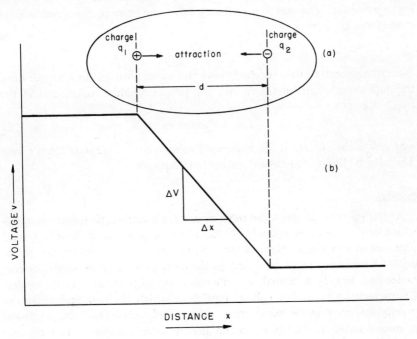

Figure 2-4. Interaction of Electrical Charges: (a) Coulomb's case; (b) field strength.

Bioelectric Potentials

At the microscopic level the most important potential differences in the living system arise from concentration differences (why they do will be seen later), and these occur almost without exception across living membranes. For example, in heart muscle cell the potential difference or voltage between the inside and outside of the cell, across the cell membrane, is about 85 mv, on the average, and cycles above and below this, as the heart beats.

The *electric field strength* (see Figure 2-4) is defined as the voltage gradient, $\mathcal{U}$, dV/dx, i.e., the voltage change per centimeter of effective thickness of membrane across which the force acts. In cells it has been variously estimated that the effective part of the membrane is only about 100 angstroms (100 Å), 100×10^{-8} cm, thick. The field strength across the membrane is therefore a phenomenal 85,000 v/cm, or over 200,000 v/in.!

Electric field strength enters many phases of biophysics, and will appear often throughout this book, e.g., whenever membranes or bioelectric phenomena, such as those which give rise to the electrocardiogram and encephalogram, are introduced.

The voltage gradient, $\mathcal{U}$, (i.e., electric field strength) is the force which causes charge to flow—for positive charges, in the direction from higher to lower potential. The rate at which they flow (the current, i) is proportional to the force $\mathcal{U}$. Thus

$$i \propto \mathcal{U}$$

Since the potential difference acts over the same path as the charges flow, the path length can be taken into the proportionality constant, and the result becomes

$$i = KV \text{ amperes}$$

where K is the current if the impressed voltage is 1 v. This is Ohm's law. Transfer of charge is discussed further in Chapter 8.

Colloids

At the microscopic level the most important electrostatic forces are those which help to stabilize colloids. Colloids are suspensions of liquid or solid particles in a liquid medium (water, in our case). The particles are of the order of microns ($1\mu = 10^{-4}$ cm) in diameter, and may be single macromolecules, heavily hydrated, or collections or agglomerates of molecules. Characteristically, stable colloid particles (which do not agglutinate or precipitate) have excess like charge, and so repel each other. The repulsion promotes stability. The excess charge usually arises ultimately from the fact that the agglomerate contains acidic and basic chemical groups (e.g., $-COO^-$, $-NH_3^+$, $-PO_4^=$) whose extent of ionization at the tissue pH ($\sim$7) depends upon electrostatic interactions with other chemical groups nearby in the molecule. Since these interactions will differ from molecule to molecule, a chemical change in the colloid, an increased salt concentration, or a shift in pH can weaken electrostatic repulsion and coagulate the colloid . . . . This is considered by some to be the mechanism by which antibodies work, and to be the reason why the blood groups are incompatible.

Intermolecular Forces

At the molecular level electrostatic interactions occur of such a profound nature that they are reflected all the way up to the physiology of the system. In this group we discuss not only charge-charge (ion-ion) forces, but also those arising from interactions involving dipoles, and even induced dipoles. With these concepts, along with that of electron dispersion in an atom-atom bond, we can then describe not only the "Coulombic forces" but also the so-called "London-van der Waals forces" operating between big molecules such as lipoproteins; and finally, with the concept of proton (H^+) exchange between neighboring groups (two oxygens, for example), we can describe the extremely important "hydrogen bond."

For reasons which are reviewed in Chapter 4, in a molecule which is not symmetric, such as CO, one end accumulates more of the electronic charge than the other. In CO, the oxygen atom has the extra bit of negative charge, and the carbon is left slightly positive, by difference. The molecule has within it a permanent charge separation, and is called a *permanent dipole*. This and its weaker sister, the induced dipole, are shown in Figure 2-5.

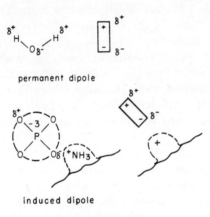

permanent dipole

induced dipole

Figure 2-5. Electrostatic Charges in Molecules.

Water is a permanent dipole, its hydrogen ends being positive to the negative oxygen. The —CONH— linkage between amino acids in proteins is also a permanent dipole, as are the —COOH groups of organic acids, and many others.

Although these are small charges, Coulomb's law applies to them, and fairly strong electrostatic forces can exist, firstly between permanent charges and permanent dipoles, and secondly between one permanent dipole and another. Water molecules attract each other, dipole to dipole, and give to bulk water a structure of oriented dipoles. Ions attract one end of the dipole and repel the other, and the result is an array of water dipoles oriented radially outwards from a central ion. The dipoles on large molecules can be hydrated by attraction to water molecules. Big molecules can be attracted to each other, or indeed have one part folded back and attracted to another part where two dipoles fall in close proximity, or where one dipole falls close to a charged group. Thus the dipolar character helps to determine not only composition but also structure.

Still weaker forces exist between induced dipoles. Even if the molecule is symmetrical about an atom, a strong positive or negative charge can some-* times induce the molecule's electrons to move a bit, so that the charge distribution becomes distorted. Such induced charge separation is called an *induced dipole*. Interactions between the mutually induced dipoles of two molecules in close proximity are called the van der Waals forces. Further, it is postulated that the electron cloud of a molecule is in continuous motion, continually varying both the size and direction of its dipole. It induces a further dipole in its neighbor, and the new "dynamic" dipole interacts with the old static one in a manner which seems to confer an extra stability on the intermolecular "bond." The extra force of attraction is called the "dispersion force," first postulated by London in 1930. Since one occurs whenever the other does, today the mutually induced dipole and dispersion forces of attraction are referred to as the London-van der Waals forces. They are very weak by comparison with Coulombic forces, principally because the charges are not only small but deformable. However, in the absence of charged groups and when two molecules can come into close proximity (< 5 Å) at a great many places over a fairly long distance (~ 15 carbon atoms in each molecular chain), considerable binding between the two has been shown to be accountable on the basis of London-van der Waals forces. Such is the case in lipoproteins in which a long hydrocarbon (and therefore with no polar groups and no permanent dipoles) chain becomes and remains intimately bonded to a polyamino acid or protein molecule. The strength and the sensitivity of this bond to interatomic spacings have been very evident in recent studies of lipoproteins in nerve cell membranes of the central nervous system. For example, one form of encephalitis is currently thought to be due to a change in binding which occurs as a result of inaccurate protein synthesis and poor binding to its lipid.

Whereas Coulombic forces are fairly long-range forces ($\propto 1/d^2$) the London-van der Waals forces are very short-range ($\propto 1/d^7$) but become important when the particles approach very close to one another (see Table 2-2).

TABLE 2-2.   Dependence of Force and Energy of Attraction Upon Distance
Between Particles

Name	Interaction	Force Proportional to	Energy Proportional to
Coulombic	ion-ion	$1/d^2$	$1/d$
	ion-dipole	$1/d^5$	$1/d^4$
	dipole-dipole	$1/d^7$	$1/d^6$
London-van der Waals	dipole-induced dipole or induced dipole-induced dipole	$1/d^7$	$1/d^6$
London-van der Waals in long-chain molecular associations	(as above)	$1/d^6$	$1/d^5$

The Hydrogen Bond

In the covalent bond two atoms are said to be held together by "shared pairs" of electrons, and the postulate that the electron of a pair can spend part of its time around each atom is thought to confer extra stability on the bond. This is the process known as "exchange." In a similar manner the hydrogen ion of an —OH group, if it finds itself in the vicinity of a second, somewhat negative oxygen, halogen, or nitrogen group may, by thermal agitation jump the gap to this second group. Ideally it may continuously oscillate between the two, and on the average assume a position half-way between them. When this occurs, the strong positive charge is equidistant from two negative charges, is attracted to them both, and so forms a bridge —a weak bond. This is the currently fashionable "hydrogen bond" (Figure 2-6). It is very versatile in the sense that, in tissues especially, which are 80 per cent water, it can be credited with much of the secondary structure

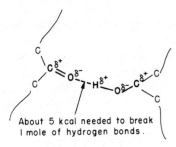

About 5 kcal needed to break
I mole of hydrogen bonds.

Figure 2–6.   Hydrogen Bond—a
Shared Proton.

of big molecules—for instance, for the paracrystallinity of the regular molecular arrays so common in tissue, such as in muscle fiber and in the aqueous humor of the lens of the eye.

Electromagnetic Force

Although we live in the magnetic field of the earth, no information exists on the response of a man to large changes in magnetic-field strength. To small changes there is no response, as far as is known. Many molecular effects are known, however, of which the recent exploitation of the so-called nuclear magnetic resonance phenomena, in which the location of a hydrogen atom in a molecule and the arrangement of atoms in molecular complexes can be learned, are exciting examples.

However, on biological systems the effects of magnetic fields are yet poorly understood. Small animals placed in fairly strong magnetic fields of $\sim$4000 gauss (at \$2/gauss, $\sim$1 lb of electromagnet/gauss) show inability to reproduce. Cell division and growth are inhibited. Interference with the collection of the mitotic apparatus in preparation for cell division is implicated. In this respect the effect of a magnetic field is similar to the effects of X or gamma rays.

The effects of electromagnetic forces—oscillating forces of unknown nature, which interact with both electric charges and magnetic poles, and with other electromagnetic forces—are better understood and are most important in the living system. In fact, the more the question is studied, the more it is realized in how many aspects of inanimate as well as animate subjects, electromagnetic forces play an important part.

Usually electromagnetic phenomena are described by their interaction energy, rather than force; this expedient enables us to by-pass their nature, and concentrate upon their effects. An "oscillating potential" permeates electromagnetic energy. It is a periodic function of time (see Figure 1-2). The amount of energy in a packet depends only upon its number of cycles per second.

Because of their importance, Chapter 4 is devoted almost completely to electromagnetic matters.

Yet will all this preoccupation with force, the physicist still is unable to cope with some really big ones, such as political "forces," and economic "pressures." In "The Razor's Edge" (1944), W. Somerset Maugham concludes: "*Goodness* is the greatest 'force' in the world!".... Unfortunately, we cannot measure it.

GENERALIZED FORCE

Although temperature is not usually thought of as a force, it is the driving force for heat-energy flow. Discussion on driving forces for several processes which occur in the living system is contained in Chapter 7.

All forces are, quite literally, "factors of energy." Thus, a generalized driving force times a quantity yields energy. Some examples are:

Mechanical force × distance   = mechanical energy or work
Gas pressure × volume of gas   = mechanical energy or work
Osmotic pressure × molar volume   = osmotic energy or work
Electrical potential × charge   = electrical energy or work
Temperature × entropy   = heat energy or work
Chemical potential × concentration = chemical energy or work

The inherent difficulties of considering both temperature in "degrees" (fractions of a length of a liquid metal along a tube!) and chemical potential (actually an energy per unit concentration) as "forces," are expounded further in Chapter 7.

What happens to a biological system when the force responsible for the acceleration due to gravity (g) is removed—that is, becomes weightless—is critically important to future space travel. The meager information on the few human beings who have so far orbited the earth is reviewed in Chapter 8.

PROBLEMS

2-1: A 200-lb football player is running full speed at a rate of 100 yd in 12 sec. Calculate his kinetic energy in ergs; in joules; in calories; in Calories or kilocalories.

If he were stopped completely in 1 sec, what power would he deliver during that 1 sec (in watts; in horsepower; in Cal/hr)? Compare this with the basal metabolic rate of 0.1 hp, or 60 Cal/hr (1 lb = 454 g; 1 cal = 4.18 jou; 1 hp = 746 w; 1 jou/sec = 1 w).

2-2: Values of the solubility of nitrogen and oxygen in water are 0.00150 and 0.00332 g of gas at 1 atm/100 g water, respectively. Approximately how many cubic centimeters of each gas are contained dissolved in the body fluids (200 lb, 80 per cent water) under 1 atm of air (20 per cent oxygen, 80 per cent nitrogen)? Neglect the fact that the solubility of gases is less in salt solutions than in pure water.

An anethetist may use a mixture up to 90 per cent oxygen, but he always retains about 5 per cent CO_2 in the inhaled gas. Why?

2-3: Assuming the total area of the adult human body to be 1 sq yd, calculate the total force due to the atmosphere (pressure 14.7 lb/in.^{2}) on the body. In dynes; in tons force.

Calculate the total force on a skin diver at a depth of 450 ft. Why is he not crushed? What precautions must he take while coming up to the surface? Why?

2-4: Make two tables showing forces of repulsion—in dynes, of two like unit charges, each with 3×10^{-10} electrostatic units of charge—at distances 0.1, 1, 2, 5, and 25 Å apart; one table for a medium of air or a vacuum (dielectric constant = 1), and the other for an aqueous solution (dielectric constant = 72). Plot the numbers, force vs distance, for each case.

REFERENCES

1. Harrington, E. L., "General College Physics," D. Van Nostrand Co., Inc., New York, N. Y., 1952.
2. Randall, J. T., "Elements of Biophysics," the Year Book Publ., Inc., Chicago, Ill., 1958.
3. Glasser, O., Ed., "Medical Physics," Vol. III, Year Book Publ., Inc., Chicago, Ill., 1960; papers by Carter, Featherstone, Lipson, *et al.*
4. Moore, W. J., "Physical Chemistry," Prentice-Hall, Inc., New York, N. Y., 1950.
5. MacIntosh, Sir R., Mushin, W. W., and Epstein, H. G., "Physics for the Anesthetist," 2nd ed., Chas. C Thomas Publ. Co., Springfield, Ill., 1960.
6. Robbins, S. L., "Textbook of Pathology With Clinical Applications," W. B. Saunders Co., Philadelphia, Pa., 1957.
7. Wolf, A. V., "Body Water," *Sci. Amer.*, **199,** 125 (1958).

CHAPTER 3

Matter Waves: Sound and Ultrasound

(On Music and Noise "from
C to C,"
On Speech and Sonic Therapy)

According to Sir Richard Paget, human speech began by the performance of sequences of simple pantomimic gestures of the tongue, lips, etc. . . . Consider the word "hither." The tongue makes the same beckoning gesture, while [one is] speaking this word, as is made with the hand.

(H. Fletcher.[3])

INTRODUCTION

Our senses of touch and hearing reveal an environment which contains a bewildering array of matter waves: the breeze; falling raindrops; noise, speech, and music; earth tremors, shock, or blast waves; the vibrations encountered when riding a horse, or when operating a jack-hammer. Bees and some other insects, and bats too, send and receive, and are guided in flight by very high-frequency matter waves.

Thus waves in matter have a great spectrum of manifestations, uses, and effects. It is the purpose of this chapter to illustrate them, for matter waves and electromagnetic radiations together comprise the most important method of man's continuous exchange of force and energy with his environment. The latter are introduced in Chapter 4. They are fundamentally very different from matter waves, although often confused with them. In matter waves the medium itself—solid, liquid, or gas—moves back and forth.

PROPERTIES OF MATTER WAVES

Definition

Matter waves are of two types, which differ only in the direction of the vibration relative to the direction of propagation. In transverse waves the vibration is perpendicular to the direction of propagation (a plucked violin string, for example). In longitudinal waves the vibration is parallel to the direction of propagation (the pressure waves from a blast, or in front of a piston, for example). Most of the matter waves which are of interest here are, like water waves, a combination of both.

The two basic properties are the pressure (force/unit area) of the wave and its rate of change with time. The former is usually called the amplitude, ψ (dynes/cm^2). The latter is usually expressed as the number of times the value of ψ cycles back and forth per second, i.e., as the frequency (cycles/sec).

All matter waves, no matter what the shape, can be expressed as a superposition of simple, sinusoidal waves, of the type discussed in Chapter 1.

There are *traveling* waves and *standing* waves (Figure 3-1 (a) and (b)). A

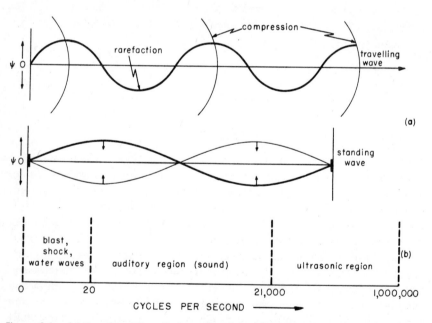

Figure 3-1. (a) Traveling Wave Such as Sound in Air; Standing Wave Such as On a Vibrating Violin String; (b) Range of Matter Waves.

sound wave moving through air travels from its source and imparts an energy to the receiver. This energy is primarily in the direction of propagation, but with scattering some of it becomes transverse.

By contrast, the standing wave can impart no longitudinal energy—it has none. But it can impart transverse energy to the medium. The generation of the sound by the vibrating violin string is an example.

The intensity, I, of the matter wave is the power delivered by it per unit area. In other words, I is the rate at which the wave expends energy. All traveling waves move at a certain velocity, v (cm/sec). Hence the product of amplitude (a pressure) times distance is the energy expended per unit area:

$$w = \psi d \quad \text{(dynes/cm}^2 \times \text{cm} = \text{ergs/cm}^2)$$

The product of amplitude and velocity is the power expended per unit area:

$$I = \psi v \quad \text{(dynes/cm}^2 \times \text{cm/sec} = \text{ergs/cm}^2 \text{ sec)}$$

The intensity or power expended per unit area by the traveling wave, is highest for those media having molecules with the greatest number of degrees of freedom in which energy can be stored—gases for example. Both the range and speed of sound are highest in solids, somewhat less in liquids, far less in gases. However, for any medium of constant density, ρ, the velocity has a fixed value. This fact results in another useful relationship, that between amplitude (pressure) and intensity (power):

$$I = \psi^2/v\rho$$

which says simply that power delivered per unit area to any medium is proportional to the pressure squared, if velocity and density are held constant.* This ($I \propto \psi^2$) is a very useful rule-of-thumb, applicable, it turns out, to all field phenomena.

Useful also is the fact that, although low-frequency waves are easily reflected and diffracted by air and hence are nondirectional (or will go around corners), high-frequency waves are only slightly scattered by air. Therefore, the latter can be beamed in a preferred direction from a source, and even focused on a particular spot by proper (saucer-like) design of the vibrating source.

---

*Dimensions:

$$I = \frac{\psi^2}{v\rho} = \left(\frac{\text{dynes}}{\text{cm}^2}\right)^2 \bigg/ \frac{\text{cm}}{\text{sec}} \frac{\text{g}}{\text{cm}^3}$$

$$= \left(\frac{\text{g cm}}{\text{sec}^2\,\text{cm}^2}\right)^2 \bigg/ \frac{\text{cm}}{\text{sec}} \frac{\text{g}}{\text{cm}^3}$$

$$= \text{ergs/cm}^2 \text{ sec}$$

(Work it through.)

Illustrations

Frequency

Matter waves have a broad range of frequency, from zero up to the current practical upper limit of about 1,000,000 cycles per sec (cps) in use in some ultrasonic-therapy and submarine-detection studies (Figure 3-1 (c)). The human ear is most sensitive from ≅50 to ≅10,000 cps; the range of man's ear, however, may be from 20 to 21,000 cps. This, then, is the auditory or sound range. Speech requires 60 to 500 cps. The piano ranges from 27.2 to 4138.4 cps. The great basso profondo, Italo Tajo, could reach a minimum of ≅60 cps; the diminutive coloratura soprano, Lili Pons, could hit 1300 cps on a good day. Of course, these are the basic frequencies, and it is understood that a basic frequency generated by any physical vibrator will contain over-tones, or harmonics, which are multiples (2×, 4×, even 8×) of the basic frequency. The quality of the tone is determined by the sum of all the components: the basic frequency plus its harmonics.

Training and youth combine to produce a receiver which can hear low-power sound up to 12,000 cps. Some musicians can detect overtones from their instruments up to 14,000 cps, but these are few. Most of us can detect frequencies up to 18,000 from a signal generator, if the signal is intense enough, and the odd person can detect up to 21,000 cps. Dogs do it with ease. Porpoises have a phenomenal sonic system in their heads which can sweep frequencies repetitively from a few cycles to many thousands of cycles —both send *and* receive.

Below and overlapping the auditory range for man is the range (0 to 50 cps) of blast and shock waves, earth tremors, water waves, and the like. The masseur will use vibrations 1 to 50 cps; a ship will roll at 0.1 cps. An air hammer operates at ∼15 cps, and we hear the overtones.

Above the range of sound, from 20,000 up to >1,000,000, lies the important range of ultrasound, and the science and technology known as ultrasonics.

Velocity

The speed of matter waves depends sharply upon the medium, and in the case of a gas, its temperature and pressure. For instance, in air at 0°C and 1 atm pressure the speed is 331 meters/sec (mps) (730 miles/hr). In water and soft tissue it is 4½ times higher than in air, and in solids it goes up to 5000 mps. The velocity of sound through fat is 1440, through muscle 1570, and through bone 3360 mps.

Velocity is independent of frequency; and it is probably just as well, otherwise the low tones of the organ might reach our ears later than the high tones of the same chord!

Amplitude and Intensity

There is a minimum pressure and power of matter waves below which the ear cannot detect the wave. This value is about 0.0002 dynes/cm², an extremely small value because the ear is very sensitive. The corresponding power or intensity limit is ∼10^{-9} ergs/cm² sec, i.e., ∼10^{-16} w/cm²! This value places its sensitivity very close to the threshold of the power in heat motion, and thus very close to the minimum background agitation of matter in our environment. The maximum amplitude the eardrum can stand, without certain irreparable damage resulting, is ∼200 dynes/cm². Therefore, the range of sensitivity of the ear is phenomenally high, one to a million. It is the most sensitive at 1,000 cps.

The sense of touch, particularly on the fingers and tongue, is not nearly so sensitive, but responds down to much lower frequencies.

To our knowledge, man has no detection apparatus for frequencies above about 20,000 cps. However, there is some evidence that ultrasound can penetrate to the brain and cause psychological aberrations, which may or may not be a result of organic damage.

One of the most convenient ways of generating matter waves of controlled frequency is by means of the vibrating crystal. Certain crystals are piezoelectric—that is, they expand or contract if an electric voltage is applied to contacts with two different crystal faces (Figure 3-2). The amount of the

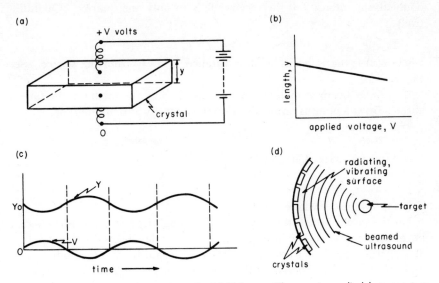

Figure 3-2. About Piezoelectric Crystals: (a) Voltage difference is applied between two opposite faces. (b) The length changes as the applied voltage is changed. (c) Varying voltage, V, gives varying length, y. (d) Concave radiator concentrates matter waves on a target.

expansion or contraction increases with increasing applied voltage. Quartz and barium titanate are currently in wide use. If the applied voltage is varied, the crystal shape varies accordingly, or vibrates, and the matter wave so established is transmitted by contact with the medium. The amplitude of the vibration is higher the higher the vibrating voltage applied. The frequency of vibration follows that of the electrical signal, if the crystal is not too big. Figure 3-2 illustrates these points.

Apparatus with output which ranges from a few to a million cycles per second, and from next to nothing up to a few hundred watts per square centimeter of crystal, has been built and used.

Constructed with a concave radiating surface (Figure 3-2 (d)), an array of piezoelectric crystals, if properly oriented, can be made to focus an intense beam of matter waves at a point a few centimeters from the radiating surface. For example, in recent therapeutic work beams of 1 Mc (1,000,000 cps) were focused on a small target, and delivered energy at a rate (intensity) of 8 kw/cm^2 of cross-section of the target!

Absorption

If waves are *diverging*, or being dissipated or scattered, the important general rule, called the "inverse square law," is obeyed. It says simply that the intensity, I, decreases as the distance from the source gets larger, in such a manner that if, for example, the distance between source and receiver is doubled, the intensity at the receiver falls to only one quarter. Quantitatively,

$$I(x) \propto 1/x^2$$

where $I(x)$ is the intensity at any distance, x, away from the source. See Figure 3-3.

If a *parallel* beam of matter waves is absorbed by the medium, the rate of absorption at a point is proportional to the intensity at that point; or

$$dI/dx = -kI$$

which integrates (see Chapter 1) to

$$I = I_0 e^{-kx}$$

if I_0 is the value of I where $x = 0$.

For the case in which the waves are diverging and also being absorbed, a linear combination of the inverse square law and the absorption law applies. The energy absorbed from the matter-wave beam by the medium contributes to the thermal motion of the molecules of the medium. The absorption coefficient, k, is intimately related to several physical properties of the medium.

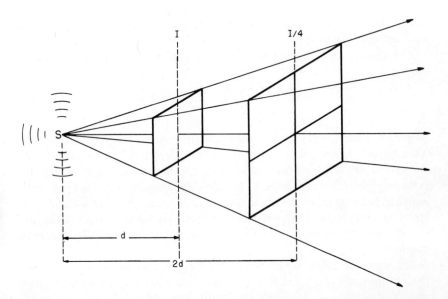

Figure 3–3. Inverse Square Law. Radiation from source S diverges. Intensity (w/cm²) at distance, *d*, is four times the intensity at 2*d* because the same radiation is spread through four times the area by the time it reaches 2*d*.

However, there are two principal mechanisms of absorption of matter waves by tissue:

(a) *Frictional resistance:* The momentum of the propagation, which is directional (Fig. 3-1 (a)), is passed to the molecules of the tissue, which become momentarily polarized by the pulse of pressure. The directed energy thus received quickly decays into random, nondirectional molecular motion. This mechanism can be called "molecular absorption." It is important at medium and high frequencies.

(b) *Elastic reactance of the bulk tissue:* Absorption occurs by movement of the bulk material; mass is displaced, and macro-oscillations result in sympathy with the impinging, oscillating pressure. Because the tissue is not perfectly elastic (i.e., the molecules will realign themselves so that they won't be polarized), the absorbed energy quickly dissipates in front of the pressure pulse as molecular motion or heat. This is the only method by which energy is absorbed at low frequencies—during earth tremors, train rumble, or massage, for example. This mechanism can be called "elastic absorption."

Reflection, due to the inertia of the tissue (its tendency to remain at rest unless forced to do otherwise—Newton's first law of motion), occurs at high frequencies for soft tissue and even at low frequencies for dense tissue such as bone. Truly elastic tissues simply reflect incident matter waves.

The absorption coefficient for molecular absorption (k) is well known for air and water:

$$k = \frac{8\pi^2 f^2}{3v\rho} \left[\eta + \frac{3}{4} \frac{c_P - c_V}{c_P c_V} K_T \right]$$

where f is the frequency (cps) of the impinging wave, v the velocity (cm/sec), ρ the density (g/cm^3), η the viscosity (dyne sec/cm^2), K_T the heat conductivity (cal/sec deg cm), and the c's are the specific heats (cal/deg g) at constant pressure, P, and constant volume, V. Hence the energy absorbed per centimeter of penetration of the impinging wave increases linearly with the viscosity or "stickiness" of the medium and with its thermal conductivity; increases very rapidly with increasing frequency; but decreases with increasing density.

For water, which is a sufficiently good approximation to soft tissue for present purposes, $k/f^2 = 8.5 \times 10^{-17}$ sec^2/cm. For air the value is 1000 times higher, because although η is 50 times smaller for air than for water, v is 4½ times smaller and ρ is 1000 times smaller. For liquids only the first term (the frictional or viscous one) is important; for gases both are important. Therefore it is useful to aerate a tissue before sonic therapy is applied, because absorption is higher.

Since reflection increases with increasing frequency, the method of application is important. In the absence of reflection, the above expressions describe the situation well. Direct application of the vibrator to the tissue assures this. However, if the sound is beamed through air, the situation is quite different: reflection occurs.

Quantitative studies on tissues are only recent. The general rule which has emerged is as follows: Beamed through air, sound of high frequency suffers little absorption, and little damage results. The depth of penetration increases with increasing frequency. Most (>95 per cent) of the incident energy passes right through, or is reflected. Some of Von Gierke's figures (1950) are: 5 to 6 per cent absorbed at 100 cps; 0.2 to 4 per cent absorbed at 1000 cps; and <0.4 per cent absorbed at 10 kc. Beamed through liquid or solid, ultrasonic radiation is easily controlled and its absorption predicted. More will be said about this later, in the section on therapy.

SENSITIVITY OF A DETECTOR, AND THE WEBER-FECHNER LAW

It is a fact that whether or not a receiver will detect a signal depends upon how much the signal differs from the background noise. The dependence is not a simple proportionality, but rather a logarithmic one. Thus, the sensation, or loudness, L, is given by

$$L \propto \log I/I°$$

where $I°$ is background intensity, and I is the intensity, over background, of the signal to be detected. This is the basic form of the Weber-Fechner law. It has many manifestations. For instance, if there are two signals equally strong, with different backgrounds, the resolution of (difference in loudness), $L_2 - L_1$, is related to the ratio of the intensities of the two backgrounds, $I_1°$ and $I_2°$, as follows:

$$L_2 - L_1 \propto \log I_1°/I_2°$$

This is a law which has rather wide application, not only in the psychological sensations but in detection of electromagnetic waves of many frequency ranges, from the radio to the infrared. Therefore its implications should be very thoroughly contemplated.

Because of this logarithmic law, it is convenient to express power ratios by a logarithmic unit, so that sensation becomes approximately linearly proportional to this unit. The unit is called the "bel," (b) and is equal to the logarithm of the ratio of two sound intensities if they are in a ratio of $10:1$. The number of bels then is given by

$$b = \log I/I°$$

For sound, the value $I°$ is arbitrarily chosen to be the lowest one which a human ear can detect (10^{-16} w/cm²; or, in pressure units, 0.0002 dynes/cm², since the same conversion factor applies to numerator and denominator). The bel unit is too large for convenience, and the decibel, one tenth of a bel, has received wider use. Therefore, the number of decibels is:

$$db = 10 \log I/I°$$

Another form of the Weber-Fechner law, then, is

$$L \propto db$$

It holds true for all sensory receptors.

Some minimum discernible *relative* changes,** $(I_t - I°)/I°$ (where I_t is threshold intensity), which man can detect are:

Brightness of light: 1 per cent
Lengths of lines: 2 per cent
Feeling of weight: 10 per cent
Loudness of sound: 30 per cent

**Remember relative error, defined in Chapter 1?

Sensitivity, S, of a detector, or discernment per decibel of signal over background, is defined as

$$S = \log I^\circ / \Delta I_t$$

where $\Delta I_t = I_t - I^\circ$. Sensitivity is higher the smaller is the value of ΔI_t. Usually when S is determined at different values of an independent variable, the result is expressed as the *sensitivity relative to the maximum value taken as unity* (S/S_{max}). The sensitivity of the ear is so expressed in Figure 3-4.

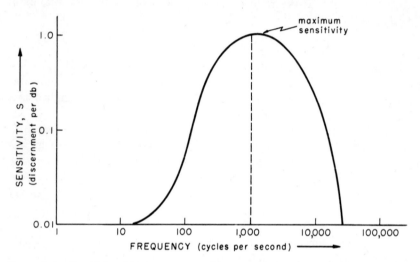

Figure 3-4.   Sensitivity of Human Ear at Different Frequencies of Sound Waves. The individual's sensitivity curve may differ markedly from this average curve.

THE BODY'S DETECTORS OF MATTER WAVES

Introduction

In this section are given an outline of the structure of the ear and a description of the mechanism of the sense of touch. This sketch is meant to show the important general features, but does not penetrate into either the depths of the mechanism nor the psychology of the resulting sensations such as loudness and pitch. A very well written and concise display of the biophysics of hearing is found in the book by Stacy *et al.*[6] An up-to-date survey of the physiology of hearing is given by Whitfield,[7] and a masterful discussion of biological transducers (converters of mechanical to electrical stimuli) was recently given by Gray.[8] To delve deeply into this aspect of the subject is, unfortunately, beyond our scope, although it is currently a very active part of biophysical research.

Notes on the Ear

The structure of the ear can be pictured, in simplest terms, as consisting of three main parts: the pinna (lobe) and external canal, the middle ear, and the cochlea. The canal and the middle ear are separated by the tympanic membrane (ear drum) which covers and protects the latter. The middle-ear cavity contains a system of three bony levers, the ossicles (the malleus, incus, and stapes) whose main job seems to be to act as a matching device transmitting matter vibrations between the two fluids: the air outside in the external canal, and the perilymph inside the cochlea. The cochlea is a spiral canal within the bone of the skull. It is divided axially into three channels by membranous partitions. Into one of these, the scala vestibuli, is inserted the end of the stapes; this chamber, then, receives directly the transmitted vibrations. Through the membranes, vibrations are passed laterally into the other two canals, the scala media and the scala tympani. These two are separated by the basilar membrane, which receives the endings of the auditory nerve, and the cells of which are the transducers that convert the mechanical energy of vibration into the electrical energy transmitted along the nerve. Most recent work has been aimed at the mechanism of action of the region of the basilar membrane, the transducer. Some of the cells on the membrane have hair-like processes projecting from their upper ends and attached to the overhanging, tectorial membrane. Relative movement between the tectorial and basilar membranes distorts the cells of both. Note Figure 3-5.

The analogy with piezoelectric crystals is usefully drawn at this point: distortion of the shape of the transducer in both cases leads to change in the potential difference between two points on the surface of the transducer—in one case the surface potential of the crystal, in the other case the membrane potential of the cell.

An accumulation of evidence now exists—Von Békésy[13] received the 1961 Nobel Prize in Physiology and Medicine for this work, done at Harvard— that a traveling wave passes along the basilar membrane during excitation. The position at which the wave achieves its highest amplitude (think of the whip) is dependent upon the frequency of the wave being detected. Therefore, nerve signals from different tones arise at different spots, each spot associated with specific nerve endings. At low frequencies the whole basilar membrane vibrates in sympathy with the incoming matter wave.

The question of membrane potential change will be considered in Chapters 7 and 10, in reference to erythrocytes and nerve cells, upon which voltages have been directly measured *in vivo*.

Deformations in the structure, or failure of the ear to respond to matter waves, is the subject matter of the otologist. Corrections are applied sometimes simply by amplification of the signal reaching the tympanic membrane, sometimes, although less commonly, directly to the cochlea by stimulation of the bone structure which surrounds it. Surgery is often necessary to free the "frozen" lever system.

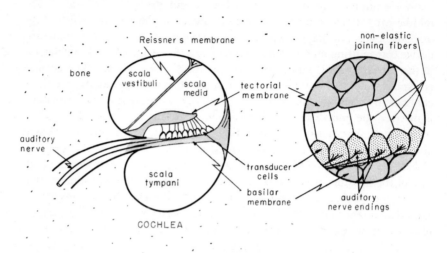

Figure 3-5. Schematic Drawing of Cross-section of the Cochlea, the Inner Ear. The three scalae are separated by deformable membranes. The transducers are fastened to the tectorial membrane by fibers. Relative motion between the tectorial membrane and the basilar membrane causes stretching of the transducer cells, resulting in change in membrane permeability, and therefore ionic composition and membrane potential. This change activates the nerve endings attached to the cells, and the impulse is carried down the auditory nerve to the brain.

The Sense of Touch And Other Mechanoreceptors

A magnificent array of mechanoreceptors (as well as photo-, chemo-, and thermal receptors) is displayed by the human body. These bring in information from the environment, and then provide a feedback of information concerning an action taken. The most sensitive transducers, other than those in the ear, are found on the tip of the tongue and on the tips of the fingers, although mechanoreceptors are located all over the body, so closely spaced that no pressure change on the surface, above some threshold value, goes undetected.

They all have three parts in common: (1) a mechanism for transmitting a pressure change to the receptor cell; (2) the deformable receptor cell, the deformation of which (apparently) changes its cell membrane potential at a point intimately associated with (3) a specialized ending of a nerve cell's axon. Speculations are rampant on the mechanism of this transposition. Transduction through changing electrical potentials across the receptor cell wall is currently a very popular generalization; but reliable details of mechanism, unfortunately, are too few.

SPEECH

Three resonators, or vibrating cavities, are responsible for the organized noise which we call speech. They are (1) the vocal chords, which close the exit used by air exhaled from the lungs; (2) the throat and the mouth; and (3) the nasal cavity. The vocal chords, the tongue, and the lips control the changes in vibration which are induced in the exhaling air stream and which are the sounds of speech. The combination of these three moving parts, each of which can take several different shapes, gives remarkable versatility in the production of sound.

The fundamental sounds of speech are divided into six classes: pure vowels, diphthongs, transitionals, semivowels, fricative consonants, and stop consonants. The subject of phonetics is well known, is heavily illustrated in any good dictionary, and needs no review here.

Amplitude and intensity are controlled mainly by the rate of expulsion of air, although secondary resonators such as the head and the chest play a small role.

Speech sounds have been analyzed on many people by the Bell Telephone Laboratories, for obvious reasons. Some of the results are contained in the classic book by Fletcher.[3] For instance "oo" as in "pool" spoken by men (by women) has a mean fundamental frequency of 140 cps (270 cps), a mean low frequency of 411 (581 for women), scattered high frequency of 3700 (4412 for women). All speech sounds have been carefully recorded and analyzed, and the sounds of the "average man" used for microphone design.

The fundamental speech sounds have a power. When one talks as loudly as possible without shouting, the average speech power is about 1000 microwatts (1 μw = 0.000001 w) at the source. When one talks in as weak a voice as possible, without whispering, it drops to 0.1 μw. A very soft whisper has a power of about 0.001 μw. Very loud speech is ~20 db over average speech power; a soft whisper is ~40 db under average.

NOISE

High-intensity noise has become one of the most disturbing problems of the modern way of life. Noise is usually defined as any unwanted sound, and hence the classification is highly subjective. High-intensity noise is usually defined as any unwanted sound greater than 85 db (see Table 3-1).

Noise has many components—matter waves of many frequencies. The "buzz" from speech in a crowded room will center in the range 300 to 6000 cps. The noise generated by a wood planer has most of its energy between 200 and 2000 cps, while a power saw will emit noise from 50 to 6000 cps.

Only low-pitched or high-pitched voices can be clearly understood. This is the crux of the problem facing communication engineers and otologists alike: to provide a sufficient sound intensity level (over background noise) to the middle ear. This question is considered in more general terms in Chapter 11.

TABLE 3-1. Some Sources of Noise*

Location	Power (w/cm^2)	Sound Power Level** (db)
50-hp siren (100 ft away)	10^{-2}	140
Submarine engine room (full speed)	10^{-5}	110
Factories	10^{-4} to 10^{-8}	76 to 128
Woodworking plants	10^{-4} to 10^{-8}	80 to 114
Subway car	10^{-7} to 10^{-8}	80 to 90
Loud radio (2 ft away)	10^{-8}	80
Speech at 2 ft	10^{-12} to 10^{-8}	60 normal, 77 shouting
Speech at 12 ft		43 normal, 61 shouting
Private office	10^{-12}	40
Average home	10^{-13}	30
Library	10^{-14}	20
"Silence"	10^{-16}	0

*After Neeley, K. K., "Noise—Some Implications for Aviation," *Cau. Aeronaut. J.*, **3**, 312 (1957).
**Referred to 10^{-16} w/cm², the threshold of hearing.

Exposure of man to high-intensity noise has several effects: change in hearing acuity, and mechanical or pathological damage to the cochlea; temporary blindness (>140 db); changes in ability to perform skilled and unskilled tasks; feelings of fear, annoyance, dissatisfaction, and nausea. Discussion of some of these effects follows in the next section.

PHYSIOLOGICAL EFFECTS OF INTENSE MATTER WAVES

The physicochemical basis of the physiological damage is fairly well understood. Five facts are important to the discussion:

(1) During the absorption of matter waves, a front of high pressure precedes a front of reduced pressure through the tissue. There is therefore a differential pressure, or a pressure gradient, along the tissue which stretches and compresses it in sympathy with the incoming wave. If the amplitude is

such that the elastic limit is exceeded, tearing can result. Thus 160 db will rupture the eardrum itself, probably the toughest part of the soft tissue of the whole organ!

(2) At high frequencies, the compression occurs so fast that energy is passed from the matter wave to the recipient molecules so rapidly that it has no time to disperse through molecular vibrations. The molecule becomes phenomenally "hot" or energetic, and may fly apart. Thus chemical bonds are broken (Figure 3-6 (a)). Water is decomposed to H_2 and H_2O_2.

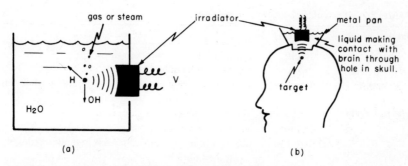

(a)   (b)

Figure 3-6. (a) Cavitation and Production of Broken Water Molecules by Ultrasound. The OH fragment is a rapidly effective oxidizing agent. (b) Irradiation of a Small Locale in the Brain. (Success with Parkinson's disease reported.)

(3) During rarefaction (low-pressure part of the wave), any dissolved gas in the tissue may coalesce into bubbles; and in fact bubbles containing only water vapor may form, breaking molecular bonds as they form, and breaking more bonds as they collapse and release their high surface energy. This is called cavitation. It occurs in water at power levels as low as 140 db. This critical power level decreases with increasing frequency.

(4) With the breaking of bonds, free radicals are produced, which, for reasons to be discussed in Chapter 4, cause a (net) oxidation reaction to occur in most aqueous solutions. Three watts of power introduced at 500,000 cps, for example, will cause oxidation.

(5) Because of general absorption of energy within the volume irradiated with matter waves, a general temperature rise occurs. This upsets the metabolism of the tissue in a manner discussed later in Chapter 8. Irradiation by 1 megacycle (Mc) at a power of 50 w/cm², for example, raises the temperature of water from 20 to 50°C in a few minutes.

Some specific observations of effects of sound waves on man are given in Table 3-2.

For obvious reasons, experiments using high-power sound are carefully and selectively done on man. However, an accumulation of experience is being gained on animals, principally guinea pigs, rats, and mice. The investigations have not been extensive enough to denote anything other than generalitites. However, at 165 db, 500 to 400,000 cps, on guinea pigs, pathological changes occur in both the inner and middle ear; lesions appear in the organ of Corti, and it is ruptured from the basilar membrane. Hemorrhages start where the malleus meets with the eardrum. Convulsions often result. The skin becomes blistered and reddened. Death is hastened by the damage.

TABLE 3-2. Effects of High-Intensity Sound on Man*

Frequency (cps)	Level (db)	Effect
100	110	stimulation of receptors in skin
2000 to 2500	>150	mild warming of body surfaces
Jet engine	130 to 155	nausea, vomiting, dizziness; interference with touch and muscle sense
100 to 10,000	105	significant changes in pulse rate
	140	pain in middle ear
	130 to 140	changes in muscle tone; increase in tendon reflexes; incoordination
	~160	minor permanent damage if prolonged
	~190	major permanent damage in short time
50	~120	vibration of muscles in arms and legs
700 to 1500	130	resonance in mouth, nasal cavities, and sinuses

*Collected by Neeley, K. K., "Noise—Some Implications for Aviation," *Can. Aeronaut. J.*, **3**, 312 (1957).

SONIC AND ULTRASONIC THERAPY

Certain uses have already been demonstrated; others await discovery, for the technique is very new to medicine. The following applications are already well known in principle, and are now being introduced in practice very cautiously—for the early 1950's saw the period of novelty wax strong, and then wane into a hard reappraisal in the mid-50's; and one now observes the gradual emergence of the place of vibrations in the medical arsenal. Details can be found in the reviews of two masters of the subject, R. F. Herrick[10] and W. J. Fry[1] and in the book edited by E. Kelly.[2]

Present Applications

(1) Subcutaneous lesions can be located by ultra high-frequency matter waves. They focus well at 1 Mc, and penetrate to a useful depth. The depth of penetration is a function of the power of the source. Since reflection of matter waves is greater the higher the density of the medium, tumors can be distinguished from normal tissue at a location deep below the surface.

(2) Based on the same principle, the rate of blood flow through the arterial system can now be measured by reflected ultrasound, in a nondestructive experiment in which all instrumentation is external to the body.

(3) Dentists have begun to apply sound to the ears of patients during drilling, because it has been found that the brain cannot perceive pain from the teeth and sound from the ear at the same time. The sound in this case acts as a local anesthetic.

(4) "Rapid massage" heat therapy is now quite common, with an assortment of low-frequency vibrator pads and belts available, and experimental models operating in the 12,000 to 50,000 cps region. For deep "massage" higher frequency ultrasound is used; it has the added advantage of comfort from noise.

(5) Certain skin diseases can be treated with beamed and focused ultrasound. Thus viruses are destroyed (literally shaken into little bits!) by ultrasound, and a future in sterilization seems assured. In this application its competitor is soft X rays.

(6) "Neurosonic surgery" is now well advanced on animals, and has received some experimental evaluation on humans. The most spectacular success so far has been achieved in treatment of Parkinson's disease, the shaking palsy. Because of its future importance,*** some details will now be given.

"Neurosonic Surgery"

The ultrasonic radiation reaches the brain through a hole cut in the skull, and the matter waves are beamed and focused on that part, deep in the brain, in which involuntary movements are controlled (Figure 3-6 (b)). The energy dissipated by the beam is concentrated at the focus of the beam, and gently destroys the metabolic activity at the site (the substantia nigra). The method, when used carefully, has the advantage over all others that it produces lesions at the focus of the ultrasonic energy without interfering with the normal blood flow from one part of the brain to another through the region irradiated. Of course this is a great advantage from the medical point of view. The techniques were worked out first on hundreds of cats and monkeys, and are now very cautiously being applied to man. Functional disruption of nervous conduction occurs within a few seconds of exposure to ultrasound of sufficient dosage to produce lesions: 980,000 cps, 1.8- to 3-sec duration, and particle velocity amplitude of 350 cm/sec, from a generator with the capability of 20 to 1000 w/cm². From the therapeutic viewpoint it has been found possible to irradiate simultaneously the four small parts of the brain which are active with respect to Parkinsonism in the four limbs.

***In spite of the fact that Parkinsonism may be dying out. Thus the average age of these patients is steadily increasing, in North America, a trend which, if it continues, would indicate that the disease may have died out naturally by 1985.

Other conditions reported treated successfully by this method at this date include a case of cerebral palsy and one of phantom limb pain. The principle is simple enough: to produce lesions, without excessive damage, at the tiny spots in the brain which control the function which appears disordered. Conversely, using this tool to inhibit temporarily the various functions controlled by the brain, one not only can obtain a micromap, in three dimensions, of the control sites, but learn something of the mechanism of control as well.

The facts of microirradiation and selective absorption and damage, augur well for the future of "neurosonic therapy" as a strong competitor to the mechanical, electrical, and chemical techniques now in use in brain disorders.

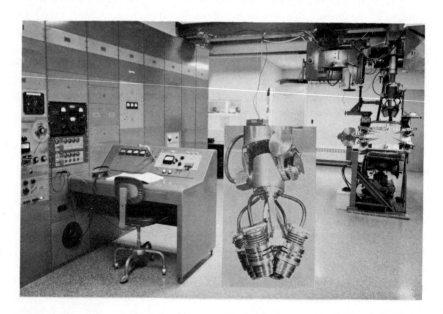

Figure 3-7. Equipment for Clinical Ultrasonic Irradiation of a Patient with a Hyperkinetic Mental Disorder. *Upper right and insert:* The multibeam irradiator itself. (Courtesy of W. J. Fry, University of Illinois Biophysics Research Laboratory.)

The Dunn-Fry Law

As the quotation from Lord Kelvin (Chapter 1) said, it is always comforting to be able to state quantitatively an important fact. On animals it has been found that the time, t, of irradiation to a chosen physiological state —in this case to paralysis of the hind legs of young mice—is related to the intensity, I (power), of the irradiating ultrasound (982 kc/sec, hydrostatic

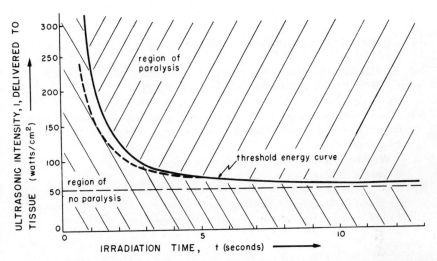

Figure 3-8. Threshold Energy for Paralysis as a Function of Ultrasonic Intensity. Solid curve shows data of W. J. Fry and F. Dunn, 1956. Broken curve shows how the threshold is much higher than expected at very short irradiation times.

pressure 1 atm, starting temperature $10°$ C) by the simple expression

$$t \propto 1/\sqrt{I},$$

the Dunn-Fry law, which says simply that the time to paralysis is shorter the higher the intensity; but that the damage occurs relatively more slowly for large intensities than for small intensities.

This is one of the best rules-of-thumb so far worked out in biophysics of ultrasound therapy. It remains to be seen whether it is of general applicability. Intuitively one would think it should be. In any case it might be well to state the following memory aid: Probably because of general heating and of molecular excitation induced by absorbed ultrasound, metabolic, physiologic, and histologic changes occur in tissues. In other words, tissues Fry until Dunn!

CONCLUSION

"Like some other agents which have been introduced into the armamentarium of clinical medicine, medical ultrasonics passed through the early stages of enthusiasm, followed by a reactionary stage of pessimism, before it achieved the stature presently accorded it. Currently there are promising developments and interesting applications of ultrasound for medical diagnosis, for therapy, and for biologic measurement." (J. F. Herrick.[12])

The next ten years should be interesting ones from this point of view.

PROBLEMS

3-1: Express in decibels the sound which delivers 150 times the power of background noise.

3-2: (a) Calculate the value of the absorption coefficient of sound in tissue at 50; 1000; 10,000; and 500,000 cycles per second (cps).

(b) Make a plot of intensity vs depth in tissue for each frequency.

3-3: How would you employ the inverse square law to "protect" yourself from an intense source of noise? Suppose you wanted to reduce the noise level by a factor of ten.

What could you learn about this problem from $a = f(\eta)$ as these terms are defined in the text?

3-4: Two signals enter your ear: one at 500 cps, with intensities I and $I°$ equal to 10^{-12} and 10^{-15} w/cm², respectively; and the other at 6000 cps with intensities I and $I°$ equal to 10^{-14} and 10^{-16} w/cm². Which will seem the louder?

REFERENCES

1. Fry, W. J., *Adv. in Biol. and Med. Phys.*, **6**, 281 (1959): a review, illustrated.
2. Kelly, E., Ed., "Ultrasound in Biology and Medicine," *Amer. Inst. of Biol. Sciences*, Washington, D. C., 1957.
3. Fletcher, H., "Speech and Hearing," D. Van Nostrand Co., Inc., New York, N. Y., 1946.
4. Ruch, T. C. and Fulton, J. F., Eds., "Medical Physiology and Biophysics," W. B. Saunders Co., Philadelphia, Pa., 1960.
5. Herzfeld, K. F. and Litovitz, T. A., "Absorption and Dispersion of Ultrasonic Waves," Academic Press, New York, N. Y., 1959.
6. Stacy, R. W., Williams, D. T., Worden, R. E., and McMorris, R. O., "Essentials of Biological and Medical Physics," McGraw-Hill Book Co., Inc., New York, N. Y., 1955.
7. Whitfield, I. C., "The Physiology of Hearing," in *Progr. in Biophysics*, **8**, 1 (1957); a review.
8. Gray, J. A. B., "Mechanical into Electrical Energy in Certain Mechano-Receptors," *Progr. in Biophysics*, **9**, 285 (1959); a review.
9. Neely, K. K., "Noise—Some Implications for Aviation," *Can. Aeronaut. J.*, **3**, 312 (1957).
10. Herrick, J. F. and Anderson, J. A., "Circulatory System: Methods—Ultrasonic Flow Meter," in "Medical Physics," Vol. III, O. Glasser, Ed., Yearbook Publ., Inc., Chicago, Ill., 1960, p. 181.
11. Gardner, W. H., "Speech Pathology," *ibid.*, p. 637.
12. Herrick, J. F., *Proc. Inst. Radio Engineers*, Nov., 1959, p. 1957.
13. Von Békésy, G., "The Ear," *Sci. Amer.*, Aug., 1957; a review.

CHAPTER 4

Electromagnetic Radiations
and Matter

The next thing is striking: through the black carton container, which lets through no visible or ultraviolet rays of the sun, nor the electric arc light, an agent (X) goes through which has the property that it can produce a vivid fluorescence . . . .

We soon found that the agent penetrates all bodies, but to a very different degree. (W. C. Roentgen, *Annalen der Physik und Chemie*, 64, 1 (1898).)

INTRODUCTION

Within fifteen years, just before the turn of the century, complacent classical physics received three rude shocks. The first was Julius Plücker's description (*circa* 1890) of the electrical discharges which take place in gases under low pressure and high voltage (the embryo of the "neon" sign). The second was Henri Becquerel's discovery of natural radioactivity in 1895; and the third was Wilhelm Roentgen's discovery of X rays, reported in 1898. In the years since then, the three discoveries have collectively engendered intense investigation of: (1) the structure of molecules, atoms and nuclei; (2) arrangements of molecules in crystals and other, less well-defined molecular arrays; (3) the electromagnetic spectrum, from X rays through visible to infrared radiation; and (4) the interactions—and in fact interconversion! —of electromagnetic energy and matter. In this chapter a review is given of those facts and theories which are useful to an understanding of the biophysics of the interactions of electromagnetic radiation and living matter.

THE STRUCTURE OF MATTER

The Elementary Particles and Atomic Architecture

Some of the key experimental facts accumulated within a few years of 1900 illustrate the bases upon which our knowledge of structure depends.

Roentgen found that his unknown, or "X," rays would cause fluorescence in zinc sulfide and barium platinocyanide; and further that they would ionize gases and darken a photographic plate. They were therefore easily detected by an electroscope, or by an increase in current through a gaseous discharge tube, or by photographic techniques. He studied penetration through paper, wood, and metals, and showed that difference in penetration is one of degree rather than of kind (cf. the quotation which opened this Chapter.)

A fluorescent screen on each end of a cylindrical gaseous discharge tube showed that particles, presumably charged, pass between the electrodes in each direction. By placing metal shields between positive and negative electrodes, and by impressing a voltage between horizontal plates placed with their plane parallel to the direction of flow, it was shown that the rays coming from the positive electrode bend toward the negative horizontal plate, and are therefore positively charged; and likewise the rays from the negative plate bend toward the positive plate, and are therefore negative. The negative particles were called *cathode rays*, and positives *canal rays*.

In 1897, J. J. Thomson (not William Thomson, Lord Kelvin) measured the deviation of the (negative) cathode rays in an electric and magnetic field, and obtained a value for the quotient of the charge to mass, i.e., e/m. This value was found to be the same (1.757×10^{14} cou/g) no matter what materials were used. Cathode rays were therefore recognized as elementary particles of matter, and were called *electrons*. The (positive) canal rays, however, were found to be different for different materials.

By an ingenious experiment in late 1897, Milliken was able to obtain an independent measure of e, the charge on the electron. One or two electrons were trapped on atomized oil particles, and the electrical force necessary to prevent each oil particle from falling under the influence of gravity was measured. Since the size of the particle could be determined from the rate of free fall, the charge absorbed by the particle could be evaluated. The smallest value obtained, 4.78×10^{-10} electrostatic units (1.600×10^{-19} cou), corresponded to one electron absorbed.

From Thomson's value of e/m, the mass could then be determined as 9×10^{-28} g. This was an astounding achievement, the fact that exact measurement of this mass was possible by these means, whereas the most sensitive chemical balance weighs to only approximately 10^{-6} g!

For the canal rays, e/m for H^+ was found to be 1820 times smaller than for the electron. Faraday in 1830 had shown by electrolysis that the charge on the hydrogen ion was equal and opposite to that on the electron (being simply the absence of an electron), and hence the mass of the H^+ was determined to be 1820 times the mass of the electron, i.e., approximately 2×10^{-24} g.

In 1896 Becquerel reported that he had accidentally discovered a penetrating emanation from uranium salts. Thus, his photographic plates, kept in a drawer, with a key in the drawer above, became exposed with the imprint of the key in the presence of some phosphorescent minerals—notably salts of uranium—lying on the top of the bench. These emanations were also found to ionize gases. The Curies, in 1898, extracted a concentrate from pitchblende which had high emissive power, and named it *radium* (hence the terms "*radium-active*" or "radioactive" elements, and "radioactive emanation").

They measured the strength of the emission by means of an electroscope. This instrument is essentially a vertical metal rod with a thin gold leaf attached to it by one end. If the electroscope is charged, the free end of the gold leaf is held out from the main shaft by repulsion of the like electrostatic charges. It falls to the shaft in the presence of ionizing radiation, at a rate which increases with the strength of the emitter, because the electrostatic charge on the metal is neutralized by charged particles formed during the absorption of radiation. Today ionization chambers based on this principle have wide use: a burst of current due to ionizing radiation is amplified and recorded. One pulse of current occurs for each bundle of emanation absorbed. Ionization chambers are discussed in Chapter 5.

In an experiment whose origin is obscure but which was refined and expanded by Rutherford (see Figure 4-1), three fractions emanating from a radioactive source such as radium were separated, and called alpha (α), beta (β), and gamma (γ) rays.

It was found that alpha rays are positively charged and are much heavier than the betas. They are completely stopped by thin paper or a few milli-

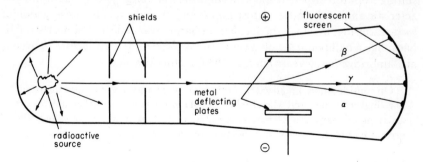

Figure 4-1. Rutherford's Separation of Alpha, Beta, and Gamma Rays, by Means of an Electric Field Applied Between the Deflecting Plates. Tube is evacuated.

meters of air, and lose one half their intensity if directed through 0.005 mm aluminum foil. By contrast, the beta rays are negatively charged, only weakly ionize gases, can travel many centimeters through air, and lose one half their intensity only if passed through 0.5 mm of aluminum sheet. The gamma ray has no charge. It strongly ionizes gases and penetrates up to 4 in. of lead.

Careful determination of e/m showed the beta rays to be fast electrons, traveling at speeds up to 0.99 times the velocity of light (3×10^{10} cm/sec). Similar experiments, and actual collection of alpha rays in a lead box, showed that the alphas are helium ions, He^{++}. Experiments on penetration and analogous properties indicated that the gammas are simply electromagnetic waves like light, except of very short wavelength, shorter (or "harder") and more energetic than X rays.

Rutherford's famous scattering experiments, performed about 1911, disclosed the inner structure of the atom. Alpha rays were used as the bullets and metal foil as the target (Figure 4-2). He surrounded the target with a

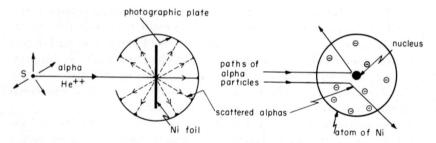

Figure 4-2.   Scattering of Alpha Rays by Nickel Nuclei. Definite scattering angles and even back-scatter were observed. See text.

cylindrical photographic plate, and observed, in addition to dark spots resulting from direct penetration through the foil, dark spots at certain characteristic angles of scatter. Most important, though, was the observation of *back*-scattering, in which the incident radiation was reflected almost straight back, like a ball bouncing off a wall. In his own words, in a lecture delivered at Cambridge many years later, in 1936, Rutherford said:

> On consideration, I realized that this scattering backwards must be the result of a single collision; and when I made calculations I saw it was impossible to get anything of that order of magnitude unless one took a system in which the greater part of the mass of the atom was concentrated in a minute nucleus . . . .

The back-scatter requires such energy that the alphas must penetrate to within 1/10,000 of the center of the positive charge in the atom; this means that the positive charge is centered in a nucleus of diameter 1/10,000 that of the whole atom. The atomic diameter calculated from Avogadro's number (6×10^{23} atoms per gram atomic weight) and the density of, say, nickel (8.9 g/cc) is found to be approximately 10^{-8} cm (1 Å). Therefore the diameter of the nucleus is approximately 10^{-12} cm. Of primary importance to an understanding of penetration of energetic radiation into tissue was the deduction: the total positive charge is centered at the nucleus, which contains also most of the weight of the atom. The negative charge, equal in magnitude to the positive but of negligible weight, is in the orbital electrons.

Atomic theory then developed rapidly, between 1910 and 1925. Max Planck suggested that light is emitted and absorbed in bundles of energy (quanta); and Niels Bohr postulated that the electrons are held in definite orbits or levels around the nucleus, bound to the nucleus by positive-negative attraction, yet held from each other by negative-negative repulsion, thus preserving a definite diameter for the whole atom.

It was in 1926 that Erwin Schroedinger proposed an expression relating energy to radius, which for the first time gave these qualitative ideas quantitative expression. It describes a model of the atom in which the electrons exist in a series of levels or orbitals, given the names K, L, M, etc., the K-shell being next to the nucleus. Figure 4-3 illustrates the spherical and

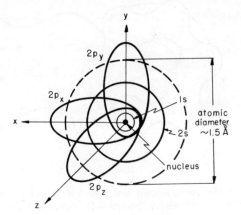

Figure 4-3. Sommerfeld's Atom with Elliptical (p) and Spherical (s) Orbitals. Three p's are at right angles to one another. Each orbital can hold two electrons, whether both from the one atom or a "shared pair" in a bond. As drawn, this "atom" could accommodate 2 electrons in the K shell (1s) and 8 in the L shell (2-level). Thus it represents atoms from hydrogen (1 electron) up to neon (10 electrons). The 3s, 3p, etc., orbitals, only slightly larger, and not shown, accommodate orbital electrons of elements higher in the periodic table.

ellipsoidal orbitals first envisioned by Sommerfeld and described by Schroedinger. Each orbital can accommodate two electrons only, according to Wolfgang Pauli's "exclusion principle." The quantitative theory has now been tested experimentally for 36 years, by observation of the "light" emitted by excited atoms, and it describes, with the most beautiful precision known in science today, the observed results (more about this later). The inference is that Bohr's guess was right. But nobody knows why!

Werner Heisenberg's introduction of the "uncertainty principle," and later his new formulation, called *wave mechanics*, in which all the elementary particles (and hence all matter) are considered to follow the undulations of electromagnetic waves, have only served to strengthen the grasp that this particular atomic model, or theory, has on science.

The model discloses that there are sublevels in which an electron may find itself within the electron cloud: the *s*, *p*, *d*, and *f* levels,* or orbitals, as they are called (Figure 4-4). In each of these the electron is confined within a certain spherical or cigar-shaped volume about the nucleus. The orbitals of the outermost electrons of the atom overlap with those of the neighboring atom, and form a "bond."

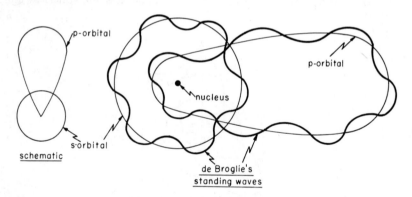

Figure 4-4. Schematic (exaggerated and distorted) *s* and *p* Orbitals with de Broglie's "Pilot Waves," Which are Thought to Guide the Electrons in Their Orbits.

Working from the inside to the outside, we discuss interatomic binding after a section in which we focus attention on the hard, heavy, positive core of the atom, the nucleus, knowledge about which is so important to the understanding of radioactivity and its biological effects.

---

*For *sharp, principal, diffuse,* and *fundamental:* descriptive codings used by spectroscopists to describe spectral lines.

The Atomic Nucleus

Since World War II much research has centered on the forces which hold the nucleus together. The nucleus carries all the positive charge and most of the mass of the atom. As a result of bombardment experiments (Figure 4-2), especially on light nuclei, by 1930 it was known to be composed of two main particles, *protons*, p, (H^+) or bare hydrogen nuclei, and *neutrons*, n, particles of the same weight as protons, but with no charge. Moseley showed in the year 1914 the correlation between atomic number and positive charge on the nucleus; and isolation and identification of *isotopes* (same atomic number, different atomic weight—i.e., more or fewer neutrons) followed at a fast pace, until today more than 600 isotopes of the 108 elements are known. Some nuclei are stable, but some are unstable, and fly apart spontaneously into fragments. These are the *radioactive* isotopes. Some unstable isotopes do not exist in nature, but can be produced artificially by nuclear bombardment (by n, p, etc) techniques. They are called artificially-radioactive isotopes.

Experimental bombardment of the nucleus and examination of the products by cloud chamber, ionization chamber, energy-balance studies, photographic, and other techniques has disclosed about 20 new particles. First came the *neutrino* and the *positive electron*, or positron, then a number of new particles, at first all called *mesons*. Named after the great theoreticians, Bose and Fermi, these are now classified into:

Bosons (spin = 1)
(a) *pi*ons, or light mesons ($\pi°$: 264.2; $\pi^\pm$: 273.2)
(b) *ka*ons, or heavy mesons ($k°$: 965; $k^\pm$: 966.5)
Fermions (spin = 1/2)
(a) leptons, or light particles ($\mu^\pm$: 206.77; $e^\pm$: 1; neutrino)
(b) barions, or hyperons and nucleons (Xi$^\pm$: 2585; $\Sigma^\pm$: 2330;
       $\Lambda°$: 2182; p$^\pm$: 1836; n$°$: 1837)

The mass (in multiples of the electron mass) and charge (°, +, or − superscripts) of these particles (π, k, Xi, p, etc.) are given in parentheses. The bosons exist in the nucleus and contribute to its phenomenal binding energy. Isolated, all but the electron, proton, and neutrino are unstable. However, the neutron persists for about 20 minutes on the average. The others last only 10^{-6} to 10^{-10} sec.

Of some particular interest may be the muon ($\mu^\pm$), well established as a cosmic-ray product in the atmosphere in which we live. It is ultimately produced by the impact of a cosmic ray proton and an atomic nucleus in the upper atmosphere. A π-meson is first produced, which in turn decays rapidly into the muon plus a gamma ray. The muon disintegrates into a fast, ionizing electron and two more gamma rays, at sea level.

The atom and its nucleus were recently detailed in delightful form by Gamov[10], in a little book highly recommended for its simple, colorful descriptions of very complex phenomena.

Molecular Structure and Binding

It is the outer, or valence, electrons of the electron cloud which are evidently involved in binding atom to atom (Figure 4-4). Two distinct cases, and one intermediate case, have been studied thoroughly. First, the valence electron in "atom 1" can jump into an empty orbital of "atom 2," leaving atom 1 positive and making atom 2 negative. Strong electrostatic binding exists (Coulomb's law) because the charge separation is small. This is the case in all salts, both inorganic and organic. The bond is called *ionic*.

Secondly, the electron from atom 1 can simply exchange, or be "shared" with that of atom 2. For instance if each of the two valence electrons is in an *s* (spherical) orbital, and the orbitals can overlap so that exchange or sharing takes place, a "sigma" bond is formed. If both are in *p* ("probing") orbitals (cigar-shaped), and if they overlap, a so-called pi (π) bond is formed (Figure 4-5). Indeed combinations of *s* and *p*, called "hybrids," are possible. For example each of the four bonds made by a carbon atom is a hybrid of one *s* and three *p* valence electrons—imagine, in Figure 4-4, the 2*s* and 2*p* electron orbitals as distorted; it is a mixture, called an sp^3 hybrid. The four are directed tetrahedrally from each other, like four long noses, each to form a bond (i.e., to share a pair of electrons) with a neighboring atom. In the case of water, each of the *p* orbitals of oxygen overlaps with *s* of hydrogen to form a bent (109°) molecule. The bond is called *covalent*.

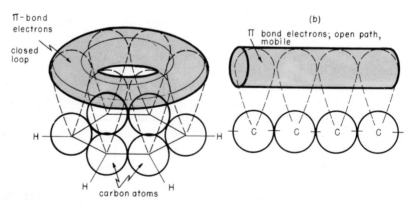

Figure 4-5. Diagrams of Overlapping π Bonds: (a) A closed loop to form a doughnut of negative charge above the plane of a benzene ring; (b) on a protein with open and ringed molecular structures, in which π-bond electrons are somewhat mobile and can transfer charge from one end of the molecule to the other, if forced.

In between the ionic and covalent bond is the *dative* bond, in which the electron of atom 1 is partially given over to atom 2, although exchange and overlap still occur. Organic-phosphorus molecules are an important example (ATP, for instance, the "mobile power supply" in the living system). The oxygens of the phosphate assume a definite negative charge because of dative bonding.

Of special importance is the π bond, formed by the overlap of two p orbitals ("probosci"). It often forms the second bond in the "double bond" of conjugated organic molecules, and restricts the relative rotation of atoms 1 and 2 if joined by the π. But the most important property of the π bond is its position, directed parallel to, but not coaxial with, the atom—atom axis (Figure 5 (b)). Although it helps to bind atom 1 to atom 2, it is an accumulation of negative charge outside the volume containing the two atoms. It therefore can form weak bonds (complexes) with positive ends of other molecules in the vicinity; but, most important, it can exchange electrons with other π bonds close by, and hence provide a pathway by which electrons can run along a molecule from a point of excess negative charge to a point of deficiency of charge. Hence some organic molecules in tissues are electronic conductors, a fact which only recently has been appreciated with respect to nerve conduction and photosynthesis. (This very important topic is pursued in Chapter 6.) Further, the possibility of different electronic states in molecules, with different types of bonds, has profound ramifications in interactions of the molecule (and the tissue of which it forms a part) with electromagnetic radiations. These very important topics are also discussed in Chapter 6.

It is obvious that the elementary particles are the building blocks of the living stuff. From the molecular point of view, however, it is not at all clear where the line is to be drawn between the living and nonliving. Usually the attributes of growth and reproduction are used to classify the living. Yet, in a supersaturated solution, copper sulfate crystals will "grow," layer upon layer; and if the temperature is allowed to fluctuate up and down with a frequency of one or two cycles per day, they will "reproduce" themselves, by "seeding," in the form of many crystallites on the walls of the container. Indeed, Teilhard de Chardin, in 1945, proposed that *all* the elementary particles of matter are living, that they have the potency to do the things which living things can do, but that this potency is, to us, masked behind the gross behavior of large numbers. The gross behavior—statistical behavior— is all that our experimental techniques can today perceive in inanimate nature. Our techniques can examine the highly organized individual man in which $\sim 10^{28}$ particles are organized and controlled from within, although this inner FORCE is not amenable to physical examination as we know it today. From the point of view of *elementary particles*, the only difference between living and nonliving matter is one of *organization*.

ELECTROMAGNETIC RADIATION; NATURE AND SPECTRUM

The electron clouds of atoms and molecules can be excited by various methods—by heat, bombardment by some charged particle, and by absorption of incoming radiations. A simple example is the flame test for sodium: if a sodium salt is heated in a flame, it glows with a characteristic yellow glow. It is not burning (i.e., being oxidized by oxygen). Rather, the valence (outermost) electron gets excited (accepts energy) and "jumps" to a higher-energy orbital, from a $3s$ to a $3p$. Imagine the next set of orbitals around the nucleus in Figure 4-3. Its lifetime there is short, however, and it falls back to the original state ("ground state"), and emits the extra energy as electromagnetic radiation (*light* in this case) of such a wavelength (5893 Å) that it excites the cone cells on the retina of the eye.

Biology is entering its electromagnetic age. Many parts of the electromagnetic spectrum are beginning to be used for diagnosis and therapy, as well as for studies which are leading to a better understanding of the roles of each of the parts in the systematized whole.

Nature of Electromagnetic Radiation

The exact nature of electromagnetic (em) radiation is unknown. What *is* known is that the wave has two component parts, an electric part and a magnetic part, moving in phase, but in direction 90° from each other—much like two vibrating strings, one going up and down while the other goes back and forth—superimposed on each other. Each oscillates about an average value (zero) at a frequency which depends upon electronic vibrations in the source. The em waves travel in a straight line, and have energies inversely proportional to the wavelength, or directly proportional to the frequency (number of cycles per second). The wave carries no net electrical charge, and no net magnetic moment, but because of the components which can interfere or react with electric or magnetic fields, it can lose or gain energy (i.e., change frequency). All em waves travel at the velocity of "light." They have both wave properties (such as the capability of being reflected or diffracted) and particle properties (such as delivering their energy in bundles or quanta.). The unit bundle of electromagnetic energy is called the *photon*. Undulations in the electromagnetic field are described by the celebrated Maxwell equations (1873).

Electromagnetic radiations vary only in frequency, and through this, in energy. Therefore their use requires handling the energy contained in the radiation. For example, we know how to handle light with mirrors, lenses, microscopes, and prisms, and to detect it by photographic plates, photoelectric cells, the eye, etc. *Handling*, or making it serve a useful purpose, is simply a question of using equipment which *does not absorb* the light. *Detec-*

tion is simply a question of providing a medium which *can absorb* the light, or a medium with which the light can interact and be partially absorbed, to appear as another, more familiar form of energy.

Electromagnetic radiation propagates with undiminished energy through a vacuum, always at the speed of light no matter what the frequency.

The Electromagnetic Spectrum—A Survey

Table 4-1 gives some properties of interest for the whole spectrum of electromagnetic radiations. Since the em radiation has both wave and particle properties, the wavelength range of the different sections is given, and the energy associated with an excitation in each section is given in electron volts (1 electron volt/molecule = 22,000 cal/mole). Common means of detecting and of handling the radiations are noted; and what happens during absorption is indicated.

If one expects to gain insight into the interactions of electromagnetic radiations and matter, one *must* study the two Tables, 4-1 and 4-2, exhaustively. There is no easier way. One will find, for example, from inspection of the dimensions of the wavelength, λ, and frequency, ν, that they are related through the velocity, c, which for all electromagnetic radiations in vacuum, no matter what the wave length, is 3×10^{10} cm/sec (186,000 miles/sec). Thus

$$\nu = 3 \times 10^{10}/\lambda \quad \text{cycles/sec}$$

Table 4-2 indicates some of the effects of the interaction of various "cuts" of the spectrum with matter. It is certainly true that radiation of short wave length (high frequency) carries more energy, is more penetrating, and can do more damage than that of long wave length. Thus, at wavelengths from 20,000 to 500,000 Å, the radiation simply tickles the molecules into a rotational and vibrational frenzy (high heat energy). Radiation of 4000 to 7800 Å excites electrons in the pigment molecules of the retina of the eye, and is visible. (Maximum sensitivity of the eye is at about 6000 Å.) Radiation of wavelength 2000 to 4000 Å (ultraviolet) excites even the bonding electrons in a molecule, and so loosens up a bond that chemical reactions may take place which otherwise could not. Wavelengths below 2000 Å, in the hard or vacuum ultraviolet, actually drive electrons out of a molecule, or ionize it; and as the wavelength gets shorter, and the radiation "harder," more and more ions are formed in the wake of the incoming radiation. In the X-ray region ($\lambda \approx 1$ Å) the electrons of even the K shell of the atom, the most tightly bound ones, can be excited or ejected; and in the gamma region (~ 0.01 Å), even the nucleus can be penetrated by the radiation, although electrons in the atomic cloud are a more probable target.

TABLE 4-1. The Electromagnetic Spectrum—Some Physical Properties

Radiation	Wavelength Range	Frequency Range (cycles/sec)*	Energy per Photon (electron volts)*	Detected by	Diffracted (bent) by
Cosmic	(secondary, due to fast protons from outer space)		billions	ionization chamber (ich); photographic plate (fp)	earth's magnetic field
Gamma	0.003 to 0.1 Å	10^{21} to 3×10^{19}	millions; 4 to 0.1 Mev	ich; fp	earth's mag. fld; and crystals
X	0.01 to 1.0 Å	3×10^{20} to 3×10^{18}	thousands; 400 to 4 kvp	ich; fp	crystalline solid (cs)
Vacuum UV	20 to 1800 Å	$\sim 10^{17}$ to 10^{15}	tens; 620 to 7	fp; photocell (fc)	cs; ruled grating (rg)
Far & Near UV	1800 to 4000 Å	10^{15}	7 to 3.1	fp; fc; scintillator	quartz prism; rg
Visible	4000 to 7800 Å	$\sim 5 \times 10^{14}$	3.1 to 1.5	fp; fc; eye	glass or quartz prism; rg
Near Infrared	7800 to 250,000 Å	3×10^{14} to 10^{13}	1.5 to 0.04	fp; fc; sense of touch	KCl prism
Far Infrared	250,000 to 1,250,000 Å	3×10^{13} to 2×10^{12}	0.04 to 0.008	fp; fc; bolometer; touch	KBr and KF prisms
Microwave (radar)	500,000 Å to 30 cm	$\sim 10^{13}$ to 10^{9}	0.024 to 4 × 10^{-6}	tuned capacitor-inductor circuit; human body	atmosphere's ionized layers; human body
Ultra high-freq.	30 to 150 cm	200 to 1000 megacycles (Mc)	4 × 10^{-6} to 8 × 10^{-7}	tuned capacitor-inductor circuit; human body	atm. ion. layers; human body
High freq. radio	300 cm to 150 m	2 to 100 Mc	4 × 10^{-7} to 8 × 10^{-9}	tuned circuit	atm. ion. layers
Broadcast radio	200 to 600 m	550 to 1650 kilocycles (kc)	(6.3 to 2.1) × 10^{-9}	tuned circuit	atm. ion. layers

1 megacycle = 1,000,000 cycles; 1 kilocycle = 1,000 cycles.   *Unless otherwise specified.

TABLE 4-2. The Electromagnetic Spectrum—Absorption

Radiation	Source	Absorbed by	Effects of Absorption
Cosmic	nuclear reactions on sun	nucleus; electron cloud of atoms and molecules	artificial radioactivity, fission, excitation, ionization
Gamma	radioactive elements	nucleus; electron cloud	artificial radioactivity, excitation, ionization
X	metals hit by high-speed electrons	electron cloud	excit. or eject. of K-shell electrons
Vacuum UV	sun; atoms hit by med. speed electrons	electron cloud	excit. or eject. of L- or M-shell electrons
Far and near UV	gas discharge tubes; sun*	electron cloud	excit. of sub-shell and valence electrons
Visible	sun; thermally excited atoms	electron cloud	excit. of valence electrons
Near infrared	red-hot bodies (e.g., fireplace); sun	vibrating permanent dipoles in molecules	increased kinetic energy of vibrat. (incr. temp.)
Far infrared	red-hot carbon; sun	rotat. and vibr. perm. dipoles of molecules	incr. kinet. energy of rotat. and vibr. (incr. temp.)
Microwave (radar)	klystron radio tubes	rotation of perm. dipoles	incr. kinet. energy of rotat. (incr. temp.)
Ultra high-freq. radio	tubes and tuned circuit	reradiated by conductors (metals, the body, etc.)	unknown; interaction with nerve?
High-freq. radio	tubes or transistors and tuned circuit	reradiated by conductors (metals, the body, etc.)	unknown
Broadcast	tubes or transistors and tuned circuit	reradiated by conductors (metals, the body, etc.)	unknown

*Estimates of the internal temperature of the sun go as high as a million degrees K. Spectroscopic measurements give the temperature of the incandescent gases surrounding the sun to be about 6000°K. A black body at 6000°K radiates some energy at nearly all wavelengths, but the maximum energy is radiated at about 5000 Å, right in the middle of the range of wavelengths visible to man. This is no coincidence, of course, for man's senses are adapted to his environment.

After absorption of the damaging short-wavelength ionizing radiation by the upper atmosphere, the total energy reaching the surface of the earth on a clear day is $\sim$ 1.25 cal/min cm². However, above the atmosphere space travelers will have to be protected against the small amounts of ionizing radiation which extend right down to wavelengths in the X-ray region. The most prominent of these is the strong emission of excited hydrogen atoms, the "Lyman-alpha" line, at a wavelength of 1215 Å.

Quantitative expression of these ideas followed Planck, who, in 1901, proposed that the energy, ϵ, contained per photon in incoming electromagnetic radiation is proportional to the frequency, ν, of the radiation. Thus

$$\epsilon = h\nu$$

where h is the proportionality (Planck's) constant, equal to 6.62×10^{-27} erg sec/photon (1 electron volt, ev, $= 1.6 \times 10^{-12}$ ergs).

Let w_1, w_2, and w_3 be the energies of binding of different atomic or molecular orbital states of the electron to the nucleus, and accept Bohr's assumption. If $\epsilon = w_1$, w_2, or w_3, absorption of the incoming radiation will easily occur, accompanied by excitation of the electron from its "ground state," or orbital of lowest energy, to an excited state. If $\epsilon \neq w_1$, w_2, or w_3, then absorption does not *readily* occur, although in favorable cases w_1 can be taken from a larger ϵ, the electron excited to state 1, and the radiation pass on with reduced energy ($\epsilon - w_1 = h\nu_2$) and lower frequency (longer wavelength). This is one aspect of the famous "Compton scattering."

If ϵ is greater than some critical value, w, the ionization energy, the electron can be ejected completely from the atom or molecule, and may have any kinetic energy up to and including $\epsilon - w$. Since the electron has a mass of 9×10^{-28} g, the kinetic energy ($1/2\ mv^2$) is less than, or equal to, $\epsilon - w$. Now a negative particle of velocity v, just like any other member of the electron cloud about a molecule, but moving with high velocity, is a very good ionizer itself. Hence the ionization process continues along a track through the tissue until all the incoming energy, ϵ, has been dissipated either as *heat* or in producing *ions*.

The Laws of Absorption

In the tables of properties of em radiations, the bases of the techniques for handling them were implied. What happens when absorption takes place was also indicated. We consider now the extent of absorption, and its converse, the depth of penetration.

In brief and in summary, absorption of electromagnetic radiations is governed only by the laws of chance. The chance that a photon will be absorbed depends only upon the number of target electrons and nuclei in its path. From the fact that the higher energy (shorter wave length) radiations penetrate deeper into any given material, it is inferred that they are more difficult to capture—have a "smaller capture cross-sectional area." Conversely, the denser the target material the greater is the number of potential targets per centimeter of the photon's path, and hence the greater is the absorption per unit length of path.

These ideas are expressed quantitatively in Lambert's law. The rate of absorption is directly proportional to the amount to be absorbed; or

$$-dI/dx = k'I$$

where x is thickness and I is intensity, or number of photons passing 1 cm^2 per sec. This is one of the natural functions (Chapter 1) for which I is expressed explicitly as

$$I = I_0 e^{-k'x}$$

where I_0 is the intensity when $x = 0$, just as the radiation enters the absorbent; k' is a constant, characteristic of the absorbent (larger, the better the absorption capacity of the medium), called the *absorption coefficient*. The plot of I vs x is shown in Figure 1-2 (c).

Since $\ln I_0/I = k'x$, conversion to common logarithms by dividing by 2.303 gives $\log I_0/I = kx$, where $k' = 2.303 k$, and k is called the "extinction coefficient."

Lambert's law is applicable over the whole electromagnetic spectrum, and, you will remember from Chapter 3, is useful also to describe the absorption of matter waves. It is an obvious but very important point that the extinction coefficient of a substance will be different at different wavelengths. From the far infrared, through to the near ultraviolet, the extinction coefficient is large only for particular wavelengths. Such specificity is a property of molecular absorption. If these molecules are suspended or dissolved in a medium, k will be directly proportional to the concentration, c (Beer's law). Thus k can now be factored into ac, where a is called the *molecular extinction coefficient*. Formally then:

$$\log I_0/I = acx \qquad \text{(Beer-Lambert law)}$$

The specificity for absorption of selected wavelengths disappears from the far ultraviolet through to gamma radiation—continuous absorption occurs accompanied by ionization—and the extinction coefficient decreases more or less linearly with decreasing wavelength (i.e., with increasing energy /photon). Thus ultraviolet light penetrates only a small fraction of an inch of tissue; and the k for tissue for near ultraviolet is very large. By contrast, soft X rays penetrate tissue with only a small amount of absorption per cm; and k is smaller. However, each photon of X rays absorbed carries roughly 1000 times more energy than each photon of near ultraviolet, and therefore only 1/1000 as much absorption is required to do the same damage. It is seen then that the important quantity is the *energy absorbed per unit volume*, because this determines the subsequent effect: warming of tissue, triggering of the optic nerve fiber, providing the energy for photochemical synthetic processes, or ionization and rupture of molecular bonds.

The molecular extinction coefficient is strongly dependent upon wavelength, as we shall soon see. The *optical transmission* is defined as 100 I/I_0 per cent. The *optical density*, often used, is defined as log (I_0/I), and increases linearly as concentration of absorber is increased.

SOME INTERACTIONS OF ELECTROMAGNETIC RADIATIONS AND LIVING MATTER

The parts of the spectrum which are of biophysical importance can be conveniently classified under four main titles: the *warming region*, the *visible region*, the *photochemical region*, and the *ionizing region*. Each of these is illustrated below. Enough of the principles are given to introduce infrared and ultraviolet therapy. The visible region is considered in more detail, for obvious reasons. X and gamma rays, and hard ultraviolet too, are introduced here in principle only. Detection and absorption are discussed in Chapter 5, and Chapter 9 deals exclusively with biological effects of all the ionizing radiations.

The Warming Radiations (Infrared)

Electromagnetic radiation in the infrared range is always associated with heat energy of those molecules which contain permanent dipoles. Its absorption results in increased rotations and vibrations, and therefore in increased temperature. Infrared radiations are then logically called "heat rays."

The penetration into tissue is appreciable, although the extinction coefficient is large. The warming effect of absorption by the very outer layers of the skin can be felt beneath the surface because of the poor but substantial heat conduction of the tissue. Infrared-lamp therapy is based on this principle. Since the tissue is 85 per cent water, the strongest absorption would be expected to occur particularly near the strong water-absorption wavelengths: (1) vibrations at 28,200 and 63,000 Å, (2) rotations from 500,000 to 1,200,000 Å, as well as (3) some absorption by mixed vibrations and rotations at nearly all wavelengths greater than about 8000 Å. Intense infrared electromagnetic radiation, when absorbed by tissue, causes gas and steam pockets which lead to lesions and blisters.

Infrared Spectra

The wavelengths absorbed often provide clues as to what rotation or vibration is absorbing the incoming radiation. In the instrument called the spectrometer a small slit of light from a continuously burning carbon arc—a good source of infrared radiation—passes through the absorbent and then on through a triangularly shaped crystal (prism) of KCl or KBr; the transmitted radiation is broken up—the longer wavelengths will be bent sharply within the crystal, the shorter wavelengths less so—and the image of the slit will appear as darkening on a photographic plate, at positions proper to the wavelengths entering the slit. Thus the absorption bands of water correspond to O—H stretching vibrations and to $H{\diagup}O{\diagdown}H$ bending vibrations. This is true for any absorber with rotating or vibrating dipoles. Many thousands of spectra have been determined, principally in organic molecules, for purposes of learning what polar groups there are in the molecule, or for identification of a particular substance in a mixture. Continuous use is now being made of this technique in investigation and control of barbiturates and narcotics, for example. Each material has a characteristic spectrum (plot of absorption *vs* wavelength), easily reproduced, in many cases easily identified. Figure 4-6 shows two examples, and gives an indication at the bottom of what rotations and vibrations within the molecule may be responsible for each absorption peak (pointing down).

Visible Radiations

This region is noteworthy for the sole reason that the animal body is equipped with a very sensitive set of living cells which can detect wavelengths of 4000 to 7800 Å coming in from excited molecules in the environment. Molecules in the environment are excited by radiation which pours in from the sun at all frequencies proper to a hot body. The reradiated energy from the excited molecules of a tree, for example, outlines its shape; the exact composition of the reradiated energy defines its brightness and what we perceive as its color.

The eye is a device by which the energy of an electromagnetic radiation pattern is converted into the energy associated with the various nerve impulses which can traverse the optic nerve to part of the brain. It is a transducer in the sense that it provides a mechanism by which electromagnetic radiation of wavelengths in the critical range can be received, focused, sorted out, and then converted into the chemical, thermal, and electrical energy which is necessary to trigger nerve propagation. In general, the energy carried by a nerve impulse is much greater than that of the light photons which trigger the propagation. This subject is considered in Chapter 10, and we confine ourselves here to what takes place before the nerve is triggered.

Architecture of the Eye

Figure 4-7 is a simplified sketch of the basic parts of the eye. It illustrates principally the roles of the lens, the retina, and the optic nerve. Light of intensity I_0 ergs/cm² from a light source falls on the *cornea*. About 96 per cent passes on through the lens, and about 4 per cent is reflected. The cornea, the aqueous humor, the lens, and the vitreous humor are essentially

84

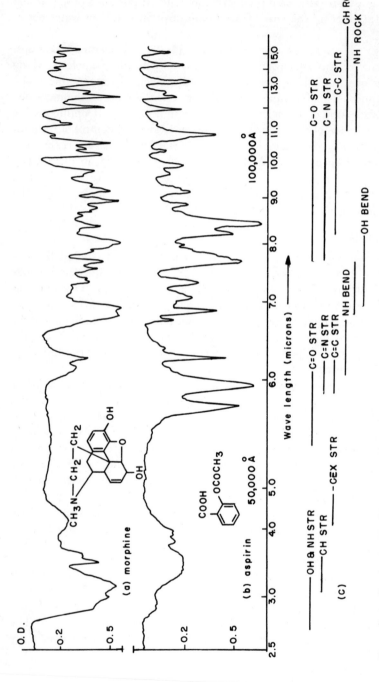

Figure 4-6. "Molecular Fingerprints." Infrared Spectra of Acetylsalicylic Acid and Morphine. Colthup's General Assignments. Assignment of a particular absorption peak to a particular rotation or vibration within the molecule is usually difficult. Spectra are reproducible in finest detail. (Courtesy of C. E. Hubley.)

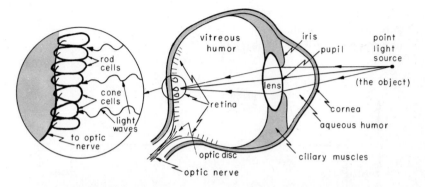

Figure 4-7.   Architecture of the Left Eye, Viewed from Above.

liquid crystal materials and are, of course, transparent. About 48 per cent of I_0 reaches the retina. The *iris* acts as would the diaphragm of a camera, controlling the area of the pupil, and hence the total energy admitted.

The incoming light, which is usually divergent from the source, is focused on the *retina* by the *lens*. The distance, q, between the lens and the image (of the light-source) on the retina is constant, but the lens-to-object distance, p, may vary widely from about 4 in. to a mile. To be versatile, then the focal length, f, defined as

$$\frac{1}{f} = \frac{1}{p} + \frac{1}{q}$$

must be adjustable if objects at different distances are to have sharp images on the retina. Now the focal length depends upon the geometry of the lens: a thick lens will have a short focal length, and a thin lens a long focal length. Because the lens is a liquid crystal much like jelly, its shape can be changed by the tension exerted by the *ciliary muscles*. This tension is in turn controlled by a nervous signal fed back from the retina, the cells of which estimate the sharpness of the image. This process is known as *accommodation*.

Photosensitive Cells

The focused light falls on two types of cells on the retina, rod cells and cone cells, named because of their shape. The rod cells (scotopic vision) are the more sensitive to light, and distinguish for us light from dark when the intensity is very low (twilight vision). On the other hand the cone cells (photopic vision) are less sensitive, can resolve large amounts of light into its components, and therefore detect details of the image, such as shape and color.

The photosensitive cells are present in large numbers, estimated at 126,000 cells/mm². Most of the cone cells are clustered close together about a center called the *fovea centralis*. The distribution of rod cells is different (Figure 4-8)—practically none at the fovea, but otherwise distributed in great numbers over the whole area of the retina.

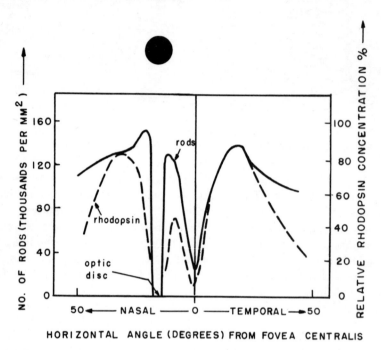

Figure 4-8. The amount of rhodopsin and the number of rods per unit area have a similar dependence on angle bounded by the incoming light and the central meridian in which incoming light falls directly on the fovea. The optic disc, where the optic nerve enters, is about 16° to the nasal side, and therefore a blind spot exists there. (Locate the blind spot in your right eye by first focusing the eye on the black dot, then turning the eye 16° to the left—i.e., about 4 in. if the dot is 10 in. from the eye.) (After Rushton.[1])

A brief discussion is now given of those molecules, known as pigments, which are not only the absorbers of the incoming radiation but also the transducers, the "machines" by which the incoming energy is trapped and "led across" into another form, not heat, which can trigger the optic nerve. Actually there are two separate subjects to discuss: twilight vision and color vision. Although much has been learned by direct experiment on *animals*, Rushton[1] complained in his recent review: "Measurements upon *human* pigments have only just begun, and it is to be hoped that far better experiments will be made." We give here a summary of the present understanding of this important vital process, keeping pretty close to the facts, by-passing the theories.

Twilight Vision

As mentioned above, cells of two general shapes are found on the retina, rod and cone, the rod cells being responsible for the very sensitive detection of light from dark when it is *almost* dark. These cells distinguish the shape of the object, and although this is their primary role, they also permit us to distinguish colors.

The pigment responsible for twilight vision is a molecule called *rhodopsin*, the classical "visual purple." It is a condensation product of the carotenoid, *retinene*, and a protein called *opsin*. Retinene is a 20-carbon, ringed compound, the aldehyde of vitamin A, and its structure is well known. However, not very much is known about opsin. Another opsin has been identified, attached to retinene in the pigment *iodopsin*. Further, an isomer of retinene has been combined with the original opsin, and *cyanopsin* formed. However, only rhodopsin is active in twilight vision.

The extinction coefficient of rhodopsin, extracted in bile solution or in digitonin, has a maximum value at 5000 Å. It drops off rapidly at both higher and lower wavelengths. Thus at 5500 Å it is already down to about 25 per cent of the maximum, and at 5800 Å is nearly zero; while at 4000 Å it is also 25 per cent of the maximum value, but then remains about the same to wavelengths below those detected by the eye (smaller than 4000 Å). The Beer-Lambert law is obeyed exactly for weak solutions of rhodopsin. Further, Figure 4-9 shows that the sensitivity of the human eye is determined directly by the absorption of light by rhodopsin. To man's eye rhodopsin has a rose color; it absorbs strongly in the green (5000 to 5800 Å) and yellow (5800 to 6000 Å) regions and to a lesser extent in the blue (4200 to 5000 Å), and reflects all the rest; it is this reflected light which falls on man's eye as he looks at the pigment, whether on the retina through an ophthalmoscope, or in solution. This is why it is "colored" rose.

It follows from the preceding paragraph that the fewest number of photons which will trigger the nerve will be those of wavelength 5000 Å, for it is here that the extinction coefficient is greatest. Incidentally, the unit of light energy falling on the retina is the *troland*. At this wavelength it amounts to about 100 quanta falling on a rod per second. However, the rhodopsin of a rod is half-bleached by about 0.03 trolands, or 3 quanta per rod. It happens that 1 troland is the retinal illumination when 0.1 millilambert (mL) is viewed through a pupil 2 mm in diameter; and 0.1 mL is the brightness of a white screen illuminated by 1 candle at a distance of 1 m.

Rhodopsin is "bleached" by white light. Its color fades rapidly through yellowish to clear. In the dark, *in vivo*, the color is restored. The process can be summarized as follows:

$$\text{photons} + \text{rhodopsin} \xrightarrow[\text{(bleaching)}]{k_1} \begin{bmatrix} \text{bleached vitamin A} + \text{energy} \\ \qquad\qquad\qquad\text{(to nerve endings)} \\ + \\ \text{retinene} \end{bmatrix}$$

$$\underset{\substack{+ \text{ energy} \\ \text{(regeneration)}}}{\xleftarrow{\hspace{4cm} k_2 \hspace{4cm}}}$$

The scheme above indicates that the greater the intensity of the incoming light, the more will the rhodopsin be bleached. In twilight most of the pigment exists as rhodopsin, and the sensitivity is greatest. In daylight, most of it will be bleached, and the sensitivity least. "Dark-adaptation" is very familiar to us all; it is slow because the speed of regeneration of rhodopsin is

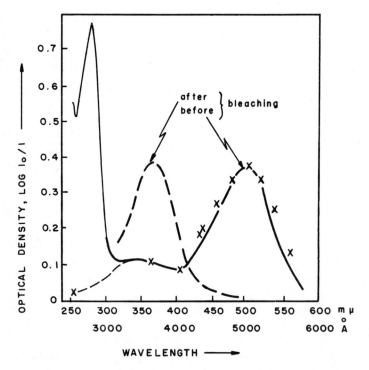

Figure 4-9. The spectrum of human scotopic (twilight) vision sensitivity (crosses), and the absorption spectrum of rhodopsin (solid curve) are the same. (After Rushton.[1])

slow. The reader is invited to contemplate the expression of the Weber-Fechner law in this organ:

$$S \propto \log I°/\Delta I_t$$

It says that the sensitivity, S, increases as the difference between the threshold intensity and that of the background decreases.

This photochemical description of twilight vision, although satisfactory in general, apparently needs revision, for serious troubles arise when quantitative description is attempted. It now seems likely that individual pigment molecules are attached to individual nerve endings, and the excitation of just one pigment molecule by incoming radiation is sufficient to trigger the nerve. Thus, although it takes upwards of half an hour for dark adaptation to occur—that is, for the bulk rhodopsin to be regenerated in man after a bleaching—the minimum time during which the eye can recover enough from a flash to see another flash is about 0.01 sec.

Color Vision

The cone cells somehow distinguish between wavelengths, and thus distinguish colors. The Young-Helmholtz theory, usually accepted, and now nearly 100 years old, suggested that three color-sensitive pigments exist, each one sensitive to one of the basic colors: red (6200 to 7800 Å), green (5000 to 5800 Å) and blue (4200 to 5000 Å); and that various intensities mix to give the colors and qualities commonly referred to as hue, brightness, etc.

The Young-Helmholtz theory is based on the experimental fact that by a proper mixture of red, blue, and green light in an object, any shade of color can be matched. The theory is that the three pigments absorb definite fractions of the visible spectrum and overlap one another, and that the optic nerve can receive and transmit signals which correspond to any and all wavelengths of the spectrum. Apparently this theory now requires major modification as a result of the very recent (1959) work of E. H. Land.[7] In some remarkable experiments he has shown in effect that the *full* range of colors can be recorded by the brain provided only that the *proper mixtures* of intensities of *two wavelengths* (one greater than, and one less than, 5880 Å (yellow)), fall on the retina! It seems that the information about colors other than the two incoming wavelengths is developed *in the retina*. The possibility that the pigment molecules are in intimate contact in the cone cells, and distribute the excitation energy among themselves in a manner controlled by the intensity pattern of the incoming light, immediately suggests itself. But more work is clearly needed following this surprising turn. Another recent surprise is that some evidence has been turned up that other molecules in the neurones, in the nerve pathway itself, contribute to the color perceived in human vision.

In spite of the credence placed in the Young-Helmholtz three-pigment theory of color vision, there is no direct evidence that three pigments exist in the cones. There is direct experimental evidence for two, however; this will now be recalled. Protanopes (color-blind people) cannot distinguish green from red. By measurement of the intensity of the light reflected from the retina as a function of incident wavelength on protanopes, it has been shown that a definite absorption by a pigment, given the name "chlorolabe," takes place with maximum at about 5400 Å.

Now the protanope can see green, but not red. This fact means that a second pigment, given the name "erythrolabe," is missing in the protanope. Difference spectra (unreliable) of two pigments in the *normal* fovea (collection of cone cells) show that the maximum absorption of the second, or missing, pigment is about 6000 Å. Thus there is good knowledge of one pigment, the chlorolabe, and knowledge of the existence of a second, erythrolabe. There is *no* experimental knowledge of a third in cones. But, of course, Land's new work indicates that only two are really necessary, one sensitive above and one sensitive below 5800 Å. The two pigments discussed have these qualifications. Recall that the optical density maximum for rhodopsin is at 5000 Å.

What the relation is between the excited pigment molecule and the color perceived is poorly known. Experimental approaches include that of measuring the electrical signals in the optic nerve (the electroretinogram, ERG) during stimulation by light, the reflection densitometry experiments mentioned just above, studies of the rates of bleaching and recovery (adaptation), visual acuity, color perception, and Land's new work. However, since the excitation energy for electrons in large molecules is so dependent upon structure, it would not be surprising if rhodopsin, chlorolabe, and erythrolabe turn out to be very similar in composition. The answer will lie in knowledge of the structure of these molecules.

Incidentally, an important new fact, bearing upon acuity especially, is that the eyeball is never still, but rather is in a state of small, almost imperceptible oscillations, such that the incoming light falls on a spot on the retina for only a few microseconds before it is deflected away. If the eyeball is fixed relative to the light source, color vision disappears.

Physical Defects of the Eye

If the lens is too thick or the eyeball elongated (myopia), the ciliary muscles are not able to make sufficient adjustment of the focal length to permit distant objects to be focused on the retina. The phenomenon is known as *nearsightedness*, and can be corrected with the aid of glasses with a concave lens of the proper focal length. If the length of the eyeball is too small, the condition is called *hypermetropia*, and can be corrected with a convex lens of proper focal length.

The lens of the eye often does not have the same curvature over all its surface, and light passing through the area of improper curvature will not be properly focused on the retina. The lens of such an eye is said to be *astigmatic*. A properly ground astigmatic glass lens can compensate.

Sometimes translucent or opaque tissue grows in or on the liquid crystal material of the lens and absorbs the incoming light before it reaches the retina. Such tissues are generally termed *cataracts*. Some can be removed by surgery; some are too extensive.

Depth Perception

Two detectors in different locations can inherently provide more information than one; and if relative information is recorded and interpreted from the two signals, more information is available from the two detectors than if each were interpreted separately. This is the reason sensory organs come in pairs. Typical of the relative information obtainable from two stations, in general, are *direction* and *distance*, or depth. Sound can be reflected, and hence the directional information provided by two stations is important. Light travels in a straight line to the eye, and therefore directional information is not important. However, the information derivable about distance or depth is important when we attempt to compare distances or develop a perspective view. Ideally the eyes may each be rotated about 50° from a central line of vision. The two have to be in focus at the same time, on a near or a far object, and this requires a facility of minor individual adjustment. If the eyes cannot be made to focus (crossed eyes), sufficient correction can sometimes be made with a suitable set of glass lenses, but often the cross must be corrected by shortening the lateral muscles or by suitable exercises designed to strengthen them.

Photochemical Radiations (Ultraviolet)

Photosynthesis

Subshell electrons are excited by the ultraviolet. The absorbed energy may be passed off to the vibrations or rotations of nearby molecules and appear as heat energy; it may be re-emitted as ultraviolet; or it may excite the molecule and make it more susceptible to chemical attack by neighboring molecules. Thus in the last case the ultraviolet may provide some or all of the activation energy needed for reaction to occur, and thereby increase the rate of reaction (treated later in Chapter 8). In fact, the photochemical mechanism is *sometimes the only* mechanism by which certain reactions can take place at a reasonable speed at biological temperature.

Because they carry more energy than photons in the visible region, the photons in the ultraviolet region are less likely to be absorbed. They penetrate deeper into the absorbent and excite molecules at the point at which they are finally caught.

Of all the synthetic biological reactions whose rate is sensitive to ultraviolet light, probably the photosynthesis of simple organic sugars from CO_2 and O_2 in plant leaves is the best understood; and yet the understanding of this basic process is not completely satisfactory. Of course if it were, we should be able to reproduce the syntheses in a test tube; but we cannot.

More important to present considerations is our knowledge of photo-catalyzed syntheses of the vitamins from basic components. Some of the vitamins have been purified, crystallized, and synthesized, and hence their chemical composition and structure are known. Consider the antirickets vitamin D_2 (calciferol) for instance. Its structure is well known: two six-membered rings and a five-membered ring attached to an unsaturated aliphatic side chain of six carbon atoms, with a molecular weight of 393. This molecule is formed through the absorption of ultraviolet radiation of 2500 to 3000 Å by ergosterol, a sterol molecule whose structure also is well known. The synthesis occurs in at least two steps. The absorption is considered to take place at a carbon-carbon double bond, and the absorbed energy to go into excitation of the π electrons which form the bond. The opening of a benzene-like ring follows, and further rearrangements of the atoms and bonds give the biochemically active vitamin B_2 structure. The reaction will not occur at all unless photolyzed.

This synthesis takes place in the human body at a location to which both the molecular components and ultraviolet radiation are accessible: that is, just beneath the surface of the skin in the living tissue serviced by the blood capillaries. Thus the principle upon which ultraviolet therapy is based, and the advantages of moderate exposure to sunlight, both become apparent.

Phototherapy

Prolonged sun bathing can damage skin pigments and can cause erythema. For instance, on the average it takes only 20 microwatts (μw) of ultraviolet of wavelength 2537 Å (from a mercury vapor lamp) falling upon the skin for 15 min to produce erythema. It is fortunate that the very intense ultraviolet radiation from the sun is attenuated (scattered, absorbed, converted into radiation of longer wavelength) by the ozone and nitrogen compounds in the upper atmosphere. Ultraviolet radiation would be a problem in space travel if it were not so readily reflected by metallic surfaces. The effects on the eye are well known and have been implied in the discussion of the chemistry of the eye: the higher-energy photons of the ultraviolet in falling on the retina can keep the rod and cone cells devoid of rhodopsin and damage the color pigment molecules. Snow-blindness and "whiteouts" are the result. Further, ultraviolet has been attributed in some cases to promoting the growth of cataracts and photothalamia, or inflammation of the cornea. However, ordinary window glass absorbs all the dangerous ultraviolet, and colored inorganic materials can be added to filter out (or absorb) any undesired range of wave lengths. Therefore, protection is no problem, if properly sought.

Ultraviolet light has a lethal effect on primitive animal and plant life. This fact is used to good advantage in destroying the bacteria, *escherichia coli* and *bacteria coli*, in foods or in our water supply. Each of these is killed by about 14×10^{-6} ergs per bacterium. Among the abnormalities successfully treated with ultraviolet light are conjunctivitis, fibrosis, acne, and surface infections of various kinds. Certain heavy metals (calcium, gold, silver, etc.) and certain highly absorptive molecules (methylene blue, quinine, etc.) sometimes increase the therapeutic value of the ultraviolet irradiation.

The shortest-wave, vacuum-ultraviolet radiation overlaps the X-ray region. The principle difference between the two regions in the present classification is whether ionization and bond rupture is the exception (ultraviolet) or the rule (X and gamma). The vacuum-ultraviolet will be discussed implicitly in the next section, for the differences between it and the X ray are of degree rather than of kind.

Ionizing Radiations (Mainly X and Gamma)

Principles

The only distinction between the radiations more and less energetic than that with a wavelength about 2000 Å is one of excitation *vs* ionization. That is, at wavelength λ greater than about 2000 Å, excitation of electrons of the electron cloud takes place as the rule, and ionization takes place only in special circumstances; while at λ less than about 2000 Å the electrons can be knocked right out of the atom by the absorbed photon. As λ decreases, the loosely held orbital electrons are the first to go, followed by the subshell electrons, and as $\lambda \rightarrow 1$ Å (X-ray region) the tightly bound K-shell electrons can be ejected.

A simple calculation will make this important point clear. It takes an input, w, of ~230 kcal to make 1 mole of ions out of 1 mole of atoms, i.e., 10 ev to make an ion out of an atom. (This is the energy carried by each photon of em radiation of wavelength 1200 Å.) Now the gamma radiation of the radioactive isotope of cobalt of atomic weight 60 (referred to the hydrogen atom as 1), Co^{60}, used in deep radiation therapy for cancer, has an energy of about one million electron volts (1 mev/photon). Therefore, each photon would leave a wake of about $10^6/10 = 10^5$ pairs of ions (or molecules which have been ionized) before it loses all its energy.

The electrons lost may have been valence, or bonding, electrons—active in holding the molecule together. In covalent bonding two paired electrons form the bond between carbon atoms, as in a sugar molecule for example. Ionization weakens the bond and perhaps breaks it; in any case the unpaired electron left is chemically very reactive and will make a new bond at any time or place. Cross-bonding of molecules, the synthesis of new molecules, polymerization of old ones, etc., all can occur. It is not hard to envisage how such reactions could adversely affect the tightly geared steady-state of normal living tissue.

It is convenient to reserve further discussion of the effects of ionizing radiations until the principles of radioactivity have been outlined. The radioactive emanations, alpha, beta, and the nucleons, are ionizing radiations, as are gamma and X, and the effects of all are conveniently discussed together.

Diagnosis by X Rays

The absorption of electromagnetic radiation increases with increasing density of the absorbent. Differentiation of diseased tissue from normal is based on this fact. The higher the speed of the electrons which impinge on the target metal, the harder the X rays so produced. Machines available today produce X rays from electrons which have been accelerated by thousands to millions of volts. In general, the greater the voltage, the greater the energy of the X-ray photons, and the greater their penetrating power.

For example, at 40,000 v (i.e., 40 kilovolt potential (kvp), in radiation terminology) almost any tissue will stop some of the X radiation and cast a shadow on the fluorescent screen or photographic plate behind it. At 80 to 100 kvp, commonly used in medical diagnosis, the radiograph displays shadows which differentiate fat and other soft tissues from air space and from bone.

Whenever it is possible to insert molecules containing heavy metal atoms into a region of interest, differentiation of tissues in the region is enhanced (Figure 4-10). Thus barium sulfate solution is commonly administered as an enema so that the lower part of the intestines may be examined (by X radiation). Iodine in a variety of compounds is also widely used to increase differentiation. For instance, in iodophthalien it is preferentially taken up by the liver and stored in the gall bladder; thus gallstones, if present, are easily seen. Similarly, the kidneys, uterus, blood vessels, and even the heart can be made visible to X-radiography (see Figure 4-10 (b), for example). Location of broken bones, of swallowed pins, of stomach ulcers and of tumors is routine.

The use of X rays for diagnosis introduces the serious question of the extent of the damage done by the rays absorbed. A complete fluoroscopic gastrointestinal examination with barium sulfate *can* be done by a competent physician with the dose to the region irradiated not exceeding 20 rads (the

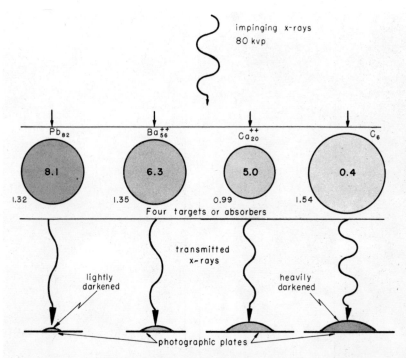

Figure 4-10a. Absorption of X Rays by Atoms. Energy of the incoming wave is trans-ferred to the electron cloud. Absorption is proportional to electron density, electrons per cubic Å (bold numbers inside). Number of electrons (i.e., atomic number - valence) and atomic weight are given, as is atomic radius (at 7 o'clock). Note shift of both ampli-tude (number of photons per sec) and frequency (energy per photon).

unit is defined later—only relative numbers are of interest now), although electronic intensification of the image now permits one to reduce this dose by a factor of ten. Although immediately measurable damage appears only if the dose is hundreds of times higher, more subtle effects, such as malignant growths, may show up years or even generations later if the greatest caution is not exercised. The effects of absorbed radiation dose can be cumulative.

These questions are considered in more detail under "Therapy" in Chap-ter 9.

MICROSCOPY

A microscope is a device which throws a large image of a small object on the retina of the eye. It does this by passing definitive light through a sys-tem of lenses. A few useful notes are now given on the two most common types. All the necessary details are set out in a very useful, practical manner in the little book by Martin and Johnson entitled: "Practical Microscopy,"[8] and in literature happily supplied by the optical companies.

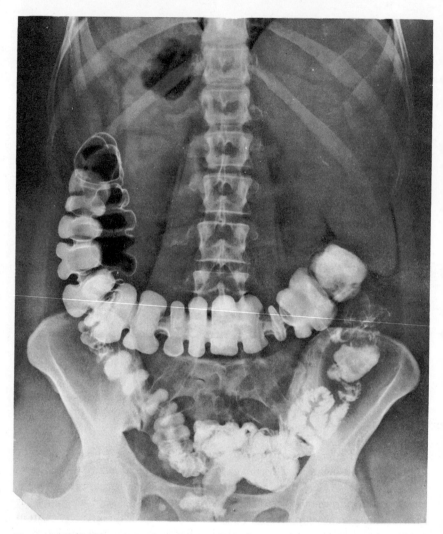

Figure 4-10b(i). Absorption of X Rays by Tissues. Abdomen with Barium Sulfate in the Colon. Note the differences in absorption of X rays by skeleton (vertebrae, sacrum, ribs, etc.), soft tissue (bottom edge of kidney, psoas muscle, liver), and gas pockets in stomach and colon. Low contrast film.

Optical Microscope

The small object to be viewed is illuminated either from above or below. In the former case reflected light, and in the latter case transmitted light, is allowed to pass through a convex objective lens of short focal length. In passing through the objective, the rays (visible region) are sharply bent, so that a bright, but small image of the object exists within a few centimeters of the objective. About 10 cm away from the objective, and in line with the object, is the "eye-piece," or condenser, another convex lens with very short focal length, which throws an image of the objective's image on the retina if held about 2 cm away.

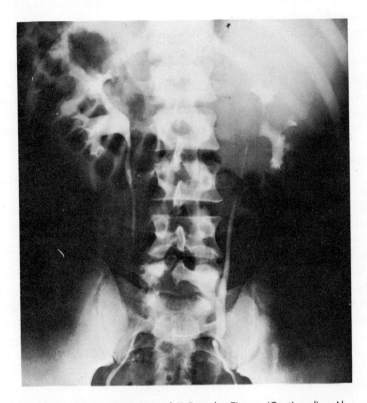

Figure 4-10b(ii). Absorption of X Rays by Tissues (Continued). Abdomen with Iodine Metabolized into the Kidneys. Note the difference between the normal calyces of the kidney (white "horse," upper left) and the defective one (upper right). High contrast film. (Courtesy of A. F. Crook, Ontario Cancer Foundation.)

Magnifications up to more than 1000× are possible with the best instruments. The preparation of the lenses is the critical thing, for it is difficult and costly to grind a large lens which will not be astigmatic. If the lenses are perfect, the limit of resolution (the smallest distance by which two objects can be separated and still be differentiated) is determined only by the wavelength of the light and the size of the aperture which admits the light.

For white light, with an average wavelength about 5000 Å and a numerical aperture of unity, the resolving power is 10,000 Å, or 10^{-4} cm, or 1 μ. One can use monochromatic blue light to improve this somewhat; and the research use of ultraviolet (λ = 2537 Å from a mercury arc, for example) with fluorescent screens, is an attempt to push the resolution down to 0.1 μ. In common practice, however, "good" microscopes used in schools and routine examination have a resolving power 5 to 20 μ.

The binocular microscope uses two microscopes in parallel, one for each eye. From this double input, one obtains depth perception.

Phase-contrast and interference features have been superimposed on the simple microscope, broadening its versatility by improving the contrast between different parts of the object under study. Contrast occurs in the normal microscope because of differences in *density*. In phase and interference microscopes, used when the density is about the same throughout (soft tissue is ∼90 per cent water), advantage is taken of the facts that the speed of light through materials, which determines their refractive index, and the amount to which the plane of polarized light can be rotated, often differ if the molecular composition of the materials is different, even though their density is the same. To take advantage of these facts, two methods are available. Both present a highly contrasted image to the eye, one in intensity, one in color.

The principles are really quite straightforward. The reader is referred to the trade literature for operating detail. Both are extensions of the normal bright-field transmission microscope; only the extensions will be noted here. In the *phase microscope*, an annular diaphragm is inserted in front of the condenser lens and therefore before the light falls on the specimen, together with a phase plate composed of a thinly evaporated ring of dielectric on a background of thinly evaporated metal. Thus light passes at different speeds through different parts of the object to be viewed, and the emerging light waves are out of phase. At one point of emergence from the object the phase difference will be such that the waves cancel each other; at another they reinforce each other. The phase plate "fixes" these differences by retarding those which pass through the dielectric, and absorbing some of those which pass through the metal. Thus identification and analysis of the structure of (unstained) *living* cells and tissues, the components of which are so similar in density that discrimination is impossible with the light microscope without killing and staining, is made possible. This instrument, invented by Zernicki in the Netherlands in 1932, is now an indispensible tool in clinical analyses — in bacteriological, histological, and, in particular, pathological studies of tumors and cancerous tissues. Note the contrast in Figure 4-11.

The *interference microscope* is a polarizing microscope, adapted so that part of the light passes *through* the object and part *around* it, the two then being

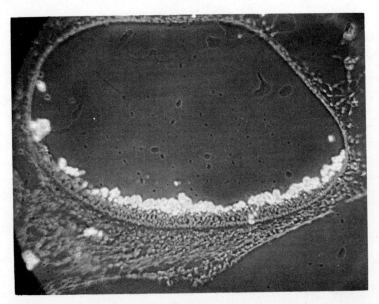

Figure 4-11. Partially Crystalline Otoconiae (stones) of the Utricular Macula (bone) of the Organ of Balance in the Middle Ear: Sectioned, and in Negative Phase Contrast. Magnification 60×. In addition to the sizes and shapes of the stones, note their darker center (glycoprotein) and the bright lamellar periphery (calcium carbonate). (Photograph courtesy of L. F. Belanger, University of Ottawa Medical Faculty, and of *J. Cytology and Cellular Comp.*)

recombined to interfere constructively or destructively (as in the case of phase, above), and to present to the eye enhanced differences in density or color. Before the light passes through the specimen it is plane-polarized by passing through a crystal in which the light in all but one plane is absorbed. The emerging, polarized light is split into two beams whose polarized planes are rotated at right angles to each other after one has passed through a second crystal (birefringent). One beam then passes through the specimen, and the other around it. The one which passes through is rotated, absorbed, and retarded in different places to an amount depending upon the arrangements of the molecules (—the term is "different optical paths"). The distorted light is then recombined with that by-passed, and their interference presents the image in different colors to the eye. If monochromatic light is used, the image appears in the form of differences in intensity; if white light is used, the image appears in the form of differences in color. Although it is not as sensitive as the phase microscope to differences in structure, the interference microscope affords a wider field of view, can show subtle differences as shades in color, and has permitted (optical) determination of the *amount* of a particular absorbing material in the field of view. Since its inception, in the early 1950's, it has been used for quantitative studies of proteins in living muscle, growth rates of cells and parts of cells, and similar problems on living tissue which can be studied only with a nondestructive tool.

Electron Microscope

This development of the last twenty years has added a new dimension to the depth to which tissues can be viewed. After fixing and staining (e.g., permanganate, phosphotungstic acid, osmium oxide), a very thin cut to be examined is placed in high vacuum, and bombarded from below by electrons (from a hot filament) which have been accelerated through a small aperture. Some of the electrons hit dense parts of the object and are scattered and absorbed—the principle is the same as for X rays (Figure 4-10 (a)); others pass on through less dense parts and fall upon a fluorescent screen or photographic plate. Proper alignment permits, in today's machines, amplifications of 500 to 100,000×, with resolution of a few angstroms.

One instrument, which can be considered typical for biological work,** gives a 15-Å resolving power; 600 to 120,000× magnification; and acceleration voltages of 100, 75, or 50 kv, to give electron beams of equivalent wavelengths of 0.037, 0.043, and 0.054 Å. The "lenses" are electric voltages between charged plates. The amplification can be increased to over 1,000,000× by photographing the screen, and enlarging the photograph.

Others

The ultraviolet microscope and fluorescence microscope have been used and improved since the early 1900's. They have some specialized uses in biological research. X-ray microscopy is useful when the sections to be studied are opaque to visible and ultraviolet light. For example, in histological sections on bone, soft (∼5 kvp) X rays are absorbed by the mineral component, passed by the organic component.

Reflection microscopy, especially the slowly developing infrared reflection techniques, may find limited use in future studies on biological material.

PROBLEMS

4-1: Draw the shapes of sigma and pi bonds.

4-2: If all 10^{28} atoms in a human being were lined up side by side, how long would be the line, in miles?

4-3: It costs an input of about 105 kcal/mole to pull the first hydrogen off a water molecule. "Light" of what wavelength will blast it off? (calculate it).

4-4: Sketch intensity *vs* distance for the penetration of electromagnetic radiation into tissue, presuming concentration of absorbent of 0.1 moles/l and molecular extinction coefficients of 0.1, 1.0, and 10.0.

**The limitations should be realized: the tissue sample is *dead*, *dry*, and *thin* while being viewed in the electron microscope.

REFERENCES

1. Rushton, W. A. H., "Visual Pigments in Man and Animals and Their Relation to Seeing," *Prog. in Biophys.*, **9**, 239 (1959).
2. Stacy, R. W., *et al.*, "Essentials of Biological and Medical Physics," McGraw-Hill Book Co., Inc., New York, N. Y., 1955, p. 262.
3. Brindley, G. A., "Human Color Vision," in *Prog. in Biophys.*, **8**, 49 (1959).
4. Evans, R. M., "An Introduction to Color," John Wiley & Sons, Inc., New York, N. Y., 1948.
5. Ruch, T. C. and Fulton, J. F., Eds., "Medical Physiology and Biophysics," W. B. Saunders Co., Philadelphia, Pa., 1960.
6. The Physics Staff, University of Pittsburgh, "Atomic Physics," 2nd ed., John Wiley & Sons, Inc., New York, N. Y., 1944.
7. Land, E. H., "Color Vision and the Natural Image," *Proc. Nat. Acad. Sci.*, **45**, 115 (1959); *Sci. Amer.*, **200**, 84 (1959).
8. Martin, L. C. and Johnson, B. K., "Practical Microscopy," 3rd ed., Blackie & Son, Ltd., London, 1958.
9. Shamos, M. H. and Murphy, G. M., "Recent Advances in Science," New York Univ. Press and Interscience Publs., Inc., New York, N. Y., 1956.
10. Gamov, G., "The Atom and its Nucleus," Prentice Hall, Inc., New York, N. Y., 1961.
11. Richards, O. W., "Pioneer Phase and Interference Microscopes," *N. Y. State J. Med.*, **61**, 430 (1961).
12. Bennett, A. H., Jupnik, H., Osterberg, H., and Richards, O. W., "Phase Microscopy," John Wiley & Sons, Inc., New York, N. Y., 1951.
13. Hale, A. J., "The Interference Microscope in Biological Research," Williams & Wilkins Co., Baltimore, Md., 1958.
14. Pritchard, R. M., "Stabilized Images on the Retina," *Sci. Amer.*, **204**, 72 (1961).
15. Hall, C. E., "Introduction to Electron Microscopy," McGraw-Hill Book Co., New York, N. Y., 1953.
16. Szent-Györgyi, A., "Introduction to a Sub-Molecular Biology," Academic Press, Inc., New York, N. Y., 1960.

CHAPTER 5

Radioactivity; Biological Tracers

Our sensory data, even with complex equipment, consists of flashes of light, of the rates of discharge of an electroscope, of audible clicks or totals from an automatic counter, of tracks of liquid particles in a small chamber, of the deposit of silver grains on a photographic film, of heat evolved, of certain color changes. From these simple observations scientists have already created a complex and exciting description of particles far too small to be seen directly . . . . (Miner, Shackelton, and Watson.[3])

INTRODUCTION

Properties of the Emanations

In 1897, we entered the golden age of nuclear physics. It was then that Becquerel, experimenting with pitchblende, which is fluorescent, accidentally discovered a new and exciting emanation from the material. The emanation was rather penetrating (through his desk-top), and darkened some photographic plates kept in a drawer below. The Curies extracted the element which gave rise to the activity—radium—and called the emanation "radium-activity," from which we derive the modern name, radioactivity. Chapter 4 has already described how three components were isolated from one another by Rutherford, and named alpha, beta, and gamma rays. The relevant properties of each as determined from scattering experiments, etc., are gathered in Table 5-1.

It is the penetrating properties of these radiations with which we are now primarily concerned. However, to understand penetrating properties of radiations from any radioactive source, we must first understand their origin (i.e., in the atomic nucleus) and their absorption, as well as the methods used to detect them, to identify them, and to measure their energy.

TABLE 5-1. Physical Properties of Nuclear Particles

Emanation	Symbols	Rest Mass (grams)	Charge	Nature	v/c	Source
Alpha	α, ⦵	7.2×10^{-24}	+2	bare helium ions	0.001 to 0.1	unstable nuclei (u.n.)
Beta	β, ●	9×10^{-28}	±1	electrons	0.1 to 0.9	u.n.; accelerators (acc.)
Gamma	γ, ⌇	(not applicable)	0	electromagnetic radiation	1.0	u.n.
Proton	p, ⊙	1.8×10^{-24}	+1	bare hydrogen nucleus	0.01 to 0.2	u.n.; acc.
Neutron	n, ○	1.8×10^{-24}	0	same, neutralized	"fast," and "thermal" (slow)	u.n.; fission
Deuteron	d, ⊙⊙	3.6×10^{-24}	+1	$n + p$		u.n.; acc.

NOTE: Charge is the number of units of 4.8×10^{-10} electrostatic units (esu) of charge.

Velocity is v; and velocity of light, c, is 3×10^{10} cm/sec. (The ratio v/c for protons in cosmic rays and in the Van Allen radiation belt above the earth's surface approaches 0.8 (or larger than that produced artificially).

The Nucleus

As has already been seen (in Chapter 4), the size of the nucleus has been measured by means of scattering experiments and found to be 10^{-12} cm, or about 10^{-4} Å. The nucleus carries all the positive charge and most of the weight of the atom. It is thus very dense.* The positive charge carried by such a dense particle is almost unimaginably high—for radium it is 88 times that of a hydrogen ion!—and it is therefore not surprising that the binding forces, whatever they may be, must be orders of magnitude stronger than those of the electron cloud of the atom; and even a minor reorganization or splitting must involve a mass-energy change. It is instructive for one to compare again (Table 4-1) the energy of visible light, ~ 1 electron volt/photon, with that of gamma rays, 1,000,000 electron volts/photon, which arise from nuclear rearrangements.

---

*This can be illustrated by a calculation of the weight of a 1-cm cube of nuclei of nickel (Ni) atoms, for instance, it being presumed that the nuclei are close-packed, side by side. Since the diameter of each is $\sim 10^{-12}$ cm, 10^{12} nuclei side by side would be 1 cm long; and the cube would contain 10^{36} nuclei. Each weighs 65 times as much as hydrogen, or $65 \times 2 \times 10^{-24}$ g. The weight of the 1-cc cube, then, is about 10^{14} g. or approximately 100,000,000 tons!

It is exactly this huge energy carried by the alpha or beta particle, or by the gamma photon (packet of light), which is responsible for its detection as well as the damage it does to the molecules of a tissue. Thus, as the emanation is absorbed by molecules of a gas, say, its energy is gradually dissipated by being passed over to the gas molecules; these in turn are at least excited, and many are ionized, a process which requires only a few electron-volts per molecule.

The number of protons in the nucleus determines its positive charge, and hence its position in the periodic table. Protons plus neutrons determine the weight of the nucleus. There may be several numbers of neutrons which can combine with a given number of protons, and thus there can be several weights of the same element. These different weights of the same elements are called "isotopes" (*iso topos*—in the same place in the periodic table). Some isotopes are quite stable, some spontaneously disintegrate. For example, carbon with 6 protons in the nucleus, may have 4 to 9 neutrons in the nucleus, to form C_6^{10}, C_6^{11}, C_6^{12}, C_6^{13}, C_6^{14}, C_6^{15}. The isotope C_6^{12} is the basic carbon in nature, and is quite stable, whereas C_6^{14} is a long-lived beta emitter also found in nature. The others are short-lived, and are made artificially by bombardment of nuclei by the "bullets" listed in Table 5-1.

IONIZATION AND DETECTION

Ionization

Positive Ions

The mechanism by which ionization takes place in the path of each emanation is important to considerations of penetration. Each mechanism is different from the others because the emanations differ so remarkably. The *alpha* $(He_2^4)^{++}$, the *proton* $(H_1^1)^+$, and the *deuteron* $(H_1^2)^+$ are very small, but dense; the alpha carries the positive charge of two protons. Upon collision with electron clouds of a target material, it easily ionizes the atoms by pulling the negative electrons after it, wasting a small fraction of its kinetic energy in the process. Since it is likely to tear at least one electron out of every atom through which it passes, it leaves a very dense wake of ionization (Figure 5-1). The alpha of radium (Ra) has a kinetic energy of 4.8×10^6 electron volts, which means that it leaves a wake of about 140,000 ionized atoms. Thus in air it can travel a few inches; in metal it can penetrate only about 0.0001 cm; and in fact can be stopped by a piece of paper! Although its path is short, the radiation damage or ionization along the path is intense. Actually, theory shows that the energy transferred per centimeter of path (called the linear energy transfer, LET) increases with increasing charge, q, and decreases with increasing velocity, v, as follows:

$$LET \propto q^2/v^2$$

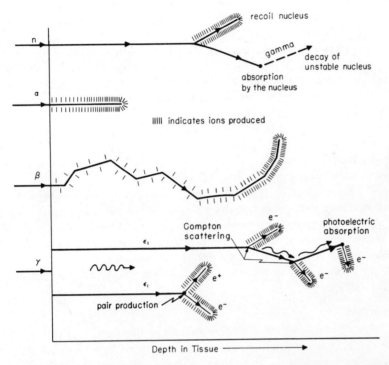

Figure 5-1. Schematic Representation of Tracks of a Neutron (n), and of Alpha (α), Beta (β) and Gamma (γ) Rays in Tissue. Note that the density of ionization increases as energy is lost from the impinging ray. The alpha trail of ionization is dense, the beta trail is spotty, and the gamma and neutron trails are composed of spurs.

From these considerations and the properties given in Table 5-1, one can understand that the differences among alphas, protons, and deuterons are more those of degree than of kind. All are positive, heavy particles with high LET.

Electrons

The *beta* is a very small particle—a very fast electron. Its charge is either negative (as is the beta from P^{32}) or positive (as is the beta from P^{30}), although the negative is the more common among biologically interesting isotopes. Because it is of light weight, with a mass only somewhat greater (relatively) than the mass of the electrons in the atom, a collision can result in energy transfer and a change in direction, similar to billiard balls in play. As a result the path traversed by the beta will be governed more or less by chance collision. It will have many changes of direction. Along the straight portions of the path, when the beta flies through the electron cloud of the atom, excitation can occur, accompanied by loss of speed, and hence loss of energy ($=1/2 \, mv^2$). The definite changes in direction result from collisions, and the energy and momentum transferred can cause ejection of the electron hit; i.e., ionization. When collisions are "favorable," the trail of ionization, although sparse, may penetrate quite deeply into a tissue; but when unfavorable, it will be very intense but very short. (See Figure 5-1.)

Very fast electrons may penetrate the atom as far as the nucleus, and by interaction with the field of force about the nucleus lose energy, with the production of secondary X rays. These X rays are called *bremstrahlung*. Hence a hard beta source may produce a secondary radiation which is much more penetrating than the impinging betas.

The initial velocities of betas from a source vary widely because the small neutral particle, the neutrino, is ejected from the nucleus along with the beta, and the energy of the disintegration is split between the two. It is the *maximum* energy of the betas which is usually given in tables of data. As a result of the energy distribution and the deflection of betas as they enter and lose energy in a target, the betas follow a nearly exponential law of penetration.

Gamma Rays

The *gamma ray* is electromagnetic radiation, like light, but of very short wavelength. Since it carries no charge, it is captured only by direct collision or wave-like interaction with a target: with the nucleus or the electrons of an atom. Some energy is transferred to the target electron and the gamma continues on, usually in a modified direction, at reduced energy ($\epsilon_i = h\nu_i$) where ν_i is frequency and h is Planck's constant. The recoil electrons are relatively slow, and are therefore good ionizers (see Figure 5-1). Just as in the case of X rays (see Figure 4-10 (a)), then, absorption of gammas arises from essentially two processes: (1) "pair production": strong interaction with the nucleus and production of a pair of electrons (e^+ and e^-)—important in water only if energy of the γ is above 3 Mev; and (2) "Compton absorption": ejection of an electron at an angle, some of the energy of the gamma being lost, and the remainder ("Compton scattering") proceeding, usually in a changed direction, and always at lower frequency. The process (2) is repeated until, finally, the energy left from a succession of collisions is absorbed by the electron clouds of atoms (photoelectric absorption) and is ultimately dissipated as heat. At energies below about 0.2 Mev, elastic (Rayleigh) scattering reduces the absorption and increases the range of the gamma in water and soft tissues.

Neutrons

The neutron is as heavy as the proton, but carries no charge. Energy is lost only by collision with light nuclei, and hence it can penetrate as deeply as X rays. The nuclei set in motion by bombardment by fast neutrons (0.1 to 15 Mev) have a high LET and leave a wake of intense ionization. Slow (thermal) neutrons are ultimately captured by nuclei; the product is normally unstable, and, for light atoms, usually emits a gamma ray. A good billiard player will attest that maximum energy transfer can take place between two neutral "particles" if they have the same weight. Therefore, neutrons are slowed down, or "moderated" best by materials containing much hydrogen—water, paraffin, etc. Thus, penetration into these materials is slight, or in other words, the absorption coefficient is high.

Neutrons are by-products of nuclear fission, or of proton- or deuteron-bombardment of light nuclei; they have a half-life of the order of 20 min, can be quite destructive of living tissue, and are difficult to detect. The damage is caused by charged nuclei set in motion by the impact of the neutron, or from artificial radioactivity induced by capture of the neutron by the nucleus (Figure 5-1).

Detection

Ionizing radiation is detected by any one of four basic methods:

(1) *Exposure of a Photographic Plate:* i.e., reduction of silver halides to silver along the path of the photon or particle. If the plate is placed in contact with a section of tissue containing a radioactive tracer, the plate will be exposed where the activity is. This method of mapping is now known as "autoradiography."

Microradiography is another interesting technique in which a large shadow of a small object is allowed to fall on a photographic plate. This technique has been used for years with X rays as the source, and recently it has been demonstrated to be feasible and useful using alpha rays as the source. Figure 5-2 shows a micro X radiograph of a section of bone—the mineral content is clearly visible—and an alpha radiograph taken of the organic part after the mineral had been removed.

(2) *Ionization of a Gas Contained Between Two Electrodes:* As the photon or particle passes through the gas it leaves a wake of ion-pairs. If there is no potential difference between the electrodes, the ions will recombine. If a potential difference is applied (Figure 5-3 (a)), each ion will migrate toward an oppositely charged plate. Those which reach the plate before recombining will be discharged and produce pulses of current in the external circuit. The higher the potential difference, the less is the recombination. Thus at an electric field strength of about $10v$/cm almost all the ions produced are "collected" at the electrodes. This is called the "saturation" condition, and most ionization chamber systems operate in this region.

If the electric field strength is increased still further, the primary ions are given sufficient energy to produce secondary ionization of the gas molecules, resulting in a multiplication of the original ionization. This is known as an

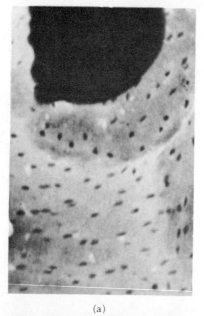

(a)

(b)

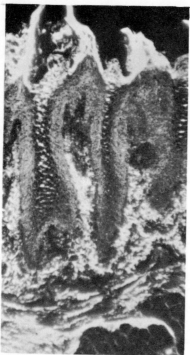

(c)

Figure 5-2. Microradiography.   (a) X-ray microradiograph (5 kvp) of a section of natural compact bone (tibia). Note the large (black) osteonic canals and the (light) mineralized regions. Magnification 500×.   (b) Alpharadiograph (source 2 mc/cm² of Po²¹⁰) of a section of the same bone demineralized. Note regions of low-density (dark) and high-density (light) *organic* material. Magnification 150×. Together (a) and (b) demonstrate directly the regions of growth of young bone around the osteonic canal: tissue mostly organic, only lightly mineralized.   (c) Alpha-radiograph showing filiform papillae (top) of the human tongue. Note the dense fibrous collagen core of the papillae and of the supporting base of the epithelium, and observe the low-density (black) mucous-forming cells at the bottom of the picture. (Courtesy of L. F. Belanger, University of Ottawa Medical Faculty, and D. H. Copp, University of British Columbia Medical School.)

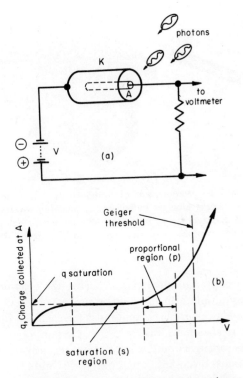

Figure 5-3. Ionization Chamber: (a) schematic design—wire anode, A, and cylindrical
cathode, K, filled with gas (e.g., Argon); (b)
charge collected at A per pulse at different
voltages. (See text.)

"avalanche" process. The multiplication factor may be as high as 10^3 or 10^4, so that the current pulse which is produced may be 10^3 or 10^4 times larger than the "saturation" pulse (Figure 5-3 (b)). Since the pulse size is proportional to the energy lost by the original photon or particle, a chamber operated in this fashion is known as a "proportional" counter.

At higher voltages, the multiplication factor for large pulses tends to be smaller than that for small pulses, and all pulses are multiplied to a constant size regardless of initial strength. The voltage at which this gaseous discharge starts to occur is known as the "Geiger threshold."

Figure 5-3 shows an ion-chamber design from which the proportional counter and the Geiger counter may be developed. Figure 5-4 is a photograph of a typical unit.

(3) *Fluorescence Induced in Solids and Liquids:* The light emitted after the absorption of ionizing radiation by a fluorescent solid is reflected on to the

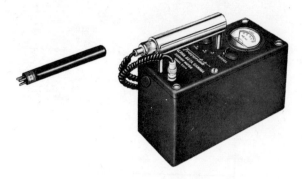

Figure 5-4. Measurement of Radioactivity. Left: thin-walled Geiger tube for alpha- and gamma-ray detection. Right: a typical survey instrument with protected, detachable detector tube. Typical ranges: 0 to 0.25 mr/hr; 0 to 2.5 mr/hr.

photocathode of a photomultiplier tube, causing the ejection of more electrons. These are multiplied in number by an internal secondary-emission system to produce a measurable current pulse for each scintillation. A typical arrangement is shown in Figure 5-5. Certain organic liquids also fluoresce, and very sensitive liquid counters have recently been developed.

Each of the counters discussed in paragraphs (2) and (3) has specific uses. For a radiation such as the 1.2-Mev gamma from Co^{60}, for instance, the scintillation counter can have efficiencies as high as 15 per cent as compared to 1 per cent for a Geiger counter. Therefore, for medical tracer applications of gamma in which the intensity is low, a scintillation counter would be preferred over a Geiger counter. However, if dosage is high, as it may be in radiation therapy, the extra sensitivity is not important. Figure 5-6

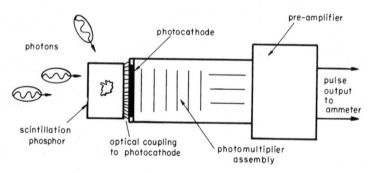

Figure 5-5. Schematic Drawing of Scintillation Counter. (See text.)

shows a lead-collimated scintillation counter, useful, for instance, for exploring the thyroid after radioactive iodine has been administered. External exploration of the organ for determination of size is known as scintography. Mechanical devices have been designed which control the exploration and print a map of the intensity of radiation from that area of the throat.

(4) *Chemical Reactions Induced in Aqueous Solutions:* Water is broken up into H and OH, and these very reactive products undergo reactions with solutes to produce new chemicals. Oxidations or reductions, molecular rearrangements, polymerization of plastics, and corrosion of metals have all been used as detectors. Important quantitative aspects of absorption of ionizing radiation by aqueous tissues are developed in Chapter 9.

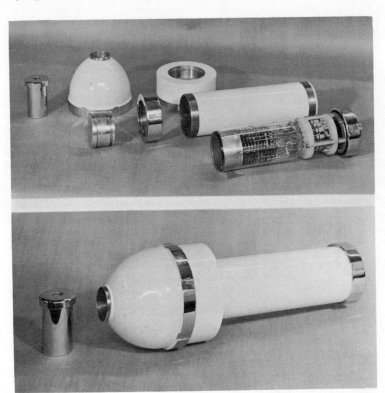

Figure 5-6. Collimated Scintillation Counter. Top: disassembled to show photomultiplier assembly. Bottom: assembled. With collimator (left) attached, the instrument can be used for scintography—for detailed external mapping of the human body, above the liver for example, following internal administration of the appropriate radioactively-labeled chemicals. (Photographs courtesy of Burndepts Ltd., Erith, England.)

DISINTEGRATION (DECAY)

Rate of Decay; Half-Life

We have no control over the disintegration of individual nuclei: if a nucleus is unstable, *it* will decay at a time which is completely unpredictable. However it is possible to describe and predict the fraction of a *large number* of unstable nuclei which will decay within a given period; that is, $\Delta N/\Delta t$ is easily measured. In fact the number of nuclei (N) which do decay within a given time is proportional to the number present which *are able* to decay.

Thus

$$\Delta N/\Delta t \propto N$$

or the instantaneous rate

$$dN/dt \propto N$$

Insertion of the proportionately constant $-\lambda$ (called the "decay constant") gives

$$-dN/dt = \lambda N$$

After the summation in the fashion indicated in Chapter 1,

$$N = N_0 e^{-\lambda t}$$

where N_0 is the number present at any arbitrarily chosen zero of time.

This expression says simply that the number, N, of nuclei which are present at any time, t, is only a fraction of the number, N_0, which were present at zero time—the fraction being $e^{-\lambda t}$. Now, it is useful and instructive to expand the fraction into the series it is, and write

$$e^{-\lambda t} = 1 + \frac{(-\lambda t)}{1} + \frac{(-\lambda t)^2}{2 \times 1} + \frac{(-\lambda t)^3}{3 \times 2 \times 1} \cdots$$

$$= 1 - \lambda t + \frac{\lambda^2 t^2}{2} - \frac{\lambda^3 t^3}{6} + \cdots$$

The value of λ differs for different radioactive elements. For Sr^{90} the value has been measured to be 0.028 yr^{-1}. After five years, for example,

$$e^{-\lambda t} = 1 - (0.028 \times 5) + \frac{(0.028 \times 5)^2}{2} - \frac{(0.028 \times 5)^3}{6} + \cdots = 0.87$$

Therefore $N = 0.87 N_0$, or the fraction of N_0 left after five years is 87 per cent.

Calculations for 10, 15, 25, 50 yr would span a time at which N is just 50 per cent of N_0. For Sr^{90} this time is about 25 yr, and it is called the "half-life"—the time it takes active material to decay to 50 per cent of the original concentration, N_0. Half-life, $\tau = \ln 2/\lambda = 0.693/\lambda$.

If two radioactive elements have been concentrated chemically to the same value of N_0, the one with the shorter half-life decays faster, has greater "activity" (higher dN/dt) at time zero, or delivers more emanations per second to the tissue being irradiated.

The unit of activity is the curie (c), that amount of radioactive material which provides 37 billion (i.e., 3.7×10^{10}) disintegrations each second. Thus 1 g of pure Ra^{226} which gives off 4.8 Mev (average of 3) alphas, has a total activity of about 1 c. $Sr_{38}{}^{90}$, which gives off only a 0.6 Mev beta, decays faster and is less dense than radium; 1 g of pure Sr^{90} provides an activity of 147 c. However, since a pure radioactive substance is always contaminated by its daughter products, the activity per unit weight is determined by the *concentration* of radioactive substance. Clearly 1 millicurie (mc) per gram might be usable in a medical application, whereas 1 mc per ton should be quite impractical. *Specific activity* is defined as the number of mc/g.

Figure 5-7 shows decay schemes for several radioactive isotopes of use as tracers in diagnosis and as irradiation sources in therapy.

Energy Distribution of the Emitted Rays

Before we come to the question of depth of penetration and extent of ionization of the rays from a radioactive source, we must consider two more factors: the energy distribution (spectrum) of the rays from any given pure source, and the number and kind of products of disintegration.

Both alphas and gammas are the result of a particular kind of fracture or rearrangement of unstable nuclei. One could consider the nuclei to be in excited states (think of an undulating water droplet), existing as such from the time of their formation (in the sun?) millions of years ago, and disintegrating at a rate which we can measure but which we are not able to vary. Thus, although half the atoms of Ra^{226} in a sample will undergo alpha decay in a definite and reproducible time, we do not understand why the disintegration of Ra^{226} is always by loss of one alpha particle, a package of 2 protons + 2 neutrons; and the most striking fact of all is that these alphas always come off with the same velocity. The similarity of this quantum-like behavior to the quantized absorption and radiation of light by the electron cloud of the atom, suggested to theoreticians that a Bohr-like model for the nucleus should be useful. Development of theory has proceeded along these lines, and has led at least to a quantitative description, if not an answer to the question "why?".

The alpha or the gamma radiation from a single elemental source occurs at discrete energies—alphas of single velocity, gammas of single frequency (Figure 5-8). However, with the beta is expelled a neutrino, a tiny neutral particle of variable velocity; and therefore the beta radiation from a single elemental source has a distribution of energies — low, corresponding to a

114

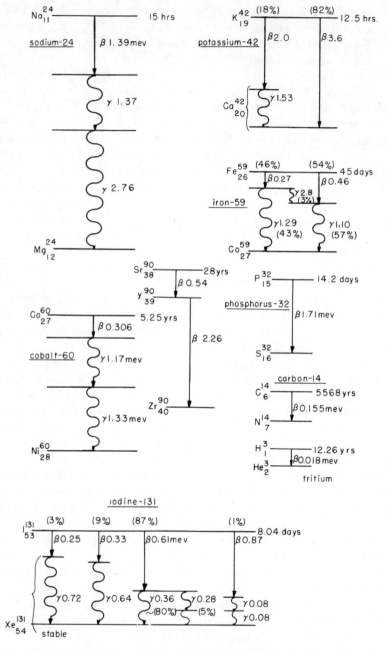

Figure 5-7. Decay Schemes for Several Radioactive Isotopes Used in Biological
Research, and in Medical Diagnosis and Therapy.

fast neutrino; high, corresponding to a slow neutrino; and reaching the largest, or maximum value when the velocity of the ejected neutrino is zero. The spectra are represented in Fig. 5-8 for pure emitters. The areas under the curves for each type represent the total emission. Table 5-2 gives the energies of the emanations from some unstable isotopes of biological interest.

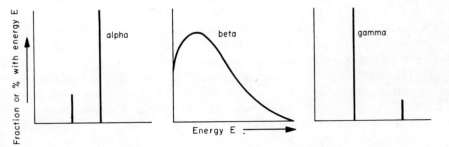

Figure 5-8. Energy Spectra of Three Emanations, Each from a Pure Source. Alphas and gammas are monoenergetic; betas come off with a range of energies (i.e., speeds).

Many biologically active chemical elements have unstable isotopes, of which the type, the speed, and the length of time over which the emanation is given off (i.e., the rate of decay) vary widely. There are now over six hundred isotopes known. Only about twenty of these satisfy the chemical, the energy, and the half-life requirements sufficiently well to be useful in biology. Of these, the uses of P^{32}, I^{131}, C^{14}, and Co^{60} are the most advanced.

TABLE 5-2. Some Isotopes Used as Biological Tracers*

Isotope	Half-life	Ray Emitted	Energy (Mev)
H^3	12 yr	beta$^-$	0.0180
C^{11}	20 min.	beta$^+$	0.97
C^{14}	5100 yr	beta$^-$	0.155
P^{32}	14.3 days	beta$^-$	1.71
I^{131}	8.0 days	beta$^-$	0.6
Co^{60}	5.3 yr	beta$^-$	0.31
		2 gammas	1.17, 1.33
Fe^{59}	46 days	2 betas$^-$	0.27, 0.46
		2 gammas	1.1, 1.3
Cr^{51}	28 days	secondary X rays	0.75
Ra^{226}	1620 yr	alpha	4.8
		gamma	0.19

*From "Radiological Health Handbook," National Bureau of Standards, Washington, D. C., 1960.

"Daughter Products": Products of Radioactive Decay

Any radioactive source, before being administered for any good reason, should be examined for the radioactivity and the chemical properties of its disintegration products. Refer to Figure 5-7. Thus, loss of an alpha means a shift downward of two places in the periodic table (e.g., radium $\xrightarrow{\alpha}$ radon); and loss of a beta means a shift upward of one place (e.g., iodine $I^{131} \xrightarrow{\beta}$ xenon^{131}), because these charged particles (electrons) are ejected from the nucleus, and it is the charge on the nucleus which determines the position of the element in the periodic table. Loss of a gamma results in *no* shift, but is simply a loss of energy during a nuclear reorganization.

The daughter products often are unstable and give rise to further disintegration. Several steps may occur before a nucleus reaches a stable state. One of the simplest disintegrations is that of Na^{24}, used in determining the role of sodium in a cell-membrane transfer. The scheme was seen depicted in Figure 5-7. The isotope Na^{24} gives off a 1.39 mev beta to become excited Mg^{24} (magnesium); but this in turn emits two hard gammas before reaching a stable product.

The Ra_{88}^{226} nucleus and its daughters produce a total *of eight alphas, eight betas, and eight gammas* before reaching the stable isotope Pb_{82}^{206} (lead). Three isotopes of polonium (Po_{84}), two of bismuth (Bi_{83}), one of thallium (Tl_{81}) and three of lead take part in the disintegration scheme! Note that all the daughters except radon are solid elements. Although all have short half-lives, they take a fleeting part in the chemistry of the molecules in the vicinity in which they are formed.

By interesting contrast with radium (Ra), Po^{210} is a pure alpha emitter, and P^{32} (phosphorus) is a pure beta emitter. I^{131} and radio-gold, Au^{198}, emit both betas and gammas. Decay schemes for some of these are given in Figure 5-7.

PENETRATION OF THE RAYS INTO TISSUE

It is preferable to discuss the penetration of the pure emanations and then to infer the effects of the mixed emission of mother and daughters.

The alpha (and also the proton and deuteron) penetrates in a straight line until it is stopped (Figure 5-1), provided of course that it does not "hit" a nucleus (Figure 4-2). Because both the α and the target nucleus are so small, the likelihood of collision is small. Since alphas are monoenergetic from a source, all penetrate to about the same depth.

Both beta-scattering and gamma-absorption are governed more or less by chance collisions in which energy is lost from the penetrating radiation. The intensity decays more or less exponentially with distance in each case (Figure 5-9). This is only true to a first approximation, however, because of scattering which is related to the geometry of the system.

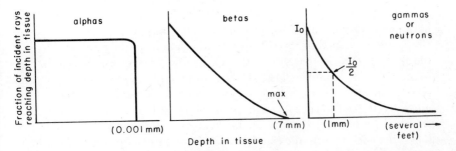

Figure 5-9. Penetration of 1 Mev Alphas, Betas, Gammas, and Neutrons into tissue.

In simplest cases, the curve for gammas is truly exponential; that for betas has less curvature and reaches a maximum value, which is the depth of penetration of the fastest betas. Note that the area under each curve corresponds to 100 per cent of the impinging rays hitting the target. The depth of penetration is radically different for the three cases.

TABLE 5-3. Ranges of Various Types of Radiation in Soft Tissue.*

Radiation	Usual Energy Range (mev)	Ionizing Particles in Tissue	Range of Radiation in Material of Low Atomic Number	
			Actual Range in Air, NTP (cm)	Equiv. Range in Watery Tissue (cm)
Beta rays	0.015 to 5	electrons	0.1 to 1000	0.0001 to 1.0
Electron beams	2 to 10	electrons	300 to 8000	0.4 to 10
X rays and	0.01	electrons	230	0.23
Gamma	0.10	electrons	25,000	4.0
rays**	1.0	electrons	23,000	10
	10	electrons	34,000	34
Fast neutrons**	0.1 to 10	protons	many meters	$\sim$10
Slow neutrons***	less than 100 ev	0.6-mev protons	0.8 (protons)	0.001
		+2.2-mev gammas	400 (electrons)	0.5
Proton beams†	5 to 400	protons	30 to 80,000	0.035 to 80
Alpha rays†	5 to 10	alphas	4 to 14	0.003 to 0.01

*From "Radiological Health Handbook," National Bureau of Standards, Washington, D. C., 1960.
**Range for absorption of half the incident radiation.
***From "Safe Handling of Radioisotopes," Health Physics Addendum," C. G. Appleton and P. N. Krishnamoorthy, Eds., International Atomic Energy Agency, Vienna, 1960.
†From G. J. Hine and G. L. Brownell, "Radiation Dosimetry," Academic Press, Inc., 1956 and W. Whaling, "The Energy Loss of Charged Particles in Matter," Handbuch der Physik, XXXIV.

In review, the nature and properties of the four main types of emanation have been considered. Positive ions and electrons lose kinetic energy by charge interaction with the electron cloud of atoms in the path: the greater the electron density the greater the absorption. Gamma rays lose energy to the electron cloud principally by pair production or Compton scattering. A neutron must hit a nucleus to lose energy. When it does, either the nucleus (charged) recoils through the medium and ionizes as a positive ion, or the neutron is absorbed by the nucleus, usually to form an unstable isotope which decays with the expulsion of beta or gamma, proton or neutrons.

The data of Table 5-3 illustrate these important principles. Note particularly the variation of the range in tissue for radiations of different type and energy. Protons are the ionizing particles in tissue which is under fast-neutron irradiation because hydrogen of water is the most plentiful target in the tissue. . . . This table should be thoroughly studied and understood.

USES AS BIOLOGICAL TRACERS

One of the simplest, and yet one of the most intriguing applications of the properties of radioactive substances has been in their use as tracers. The age of the earth, the authenticity of oil paintings, the courses of water and wind currents, have been probed simply by analyzing for the pertinent radioactive isotope in the proper place in the proper manner.

Three uses as tracers concern us here: (1) as an aid in determining the steps and paths by which molecular reactions occur, whether simple hydrations of ions, or the more complex syntheses and degradations of large biochemicals; (2) in plotting the course of fluid flow, through the blood capillaries, across cell walls, etc.; (3) in plotting the time and space distribution of biologically active chemicals. Examples of each are now given to illustrate the principles. The book by Kamen,[5] now a classic in the subject of tracers, is highly recommended for further study.

Tracers of Molecular Reactions

The first use of isotopic tracers on a biological problem was reported by Hevesy in 1923; this was a study of lead metabolism in plants. When heavy water (D_2O) became available in Urey's laboratory after the discovery of deuterium there in 1932, many biochemical problems were attacked: hydrogenations and dehydrogenations, cholesterol synthesis from smaller fragments, conversion of phenylalanine to tyrosine, etc. Then, by 1942, ammonium sulfate containing N_7^{15}, instead of the more common N_7^{14}, became available, and compounded the possibilities for biochemical investigations. Thanks to the nitrogen tracer, the fate of amino acids in protein synthesis could be followed. Probably the most important of all these investigations, from the point of view of biology, was the demonstration that protein molecules are in a dynamic equilibrium with their environment: they are not fixed end-items, but rather they are continually breaking apart here and there, accepting new amino acids and rejecting old. The same thing has now been found in lipid and carbohydrate metabolic reactions. Thus a dynamic steady-state must now be considered well established in the biochemistry of life, even at the molecular level, a fact which could be established only by this unique tool, the isotopic tracer.

To be useful as a tracer, the only requirement is that the isotope be present in an amount different from that occurring in nature. If the isotope is radioactive, its presence is easily detected by the ionization caused by its disintegration product. If it is not radioactive (deuterium, H_1^2, and nitrogen-15, N_7^{15}, are examples), it can be detected by two methods: (1) In the highly evacuated mass spectrograph, the atom is ionized by bombardment by electrons, and then, after the ion has been accelerated in an electric field to a prechosen velocity, it is allowed to enter the space between the poles of a strong magnet. It is deflected there by the magnetic field, by an amount determined by the weight of the flying particle: the heavier the particle the less the deflection. (2) By neutron activation: In some cases—N_7^{15} is an example—the nonradioactive isotopic tracer can be made active by bombardment with thermal neutrons, and then its quantity measured as the radioactivity of the product, N_7^{16} in this case, a hard beta and gamma emitter with a half-life of only a few seconds.

Tracers of Fluid Flow

The classical method of determining the flow pattern in the circulation system is to inject nitrous oxide, N_2O, at one point and then sample at various times and places after the injection.

The isotopic dilution technique, described under (1) and (2) above, has been used to map blood flow in the brain, advantage being taken of the fact that no new chemical reactions are introduced into the system in the materials injected.

During the past five years, the radioactive isotope method has also been applied to the very difficult problem of measuring the rate of flow of blood through various parts of the brain, and although these experiments have not been done as yet on man, the work (mainly on cats) is interesting and instructive, and illustrates the power of the method. The chemically inactive, freely diffusible gas, CF_3I^{131}, has β and γ emanations well-suited to the detection techniques already described. For example, ~ 300 microcuries (μc) are administered, either by injection into the blood stream in about 10 cc of salt solution, or inhaled from a prepared air mixture. The blood can be shunted through a glass tube from one part of an artery to another, and the activity of the shunted blood determined with a counter attached to the glass.

Alternatively, autoradiographic techniques on deep-frozen sections of sacrificed animals can give quantitative information on blood flow at different depths in the tissue and at different times. For example, through both superficial and deep cerebral structures the flow rate is about 1.2 cc/min per g of tissue—in all but the white matter, through which the rate of flow may be as low as 0.2. In the spinal cord the flow rate in the gray matter is 0.63 cc/min per g; in the white matter it is 0.14. Under light anesthesia these values are reduced about 25 per cent. All these values are given in terms of flow through 1 g of tissue, because there is just no good way to determine the number and dimensions of the blood capillaries in these tissues.

Studies on Metabolism: Time and Space Distribution of Biologically Active Chemicals

For information subsequently to be used in therapy of one sort or another, tracer studies on metabolism are probably the most important. Every tissue or organ has a definite turnover rate of its molecular components. Every substance which enters through the gastrointestinal tract or through the lungs into the blood stream, or is introduced directly into the body fluids through hypodermic needles, has one or more locations to which it goes, and a definite time (on the average) it stays there before being rejected in favor of new material. In practice, radioactive atoms are introduced into the molecules which compose the material to be studied.

Where this material goes, and how long it stays there, as well as in what form it is rejected, can all be answered by proper use of isotopic dilution or radioactive labeling technique. For example, studies have been made on the metabolism of proteins, such as the rate of protein synthesis and nitrogen (N^{15}) transfer; on the intermediary carbohydrate metabolism (C^{14} and P^{32}); on the intermediary metabolism of lipids—the pathways of fatty-acid oxidation and synthesis (H^3); on healing of bone fractures; on iodine metabolism (I^{131}) in the liver and in the thyroid; on turnover rate and growth rate of normal** and diseased tissue (C^{14}, H^2, O^{18}, Fe^{59}, Au^{198}); on the metabolism and turnover in teeth (P^{32}); and on blood circulation in the brain (I^{131}).

In more detail: the metabolism of nitrogen in the living system has been studied by the introduction of N^{15}-labeled glycine or other amino acids, ammonia, or nitrates, into food. Measurement of the N^{15}—by either activation or mass spectrometry (since N^{15} is a stable isotope)—as it appears in the urine, as well as analysis of the molecules in which the nitrogen is contained, has shown that the cellular proteins and their constituent amino acids are in a state of ceaseless *movement* and *renewal*. The proteins and amino

---

**Other isotopes now in use in metabolic studies include: Cr^{51}, Na^{24}, S^{35}, Cl^{36}, K^{42}, Ca^{45}, Mn^{54}, Zn^{65}, Br^{82}, Rb^{86}, I^{128}.

acids are continually being degraded, and being replaced by syntheses. That the rates of breakdown and resynthesis are the same is attested by the fact that the concentrations are maintained constant during life. About 60 per cent of N^{15}-containing protein has been shown to appear as glycine in the urine within 24 hr after a high-protein diet has been eaten; about 80 per cent appears within 60 hr. Liver, plasma, and intestinal-wall proteins are regenerated much faster than those of muscle and connective tissue.

The nitrogen that goes into ringed structures such as the porphyrins, which enter complexes with Fe^{+2} and Fe^{+3} to form the hemin of red-blood cells, turns over quite slowly: it takes 10 days for the hemin to be synthesized from isotopically tagged glycine; and then nearly 140 days before the degradation process (cell replacement in this case) reduces the concentration of tagged nitrogen to half the peak concentration (see Figure 5-10).

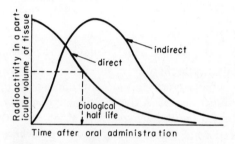

Figure 5-10. Radioactivity in a Particular Volume of Tissue as a Function of Time After Administration. Time and height of the maximum depend upon location of the volume, upon what chemical compound is given, its normal biochemistry, where it was introduced (direct or indirect), and the half-life of the isotope.

Other uses of radioactive tracers include the investigation of the effects of drugs and hormones on the turnover rate in particular tissues or organs. A subject of particular interest in recent years has been the role of insulin in the control of diabetes. In a diabetic, sugars are transported across the membrane and into the cell abnormally slowly, and they accumulate in the plasma, useless for supplying energy, via oxidation, inside the cell. Insulin, a medium-sized protein molecule whose structure has been well known since it was first synthesized in 1956, has been tagged with I^{131} and introduced into the blood stream. Within minutes, more than a third accumulates in the liver and the kidneys. However, a fraction adsorbs in a nonspecific manner on all membranes accessible to blood plasma and intracellular fluids. Cell walls are no exception; and the adsorption of insulin has been associated with an increase of the rate of sugar penetration (a process which itself has been followed by C^{14}-tagged sugars). Whether the control exercised by insulin is simply by opening the access to pores, or whether it controls in a more subtle manner by increasing the activity of the enzyme (hexokinase) also thought to be adsorbed on the membrane, has not yet been settled. However, it can be seen that the use of radioactive tracers in such a pharmacological problem can make a valuable contribution to our knowledge of the processes involved.

The pioneering work of Huff and Judd on the quantitative analysis of the time and space distributions of Fe^{59} in blood plasma, will be discussed in Chapter 11 as a concrete example of how possible methods of action can be analyzed with a computer if it is fed reliable experimental measurements of where the Fe^{59} goes and how long it stays there. We learn a little about what the iron does, and also something about just what processes are interfered with during blood diseases.

Radioactive Mapping

Administration of compounds of I^{131}, followed by external measurements of beta-ray intensity in the thyroid region of the neck, has been introduced in some centers as a replacement test for determining whether the thyroid is normal, over-, or under-active. A hyperactive thyroid may absorb up to 80 per cent of the tagged iodine; a hypoactive gland may absorb as little as 15 per cent before normal biochemical turnover elsewhere in the body reduces the concentration via excretion. Mapping of the thyroid by I^{131} scintography is common practice. Both the outline of the organ, and its turnover rate can be obtained from maps made at different time intervals after administration. The maximum activity of the emission is a direct measure of the uptake of iodine by the thyroid.

The flow of fluids through various critical parts of the system can also be mapped satisfactorily by dissolving in the fluid a small amount of gas which contains a radioactive emitter, and mapping from the outside with a collimated scintillation counter (Figure 5-6).

Conclusion

A great many elementary biochemical reactions are being studied via the tracer technique, and a few physical processes also. Some of these will be found mentioned as examples in different parts of this book. The techniques are reliable and extremely sensitive, and have the unique advantage that the introduction of the radioactive element can be done in such a manner as not to upset the chemistry or the physics of the process *in vivo*. Already in extensive use in biological research—in his review Kuzin[12] was able to collect 358 references to new work published in 1959 alone!—now, led by successes with I^{131} and P^{32}, radioactive tracer techniques have a wonderful future in medical diagnosis.

As it does in so many subjects, the National Bureau of Standards, in Washington, periodically publishes reliable definitions of terms, values of universal and experimental constants, and tables and graphs of collated data on radiologically important parameters. The "Radiological Health Hand Book" is indispensible to further study of this subject, as a quantitative supplement to the classic work of Kamen.[5]

PROBLEMS

5-1: (a) What element is formed by the radioactive disintegration of:

$P^{32} \xrightarrow{\beta^-}$ $\qquad$ $Co^{60} \xrightarrow{\beta^-}$ $\qquad$ $P^{30} \xrightarrow{\beta^-}$

$I^{131} \xrightarrow{\beta^-}$ $\qquad$ $S^{35} \xrightarrow{\beta^-}$

$Na^{24} \xrightarrow{\beta^-}$ $\qquad$ $Ra^{226} \xrightarrow{\alpha}$

$Po^{210} \xrightarrow{\alpha}$ $\qquad$ $Na^{22} \xrightarrow{\beta^+}$

(b) Is the product radioactive too?

5-2: (a) Make a graph showing activity (counts per minute) against time, for uptake, utilization, and elimination of I^{131} by the thyroid.

(b) List five important reasons why I^{131} is used in irradiation-therapy of goiter.

5-3: The 1.70 mev β-ray of P^{32} penetrates about 7 mm into tissue. The half-life is 14.3 days. A 1-millicurie (mc) source will deliver about 1 rad (radiation absorbed dose) per minute.

How long would it take for a 1 mc of $NaHPO_4$, composed of P^{32}, taken orally as a solution in water, to administer 6000 rads to an organ in which it concentrates?

REFERENCES

1. The Staff, Physics Dept., Univ. of Pittsburgh: "Atomic Physics," 2nd ed., John Wiley & Sons, Inc., New York, N. Y., 1944.
2. "Atomic Radiation (Theory, Biological Hazards, Safety Measures, Treatment of Injury)," RCA Service Co., Camden, N. J., 1959.
3. "Teaching with Radioisotopes," H. A. Miner, et al., Eds., U. S. Atomic Energy Commission, Washington, D. C., 1959.
4. Scientific American, issue on "Ionizing Radiations," Vol. 201, September, 1959: papers by S. Warren, p. 164, and R. L. Platzman, p. 74.
5. Kamen, M. D., "Tracer Techniques in Biology and Medicine," Academic Press, New York, N. Y., 1960.

6. Glasser, O., Ed., "Medical Physics, Vol. III," Year Book Publishing Co., Chicago, Ill., 1960: several short articles, p. 302–364. See especially: "Localization of Brain Tumors with β-Emitting Isotopes," by Silverstone and Robertson.

7. Kity, S. S., *Methods in Med. Res.*, **1**, 204 (1948).

8. Munck, O. and Lassen, N. A., *Circulation Research*, **5**, 163 (1951).

9. Clarke, H. T., Urey, H. C., and 16 others, "The Use of Isotopes in Biology and Medicine," in the *Proceedings* of a Symposium on the subject, The Univ. of Wisconsin Press, Madison, Wis., 1948.

10. Huff, R. L. and Judd, O. J., "Kinetics of Iron Metabolism," in *Adv. in Biol. and Med. Phys.*, **4**, 223 (1956).

11. Freygang, W. H. and Sokoloff, L., "Quantitative Measurement of Regional Circulation in the Central Nervous System by the Use of Radioactive Inert Gas," *Adv. in Biol. and Med. Phys.*, **6**, 263 (1958).

12. Kuzin, A. M., "The Application of Radioisotopes in Biology," *Review Series, No. 7*, International Atomic Energy Agency, Vienna, 1960.

13. "Scintography—A collection of Scintigrams Illustrating the Modern Medical Technique of *in vivo* Visualization of Radioisotope Distribution," R-C Scientific Co., Inc., Pasadena, Calif., 1955.

14. Cork, J. M., "Radioactivity and Nuclear Physics," 3rd ed., D. Van Nostrand, Inc., New York, N. Y., 1957.

CHAPTER 6

Big Molecules

(Structure of Macromolecules and Living Membranes;
Isomers and Multiplets;
Codes and Molecular Diseases)

A score of diseases (including sickle cell anaemia and phenylketonuria)
have so far been recognized as enzyme diseases, presumably resulting from
the manufacture of abnormal molecules in place of active enzyme molecules.
I think that it is not unlikely that there are hundreds or thousands of such
diseases.

I foresee the day when many of these diseases will be treated by the use of
artificial enzymes . . . . When our understanding of enzyme activity becomes
great enough, it will be possible to synthesize a catalyst, etc. . . . .

Thus did Linus Pauling emphasize to an international symposium of enzymologists in Chicago, in 1956, the relationship
between the structure of the macromolecule and its chemical and
physical roles in the living system.

INTRODUCTION

The structure of macromolecules and of arrays of them in living membranes and other tissues has occupied the attention of an important class of
biophysicists for the past ten years. Using modern rapid-flow, quick-freeze-
drying, and micromanipulation techniques, and armed with the phase and

interference microscopes, the X-ray diffraction camera, and the electron microscope—the last now in such an advanced stage of development that, in proper hands, it can resolve or "see" small particles just a few atomic diameters apart—researchers have been able to gain new insight into the actual shape of the molecule in the tissue, and even into the positions of atoms and groups of atoms within the molecule.

Running concurrently with these physical researchers have been chemical studies which have finally solved the puzzle of the complete chemical composition of a few large, biologically important molecules. For example, although the hormone, insulin, has been known and used widely in the treatment of diabetes for nearly forty years, it was only in 1955 that Sanger and his colleagues at Cambridge were finally able to write down the complete structural formula. It contains 777 atoms! Since then, ribonuclease (RNAse), an enzyme containing 1876 atoms and which catalyzes the cleavage of ribonucleic acid, has also yielded the secret of its composition to the attack of persistent chemists. This completes the first big step toward knowing how this molecule works as a catalyst, although details of the structure at and around the active site(s) are not yet known. This is the next big task, for if more than one of the chemical groups must exert their chemical effects on a specific part of the molecule whose hydrolysis is to be promoted, then their spatial arrangement must be very important. Not only must they be present, but they must be present at the proper positions in space if the catalytic activity of the site is to exist. In other words, if one of the players is out of position, the game is lost.

Table 6-1 gives a spectrum of biologically important organic molecules, small and large—some containing a metallic oxidizable and reducible ion which enters the chemical reactions of the molecule. Although some details are given in the following sections, the discussion is just an indication of the scope of the subject. There are excellent reference sources: for example, the recent book of Tanford.[16]

STRUCTURE

Our purpose, first, will be to outline the structure of two big molecules of critical biological importance, myoglobin and hemoglobin, learned in the recent work of the schools of Kendrew and Perutz, respectively. The method used was X-ray crystallography, and although the chemical composition has not yet been fully worked out for these two molecules, X-ray crystallographic studies have completely outlined the form of the molecule in the dry crystalline state.

The second part of this section on structure is concerned with the cross-linked structure of liquid crystals, such as in the aqueous humor of the lens of the eye, and of membranes—those of the erythrocyte cell wall which are relatively homogeneous, and those patchy, mosaic membranes exemplified by the wall of the small intestine.

Crystalline Macromolecules

Diffraction of X rays by the regular arrays of the electron clouds which surround the atoms or ions of a crystalline substance was introduced in Chapter 4. The X rays diffracted from a single crystal interfere with one another in a manner which is determined solely by the position and electron density of the target atoms in the crystal. If the diffracted rays are allowed to fall upon a photographic plate, from the position and darkness of the spots on the plate, one can (at least in principle) locate the position and electron density of the diffracting atoms in the crystal. The position of the spot tells the angle, Θ, of constructive scatter of the X rays of wavelength, λ; and the Bragg interference equation, $n\lambda = 2d \sin \Theta$, relates these values, the "order" of interference, n, and the wavelength, λ, to the spacing, d, within the crystal responsible for the scatter. The blackness of the spot gives the amplitude. The superposition of those waves which give rise to the one which emerges from the crystal, however, must be inferred from positions of the atoms in the crystal. This is done by a trial-and-error mathematical method involving superposition of infinite series, a method which will not be described here.

It was in 1951 that Pauling and Corey made the big break-through in our understanding of structure of proteins: they were able to determine from X-ray diffraction patterns that synthetic polypeptides formed of alpha amino acids all have a coiled, helical form. In other words, the back-bone of the polypeptide chain coils around and around, to form a cylindrically shaped molecular helix. This can be easily understood now, in retrospect, as follows. Since all the alpha amino acids have the structural formula

$$
\begin{array}{cc}
H & R \\
| & | \\
N-C-COOH \\
| & | \\
H & H
\end{array}
$$

and since these condense through the —CONH— linkage (Figure 6-1) in the form

$$
\cdots -\underset{1}{N}-\underset{2}{\underset{|}{C}}-\underset{3}{C}+\underset{4}{N}-\underset{5}{\underset{|}{C}}-\underset{6}{C}- \cdots
$$

the atoms of the backbone of the chain, —N—C—C—, are repeated over and over again. The bonds can be bent around only so far, and, in the limit,

TABLE 6-1. Some Molecules, Small and Large, of Biological Importance.

Molecule	Mol Wt	Metal	Organic Part	Physical Structure
Water	18	none	none	108° angle
Adrenalin	135	none	HO, HO— ...—$CHOHCH_2NHCH_3$	crystals well known
Aspirin	180	none	COOH, $OCOCH_3$	crystals well known
Morphine	285	none	4 rings (Figure 4-6)	crystals well known
Cholesterol	324	none	a lipid, a 4-ringed alcohol	structureless
β-carotene	536	none	a lipid, a highly unsaturated hydrocarbon	structureless
Hemin	652	Fe^{+3}	porphyrins (Figure 6-3)	crystals well known
Chlorophyll	893	Mg^{+2}	4 substituted porphyrin rings	flat, planar molecule
Vitamin B_{12}	1357	Co^{+3}	multi-substituted, N-containing ringed cpd., completely known. Synthesized in 1956	crystals well known
Glucagon	3647	none	a protein hormone: 29 amino acid residues	structureless
Adrenocortico-hormone (ACTH)	4540	none	protein: 39 amino acids, sequence known since 1958	structureless
Insulin (monomer)	5733	Zn^{+2} (or Co^{+2}, or Cd^{+2})	protein: 51 amino acids, double chain, 2 disulfide cross bonds, known completely since 1956; dimerizes readily	two structureless, cross-linked chains

Table 6-1 (contin.)

Molecule	Mol Wt	Metal	Organic Part	Physical Structure
Ribonuclease	12,000	none?	an enzyme: 124 amino acid residues; 4 disulfide bonds; sequence 90% known since 1959.	unknown; variable
Cytochrome-C	13,100	Fe^{+3}	porphyrins plus protein, sequence partly known	unknown
Myoglobin	26,000	Fe^{+3} (one)	porphyrin plus 238 amino acid residues, sequence almost completely known	completely known since 1958 (Figure 6-3)
Hemoglobin	67,000	Fe^{+3} (four)	about the same as above; sequence largely unknown	known down to 6 Å resolution; 4 polypeptide chains
Cellulose	$324\,n$	none	a polysaccharide of n residues of β-cellobiose	many forms; fibers, sheets, etc.
Collagen	360,000	Ca^{+2} (not essential)	3 intertwined protein helices which polymerize	macromolecule about 3000 Å long and 30 Å diameter; polymers in tendon, cartilage, leather, etc. (Figure 6-8)
Desoxyribose nucleic acid (DNA)	~6,000,000 and up	none	organic pyridine and pyrimidine bases attached to a helical ribose-phosphate framework	2-stranded helix postulated; much known by inference (Figure 6-10)
Lipoproteins Glycoproteins Lipopoly- saccharides Nucleoproteins	10^3 to 10^8	none essential	condensation products of simpler molecules	unknown

carbon *6* falls almost directly above nitrogen *1*, and the two are hydrogen bonded about 1.5 Å apart. The diameter of the helix so formed is about 8 Å. The helix has an open core, about 2 Å across, and the R-groups, or side chains to the main structure, jut out radially from the central axis of the cylinder.

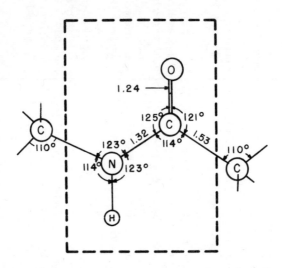

Figure 6-1.   The Planar —CONH— Linkage (boxed) Between Amino Acids in a Protein. Lengths in angstroms.

Since the helical shape is a property of poly*alpha* amino acids, it was given the name "alpha-helix," and it is now probably the most famous structure of macromolecular physical chemistry. Figure 6-2 is a drawing, similar to the original disclosure, which shows the main chain (bold bonds) and the positions of attached groups (—R); and which indicates the positions of the hydrogen bonds, the "bones" which give the helix rigidity.

It is now known to be the main structural component of α-keratin, hair, wool, nail, muscle, and connective tissue, etc. Recently it has been traced in muscle to the contractile enzyme, myosin itself. Because of the unique role of myosin, some of its physical and chemical properties are expounded in Chapter 10.

One protein, of unquestioned importance, which has intrigued biological investigators for years, is hemoglobin, the "oxygen carrier" of the respiratory enzyme system, first crystallized and purified by Hoppe-Seyler in 1862. However, with a molecular weight of 67,000, its amino acid sequence and the physical structure of the molecule have only slowly yielded to persistent

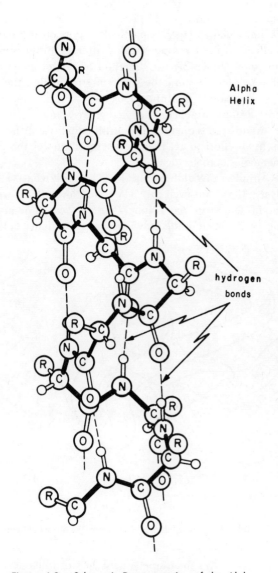

Alpha
Helix

hydrogen
bonds

Figure 6-2.   Schematic Representation of the Alpha
Helix of Protein.   Three complete turns are shown.
They start at the bottom C, wind out toward the reader
through the next —N—C—, then back in through
the plane of the paper, etc. (After Pauling and Corey,
1953.)

investigation. The X-ray diffraction pattern of even single crystals was too formidable for analysis until M. F. Perutz, about 1950, began to substitute heavy metals ions such as Hg^{+2} at particular spots on the molecule and to analyze the effects of these strong X-ray scatterers on the spectrum. With this technique, now known as the "method of isomorphous replacement," it was possible by 1960 to show the surprising result that the protein of the molecule at 6 angstroms' resolution looks like several intertwined worms, with the heme groups attached—not a regular array at all. Studies continue on the amino acid sequence, and on the analysis of the X-ray diffraction pattern, in an effort to get even better resolution of the detailed structure of the hemoglobin molecule.

Inherently simpler, myoglobin (one Fe^{+2} ion only) has yielded not only to 6 Å analysis (1956) but even to 1.5 Å resolution (1958), work for which Kendrew and his team received a Nobel Prize in 1961. The main features of this molecule are depicted in the drawing shown in Figure 6-3. The α-helix

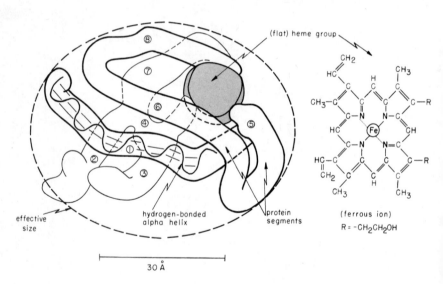

Figure 6-3. Molecule of Myoglobin. (Drawn from the Model of Kendrew, 1958.)

hydrogen-bon(d)ed, forms the framework of the worm-like segments, sudden turns in which are thought to be associated with the proline groups—an amino acid residue of odd structural configuration. The heme group sits exposed, with the iron ion ready for oxidation or reduction, or, preferably, simply complexing with O_2 picked up from air.

Although this is the configuration of *crystalline* myoglobin, the shape of the molecule dissolved in salty water may be quite different—for example, one can readily imagine the legs of this molecular octopus unfolding in the blood stream.

Structural knowledge of many other big molecules is rapidly becoming available. This is a subject of intense interest. Straight chains and helices, some coiled into balls, some folded back and forth to form rods, others with randomly coiled shapes, are known or imagined. These forms are illustrated in Figure 6-4.

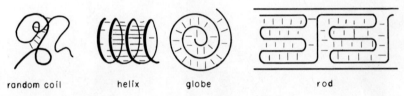

random coil   helix   globe   rod

Figure 6-4. Some Molecular Shapes in Solution (schematic). Transitions one to another can be effected by change in pH, ionic composition, or temperature.

Receiving much attention in the hands of F. O. Schmitt and the MIT School has been collagen, the structural component of connective tissue, tendon, skin, cartilage, etc. (Figure 6-5). Formed of three interwound molecular helices of protein, with molecular dimensions approximately 3000 Å long × 30 Å in diameter, it cross-links end to end to form fibers, and then side to side to form either sheets (two dimensions) or blocks (three dimensions) of connective tissue with very varied physical properties: for example, tensile strength up to 100,000 lbs/in^2, equivalent to that of a steel wire of the same dimensions!

Now thought to be the basic information-carrier of the gene, and an extremely important component of the nucleus of the cell, is desoxyribose-nucleic acid (DNA). At about 70 per cent relative humidity, it is an extended, double-stranded helix, of molecular weight in the millions. Further discussion of the structure of DNA, and its sister nucleic acid, ribosenucleic acid (RNA), appears later in this chapter.

Now, the backbone of the helices of DNA and RNA is ribose, a sugar, polymerized through phosphate groups. Polymerized sugars are the second major structural component of living tissue—cellulose and chitin are examples. Hyaluronic acid and glycogen are polysaccharides which take an integral part in the biochemistry of life. Thus glycogen is the form in which sugar is stored as an energy reserve in the liver. Polysaccharides, like proteins, take many forms in tissue. One which seems to be unique is the pleated sheet of cellulose.

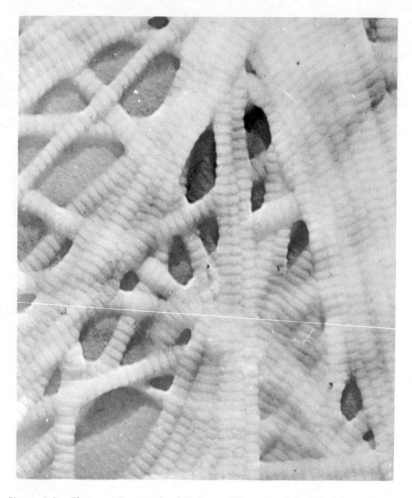

Figure 6-5.   Electron Micrograph of Collagen Fibers Carefully Lifted from Human Skin. Note how they are individually cross-segmented and collectively fused (Courtesy of J. Gross, Massachusetts General Hospital, and of *Scientific American*.)

Lipid molecules themselves are generally small, by comparison with the macromolecules discussed in this section (see Table 6-1). However, they condense with proteins to form macromolecular lipoproteins, and with cellulose to form lipocelluloses, and thus also play a primary role in the structure of tissue.

Metal-organic molecules are varied and important in living tissue (Table 6-1). The bright light from the point of view of our knowledge of structure is vitamin B_{12}, a substituted cyano-cobalt amide of molecular weight 1357, used in treating pernicious anemia, growth failure in children, etc. The complete chemical composition was disclosed in 1955, and culminated with X-ray diffraction analysis of structure three years later.

Dissolved Macromolecules

Unfortunately, when crystals such as those described in the previous section are dissolved in water, the molecules are subjected to a number of new and powerful forces of hydration and of polarization by ions, and the configurations of many molecules change. Since water has a diffuse diffraction pattern of its own, the X-ray technique used in crystals cannot be employed to advantage on solutions of these molecules, and other methods which indicate structure must be sought. All those to be described are useful, but each has its limitations.

The problem in solution is complicated by three other facts: (1) The molecule will not usually, unless it is globular-shaped, have a unique molecular weight; but rather will its molecular weight vary, some molecules in the solution having weights above, and some below an average value. The dis-

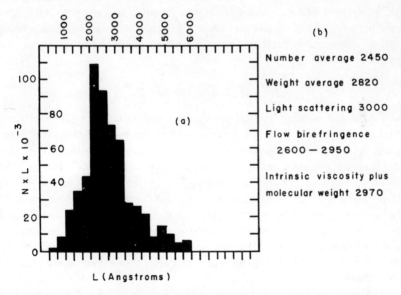

Figure 6-6. Ichthyocol (a Protein Food Supplement from Fish): Direct Measurements of Molecular Size by Electron Micrographs, Compared with Results from Indirect Methods. Number (N) with length (L) multiplied by L gives total amount of protein with particles of length L. Molecular weights, M_n and M_w, are derived from data plotted. (Data of Hall and Doty, J. Amer. Chem. Soc., **80**, 1269 (1958).)

tribution shown in Figure 6-6 clearly shows this. Number-average, or weight-average molecular weights are obtained, depending upon whether the number of particles or their size is reflected by the measurement. (2) The configurations which the macromolecule can take in solution can vary, depending upon hydrogen ion concentration (pH), cation content, and other factors which imply strong electrical effects. (3) Many macromolecules are themselves polymers, and in turn may polymerize further in solution.

From this discussion it is easy to see that the elucidation of the exact size and shape, or structure, of a particular macromolecule in a particular solution is probably still a long way off. Some physicochemical experiments which throw light on this vexing but important problem will now be outlined. We follow, in part, Paul Doty in this outline, and recommend highly his clearly written reviews[5] of 1956 and 1960 to the reader who wishes to pursue the subject beyond the bare outline given here. The methods are divided conveniently into static (or equilibrium) and dynamic methods. All give molecular weight and/or dimensions.

Static Methods

Osmotic Pressure. This is the most sensitive property of dilute solutions of macromolecules, but since it is a colligative property it is strongly influenced by the presence of any molecules or ions other than the macromolecule being studied. The osmotic pressure, π, as a function of concentration, c, can be expressed

$$\frac{\pi}{cRT} = \frac{1}{M} + \frac{B}{M^2} c + \frac{C}{M^3} c^2 + \cdots$$

where M is the number-average molecular weight, B and C are constants related to molecular size and interactions, R is the gas constant, and T the absolute temperature. Measurements* of osmotic pressure at several concentrations can be plotted as π/cRT vs c, as is shown in Figure 6-7, Doty's 1960 data on collagen at $2°C$. Extrapolation to zero concentration, where the polymer molecules have no influence on one another no matter how uncoiled they may be, gives the first term, $1/M$, the reciprocal of which is the number-average molecular weight, M_n, in this case 300,000. The parameters B and C are not zero because the macromolecules can physically coil around each other and, furthermore, interact with each other's electrically charged groups of atoms.

Light Scattering. We saw in Chapter 4 that light is scattered and absorbed by molecules in solution (Rayleigh scattering of light, and the Beer-Lambert law of light absorption). For macromolecules the loss is explicitly stated

---

*Refer back to Figure 2-3 and the discussion on page 36. If c is expressed in g/l, π in atm, and R as 0.082 l atm/deg. mol, M has units of g/mole.

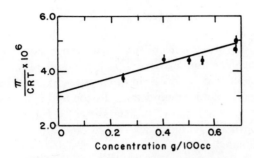

Figure 6-7. Determination of Molecular Weight
of Collagen by Osmotic Pressure (π) Measurements. The intercept at c = 0 is equal to $1/M_n$.

through a derivation due to Einstein and Debye. The resulting expression
relates the intensity of the light scattered (R_{90}) at right angles $(90°)$ to the
incident light and the concentration of the scatterer in solution:

$$\frac{Kc}{R_{90}} = \frac{1}{M} + \frac{2B}{M^2} c$$

where K is a constant depending upon the wavelength of the incoming light,
the index of refraction of the solvent, and other factors, all of which can be
measured. A plot of Kc/R_{90} vs c, then, has an intercept (value at $c = 0$) of
$1/M$, the reciprocal of which is the weight-average molecular weight.

Sedimentation Equilibrium. Perhaps the most versatile of them all, this
method of measuring molecular weight can give a reliable value indepèn-
dently (almost) of the shape.

In the ultracentrifuge, which spins so rapidly that the centrifugal force
can be higher even than 100,000 times that of the gravitational attraction
to the earth when the suspension is at rest, a macromolecule can reach a
stable position at which the centrifugal force is exacly balanced by a force in
the opposite direction which is proportional to the number of buffeting molecules per cc (Brownian motion). Heavy molecules come to equilibrium at a
position near the bottom of the centrifuge tube, light molecules toward the
top.

After the solution has spun long enough for the macromolecules to assume
their equilibrium distribution (usually some days for big molecules), the
concentration, c, and concentration gradient dc/dx along the linear axis, x,
of the tube (measured from the center of rotation), are measured, usually by
a light-refraction technique. Use of the expression

$$\frac{(1 - \bar{\rho})\omega^2 x c}{RT \, dc/dx} = \frac{1}{M} + \frac{B}{M^2} c + \cdots$$

at various concentrations and extrapolation to zero concentrations so that intermolecular interactions cannot interfere, gives the value of M, as before. Here $\bar{\rho}$ is the ratio of densities of solvent to solute, and ω the angular velocity of the centrifuge (radians/sec).

A more rapid method, used within the past few years, takes advantage of the fact that small volumes bounded by the top and the bottom of the tube reach equilibrium very rapidly; measurements of concentrations in these volumes can be made within a few hours, and an "average" molecular weight then evaluated.

Direct Measurement of Size and Shape via the Electron Microscope. For those polymers whose shape and weight are the same, dry or wet, the direct measurement by the electron microscope is possible. A comparison of the results of different methods on the globular molecule icthyocol is shown in Figure 6-6. The nonequilibrium methods will now be outlined.

Dynamic Methods

These are based on four transport processes which are discussed as a group in more detail in Chapter 8. The following outline suffices here:

Diffusion under a concentration gradient and *sedimentation* under a centrifugal force can both be stated as the speed of the process under specific conditions, and these speeds expressed as D and s, respectively. An argument involving frictional force offered by the water against movement of the macromolecules shows that the ratio of the two speeds, D/s, is related to the molecular weight, M, by

$$\frac{(1 - \bar{\rho})}{RT} \frac{D}{s} = \frac{1}{M},$$

an expression originally derived by Svedberg. Measurements of D and s, and of the densities of solid and solute permit evaluation of molecular weight.

Intrinsic Viscosity. This property, $\dfrac{\eta - \eta_0}{\eta_0}\bigg/ c$ as $c \rightarrow 0$ (where η_0 is the viscosity of the solvent and η that of the solution), can be related to the volume of the molecule and molecular weight by two expressions which in simplest form are:

(1) $[\eta] = 2.5 \ \overline{V}$ for spheres (7000 $\overline{V}$ for a big, randomly coiled molecule such as DNA)—here $\overline{V}$ is cc/g; and

(2) $[\eta] \propto M^{\alpha}$ where α is an empirical constant, usually 0.5 to 1.0.

Although measurement of viscosity is easy enough, the proportionality constants have an empirical character, and hence one always suspects the absolute values of size and shape so obtained. However, they are quite reliably indicative of *change* in molecular shape as environment is changed, and it is in this manner that they are usually used.

Speed of rotation of a big molecule about an axis can be inferred by an optical measurement called *flow birefringence*, and the result related to molecular weight. Both the optical technique involved and discussion of the proportionalities are beyond the scope of this outline, for they are very specialized.

Proper use of the techniques outlined have shown many interesting properties about certain biologically active molecules. Compare now the results of the dynamic methods with those of static methods. Table 6-2 gives average weight and dimensions of collagen, measured by five different methods, and of erythrocyte DNA by two methods. Our well-worked illustration, Figure 6-6, shows the results of the direct measurements of size of dried ichthyocol** rods by electron microscope techniques as compared with the indirect measurements by light scattering, flow birefringence, and intrinsic viscosity methods.

TABLE 6-2.   Dimensions of Molecules of Collagen and DNA.

Molecule	Method	Mol Wt	Length	Diameter
Collagen*	Osmotic pressure	310,000	—	—
	Light scattering	345,000	3100 Å	13.0 Å
	Intrinsic viscosity	—	2970	13.6
	Sedimentation and viscosity	300,000	—	12.8
	Flow birefringence and viscosity	350,000	2900	13.5
DNA**	Light scattering	4.7 to 6.2 million	—	—
	Sedimentation and viscosity	5.3 to 17.4 million	2030–2350 Å	—

*The chief constituent of connective tissue (cartilage, tendon, etc.). (After Doty, Oncley, *et al.*, Eds. (1959).)
**Extracted from human erythrocytes. (After Butler, *et al.* (1960).)

These are particularly pleasing results, one result confirming the other. Such is often not the case for randomly coiled molecules for which the results of different methods may disagree violently with one another. Carbohydrates are particularly perplexing from this viewpoint. Again, in solution DNA is a very large, randomly coiled molecule, an extended doublestranded helix, apt to polymerize and take any shape at all in response to its environment. Therefore the study of nucleic acid reproduction as a molec-

** As the name implies, ichthyocol is a collagen from fish, used as a food supplement, as are gelatin from animals and glutin from wheat.

ular reaction, like reactions of other randomly coiled molecules in solution, is made just that much more difficult. Some very fine X-ray diffraction work has been done on crystalline DNA, but even in crystalline form it may assume several structural arrangements, depending upon the humidity.

Molecular Structure of Living Membranes

There are two main subjects of interest in membrane biophysics: the structure of the membrane, and its penetration by small and large molecules and ions. They are closely interrelated. Thus there exist, in the human body, membranes which have every degree of specialization—from the quite nonspecific mosaic membrane of the small intestine to the highly specific membrane of nerve cells which not only can distinguish sodium ion from potassium ion (a trick which analytical chemists have only recently learned to do) but even change the rate at which it lets them through! We confine ourselves here to considerations of structure only. Penetration is discussed in Chapter 10.

From analytical and electron microscopic work, it has been found (Danielli and many others) over the past twenty-five years that most living membranes*** are laminar, composed of at least three, sometimes five, layers. The heart of the membrane is a bimolecular layer of lipid, flanked by thin layers of protein, or cellulose, or both (Figure 6-8 (a)). The cellulose, if pres-

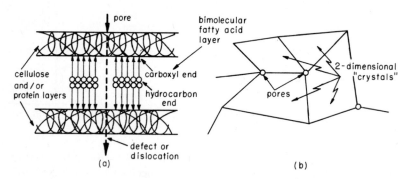

Figure 6-8. Schematic Representation of Layers in the Living Membrane. For many membranes the total thickness is about 75Å. (a) Note the position of the defect or pore. (b) Plan view of lipid film.

ent, seems to be there simply for structural reasons—to make the membrane mechanically strong. The protein layer can also provide strength. However, various metal ions and water form complexes with the protein, and some protein of most membranes has enzyme activity, a property which is cur-

---

*** For example, the cell wall, the endoplasmic reticulum within the cell, etc.

rently thought by some to be associated with control of the size of the holes through which penetration of ions and molecules occurs.

Although the membrane may have a total thickness of hundreds of angstroms, the hydrophobic lipid layer, probably continuous, (and certainly the well-protected center layer), is estimated to be only 75 Å thick. Figure 6-9 is an electron micrograph of two membranes touching each other, from which the 75 Å figure can be directly measured. This is a pattern which has been found in practically all the living membranes so photographed. The membrane is not perfectly symmetrical, as different staining methods have shown; and in some cases—the erythrocyte wall, for example—there is definitely an assymetry.

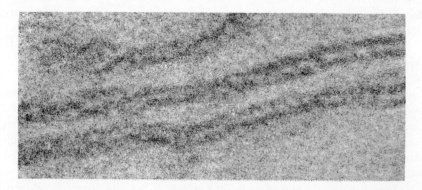

Figure 6-9. Electron Micrograph of the Double Membrane of a Nerve. Osmic acid stains the outer protein layers (see also Figure 6-8), and scatters electrons (dark ridges), but does not absorb into the (light) lipid layer in between. Total distance across one membrane is about 75Å. Magnification: 880,000×. (Courtesy of J. D. Robertson, Harvard Medical School.)

When ones tries to penetrate deeper into the structure of the membrane, one runs into singularly difficult problems. Although it must be made up of macromolecules of protein, cellulose, and lipid, those molecules probably are distorted and stretched, or cross-linked into a planar structure. Neither the structure nor the properties of degraded or dissolved membrane molecules would therefore be expected to reflect those of the living membrane by conventional techniques of analysis. And yet not only are the complete membrane structures too thin to be studied in bulk, but also they degenerate when dried for X-ray or electron-microscopic study. In other words, good techniques for studying living membranes *in vivo* are still needed. Certain very specialized membranes, such as those enclosing nerve and muscle cells, and the rod and cone cells of the retina, can be studied through examination of the details of their specialty. For instance, much progress has recently been made in elucidating the structure of the mitochondrion membrane because of its unique function in electron transport in the step-wise oxidation of foods. But the general problem of direct knowledge of the structure of living membranes probably awaits more knowledge of the structure of macromolecules in solution.

Indirect methods—i.e., studies of penetration of the living membrane by water, ions, and molecules—are proving to be very helpful to studies of structure, because from such studies one can infer some properties of the membrane *in vivo*: pore size, for example. An estimate of pore size (length and area) requires at least two independent experimental measurements, because there are two-dimensional parameters, area and length, to be evaluated. Both the rate of diffusion of a substance down a concentration gradient and the rate of flow of a fluid under a mechanical pressure, should be larger the larger the area of the hole in the membrane and the shorter its length.

Although the rate of transport of water through the cell membrane of erythrocytes is very rapid, both rate of diffusion and rate of flow have recently been measured accurately enough to determine a value for average pore diameter in the erythrocyte wall *in vivo*. Diffusion rate of water was found by measuring the rate at which radioactively labeled water is picked up by the cells within a few milliseconds of being bathed in the labeled water. A fast-flow apparatus had to be used, the ingenious details of which are best described in the original papers.[8] Then the rate of flow into the cell was measured by suddenly changing the osmotic pressure (salt concentration) outside the cell, and following the change in cell diameter by means of a light-scattering technique.

From the results, an analysis gives about 7 Å as the diameter of the pores in the erythrocyte wall. The beauty of this kind of experiment is that it is a measure of a physical property of the membrane while it is living and functioning normally. The limitation is that the analysis involves certain assumptions which may or may not turn out to be absolutely correct. In the next few years it will be supplemented by the so-called "differential osmotic pressure" approach of Staverman, in which pore size can be inferred by the "leakiness" of the membrane to certain ions; and by the molecular- or ionic-sieve approach, in which a large number of ions of various sizes are tested for their penetration. The diameter of the largest one which can penetrate the membrane is the effective diameter of the pore.

Further support for the pore theory comes from examination of monomolecular layers of large fatty acids and lipids. The lipid is spread out on water in a pan with a moveable boom (the so-called "Langmuir trough"). The boom is then made to reduce the area which the spread lipid must cover, and the force required to move the boom is measured on a sensitive torsion balance. When the layer has closed in completely, the resistance to movement of the boom increases sharply, and thus the continuous mono-molecular layer is formed. By means of electron microscopic examination it has been found that the molecules assume a two-dimensional crystal struc-ture, with many crystallites. Where these meet there is indication of defects or dislocations which could be the precursor of pores in the membrane—see Figure 6-8, (a) and (b).

All these approaches presume that pores really exist, and ignore Beutner's old (1911) idea that the membrane's lipid layer is a continuous barrier *through* which ions and molecules penetrate by either chemical reaction or solution in the lipid layer. This idea still has much appeal, especially in view of what is now known about the changes in transport mechanisms through a film across which a large electrical voltage exists. Thus a typical membrane potential of 100 mv across a membrane whose thickness is 100 Å, would exert an electrical field of 100,000 v per cm across the membrane, and *nobody* knows yet what that would do to a continuous lipid layer. Perhaps acidic and basic organic molecules are formed by electrical discharge, simi-lar to the reactions known in organic transformer oils, to give the layer more of an ionic character so that water and ions can more easily dissolve.

Structure within the living membrane is a treacherous problem for study; but no problem is more intriguing, and none in biophysics more important.

ISOMERS AND MULTIPLETS

This section is concerned with (a) the *stereoisomerism* which is expected to occur in macro-organic molecules as well as in classical organic molecules; and with (b) *excited states* which one supposes to exist in macromolecules, by analogy with the properties of smaller ones. These subjects have a bearing on the physical structure of the molecules and their chemical reactivity; but the current practical interest is in their relationship to inherited characteris-tics, to disease, and to benign (passive) and malignant (invasive) tumors. Unfortunately this subject is, experimentally, still in its infancy, although the general principles had been discussed at some length by Delbrück and Schroedinger[6] by 1944. Since the principles are fairly straightforward, and the experimental work by contrast very complicated and as yet not too definitive, we outline first the principles, and relate them to a model, or working hypothesis.

Isomers

Stereoisomerism—the existence of two or more chemicals with the same composition and differing only in the arrangement of the atoms—has been known in organic chemistry for a hundred years. Such isomers are truly different compounds, having differing physical and chemical properties. The propyl alcohols will illustrate this basic point. Thus normal propyl alcohol has the following atomic arrangement:

$$\begin{array}{c} \text{H} \quad \text{H} \quad \text{H} \\ | \quad\; | \quad\; | \\ \text{H}-\text{C}-\text{C}-\text{C}-\text{OH} \\ | \quad\; | \quad\; | \\ \text{H} \quad \text{H} \quad \text{H} \end{array}$$

However, in isopropyl alcohol the OH group is attached to the central carbon atom instead:

$$\begin{array}{c} \text{H} \quad \text{OH} \quad \text{H} \\ | \quad\;\; | \quad\;\; | \\ \text{H}-\text{C}-\text{C}-\text{C}-\text{H} \\ | \quad\;\; | \quad\;\; | \\ \text{H} \quad \text{H} \quad \text{H} \end{array}$$

"Normal" melts at $-127°$ and boils at $98°C$, while "iso" melts at $-89°$ and boils at $82°C$. Normal chlorinates slowly in PCl_3, iso chlorinates rapidly.

Not all isomers are so obvious. Consider adrenaline, which has the structural formula

$$\text{HO} \diagdown \diagup \text{C HOH CH}_2 \text{ NH CH}_3$$

Two forms exist, which differ only in the arrangement of the groups of atoms attached to the tetrahedral carbon atom starred. The two forms differ in optical rotation. One is physiologically active; the other is not.

As we proceed through the higher alcohols—for example, those with four carbon atoms or more and two OH groups—the stereoisomeric possibilities mount. In the sugars and celluloses in which rings of carbon atoms are linked to one another to form long chains, each carbon having an OH group, physical interference with free rotation about an interatomic bond adds further to the number of possibilities. In molecules of the size of nucleic acid molecules, the number of structurally different possibilities is enormous.

Thus (the example is Schroedinger's) the two characters of the Morse code, dot and dash, can be arranged in groups of four-character letters in 30 different ways. If, however, we have a system of even five characters, and if five copies of each of the five characters are arranged into linear codescripts of 25 characters, the total number of possible 25-character codescripts is an astronomical 63×10^{12}—that is, 63 million millions! Note that even though the total number of characters chosen to define uniquely the "isomer" is only 25, the number of possibilities is hard to envisage; and indeed this number does not count any arrangements with either side-chains or rings, and is limited even further in that it excludes anything but five copies of each character to make up the 25! Of course, not just *any* arrangement of atoms gives a stable molecule; but on the other hand the number of chemical groups of which a macromolecule is composed ($-CH_2$, $-NH$, $-CO$, $-C-S-$, etc.) is certainly far more than five! .... One concludes that the number of stable isomers of a macromolecule must be huge, but at this stage of knowledge one really has no idea how many there are. Each must have a unique set of physical and chemical properties. Just as in the case of the simple alcohols, each must be a stable molecular entity.

Excited States

No molecule, even if anchored at some point, must be completely quiet if $T > 0°K$. Indeed, in an environment at 98°F (37°C) such a molecule, even if initially at rest, or quiet—i.e., in its vibrational and rotational "ground state" as it is called—will soon be buffeted into motion by neighboring molecules of gas, liquid, or solid, until its energy level or temperature is, on the average, that of the environment. Heat energy enters the molecule as the energy of rotation or vibration if the molecule is anchored, and enters also as the kinetic energy of translation (linear motion) if the molecule is free. The vibrations and rotations may be thought of as standing or traveling matter waves moving across the molecule. Parts of the molecule can be fixed and immobile; other parts can be free. The distribution of energy within the molecule will be continuously changing.

Macromolecules accept and give up energy to the surroundings in discrete bursts or bunches or quanta, if the quantum theory applies here as it is known to apply to 2- and 3-atom molecules. However, the energy differences between mechanically excited states must be very small—so small that almost a continuous exchange of energy must be possible.

The important point is that all of the configurations which result from heat exchange are configurations proper to one isomer; in principle the isomer may assume many shapes. Consider the random coil configuration of protein as an example. The one chemical entity may assume many shapes simply as a result of thermal exchange.

Electronically excited states also exist but these are different. It was seen in Chapter 4 that electrons which make the bonds of molecules can absorb and re-emit electromagnetic radiation, and that some excited states can be reached by the absorption of such small amounts of energy that even local heat energy sometimes will do the trick. It is a general rule-of-thumb that whenever a bonding electron accepts energy of any kind and becomes itself "excited," the bond is weakened. Once weakened, it is more susceptible to thermal buffeting and to chemical attack. Its "defense" is to rid itself of the extra energy and get back into the bond; this it does by reradiation, or by transfer of energy into the mechanical motion of the molecule.

The salient point is the following: *If the extra energy in the molecule is large enough, quite by chance it may collect at a critical bond and loosen it sufficiently so that a rearrangement of groups within the molecule can occur, and thus produce a different isomer. When this occurs in the DNA molecule of the gene, a mutation is the result.*

There are many other biological processes which seem to involve excited electronic states of molecules: oxidations seem to be in a class by themselves because of the number of reactions of molecule + O_2 + light which have been demonstrated. In some reactions light is absorbed, and then immediately (within 10^{-12} sec) re-emitted, at least in part (fluorescence); in others the absorbed energy is retained for some appreciable time, perhaps a few seconds (phosphorescence). However, the extra energy to excite electrons in a molecule may also be derived from chemical reactions in the metabolism, for there is plenty of it there! This obviously occurs in some bacteria (pseudomonas, vibrio, etc.), some crustaceans, the elaterid beetle, and the firefly, for these animals are chemiluminescent.

That human beings are not luminescent may be a subtle reminder of two important facts: (a) in man the energy-producing metabolic reactions are more carefully delineated by enzymes, constrained to occur in many small steps, each one linked intimately with an energy-consuming metabolic process; and (b) there are electron and proton transfer reactions along large molecules, transfer mechanisms which can conduct the "energy" to where it can be used. In other words, in humans, because of the extra complexity of the system, the extra energy of excitation of molecules need not be radiated and lost; there is a mechanism provided by which it can be used.

This can be illustrated further. Although most proteins *in vitro* have no phosphorescence at room temperature where molecular mechanical motion is relatively large, at low temperature ($77°K$) all the following proteins, plus at least 18 amino acids, show phosphorescence: fibrinogen, γ_2 globulin, keratin, gelatin, zein, and bovine serum albumin, as well as egg albumin and silk fibroin. Aromatic rings with π (Pi) bonds in the molecules are a necessary condition for the phosphorescence.

In some simple organic molecules (certain ketones, for example) the extra energy has been found to excite one of the unshared pair or nonbonding (n) electrons on the oxygen atom. Its excited position is one of the so-called π positions or orbitals of the molecule. The transition is called an "$n - \pi$" transition (Figure 6-10). The energy absorbed during an $n - \pi$ transition is about 80 kcal/mole, and can be produced by ultraviolet light of wave length about 3000 Å.

The unshared pair of electrons form no bond, but they are paired in the sense that they have opposite "spins." The molecule which contains only paired electrons is said to be in a "singlet" state ($S = 2n + 1$, where n is

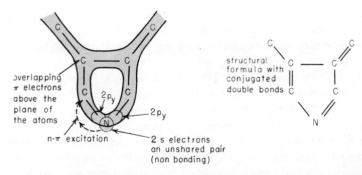

Figure 6-10. The *n-π* Electronic Transition (schematic).

the number of unshared electrons). When excited, however, the promoted electron, now in a formerly empty π orbital, is unpaired; $S = 3$, and the molecule is said to be in a "triplet" state. Triplet states are important because they sometimes retain the extra energy, without radiating it, for relatively long periods of time. Thus molecules in the triplet state sometimes have time to collide with others which are similarly excited, and the total energy of the collision may be sufficient to cause the isomeric or mutation reaction.

Based on the work of M. Kasha, Reid[10] has listed a few types of molecules (containing N, O, P, S) whose $n - \pi$ transition and the subsequent triplet states probably are energy carriers in biological processes:

Amides	Pyridines		Carbonates
Aldehydes and	Diazines and	possibly	Nitrates
ketones	triazines		Nitro-compounds
Amides	Azo- and		
Quinones	diazo-compounds		
Thioketones	Nitroso-compounds		
	Pyrimidines		

The mechanism of some isomeric reactions in which a triplet excited state is an intermediate is now fairly well understood. For large macromolecules, however, pertinent information remains for the future. Nevertheless the direction and importance of such work is now clear.

REPLICATION AND CODE-SCRIPTS

There are now four types of experiment which support the contention that genetic information is carried by the nucleic acids, DNA and RNA. There is still little direct evidence from any species higher than virus or bacterium.

The celebrated French work on the transplanting of DNA in ducks seems to open the doorway to studies on higher animals. The long extrapolation to humans may turn out to be correct, although it is certainly not yet justified, for this will take generations to prove.

Bacterial transformation: If pure DNA, extracted from a suspension of bacteria of one type (A) is added to a suspension of another type (B), the progeny of the thus-infected B type have characteristics of A.

Virus reproduction: Bacteriophage T_2, a virus, which can reproduce only after it has entered into a living bacterial cell, can be split—the protein part from the nucleic acid part (DNA). The DNA, shorn of its protein, can enter the bacterial cell and rapidly reproduce the intact T_2 phage particles again.

Virus "synthesis": Tobacco mosaic virus can be split chemically into protein + RNA. One can then reconstitute the virus, using protein of strain A and RNA of strain B. The progeny are of strain B only, having resnythesized their original protein.

Genetic recombination of bacteria: In fertile strains of bacteria, in which DNA can be passed from the donor to recipient cells, the extent of the appearance of the characteristics of the donor in the progeny is proportional to the amount of DNA transferred.

Some Properties of DNA and RNA

These "nucleic" acids (found in the cell nucleus and in the cytoplasm) are substituted sugar molecules which are polymerized through phosphate linkages. In DNA the sugar is desoxyribose; in RNA it is ribose. Both have 5-carbon rings. The substituent groups on the sugar molecules are organic nitrogen bases. These are ringed compounds with two nitrogen atoms in the ring, and are four in number: adenine, guanine, cytosine, and thymine (in DNA) or uracil (in RNA). Linkages, etc., are shown in Table 6-3.

From X-ray diffraction studies it is known that DNA is a helical molecule with 10 sugar residues per turn of the helix. In the "dry" (70 per cent RH) crystalline state two helices are found interlocked (Figure 6-11), each with its phosphate-sugar chain facing to the outside, and the purine and pyrimidine bases, hydrogen-bonded together, facing to the inside.†

At cell division, the two interlocking helices separate, and each reproduces, probably by a process analogous to crystal growth, as though each helix, separated, acts as a template or a die for the "casting" operation which forms the new molecule. That this occurs at mitosis, suggests that the helices are pulled apart by a force which exists only at mitosis. For instance if two ends, one from each helix, are attached to the membrane which encloses the nucleus, in the expansion before division (25 per cent by one measurement) the DNA helices could be pulled apart; then if each template reproduces its opposite by "condensation," two DNA molecules

---

† A single-stranded DNA is known, in phage ϕX 174.

TABLE 6-3:   Components of the Nucleic Acids (Linkage at *).

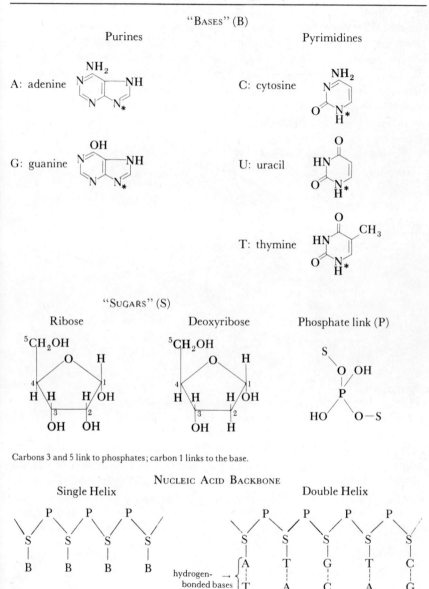

"BASES" (B)

Purines

A: adenine

G: guanine

Pyrimidines

C: cytosine

U: uracil

T: thymine

"SUGARS" (S)

Ribose

Deoxyribose

Phosphate link (P)

Carbons 3 and 5 link to phosphates; carbon 1 links to the base.

NUCLEIC ACID BACKBONE

Single Helix

Double Helix

hydrogen- →
bonded bases

will exist, one for each daughter cell after mitosis. There is now some evidence that the condensation reaction is enzyme-controlled, and, current with the times, someone has humorously suggested that an enzyme called "untwisterase" controls the uncoupling of the two DNA strands. The reaction is quite sensitive to salts and to pH, which usually indicates that strong electrical forces along the structure are important. There is also some evidence that RNA is formed by condensation around the two-stranded DNA, as a third party. DNA itself is not only synthesized by an enzyme, but is also degraded by one called DNAse.

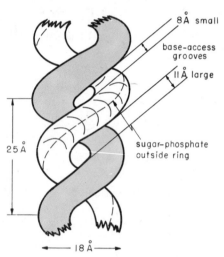

Figure 6-11. Schematic Drawing of Twin-Coiled DNA Molecule. (Refer to Table 6-3 for detailed structure.)

Much has been learned within the past eight years about these important molecules. However, more than what has been said is beyond our scope here. It is currently a very active and popular phase of the study of big molecules. They *are* big, too: molecular weight 5 to 125 million! If uncoiled, the DNA of a human cell would stretch out to a full length of about 1 mm.

Coding Theory

The manner in which DNA and RNA molecules can carry genetic information and control the sizes, shapes, and functioning of all the parts of the complete living system is still a mystery, although some progress has been made in understanding how this is done.

The coding problem is simply enough stated as follows: Since there are only four different pyridine and pyrimidine bases in the nucleic acid molecule, and yet there are 20 or more amino acids which must be arranged in the proper order if the correct protein is to result, in what way can the four be arranged so that they carry, and can transfer, information on how the 20 amino acids should be organized to form such a great variety of proteins? The answer to the question is not so simple. There are several theories, but just a few definitive facts, and information is accumulating. The evidence is now that it is RNA which actually acts as the template or die for protein synthesis. The RNA in turn obtains its exact configuration, before its job, by contact with the code-bearing DNA molecule. Its structure has to be well fixed, for it must guide without error the condensation or linking of (of the order of) 100 amino-acid residues in even a smallish protein molecule of molecular weight ~ 1000. For if one of the components falls into the wrong slot, the whole molecule may be biochemically useless to the living system—a "bad molecule." There are many pitfalls, for the number of possible arrangements in a chain of even 100 units made up of 20 different kinds is enormous.

During protein synthesis the RNA is located in the cytoplasm primarily in the microsomes (ribosomes) (see Figure 6-12), and it is here that the bulk of the protein synthesis take place. Energy for the synthesis is provided by the adsorption on RNA of the amino acids, the "mobile power supply," ATP, and an enzyme, there being one specific enzyme (site) for each amino acid.

The replication process is supposed to go as follows: Sometime in the late stages of the period between cell divisions, during the early part of the prophase when the mitotic apparatus is collecting in preparation for division of the cell, the DNA molecules—which have been depolymerized and dispersed throughout the cell and are presumably attending to the business of synthesis of big molecules—begin to polymerize and collect into thread-like bodies called chromosomes. (There is some evidence that this process itself is controlled by a large protein.) During this collection process, the DNA's intercoiled helical strands are pulled apart or unwound, and each acts as the template for the condensation of another helical partner, formed from nucleic acid residues in the fluid of the cytoplasm. The process is completed as the resulting pairs of chromosomes are lined up (by contractile protein?) midway between the asters of the mitotic apparatus, and perpendicular to the spindles which join the asters, just before the actual division takes place.

Replication of DNA and of the whole chromosome requires the action of subtle physical forces: the DNA helices must be pulled apart for individual replication, before they are polymerized to form the chromosomes, which in turn are lined up in a predetermined fashion in the mitotic apparatus; and this is then forced to split in two. The nature of the forces which do these jobs, and of the guiding principle which controls the order and speed with which they are done, are essentially unknown. However, contractile forces of molecular origin are now well known in myosin, and may be important here; chemical condensations and osmotic pressures, changed as the nuclear membrane disappears and the fluid of the cytoplasm enters, are other candidates. The forces seem to be too long-range to be electrical in nature.

The essential feature of the replication of the "code" or specification for the animal seems to be the reproduction of the DNA itself. It is now surmised that this is a cooperative action of four molecular parts: (a) one of the uncoiled DNA helices, (b) an enzyme, on which has been absorbed (c) the energy carrier, ATP, and (d) the basic polyacid which is to be "stamped" onto (or better: is to condense with) the DNA at the proper spot on the chain. This "enzyme" may be nothing more than one of the proteins synthesized already through RNA; it may have a series of "active sites" when uncoiled, one for each of the polyacids which is to be stamped onto the DNA helix.

Thus, at least in principle, the replication process and protein synthesis have many features in common:

Replication: DNA + enzyme + ATP + basic polyacids

Protein Synthesis: RNA + enzyme + ATP + aminoacids

The key or code for both is carried by DNA, and thence RNA; and sometimes by RNA alone.

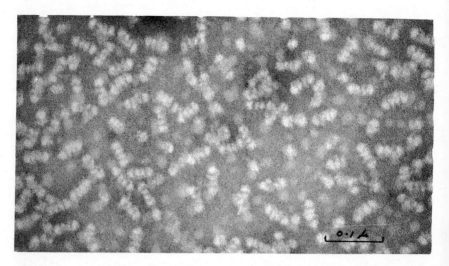

Figure 6-12.   (a) Electron Micrograph of Ribosomes (containing RNA plus small protein molecules called histones) of *Escherichia coli*: extracted from the pulverized bacteria by ultracentrifugation from a solution 0.01 m in magnesium ions; fixed in formalin; and mounted on carbon-filmed grid negatively stained with phosphotungstic acid to give a dark background. Most particles consist of four segments about 125Å wide. Magnification 160,000×, scale: 0.1 micron.

A. In 0.002 M - Mg^{++}: m$_A$ 30 50 70 100

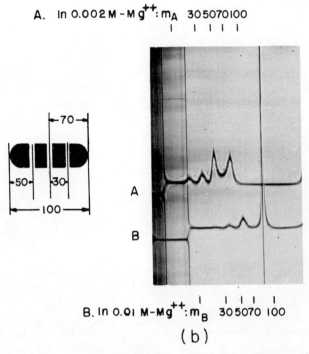

B. In 0.01 M - Mg^{++}: m$_B$ 30 50 70 100

(b)

Figure 6-12. (b) Two Sedimentation Patterns (A and B) of the Ribosomes shown in (a). Note how the binding of these little particles is so dependent upon the medium. The numbers are the sedimentation rates (in svedberg units) of the different particles in the ultracentrifuge: the larger particles fall faster. (Photographs (a) and (b), courtesy of S. T. Bayley, National Research Council's Biophysics Section, Ottawa.)

"Cogs" and "Cams"

It is generally assumed that the code is contained in the arrangement of the four basic (2 pyridine and 2 pyrimidine) groups in the nucleic acid chain. There are at least 20 amino acids which must be distinguished. The smallest number of 4 basic groups which could be arranged in enough different ways to distinguish 20 amino acids is 3; and 3 in principle could distinguish as many as 64 amino acids (4^3).

Two suggestions have been made in which it is shown that, of the 64 possible ways or arrangements, only about 20 are unique in a chain. One suggestion was made by Gamov, Rich, and Ycas in 1953, who postulated that the cyclic, helical structure of DNA would give rise to arrangements in which the 4 pyridine and pyrimidine bases jut out from the helix to form the 4 corners of a diamond on the external surface of the helix. Only 20 unique arrangements of the 4 bases could exist. Let us call this the *cam* theory partly because one thinks of a cylindrical cam with coding on its walls (Figure 6-13), and partly because it is a degeneration of *Gamov*!

The other suggestion, made by Crick, Orgel, and Griffiths in 1957, was that in a linear arrangement of only 4 characters, only about 20 unique groups of 3 could be written, provided that no character be counted as belonging to more than one group of three—that is, if there is no overlap. We think here of a helical molecule with 20 arrangements of 3 bases which define the code information along the chain. Partly because the process resembles the meshing of carefully fitted gears, and partly because of the initials of the inventors of the theory, let us call it the *cog* theory. Figure 6-13 is a schematic representation of the cam and the cog.

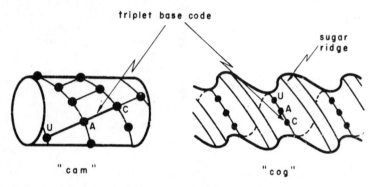

Figure 6-13. Cogs and Cams for Coding on DNA. Each spot represents a pyridine or pyrimidine base.

Both theories have serious drawbacks, not yet resolved. In the Crick model, the amino acids in solution must "know" that they are forbidden to indulge in overlap; while in the Gamov model a severe geometric restriction exists, viz., the DNA molecule (and hence the RNA whose shape is determined by DNA) must always hold a very specific and rigid helical structure if the diamond arrays are to persist on the surface.

However, successes in a flurry of investigation, genetic and biochemical, have engendered the belief that the basic facts of the amino-acid code carried by DNA may be completely known by 1963! There have been three recent remarkable disclosures. First, Nirenburg startled the International Biochemical Congress in Moscow in the Summer of 1961 by announcing that polyphenylalanine (a polypeptide) could be produced by adding polyuridylic acid (i.e., an RNA, the pyrimidine bases of which are all uracil) to a cell-free solution of phenylalanine. This showed that a sequence of uracils (probably three of them) codes phenylalanine. Secondly, from elegant genetic studies, Crick *et al.* argued that:

(a) A group of three bases (or, less likely, a multiple of three bases) along the DNA helix codes one amino acid.

(b) The sequence of bases is read from a fixed starting point along the helix. This determines what groups of three in sequence code an amino acid.

(c) The triplets do not overlap each other.

(d) Probably more than one triplet of bases will be found to code a single amino acid (that is, the code is "degenerate").

Lastly, Ochoa *et al.*, in March 1962, disclosed a three-base coding for each of the 20 amino acids, a code based on the increased rate of amino-acid uptake by *E. coli* protein to which had been added the polymerized bases of known composition. Other laboratories have been publishing partial codes also. Although they may be revised even before this book is printed, Table 6-4 lists tentative codings published by four different laboratories. Underlined are the codes in which the authors have expressed greatest confidence.

TABLE 6-4. Triplet or Three-Base Codes for Each of the 20 Amino Acids of Proteins

Amino Acid	Symbol	Tentative Codes (1962)			
		Ochoa et al.[20]	Zubay et al.[22]	Gamov et al.[11]	Woese[23]
alanine	ala	UCG*	UCG	AAC	UAG
arginine	arg	UCG	UGC	AGG	AGG
asparagine	asp N	UAA ⎫	UCA	AGU	GAU
aspartic acid	asp	UAG ⎭			
cysteine	cys	UUG	?CG		
glutamic acid	glu N	UAG ⎫	UUA	AUU	UAU
glutamine	glu N	UCG ⎭			
glycine	gly	UGG	UUG	CUU	GAG
histidine	his	UAC	UGU		
isoleucine	ileu	UUA	UAC		CAU
leucine	leu	UUC	UCU	AGC	UCG
lysine	lys	UAA	UGA	CCC	CCG
methionine	met	UAG	UAU		CUU
proline	pro	UCC	UCC	CCU	CCC
serine	ser	UUC	UGG	CGU	AAG
threonine	thr	UAC	UAG	ACU	CAC
tryptophane	try	UGG	UAA		
tyrosine	tyr	UUA	?AU		UUU
valine	val	UUG	UUG	AAU	CAG
phenylalanine	pha	UUU	UUU	GUU	UUG

U: uracil   C: cytosine   A: adenine   G: guanine

*Underlined codes are those thought by the respective authors to be very reliable. Degeneracy?

There are extensions and modifications of the *cog* and *cam* theories, and even other theories of the physical arrangements on DNA and RNA. The experimental problem is not made simpler by the fact that there are $20 \times 19 \times 18 \cdots = 2.3 \times 10^{17}$ different ways in which 20 different amino acids can be hooked together! Some "selection rules" must therefore follow from a code, for; as Gamov says "if one could spend only one second to check each assignment, one would have to work continuously for about five billion years, which is [estimated to be] the present age of our Universe!"

Other experimental work has brightened the picture still further. For instance, only with a specific enzyme does an amino acid form a complex with ATP; polymerization and depolymerization occur in DNA and RNA; complex formation occurs between the low-molecular-weight, soluble (or "transfer") RNA and the DNA molecule; the helical shape of DNA is well established in moist air; and chemical analyses have been made of certain molecules. All these are experimental facts. There are many, many variables, better knowledge of which will clarify the theory.

MUTATIONS AND MOLECULAR DISEASES

The idea of "sick people from bad molecules" is not really new, although it certainly has been experimentally demonstrated in very convincing fashion and exploited heavily since 1948. While Washington was busy on the Delaware, Scheele in Germany showed that there is a good and bad form of adrenalin. By 1913, F. G. Hopkins was able to state with some biochemical authority: "Metabolic processes on which life depends consist *in toto* of a vast number of well-organized and interlocking enzymic reactions, interference with any one of which can product deleterious effects ...." The quotation from Pauling, with which this Chapter began, concerning the need for better understanding of macromolecules and catalysts, is the modern approach to this question.

We have seen that, because of structural and/or compositional changes in macromolecules, the following results may accrue:

(1) Change in rate of chemical processes
(2) Change in rate of physical processes
(3) Introduction of new side reactions

A simple example of (3), introduced before recorded history and persisting faithfully to our day, is offered in the different blood types in man: O, A, B, AB. These differ from each other only in that the colloidal-stabilizing mechanism of the macromolecules of the blood plasma is different: for if two of the types are mixed, they agglutinate or gel; the mixture becomes thick and refuses to flow. The physical nature of this subtle difference which makes them incompatible still escapes us. The production, by each individual, of antibodies (big molecules?) which are specific to that individual, and incompatible with those built by any other individual for the same purpose, is a well known phenomenon. Thus each individual has a specific biochemistry and a biophysics of his own, which becomes manifested in many ways. It is not surprising, then, that even small changes in structure or composition of certain large molecules can sometimes have disastrous results.

A few examples will illustrate the point. No attempt is made to be exhaustive. Lathe's thesis[1] reviews several other molecular diseases.

Molecular Diseases

There is both a broad, generic connotation and a rather restricted, specialized one associated with the term "molecular diseases." In the sense that all diseases involve molecules which are incompatible with the chemistry or the physics of the system, all diseases are "molecular." However, in the more restricted sense, the term has evolved to mean diseases caused by apparently small modifications of the chemical composition or the physical structure of a particular molecule. The hemoglobin diseases, recognized only within the last decade, are now the classic example.

Hemoglobins: There are at least ten known modifications of the hemoglobin molecule, each of which is associated with a pathologic condition. The normal molecule is characterized by certain values for sedimentation and diffusion constant (thence molecular wt.), electrophoretic mobility, electric charge as a function of pH (determined by titration), solubility, ultraviolet absorption spectrum, etc. The most celebrated variant, *S*, which is found in erythrocytes from people with sickle-cell anemia, differs from the normal, *A*, principally in the manner in which it moves under the influence of an electric field: it moves faster, and at pH $= 7$, toward the cathode, whereas *A* is negatively charged at pH $= 7$ and moves toward the anode.

Some of the pertinent characteristics of ten different forms of the hemoglobin molecule have been collected in Table 6-5. Although the differences were first observed clinically, and then correlated with differences in physical properties, recent work has established that the differences arise because of different composition or arrangement in the amino-acid sequences of the protein. There are about 600 amino acids in the molecule. X-ray diffraction studies have shown that type *A* (normal adult human hemoglobin) molecules consist of four intertwined polypeptide chains. Two of these have a valine, then a leucine residue just prior to attachment to the nitrogen of the porphyrin (heme) group; two others have a valine, histidine, leucine sequence before attachment to the (iron-containing) porphyrin group. It is now known that modifications occur right at that point: a different sequence, or even different amino acids in the sequence, can occur.

TABLE 6-5. Some Known Molecular Modifications of Hemoglobin

Disease	Symptoms	Hemoglobin Modification	Electrophoretic Mobility, l, pH = 8.6	Electric Charge pH = 8.6	Peptide Chains**	Other Characteristics
None*	none	A (normal adult human)	l	−13	two α's; two β's	Two —SH groups
Sickle-cell anemia	anemia, sickling cells	S (sickle-cell anemia)	$l − a$	−10	same α's; glutamine instead of leucine in β's	three —SH groups, solubility (sol.) different from A
Mild hemolytic anemia	mild anemia	C	$l − 2a$	−8	same α's; lysine instead of glut. acid in β's	
Unnamed (rare)	mild form of S	D	$l − a$	(−10)	different amino-acids in α's and/or β's	l as of S; sol. as of A
Unnamed (very rare)	mild anemia	E	$l − 2a$	(−8)	different amino acids in β's only	very large change in l with change in pH; uw spectrum similar to A; l similar to C; resistant to alkali; unique uw absorption spectrum.
None (foetal)	none	F	$l + a$			
Hopkins	jaundice	G and Hopkins − 2			different amino acids in α's only (?)	
None	none	H			four normal β's	
None	none	I			different amino acids in α's only	

*However, slow manufacture of A, gene controlled, leads to a serious anemia called thalassemia

** α's have terminal sequence of valine-leucine amino acids; β's give terminal sequence valine-histidine-leucine. There are...

There may be other modifications out farther in the protein, but this is not yet known. Likewise there may be many more modifications of hemoglobin than those listed. The work is really quite new. Unfortunately, practically nothing is known of the shapes of these molecules—and won't be until more is known of their structure. Sufficient familiarity with the physiological reactions has been estimated to be about ten years away.

The sickling of erythrocytes occurs when the hemoglobin-S is in an atmosphere low in oxygen, and is a remarkable example of what "bad" molecules can do. It is now fairly well established that these bad molecules are so shaped that they can fit into each other and be piled up like a stack of saucers. In so piling, their strength is sufficient to push out the sides of the erythrocyte and cause it to buckle in the middle, i.e., to become sickle-shaped. On oxygenation, the stack collapses, presumably because the molecular shapes are no longer so nicely complementary. Apparently the process resembles the growth of a crystal. The reader is asked to meditate on the known structure of myoglobin (Figure 6-3), and to study the pictures of Perutz et al.[24] on hemoglobin, before pressing further into this subject via Reference 25.

Others. There are well over 20 diseases for which a "bad" molecule has been postulated as the cause. One other which is receiving considerable attention now is phenylketonuria. This is associated with mental deficiencies, and has been traced to the fact that one of the enzymes which catalyze the oxidation of phenylalanine through various steps toward pyruvic acid is not doing its job fast enough. Whether the offending enzyme molecule is not being synthesized, or has some physical deformity which renders it only partially active; or whether it or the substrate is not being transported fast enough to the place of catalysis, is not yet known. However, the result is accumulation of phenylalanine in the blood stream, and interference with synthesis of nerve tissue.

PROBLEMS

6-1: Erythrocyte DNA has a molecular weight of above five million. Calculate the diameter of the smallest sphere into which one molecule could be compressed. (Assume an average atomic weight of 12: it has C's, N's, O's, H's, and a few P's and S's. Assume also that each atom occupies a cube 1.2 Å on each side.)

   If it were stretched out, the atoms end to end, what would be the total length of the chain?

6-2: Have *you* figured out how the two helical strands of DNA can unwind: for replication, or for coding transfer-RNA?

6-3: Describe the four possibilities open to a big molecule in an electronically excited state.

REFERENCES

1. Lathe, G. H., "Defective Molecules as a Cause of Diseases," Thesis, Leeds Univ. Press, Leeds, England, 1960.
2. Dixon, M. and Webb, E. C., "Enzymes," Academic Press, New York, N. Y., 1958.
3. Pauling, L., in "Enzymes: Units of Biological Structure and Function," edited by Gaebler, O. H., Academic Press, 1956.
4. Putman, F. W., Ed., "The Plasma Proteins, I: Isolation, Characterization and Function," Academic Press, 1960.
5. Oncley, J. L., *et al.*, Eds., "Biophysical Science—A Study Program," John Wiley & Sons, Inc., New York, N. Y., 1959; papers by Kendrew, Doty, Rich, and many others.
6. Schroedinger, E., "What is Life?", Doubleday Anchor printing, 1956, of Cambridge Univ. Press book, 1944.
7. Butler, J. A. V., "Inside the Living Cell," Basic Books, Inc., New York, N. Y., 1959; Butler, J. A. V., *et al.*, *Proc. Royal Soc.*, A, **250**, 1 (1960).
8. Solomon, A. K., *Scientific American*, **203**, 146 (1960), and references.
9. Hoagland, M. B., *Scientific American*, **201**, 55 (1959).
10. Reid, C., "Excited States in Chemistry and Biology," Butterworths Sci. Publ., 1957.
11. Gamov, G., Rich, A., and Ycas, M., *Adv. Biol. Med. Phys.*, **4**, 23 (1956).
12. Davson, H. and Danielli, J. F., "The Permeability of Natural Membranes," 2nd ed., Cambridge Univ. Press, 1952.
13. Shooter, K. V., "The Physical Chemistry of Desoxyribosenucleic Acid," *Prog. in Biophysics and Biophysical Chem.*, **8**, 309 (1957).
14. *Scientific Amer.*, Issue on "Giant Molecules," **197**, No. 3, 1957; articles by Doty, Crick, Schmitt, Debye, and others.
15. St. Whitelock, O., Ed., "Cellular Biology, Nucleic Acids and Viruses," N. Y. Acad. Sci., 1957.
16. Tanford, C., "Physical Chemistry of Macromolecules," John Wiley & Sons, Inc., New York, N. Y., 1961.
17. "The Merck Index," 7th ed., Merck & Co., Inc., Rahway, N. J., 1960.
18. Bonnar, R. U., Dimbat, M., and Stross, F. H., "Number Average Molecular Weights," Interscience Publishers Inc., New York, N. Y., 1958.
19. Crick, F. H. C., Barnett, L., Brenner, S., and Watts-Tobin, R. J., *Nature*, **192**, 1227 (1961).
20. Speyer, J. F., Lengyel, P., Basilio, C., and Ochoa, S., *Proc. Nat. Acad. Sci.*, **48**, 441 (1962).
21. Nirenberg, M. W., and Matthei, J. B., *ibid.*, **47**, 1588 (1961).
22. Zubay, G., and Quastler, H., *ibid.*, **48**, 461 (1962).
23. Woese, C. G., *Biophys. and Biochem. Res. Com.*, **5**, 88 (1961).
24. Perutz, M. F., Rossman, M. G., Cullis, A. F., Muirhead, H., Will, G., and North, A. C. T., *Nature*, **185**, 416 (1960).
25. Itano, H. A., Singer, S. J. and Robinson, E., in "Biochemistry of Human Genetics," G. E. W. Wolstenholme and C. M. O'Connor, Eds., Churchill Ltd., London, 1959; p. 96 ff.

CHAPTER 7

A Conceptual Introduction
to Bioenergetics

Thermodynamics is a queer science. It is a system of logic based on three postulates which have never been proved or disproved. By clever juggling with symbols and ideas, it establishes relations between different forms of energy. . . . These are most interesting relations which allow us to peep behind the scenes of Nature's workshop . . . . Thermodynamics may yet tell us how Nature molds such complex phenomena as muscular contraction out of simpler reactions. (A. Szent-Györgyi.[7])

INTRODUCTION

Scope

The manipulation of the energy available from many natural sources has been a problem of deep concern to man since the realization of the facts of motion. Then came the mastery of fire; the kinematic machine; the use of chemicals for ballistic purposes; and the water wheel for milling, and later for producing the most versatile energy form of them all: electricity. Our age is witnessing the development of the peaceful uses of atomic energy, the energy of nuclear reactions; and a slower but perhaps more far-reaching development of methods of trapping and storing the sun's radiation as heat, and chemical and electrical energy.

Thermodynamics is the study of general principles which relate to transfer of energy from one form to another (Figure 7-1). By contrast with some of the more clearly understood systems, bioenergetics is still in its infancy, although biochemists have done much toward describing the energetics of

161

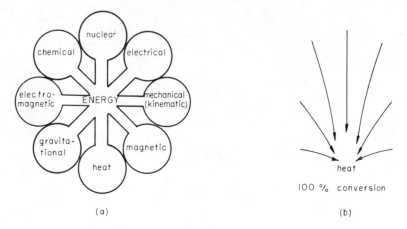

100 % conversion

(a)   (b)

Figure 7-1. Energy Interconversion, (a); (b) Degradation of Different Forms of Energy into Heat Energy (the "Heat Death").

some pertinent chemical transformations, and physiologists have done something toward relating chemical energy and work. The many relationships which must exist in living systems among mechanical, electrochemical, chemical, and heat energies are as yet poorly known. This chapter attempts to summarize the conclusions which arise from a generalized approach to energy transfer, and to indicate how far they can be carried into a description of the living system.

In this account, use will be made of three different types of symbols, small-case letters, capital letters, and script capital letters, which usually refer to 1 gram, to 1 mole, and to the whole system, respectively. The capitals and script capitals have the further property of being "variables of state"—being variables the value of which help to define the state or condition of the system or subject, irrespective of past history. This will become more clearly understood as the subject is developed.

Some Useful Definitions

Energy (from the Greek word meaning "active in work")—usually defined as the potency for doing work. Remember the difficulties with definition raised in Chapter 2?

Kinetic Energy (KE)—energy of motion; energy contained within a boundary by virute of the motion of the parts contained therein.

Potential Energy (PE)—literally "energy of position"; more generally energy stored in any metastable but convertible form.

Heat Energy (HE or q)—in terms of the kinetic theory, identically equal to the kinetic energy of motion (rotations, vibrations, translations) of the component molecules.

Specific Heat (c)—the heat energy required to raise 1 g of a substance one degree in temperature. A particularly important specific heat is that of water, by which the unit of heat energy is defined: One *calorie* is the amount of heat energy required to raise 1 g of pure water 1°C, from 3.5 to 4.5°C (where it is the most dense) at 1 atm pressure.

Heat Capacity (C)—the heat energy required to raise 1 molecular wt of substance 1 deg in temperature. The units of specific heat, c, are cal/deg Cent. g; and of heat capacity, C, are cal/deg Cent. mole.

Other forms of energy to be discussed are mechanical, electrical, gravitational, chemical, nuclear, etc. Energetics or thermodynamics is the study of interconversion of these. In biological systems the subject is usefully called bioenergetics. That part of the subject dealing with electromagnetic and matter waves was considered in Chapters 3 and 4, and is expanded in Chapter 9.

LAWS OF THERMODYNAMICS

Statements of the Three Laws

There are three general principles which summarize human experience with energy interconversion. They are negative laws in the sense that they cannot be proved always to hold, but nevertheless never have been known to be violated.

The First Law: The first law states simply that energy can be transformed from one form to another but cannot be created or destroyed. After the equivalence of matter and energy were recognized (and proved in nuclear reactions), the law was generalized still further to read: "mass-energy" instead of "energy."

The Law stands as written, needing no extension, for all cases in which any form of energy is converted into heat: 100 per cent conversion can always be realized. In Figure 7-1 (b) each of the arrows originates in a form of energy other than heat.

The Second Law: For any machine which converts heat into mechanical work, chemical into electrical energy, or the like, it is a universal experience that only a fraction can be converted; the rest remains unavailable and unconverted. There is thus an amount of *unavailable energy* as well as *available energy* from the conversion. The unavailable, it would be logical to assume, is the heat energy which must remain in the molecules of which the final state (i.e., the product) is composed.

The Third Law: At 0°K (-273.16°C), the absolute zero of temperature, at which all molecular motion has ceased, matter should be in a state of perfect order, the molecules being perfectly aligned or oriented, and perfectly quiet. This law is concerned with the absolute heat energy contained in molecules at any temperature. Although our present interest is in *changes* from one state to another, rather than absolute quantities in any state, the absolute quantities disclosed via the Third Law permit easy evaluation of the changes.

More Detailed Consideration of the First Law. Enthalpy or Heat Content

The *internal energy* of a body is defined as the sum total of all the kinetic and potential energy contained within the body. When expressed per gram molecular weight it is given the symbol U cal/mole, and is a "state variable," that is, one whose value depends only upon the temperature, pressure, and composition, irrespective of how it arrived at this condition. Heat energy, (that contained in the motion of the molecules), potential energy of the electron cloud of the atom, and the binding energy of the nucleus all contribute to the internal energy.

If a transformation takes place in one molecular weight of a substance, two things in general can occur: energy can be taken in by the substance, and work can be done. If an amount of energy, q, is taken in, and an amount of work, w, is done, the difference, $q - w$, must be the *increase* in energy of the substance during the process; this difference must be stored as internal energy, and hence the change in internal energy is:

$$\Delta U = q - w$$

where

$$\Delta U = U_2 - U_1 \text{ or } = U_{final} - U_{initial}$$

Now $\Delta U = q - w$ is the concise, algebraic statement of the First Law. The concepts are illustrated in Figure 7-2.

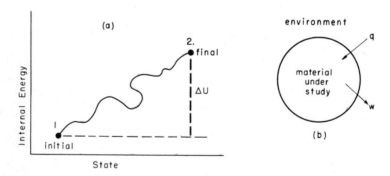

Figure 7-2. The First Law of Thermodynamics: (a) a state diagram showing internal energy change, ΔU, during a process; (b) the process: heat taken in, q, and work done, w.

One could generalize to complex, nonmolar quantities of varied composition; the law would still be conceptually the same:

$$\Delta \mathcal{U} = q - w$$

More will be said about this generalization later.

The first law can be extended into a more useful form for processes taking place at constant pressure. Since any substance, this book, for example, has an individual and independent existence in space, and since it occupies a certain volume and has an area upon which the air pressure (i.e., weight of the column of air above it) is 15 lb/sq in., the book does not have as much internal energy as it would have if it were in a vacuum, because it already has done a considerable amount of work against atmospheric pressure. That is, it has already expended enough energy (or "work of expansion"), W, to roll back the atmosphere and create a hole or vacuum in which it can exist. Hence the internal energy

$$U = KE + PE - W$$

The work of expansion, W, can be easily evaluated. Consider the cylinder with frictionless piston of area, A, enclosing a volume of gas, V. From the definition of work:

$$\text{Work} = \text{force} \times \text{distance}$$

$$= PA \times \Delta V / A$$

$$= P \Delta V = P(V_2 - V_1)$$

Since we are considering an initial state, V_1, of zero volume, in general $W = PV$. Substituting,

$$U = KE + PE - PV$$

$$= H - PV$$

where H is the internal energy contained per mole in a vacuum (when $P = 0$). The quantity, H, is called *heat content*, or preferably *enthalpy* because really potential energy as well as heat kinetic energy is included.

A little thought about the definition will lead one to the conclusion that H should be a very useful quantity for comparison purposes because its value is independent of any volume change which may accompany a transformation or process. Further, for the case of chemical reactions, $\Delta H = H_2 - H_1$ (note the parallel with ΔU) must be identical with q, the heat taken in during the process for the case in which the only work done is that of expansion; i.e., $q = \Delta H$. Many biological processes occur in solution, with no appreciable change in volume, and in these cases $\Delta U = \Delta H$.

Now $\Delta H = q$ may be positive or negative depending upon which is larger, the enthalpy of the final or of the initial state. The former characterizes an *endothermic* reaction; the later an *exothermic* reaction. As a general rule anabolic reactions are endothermic; catabolic reactions are exothermic. More specifically, the synthesis of proteins in the metabolism of the living system is endothermic; the combustion of glycogen and other food stores is exothermic.

For chemical reactions the value of q or ΔH, the "heat of reaction," can be measured calorimetrically, and quite accurate values obtained. For instance, for the simplest reaction

$$H_2 + 1/2\, O_2 = H_2O$$

the heat of reaction

$$\Delta H = H_{\text{final}} - H_{\text{initial}}$$

$$= H(1 \text{ mole } H_2O) - H(1 \text{ mole } H_2 + 1/2 \text{ mole } O_2)$$

and although the absolute value of the enthalpy (or internal energy) for neither reactants nor product is known (Who knows how to determine the sum of all the potential energies in the nucleus, for example?), the *difference*, ΔH, can be obtained with great precision: $-57{,}798$ cal/mole at $25°C$, the minus sign indicating that the reaction is exothermic.

An especially useful heat reaction is the heat of formation, ΔH_f, the enthalpy change which occurs during the reaction by which the molecule of interest is formed from its elements. Actually the example above was a formation reaction. Another now follows:

$$6\,C(s) + 6\,H_2(g) + 3\,O_2(g) = C_6H_{12}O_6 \text{ (glucose)}$$

$$\Delta H_f = -279{,}800 \text{ cal/mole}$$

From a table of heats of formation, heats of reaction can be computed as

$$\Delta H = (\Delta H_f)_{\text{products}} - (\Delta H_f)_{\text{reactants}}$$

The heat of combustion or burning of glucose could be computed, from heats of formation, from the following reaction:

$$C_6H_{12}O_6 + 6\,O_2(g) = 6H_2O\,(l) + 6\,CO_2(g) \qquad \Delta H = -669{,}580 \text{ cal/mole}$$

The fuel value of foods is usually expressed in units of thousands of calories: i.e., kilocalories (kcal), kilogram calories (kg cal), or Calories (Cal). Hence the fuel value of glucose is 669.58 kcal/mole. Other examples are given in Table 7-1 (A), from which is readily apparent the origin of the very useful "4-9-4 rule": the fuel values of carbohydrate, fat, and protein, are respectively, about 4, 9, and 4 Cal/g.

TABLE 7-1.

A. Heats of Combustion, or Fuel Values in Large Calories (kcal or Cal).

"Fuel"	Heat Given Out per Mole $(-\Delta H)$	Heat Given Out per Gram
Acetic acid: CH_3COOH (liq)	207.9	3.45
Carbon; graphite; coal: C (solid)	94.5	7.83
Hydrogen: H_2 (gas)	68.4	34.2
Propane: C_3H_8 (gas)	530.6	12.1
Glucose, a sugar: $C_6H_{12}O_6$ (solid)	669.6	3.72
Sucrose, a sugar: $C_{12}H_{22}O_{11}$ (solid)	1349.6	3.95
Alcohol: C_2H_5OH (liq)	326.7	7.10
Salicylic acid: HOC_6H_4COOH	723.1	5.96
Carbohydrates (sugars, starches, etc.), generally*	—	3.7 to 4.3
Fats (and oils), generally*	—	9.5
Proteins, generally*	—	4.3

B. Heat Given Out During Neutralization of Acid with Base at 25°C.

Acid	Base	$-\Delta H$ Cal/mole
HCl	NaOH	13.7
HCl	NH_4OH	12.4
HAc	NaOH	13.3
HAc	NH_4OH	12.0

C. Heats of Transition from One State to Another—"Latent Heats."

	cal/gram	$-\Delta H$ Cal/mole
Ice at 0°C to water at 0°C—*melting*	80	1.44
Liquid water at 37°C to vapor at 37°C—*vaporization*	575	9.85

*Mixtures, and therefore of no constant molecular weight.

Note use of both small and large calories in this table. The large "fuel" calorie = 1000 small calories defined with reference to 1 g H_2O.

Within the general framework of the First Law one can make some observations on the whole animal. The goal of the sum of all the metabolic processes in the living system is to maintain the internal energy, $\mathcal{U}$, and the enthalpy, $\mathcal{H}$, at constant values; that is, to maintain $\Delta \mathcal{U} = 0 = \Delta \mathcal{H}$ despite the input of energy and the output of work. The attempt is always made by the full-grown living thing to maintain a daily balance between the net energy taken in as food (q), and the work done (w). This work may be external physical work, or it may be internal work such as transport through the circulatory system, internal·muscle movements of the heart and stomach, chemical transformations, etc. . . .

The quantity of heat given off by living animals can be measured either calorimetrically or by the CO_2 produced, (The two measurements agree!), and when measured under conditions of a carefully defined rest, give a value related to the internal work required to keep the living system alive. This *basal metabolic rate* is about 70 kcal/hr, (about 1400 kcal/day) for a normal man. In other units, the basal metabolic rate amounts to about 0.1 horse-power (hp) continuously.

It is readily apparent that if an animal is ill, certain processes are running at too high a rate; heat energy accumulates, and the temperature rises. The rate of energy loss is increased. By contrast with the normal animal in which $\Delta \mathcal{U} = 0$, and $q = w$, in the ill animal w is much larger than q, the quantity $(q - w)$ is negative, and $\Delta \mathcal{U}$ is negative. Thus the animal lives at the expense of its internal energy, with resulting loss of weight—about 2 lb/day for a human, assuming complete breakdown of assimilative processes and food stored as glycogen and ignoring water loss. The quantities $\mathcal{U}$ and $\mathcal{H}$ decrease with time before the "turn" or "crisis," then increase more or less slowly back to normal because the animal begins to assimilate again during the recovery period.

The ideas outlined in the preceding paragraphs show the versatility and the usefulness of the First Law, that energy must be conserved, but of course do not illustrate all its facets. Note parts B and C of Table 7-1 for other examples.

More Detailed Consideration of the Second Law. Free Energy and Entropy

The Second Law of Thermo. does not violate the first, but rather extends it. It says: Whenever energy is transformed from one kind into another, only a fraction of the internal energy (enthalpy, if pressure is constant) change is available for doing useful work; the rest remains as heat energy of the molecules left at the completion of the reaction. Corollaries, although seemingly unrelated, are the following: heat energy always passes from the hot to the cold body; water always runs downhill; if energy available for doing work can decrease during the course of a process, the process will proceed spontaneously, although not necessarily at a fast rate. (That last phrase is a very important one!)

In algebraic terms, the Second Law can be expressed as:

$$\Delta H = \Delta F + Q$$

Here ΔF is the maximum available work, the "free" energy, which can be extracted from ΔH, and Q is the unavailable energy. Note that both ΔF and Q, as does ΔH, have units kcal/mole (i.e., Cal/mole).

The word "maximum" needs amplification. It is a fact of common experience that any mechanical job can be done in several ways, some ways more efficient than others. If the job is done by the hypothetical frictionless machine, with minimum loss of energy, it is then done the most efficiently. By analogy, work can be extracted from a process in many ways, some more efficient than others. The hypothetical conditions of no waste are given the special name, *reversible conditions;* ΔF is therefore the maximum work available under reversible conditions. One practical system from which nearly maximum work can be extracted is the electrochemical one, a battery for example; or, more pertinent here, the concentration cells which exist and deliver energy at living membranes.

Very common are the processes which occur under nonreversible conditions. The expression then becomes

$$\Delta H = \Delta F' + q' + Q$$

for the reaction of 1 mole, or

$$\Delta \mathcal{H} = \Delta \mathcal{F}' + q' + \mathcal{Q}$$

for the living system as a whole. Here $\Delta F'$ (or $\Delta \mathcal{F}'$) and q' refer to the externally available work and "frictional" loss, respectively. The latter of course shows up as heat energy, which must be dissipated to the environment by any of the well-recognized methods of perspiration, excretion, respiration, etc., which will be discussed later.

A useful efficiency can be defined as:

$$\mathcal{E} = \Delta F'/\Delta F, \quad \text{or} \quad \mathcal{E} = \Delta \mathcal{F}'/\Delta \mathcal{F}.$$

This ratio is the fraction of the reversible free energy change which is realized as useful work in the process. The value can easily be demonstrated with a flashlight dry-cell; it ranges from 0 per cent if the dry-cell is short-circuited by a screwdriver across the terminals; through any value up to about 70 per cent when operating in a flashlight; to close to 100 per cent when used only as a source of voltage with almost no current being drawn. Corresponding values for man cannot be given numerically, but must range from nearly zero for a football team which expends an unimaginable amount of energy to move a 2-lb football a few feet, to very high values for the nerve transmission and mental activity which occur during computation. Other examples will be given later.

The thermodynamic ratio $\Delta F/\Delta H$, defined as Υ, is fixed by the value of the unavailable energy, Q. It is a more fundamental quantity than $\mathcal{E}$, in the sense that it does not depend upon the frictional losses in the engine, or upon the inefficiencies of the living machine. All processes of energy conversion are producers or consumers of heat energy, and the conversion can take place only as long as heat can be transferred from one part of the system to another. When finally no further transfer is possible, the process ceases. It is evident that the heat capacities of reactants and products help to determine the position of equilibrium. Thus if a product is formed which has more degrees of freedom (i.e., modes of vibrations, translations, rotations) than the reactant, the product can store more energy as kinetic energy (as energy unavailable for work); then ΔF is less than H, and Y is less than 1. In other words the products, once formed, have to be heated up to the same temperature as the environment, and are heated by an energy which could have performed useful work were this not necessary. On the other hand if the products can store less heat energy at 37° than the reactants, then ΔF is greater than ΔH and Y is greater than 1. The unavailable energy in a process depends upon the temperature and upon the heat capacities of reactants and products. This special heat capacity, S cal/deg C. mole, is called *entropy*. A list of different types of energy and their factors is given in Table 7-2. Note that heat energy is the only one listed for which the intensive factor does not have the dimensions of a force. Perhaps it should be listed as $d(TS)/dx$.

TABLE 7-2. Factors of Several Kinds of Energy.

Type of Energy	Intensive (Force) Factor	Extensive (Capacity) Factor (s)
Electrical (joules)	dv/dx (volts/cm)	q coulombs $\times$ x(cm)
Mechanical (ergs)	F' (dynes)	d(cm)
	P (dynes/cm^2)	V(cm^3)
Chemical (cal)	$\partial F/\partial \xi$ (cal/mole · cm)	ξ(cm) $\times$ n(moles)
Thermal (cal)	T (deg)	S(cal/deg. mole) $\times$ n

Explanation:
ξ = reaction path length. F is free energy. Mechanical force, above, is given the symbol F' (in this Table only).

For the reaction or process under consideration,

$$Q = TS_2 - TS_1$$

where 2 and 1 refer to final and initial states. Then

$$Q = T\Delta S$$

Substitution in $\Delta H = \Delta F + Q$, gives

$$\Delta H = \Delta F + T\Delta S$$

which is the algebraic statement of the *Second Law*.

Table 7-3 lists values obtained experimentally for ΔH, ΔF and ΔS. An example of particular biochemical and physiological importance is the hydrolysis of adenosine triphosphate, ATP. At pH = 7 and 37°C:

$\Delta F = -7.73$ kcal/mole; $\Delta H = -4.8$ kcal/mole, and $\Delta S = 0.45$ cal/deg mole. If the reaction occurs in a test tube, no energy is converted into useful work, and the heat produced is 4.8 kcal/mole. If, however, it is carried out in the presence of an activated actomyosin filament (the contractile unit in muscle), mechanical work (lifting a weight, for example) can be made to occur, and the amount of work done can be anything up to 7.73 kcal/mole, depending upon how it is done. If done reversibly (infinitely slowly), 7.73 kcal/mole is done, and $\mathcal{E} = 100$ per cent; if done more and more rapidly, $\mathcal{E}$ becomes less and less.

The Production of Entropic Heat

Note that S is a state variable, like F, H, and U, and note that ΔS may be positive or negative depending on whether the heat capacity of the products is greater or less than that of the reactants. Note further that if ΔS is negative, and it often is, ΔF will be greater than ΔH. This is really not surprising if one remembers that the extra energy for work was bound up as extra heat energy of the reactants. Note also that the greater the number of rotations, vibrations, and translations of which a system is capable, the greater the heat capacity and hence the greater the entropy. Therefore *entropy* (a heat capacity) *is often used as a measure of disorder:* the greater the entropy, the greater the disorder.

For the living system, we write

$$\Delta \mathcal{H} = \Delta \mathcal{F} + T\Delta S$$

under reversible conditions, and

$$\Delta \mathcal{H} = \Delta \mathcal{F}' + q' + T\Delta S$$

for practical conditions, in which not the maximum work, $\Delta \mathcal{F}$, but rather a lesser amount, $\Delta \mathcal{F}'$, is realized. An amount of energy, q', shows up as heat energy and adds to the reversible, unavailable heat energy, $T\Delta S$ kcal. Of course q' itself will factor into $T\Delta S'$, since it is a heat energy. Then if ΔS is the reversible entropy increase, $\Delta S'$ is the extra entropy increase because of the irreversibility of the process. Although q' is, strictly speaking, a waste, it is the heat energy which maintains the temperature of a man some 10 or more degrees C above his environment in spite of a steady heat energy loss to the environment. Now, the work done may be internal work, $\Delta \mathcal{F}'_{int}$, or external work, $\Delta \mathcal{F}'$. The internal work, however, is degraded into heat *internally*, and forms part of q'. (Consider the pumping work of the heart, for example: blood is forced along the circulatory system against a frictional resistance, and the energy is finally expended as heat in the vessel walls.) If we exclude growth and mental work for the moment (these hopelessly complicate the argument), the contribution made by internal work to the

TABLE 7-3.   Heats of Reaction, Free Energy, and Entropy Changes for Some Biologically-Important Processes.

	ΔH (kcal/mole)	ΔF (kcal/mole)	ΔS (cal/deg mole)
A. Illustrative Reactions (very accurately measured)			
(1) Combustion of hydrogen in a fuel cell, 25°C: H_2(1 atm) + $\frac{1}{2}O_2$(1 atm) = H_2O (gas, 1 atm)	−57.798	−54.638	−10.5
(2) Clark Standard Cell, 25°C: $Zn + Hg_2SO_4 = ZnSO_4 + 2\,Hg$	−81.92	−66.10	−54.9
(3) Combusion of glucose, a pure sugar, 25°C: $C_6H_{12}O_6 + 6\,O_2$ $= 6\,CO_2 + 6\,H_2O$ (liq)	−669.58	−823.86	+514.
B. *Free Energy-producing Biological Reactions*			
(1) Combustion of glycogen, per $C_6H_{10}O_5$ unit, 37°C: glyc (1% soln) + 6 O_2 $= 6\,CO_2 + 5\,H_2O$ (under 0.003 atm CO_2 and 0.2 atm O_2, as in tissue)	−682.4	−703.0	+66.5
(2) Glycolysis, per $C_6H_{10}O_5$ unit, 37°C: glyc (1% soln) = 2 lactates (0.18% soln)	−32.4	−60.4	+90.3
(3) Binding of copper ion by albumin, a protein (P): $Cu^{++} + P = PCu^{++}$	+1.05	−7.06	+27.2
(4) Dephosphorylation of adenosine triphosphate (ATP) in muscle, 37°C: $ATP^{-4} + H_2O$ $= ADP^{-2} + HPO_4^{-2}$	−4.80	−7.73	+9.4
(5) Hydrolysis of acetylcholine (ACh) in nerve: $ACh + H_2O$ = acetic acid + choline	−1.09	−0.82	+6.4
(6) Reversible denaturation (D) of a normal (N) globulin (a trypsin-inhibitor in soybean): $N \rightleftharpoons D$	−57.3	−111.3	+174.

TABLE 7-3.   (Contin.)

	ΔH (kcal/mole)	ΔF (kcal/mole)	ΔS (cal/deg mole)
(7) Perfect osmotic system, osmotic pressure difference due to difference of 1 mole of solute between the two solutions. Water flow to equilibrium	0	-1.38	$+4.6$
(8) Relaxation of stretched, elastic tissue, per kcal of work done	$ca\ -1000$	-1.0	$ca\ +400$
C. *Free Energy-consuming Biological Reactions*			
(1) Peptide bond formation in protein synthesis: $R - COOH + NH_2 - R'$ $= R - CONH - R' + H_2O$	—	$+3.0$	(negative)
(2) Pyruvate or acetoacetate synthesis: $R - COOH + R'COOH$ $= R - CO\,R' - COOH + H_2O$	—	$+16.0$	(negative)
(3) Blood flow, per complete cycle	—	$ca\ +0.002$	(positive)
(4) Man walking at 2 miles per hr	—	$ca\ +0.010$	(positive)

NOTE: The values given under B and C are difficult to measure, depending as they do on pH, buffer, etc., and are subject to revision. For example in B (4), the hydrolysis of ATP in muscle, values of -9.2 and -10.5 for ΔF have also been measured, and O. Meyerhof's (1927) experimental value of $\Delta H = -12.0$ is quoted extensively. The values change markedly with dielectric constant of the medium. (Some values have been taken from the review by Wilkie, 1960.)

metabolic heat loss, q', is numerically equal to the internal work done, $\Delta \mathfrak{F}'_{int}$. The rest of the metabolic heat loss, q'_{irr}, is a result of irreversibility in the chemical and physical processes (i.e., less than 100 per cent. The efficiency is *not* 100%, as is often implied in disucssions of this sort). Therefore

$$q' = \Delta \mathfrak{F}'_{int} + q'_{irr}$$

and both q'_{irr} and $\Delta \mathfrak{F}'_{int}$ make appreciable contributions to q'. An estimate of $\mathcal{E}$ for one specific case is given later. The value, 37 per cent, is probably an upper limit to $\mathcal{E}$, because it refers to a very efficient part of the human being—the respiratory enzyme system.

For purposes of cataloguing further, the metabolic heat loss, q', can be considered to be the sum of two parts: (a) the basal metabolic heat, q'_{bm}, and (b) the extra heat, q'_{ex}, in excess of the basal metabolic heat. The former is a minimum value, measured under carefully defined conditions of rest. Thus $(q'_{ex} + q'_{bm})$ is the heat loss (measurable) from the body during exertion; and q'_{bm} is the value measured when q'_{ex} is zero.

Although the principles are straightforward enough, measurement of the quantities in these expressions is difficult. Let us make some guesses for illustrative purposes. For a normal man in North America the food intake, $\Delta \mathcal{H}$, is about 3000 Cal/day, and the basal heat loss, q'_{bm}, about 1400 Cal/day. These are measured values. Since the Second Law says:

$$\Delta \mathcal{H} = \Delta \mathcal{F} + T\Delta S$$

$$= \Delta \mathcal{F}' + q'_{bm} + q'_{ex} + T\Delta S$$

then

$$-3000 = \Delta \mathcal{F}' - 1400 + q'_{ex} + T\Delta S$$

If the food taken in and burned was glucose, for example, $T\Delta S$ can be evaluated as follows. A $\Delta \mathcal{H}$ of -3000 Cal arises from 4.5 moles of glucose (Table 7-3), and therefore

$$T\Delta S = 310 \deg K \times 4.5 \text{ moles} \times 514 \text{ cal/deg mole} = 700 \text{ Cal}$$

Our problem then reduces to $q'_{ex} + \Delta \mathcal{F}' = -2300$ Cal.

The value of total rate of heat loss has been measured for man in many aspects (look ahead to Table 8-11), and in an average day q'_{ex} can be at least as large as the basal metabolic heat loss, and usually runs in excess of 2000 Cal. Therefore $-\Delta \mathcal{F}'$ will be less than 300 Cal. The external work $\Delta \mathcal{F}'$ can be roughly estimated, especially for an unskilled laborer. Suppose he is required to dig a hole 8 ft square and 4 ft deep; the work of lifting alone is about 30 Cal, and this represents at most a third of the total work expended in loosening, picking, and lifting operations associated with the job. Locomotion, eating, and the other daily external expenditures probably account for the rest of the 300 Cal of external work.

An estimate of the internal work done per day can also be obtained. In our example above, the total free energy available was 3700 Cal (3000 + 700). If the efficiency, $\mathcal{E}$, was 37 per cent, then

$$\Delta \mathcal{F}' + \Delta \mathcal{F}'_{int} = 1370$$

Of this, about 300 Cal was external work, $\Delta \mathcal{F}'$, as we saw above; and therefore the internal work, $\Delta \mathcal{F}'_{int}$, which kept the metabolic process running, was about 1170 Cal, 34 per cent of the metabolic heat loss, q'.

The reader is invited to consider other aspects of man's life and work from this point of view: to put other estimated values into the Second Law and juggle them about, hence to become familiar with both the clarity of concept and the difficulty of successful detailed application at the present state of knowledge.

THE DRIVE TOWARD EQUILIBRIUM

The Driving Force

It is a familiar fact that if two mechanical forces of different magnitude oppose each other at a point, the resulting movement will be in the direction of the larger force. Similarly, it seems almost axiomatic that if two systems of different free energy, F, are made to oppose each other, provided they are able to interact, the interaction will proceed in the direction of the larger. For chemical reactions, if the free energies of formation for reactants and products are known, then the free energy of reaction, ΔF, is simply the difference between the two. This value, ΔF, represents the maximum amount of work available from the reaction of 1 mole of reactant into product. Since $\Delta F = F_{final} - F_{initial}$, a negative value of ΔF means that the reaction will proceed spontaneously from reactants to products. Such a reaction is said to be *exergonic*. If (see Figure 7-3) ΔF is positive, free energy must be supplied from the outside—another reaction perhaps—before reactants will go into products; the reaction is said to be *endergonic*. The analogy with exothermic (negative ΔH) and endothermic (positive ΔH), introduced earlier, is obvious.

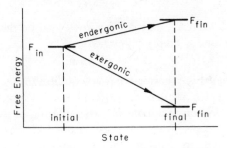

Figure 7-3. Free Energy of Initial and Final States. For exergonic (free energy-producing) processes, ΔF ($= F_{fin} - F_{in}$) is negative; for endergonic (free energy-consuming) processes, ΔF is positive.

The energy-producing reactions in the living system are numerous. Nearly all the primary sources are the combustion of food products. By suitable carriers the free energy required by the endergonic syntheses of anabolism is trapped and carried through the blood stream to the locations at which the synthetic processes take place.

Naturally, free *energy* is not a driving *force*, although it is often considered as such. Nor is the partial molal free energy, $(\partial F/\partial n)_{T,P,n_2...}$, often called *chemical potential.* These are both energies. Force is energy change per unit distance, ξ, along some reaction path; eg., $dF/d\xi$. Since this quantity cannot be determined for chemical reactions, it is usually tucked away (and forgotten) in a proportionality constant. In diffusion, heat conduction, and other physical processes, however, it can be evaluated, as will be seen in the next chapter.

The Free Energy Released During the Drive Toward Equilibrium

Internal energy, U, enthalpy, H, entropy, S, and free energy, F, all refer to 1 mole of the substance or system under consideration. In any real system the value depends upon the amount of substance present. During the drive toward equilibrium, as a reactant, A, begins to decompose to product B, the concentration $(1 - x)$ of A at any time, t, becomes less than the original concentration, while the concentration, x, of B builds up. Hence the free energy difference decreases toward zero as equilibrium is approached, and the position of equilibrium will be determined by the concentrations, x_{eq} and $(1 - x)_{eq}$, at which $\Delta F = 0$. Thus,

$$K_{eq} = \frac{x_{eq}}{(1 - x)_{eq}}$$

The relation between K_{eq} and ΔF per mole can be derived from fundamental principles, and is simply stated here:

$$-\Delta F = RT \ln K_{eq}$$

Strictly speaking this "thermodynamic equilibrium constant," K_{eq}, is a ratio of *activities*, which are defined as *effective concentrations*, it being remembered that the hydration of a molecule, the splitting of salt into ions, etc., makes the effective concentration somewhat different from that determined from the composition. In terms of activities, a, then, at equilibrium:

$$-\Delta F = RT \ln(a_B/a_A)$$

which separates out to

$$-\Delta F = -\Delta F^0 + RT \ln (a_B/a_A)$$

if ΔF^0 refers to the standard state in which the activities are 1 mole/l, and the second term corrects for deviations from an activity ratio of unity.

More generally, a_B is replaced by the product of the activities of the products, and a_A is replaced by the product of the activities of the reactants. Figure 7-4 indicates how the position of equilibrium can be quite different for different processes.

ATP: The Mobile Power Supply

An ubiquitous wanderer and a molecule of unrivalled versatility is adenosine triphosphate (ATP), a condensation product of adenine with a pentose

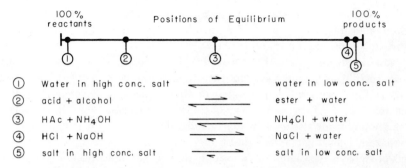

Figure 7-4. Positions of Equilibrium for Several Processes.

and 3 phosphate ions. The molecule has the following structure:

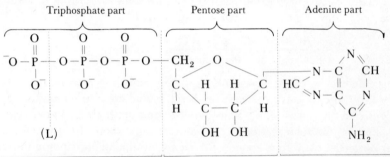

It enters many chemical reactions in the living cell, coupling, in some unknown manner, in such a way that the free energy of hydrolysis (splitting off
the terminal phosphate group at L), or dephosphorylation as it is often
called, -7.7 kcal/mole, is passed to the reaction to which it is coupled. For
example, adsorbed on the enzyme myosin in muscle, the molecule hy-
drolyzes, and the free energy appears as the mechanical work of contraction
of the muscle; coupled with RNA it supplies energy for protein synthesis.
Its hydrolysis products are adenosine diphosphate (ADP) and phosphate
ion (P).

To become rephosphorylated, as it must, it is carried to the "energy factory" of the cell, the mitochondrion (there are 50 to 5000 of these little
double-membraned, 2- to 5-micron bodies per cell), and there the ADP and
P are coupled with some step of the respiratory enzyme's oxidation of
glucose by O_2, receiving the 7.7 kcal of free energy needed to force the expulsion of water and the regeneration of ATP. In plants, the recoupling can
occur photochemically through chlorophyll and its enzyme system. The reaction can be represented as:

$$\text{ATP} + \text{H}_2\text{O} \xrightleftharpoons[\text{``charging''}]{\text{``discharging''}} \text{ADP} + \text{P}$$

and it is reversible. Left to right, it couples in wherever free energy is needed throughout the living system. Right to left it becomes "charged back up," ready to supply energy at another site.

Now the living system is not wasteful of free energy without a good purpose, such as to keep the system warm in a cold environment. Thus most endergonic processes occur in steps of about 8 kcal/mole, or slightly less, making full use of the free energy of the hydrolysis reaction. Likewise the oxidation of foods also goes in steps of slightly more than 8 kcal/mole each, so that the charging reaction is also not wasteful. Indeed, the very complex sets of steps in the oxidation of carbohydrates, fats, and proteins seem designed so that at several stages of each the ADP + P can couple in and be condensed into ATP. This is the principle of the Krebs (citric acid) cycle, for instance, in which it is estimated that 38 ATP's are reformed per molecule of glucose oxidized to CO_2 and H_2O. This number permits an estimate of the efficiency of the recharge process to be made:

$$\frac{8 \text{ kcal/mole of ATP} \times 38 \text{ ATP's}}{824 \text{ kcal/mole of glucose}} \times 100 = 37 \text{ per cent}$$

This efficiency is very respectable, especially since the reactions are going very fast. By contrast, a steam or diesel engine could probably do 20 to 30 per cent on glucose (for a short while!), and up to about 35 per cent on gasoline or oil; solar batteries can convert only about 10 per cent; and thermoelectric converters about 5 per cent from the fuel (including nuclear, or radioactive fuels). Other (like ATP/ADP) electrochemical devices—eg. batteries and fuel cells—are able to give very high efficiences (>80 per cent) if operated slowly, much less if required to operate very fast.

A simple calculation (note the approximations) will emphasize the important point of how efficient the human machine really is. Man's basal metabolic rate is about 70 kcal/hr. If this is all expended through ATP, the turnover (charge-recharge) rate is 70/8 ≈ 9 moles ATP/hr. If we assume that a 150-lb man of density about 1 g/cc contains on the average 10^{-4} moles ATP per liter, the turnover time for ATP is:

$$\frac{150 \text{ lb} \times 454 \text{ g/lb} \times 1 \text{ l/1000 g} \times 10^{-4} \text{ moles/l}}{9 \text{ moles/hr}} \times 3600 \text{ sec/hr} \approx 30 \text{ sec}$$

That is, each ATP molecule in the body is hydrolyzed and reformed about once every 30 sec! At this speed of discharge and charge, a man-made battery would have an efficiency well below 1 per cent. Indeed, it would burn up in the attempt! Hence 37 per cent in the living system is truly remarkable. To supply the basal energy, it burns the *equivalent* of $\frac{70 \text{ kcal/hr}}{\sim 4 \text{ kcal/g}} \approx 17$ g glucose each hr, 24 hr a day.

The ATP-ADP system is one of a class of oxidation-reduction (redox) or electron-transfer systems operating in the living being.   There are many others.

REDOX SYSTEMS; ELECTRON TRANSFER PROCESSES

Equivalence of Electrical and Chemical Energy

Oxidation-reduction reactions have very wide exemplification in living systems: They bring about energy-producing oxidations of food; electrochemical reactions in the brain and nerve; hydrogenation of oils and dehydrogenation of fats and sugars, etc.   Some are simple electron-transfer reactions, the reaction

$$Fe^{+2} \longrightarrow Fe^{+3} + e^-$$

for example.   The free energy of this *half*-reaction (There must be a place for the electron to go!) can be trapped as un-neutralized electrons—i.e., as electrical energy.   In fact if a metallic or molecular electron-acceptor is present at the site, such as

$$H^+ + e^- \longrightarrow 1/2\ H_2$$

the chemical free energy of the total reaction

$$1/2\ H_2 + Fe^{+3} \longrightarrow H^+ + Fe^{+2}$$

can be drained off as electrical energy.   This transformation is almost reversible (and therefore highly efficient), even at fairly high speed.   The free energy of oxidation of foodstuffs is guided by a series of redox enzymes through a particular reaction scheme, in which each step of the process is a fairly efficient redox process.   Most of the free energy of each step is trapped as an electron per molecule, and then passed on at the site where it can be used.

Equivalence of electrical and chemical energy is a requirement of the First Law.   Thus ΔF calories/mole of reaction must be equal to the electrical energy derived per mole of reaction.   Now Faraday showed about 1830 that 96,500 coulombs (amperes $\times$ seconds) are required to oxidize or reduce one equivalent weight of redox substance; and one equivalent weight is defined as the weight which will transfer *one* electron per molecule.   Hence if the number of electrons transferred per mole, or the number of equivalents per mole, is n, and if 96,500 cou/equiv is abbreviated to $\overline{F}$, then the product $n\overline{F}$ is the number of coulombs required to oxidize or reduce 1 mole.   But electrical energy in joules is volts $\times$ coulombs.   Therefore

$$-\Delta F = n\overline{F}\ E$$

What voltage is E? It is the voltage measured between the hydrogen end and the ferrous-ferric end of the reaction cell. To make this measurement, and thereby to measure ΔF, one might simply bubble hydrogen over a piece of platinum (the metallic contact) in $1 N$-acid solution; and attach the platinum through a voltmeter to another platinum piece sitting in equimolar ferrous and ferric salt solution. The two solutions must be connected if the circuit is to be complete. The value measured in this case is 0.77 v, consistent with a free energy of reaction of about 40 kcal per mole of hydrogen consumed. The ferric end is positive to the voltmeter, the hydrogen negative.

The concentrations may not be as stated, however, and we would expect, and indeed find, that the voltage measured would then differ from 0.77. The conditions specified in our example are arbitrarily chosen "standard state conditions": unit (1) activities of reactants and products, 1 atm pressure, $25°C$; and reversibility. We have already seen what a deviation from unit activity ratio will do to ΔF.

Purely as a matter of convenience and of convention, since the absolute value of *no* redox system is known, the normal hydrogen electrode (NHE) (1 atm pressure, normal acid, and H_2 on platinum) has been chosen as the standard reference, and defined as zero volts. All other redox systems are referred to this standard. In fact a table has been drawn up of known standard redox potentials, E^0's, and is called the electromotive series. However, a special table has been drawn up for biological redox systems. It differs from the standard E^0's, referred to the NHE, in two ways: all the redox reactions are measured against hydrogen at pH = 7, not zero; and since the effective concentrations or activities are not usually known for biological molecules, measured concentrations are used instead; and the tabulated values, E_{m7}, refer to equal concentrations (midpoint, m) of oxidized and reduced form (i.e., material 50 per cent oxidized). Table 7-4 lists some of these. A very complete discussion of biological redox systems is given in the remarkable book of W. Mansfield Clark,[2] who has spent a lifetime making a systematic study of, and attempting to organize our knowledge of this subject.

Free Energy and Concentration. The Nernst Equation

The free energy of reaction, and hence the emf, E, of reaction, varies with the concentrations, as is evident from the relation between ΔF and K_{eq} given above. Insertion of $n\bar{F}E^0$ for $-\Delta F^0$, and $n\bar{F}E$ for $-\Delta F$, and rearrangement gives the famous expression of the emf as a function of concentrations, introduced just before the turn of the century by Walther Nernst:

$$E = E^0 - \frac{RT}{n\bar{F}} \ln (a_{ox}/a_{red})$$

TABLE 7-4.   Redox Potentials E_{m7} of Some Important Biochemical Reactions.

Steady-state Redox Process	E_{m7}	Redox Catalyst
Hydroxide ions - oxygen	+0.80	
	+0.35	
Ferrous - ferric	+0.29	cytochrome A
	+0.25	cytochrome C
	+0.14	hemoglobin
Succinate - fumarate	0.00	
	−0.04	cytochrome B
Alanine - ammon. pyruvate	−0.05	
	−0.06	flavoprotein
Malate - oxalo acetate	−0.10	
Lactate - pyruvate	−0.18	riboflavin
Ethyl alcohol - acetaldehyde	−0.20	
Hydroxy butyrate - acetoacetate	−0.28	
	−0.32	DPN (diphosphopyridine nucleotide)
	−0.35	glutathione (estimated)
Cystine - cysteine	−0.39	
Hydrogen - hydrogen ions	−0.42	
Pyruvate - carbonate + acetyl pH	−0.48	
Acetaldehyde - acetate	−0.60	

NOTE: At pH 7, and at 50 per cent oxidation, measured against the normal hydrogen electrode.
    Values given are approximate. Complete data on these and many other biological redox systems are given by Clark.[2]

E^0 is the value when the ratio of activities of oxidized and reduced species is unity (ln 1 = 0), and the second term is the correction for any ratio not equal to unity.

Usually T is 37°C (310°K); R is always 8.3 jou/deg mole, $\overline{F}$ is always 96,500 cou/equiv; and ln x = 2.303 log x. Insertion of these numbers gives the common form of the Nernst Equation

$$E = E^0 - \frac{0.060}{n} \log (a_{ox}/a_{red})$$

For the simplest case,

$$H_2 = 2H^+ + 2e^-$$

the $a_{red} = 1$, being an element; $n = 2$; and since pH $= -\log (a_{H^+})$, and $E^0 = 0$ by definition, the emf of the hydrogen electrode, referred to the *NHE*, as a function of pH is:

$$E = -0.06 \times pH \text{ volts}$$

Plots of E vs a_{H^+} and of E vs pH are shown in Figure 7-5. It can be seen that at the physiological pH of 7, E_{m7} on the NHE scale is -0.42 v.

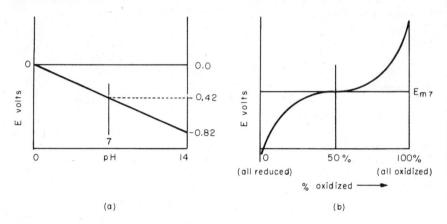

Figure 7-5. Reversible Potential of an Oxidation-Reduction Reaction: (a) as a function of pH, on the normal hydrogen electrode (NHE) scale; (b) as a function of per cent oxidation. Definition of E_{m7}: potential (on the NHE scale) when pH = 7 and when the redox system is 50 per cent oxidized.

As a further clarification and as a summary, Figure 7-6 shows schematically the relation between the NHE scale of E^0's (pH = 0), to which ΔF values have been traditionally related through $-\Delta F = n\overline{F}E$, and the physiological scale, E_{m7} (pH = 7). The latter is now commonly used as a *relative* measure of free energy changes in biological reactions. The values in Table 7-5 have been measured simply by putting a platinum wire into a mixture of equal concentrations of sodium succinate and sodium fumarate at pH 7, containing an enzyme and a mediator (discussed later), and measuring its voltage against a hydrogen electrode in the same solution. Such measured values can be used to predict the direction of reaction, or as a basis for comparison, but not for the determination of ΔF, because the effective concentrations (activities) are not known. It is well to be clear on this limitation of the E_{m7} listing.

Difficulty often arises in this subject because of notation. Different authors use different subscripts and superscripts. In this book we have defined, and use, only E, E^0, and E_{m7}. One should be aware of the variations which one may find. Further, one should understand clearly that the values given in the table for intermediary processes of oxidation are midpoint values; that although these redox systems are generally poised at their most stable point (Figure 7-5), a tight control must be kept by the living system at all times on the concentration of oxidized and reduced states of *each* system;

that too much variation could cause a normally proceeding reaction actually to go *backwards*!

A special application of the Nernst Equation is discussed under concentration cells.

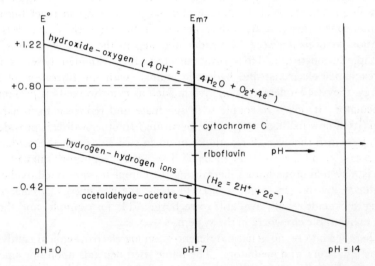

Figure 7-6. E_{m7}'s (center vertical line), and Their Relation to the Corresponding E^o's. (See text and Table 7-4.)

Balky Redox Reactions

There are three tricks provided by nature to promote electron exchange in oxidation-reduction reactions. The first is *catalysis*: providing a surface or a site on which the exchange can rapidly take place. For example, electrons exchange immeasurably slowly between H_2 and H^+ in solution, but if a surface such as finely divided platinum metal is added, electron exchange is rapid, and the potential readily manifested.

The second trick is the use of an *indicator redox system*. If one wishes to know the redox potential of a solution in which the electron transfer is slow or sluggish, one can add a very small amount of an entirely foreign redox system, which exchanges electrons rapidly with the system of interest, and which is either itself highly colored or exchanges rapidly at a metal electrode. In the first case the depth of color of the resulting solution can be related to the redox potential; and in the second case the potential can be read directly against a reference electrode. Methylene blue, a colored redox dye, is one of a class of dyes commonly used for this purpose, while the addition of a small amount of potassium iodide often will permit direct measurement of the redox potential of the solution against some suitable reference electrode. If the redox indicator (KI, for example) is present to an amount much less than the redox systems in the solution to which it is added, it can exchange electrons (KI → I_2) until its potential (determined by a_{I_2}/a_{KI}) is the same as that of the solution.

The third trick is really a combination of the first two. If a solution contains two reactants, such as glucose and oxygen, which can react together spontaneously (negative ΔF), the reaction will be extremely slow unless the solution contains *mediators*. Consider one step in the over-all process, for example succinate added to pyruvate in a test tube. Although these two ions *can* exchange electrons (and hydrogen atoms), with the liberation of free energy, they *don't* unless a redox system such as cytochrome-C is present as a mediator. Its job is to couple with succinate and reduce it to fumarate, then (itself now oxidized) to oxidize pyruvate. In other words it provides a path by which the over-all reaction can go in two steps, via the mediator, whereas it could not go at all in one. The whole respiratory enzyme system is a system of mediators, permitting the complete, controlled oxidation of glucose by oxygen to go in discrete steps, the free energy of each step being thus made readily available to recharge ATP, for example, and therefore to be usable elsewhere in the system.

There seem to be no generic differences among electrochemical catalysts, redox indicators, and mediators. The name used depends upon one's point of view. Indeed, in his classical work on the succinate-fumarate system, Lehman (1930) called succinic dehydrogenase the catalyst and methylene blue the mediator.

MEASUREMENT OF ΔH, ΔF, AND $T\Delta S$

The simplest way to measure all three energies is in an electrochemical redox cell, described in the previous section, if indeed the reaction is an oxidation-reduction reaction. Thus ΔF is directly related to the voltage on the NHE scale by $-\Delta F = n\overline{F}E$, and ΔS is directly related to the rate of change of ΔF with temperature through the relationships'

$$\frac{d(\Delta F)}{dT} = -\Delta S; \quad \text{and} \quad \Delta S = n\overline{F}\frac{dE}{dT}$$

Since ΔF and ΔS can be so determined, ΔH can be obtained from the Second Law:

$$\Delta H = \Delta F + T\Delta S$$

However, ΔH, the heat of reaction, is itself hard *not* to measure! If no work at all is extracted in a calorimeter experiment, as a process is allowed to go spontaneously to equilibrium, all the free energy is wasted away into heat, and ΔH is the quantity of heat measured in the experiment.

Measurement of the equilibrium constant, in the usual manner, gives a measure of ΔF, since

$$-\Delta F = RT \ln K_{eq}$$

Further,

$$\frac{d \ln K_{eq}}{dT} = -\frac{\Delta H}{RT^2}$$

and therefore measurement of the equilibrium constant at several temperatures allows evaluation of ΔH by an alternative method.

The Third Law, stated early in this chapter, provides another avenue for the determination of the thermodynamic energies. The law says that the entropy of all elements in their stable states (viz., S_0^0) is zero at absolute zero temperature (where all molecular motion ceases). Thus the entropy of all pure substances at $0°K$ is also zero. Further, the entropy at the normal body temperature of $37°C$ is the sum of all the little ways heat energy can be stored by the material; and it can be evaluated from the heat capacity, C_p, of the substance measured at different temperatures from $37°C$ down to absolute zero. Within the past 25 years, literally thousands of "third-law entropies" have been so evaluated. Table 7-5 lists some of these values for biologically important molecules. Then, as Szent-Györgyi,[13] the energetic contemporary physiologist, so aptly stated in the quotation which opened

TABLE 7-5.   Some Free Energies of Formation and Third Law Entropies.

	$-\Delta F_f^°$ (Cal/mole)	S_0^0 (cal/deg mole)
H_2O (l)	56.7	16.75
H_2O (g)	54.7	45.13
NaCl (s)	91.7	
C_2H_5OH	40.2	38.4
$C_{12}H_{22}O_{11}$ (sucrose)	371.6	
CO_2 (g)		51.08
HAc	94.5	38.0

this chapter, a large, formal system of very useful numbers has been calculated and tabulated from known experimental results. The National Bureau of Standards, Washington, D. C., has published handbooks of useful data. Tables 7-1 and 7-3, as well as 7-5, present very carefully selected samples, of biological and medical interest.

CONCENTRATION CELLS; MEMBRANE POTENTIALS

If two vessels containing different concentrations (two glass vessels containing O_2 at different pressures joined by a closed stopcock; or two salt solutions of different concentrations separated by a suitable membrane, Figure 7-7) are allowed to interact, the difference in free enegery, ΔF, can be manifested by transport or movement of molecules or ions. By a rather neat argument involving the dependence of electrical potential upon concentration of ions, it can be shown that the ΔF can also be manifested as a potential difference in such a system. With suitable electrodes the value can be measured. A form of the Nernst equation relates the emf of this concentration cell to the ratio of the salt activities. Thus

$$E_{conc} = \frac{0.060}{n} \log (a_1/a_2)$$

This equation shows the relationship between the potential and the activity ratio for condition of no transport across the interface. For example, for a cell composed of $1 N - NaCl : 0.1 N - NaCl$, in which the activity ratio is about 10, the value of $E_{conc} = 0.060$ v $(=60$ mv$)$.

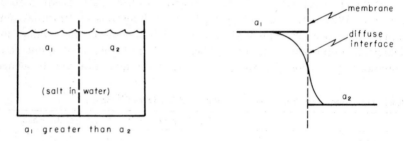

Figure 7-7. Concentration Cell (left); with Transport (right).

If flow or transport of ions or water occurs, and it usually does to some extent across living membranes, the value observed, E, differs from E_{conc} by a "diffusion potential," E_{diff}, which can be approximated by either the Henderson (1911) or Planck (1915) equations, and measured, approximately, under certain rigorous experimental conditions. Thus,

$$E = E_{conc} - E_{diff}$$

Values 50 to 100 mv are found routinely in living systems, across the membranes of nerve cells and red blood cells, for example (see Table 7-6). These values are due principally to potassium chloride concentration differences across the membranes. It is interesting to note that in the electric eel, similar cells are arranged in *series*, and potential differences of 200 to 1000 v are usually observed! In nerve, the stationary values of about 80 mv are modified rapidly with passage of a stimulus, due to a change in permeability.

TABLE 7-6.   Membrane Potentials, E, Observed, and Calculated from Measured
Concentration Ratios Across Cell Walls.

System	KCl conc / KCl conc inside / outside	E (millivolts)	
		Observed	Calc by Nernst Eq.
Loligo (squid) nerve axon	19 : 1	50 to 60	74
Sepia (cuttlefish) axon	21 : 1	62	77
Carcinus nerve cell	34 : 1	82	89
Frog muscle cell	48 : 1	88	98
Human muscle cell	50 : 1	85 to 100	99

Actually, any activity difference between two solutions separated by a membrane is a sufficient condition for a membrane potential to exist.   Three
cases will give rise to a potential difference:

(1) Two concentrations of the *same* salt (restricted flow).
(2) The same (or different) concentrations of two *different* salts.   Even
     though the concentrations are the same, the effective concentrations
     or activities differ because of different interactions with the solvent
     and with each other.
(3) Free flow through the membrane, except for one macromolecular ion.
     This is a rather famous equilibrium, exemplified across living cell
     walls, and described quantitatively by Donnan.

To sort out these possibilities on living membranes is one of the hardest
tasks in biophysics today.   The subject will be considered one step further:
the time-variation of the potential across nerve-cell membrane (Chapter 10).

NEGATIVE ENTROPY CHANGE IN LIVING SYSTEMS

The concept and the quantity entropy has been very carefully introduced
in a simple manner, as a specific heat—a very special specific heat, to be
sure—and this idea of entropy is sufficient for many considerations.   But the
implications are more far-reaching than at first suspected.   Thus, an increase
in entropy during the course of a reaction was described as meaning that
the modes of rotation, etc., of the products were more numerous than those
of the reactants.   This interpretation means that the amount of complexity
in the system has increased with reaction, and could be rather loosely extended to mean that the amount of *disorder* in the system has increased.   Thus
the extra heat, q', lost during a process done in a nonreversible manner contributes quantitatively to the disorder of the system and its environment.

The idea of entropy being associated with disorder or randomness can be
introduced systematically and logically through statistics.   Briefly, the

method takes the following form: The properties of a quantity, ln Ω, are considered in some detail, and it is shown that ln Ω has the two fundamental characteristics of thermodynamic entropy: (1) that ln Ω for two or more independent systems is the sum of the ln Ω's for all the individual systems— that is, that ln Ω is an extensive property dependent upon quantity; and (2) that ln Ω increases for all spontaneous changes occurring in a system for which the quantity of material and the energy are held constant. Both these properties have been introduced earlier, although not in just this form. The proportionality constant, R (cal/deg mole), then is introduced to relate S and ln Ω:

$$S = R \ln \Omega$$

In this development Ω is a pure number, the number of ways in which the particles or parts of the system can be arranged (organized or disorganized). For one of a pair of playing dice the number is 6 (six sides). For a mole, which contains 6×10^{23} molecules, this number, Ω, could be counted out, if we were clever and patient enough! However, approximations can be made through the methods of statistics which give closely enough the number of ways the particles can be arranged. Hence the expression above means that the entropy, S, of a system increases as the number of ways in which the system can be arranged increases. The greater the chaos or disorder, the greater the number of ways; and the greater the entropy of the system.

It has already been shown that all naturally occurring processes, which occur irreversibly, make a positive contribution to the entropy and hence the heat energy of the universe. If there are no violations of the Second Law elsewhere in the universe, the available energy is decreasing all the time, and the universe is approaching the ominous "heat death" or "entropic death," in which the free energy will have reached zero and the entropy a maximum or upper limit. We have then the two interesting possiblities: a *one-step* creation during which the whole was wound up, from which condition it has been slowly running down ever since; or the *continuous* violation of the Second Law is occurring somewhere in the universe. An interesting question, then, is: Is continuous creation occurring within the living thing?

Hence, one of the more important aspects of this study of entropy changes centers on the fact that, although the net result of any physical process must be (Second Law) a positive entropy contribution to the universe, there are some processes in which the entropy definitely *decreases* within a limited space; and it is not very obvious where the overriding increase, if any, occurs to the universe. The process referred to is the creation of the living thing (Figure 7-8), which, although very complex, is certainly not disordered. In fact it is much more highly ordered than the components from which it is made. Growth of the living system, controlled from the outset by a molecule such as DNA (desoxyribonucleic acid), must be one of the great "consumers of entropy" or "producers of negative entropy".... Is it in the growth of an ever-increasing number of living individuals that we find our continuous creation?.... Although during death and decay the order of life is gradually replaced by disorder, the quantity of physical order existing at any one time seems to be increasing each generation, and higher social and economic order runs parallel with the higher physical order of a larger population.

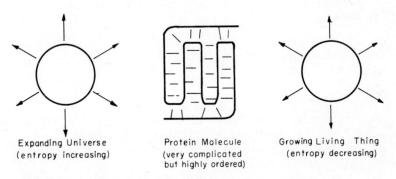

Expanding Universe   Protein Molecule   Growing Living Thing
(entropy increasing)   (very complicated   (entropy decreasing)
                            but highly ordered)

Figure 7-8. Entropy Changes.

Some attempts have been made go give quantitative expression to these ideas. Most of these attempts since 1930 involve the concept of the "steady-state," which is treated in the next chapter; but even these attempts do not permit the use of numerical examples, and although inherently very interesting, cannot be treated quantitatively in this book. On the other hand, perhaps Teilhard de Chardin was right when he suggested that, taken as a whole, the universe is evolving toward a single, highly organized arrangement in which all the ("living") elementary particles of matter have achieved their ultimate state of development; that as living systems organize themselves more and more, over many more thousands of years, the statistical expression of behavior in terms of the average of random motion of many subparticles, will gradually give way to expressive dominance by the grand ensemble of organized living things. Unfortunately we simply have no way at all of evaluating the sociological and economic interaction energies, nor indeed the psychological, spiritual and moral energies of our own minds.

Armed with the background presented in Chapters 4 to 7, the reader will now want to push on more deeply into certain aspects of energy transfer in living systems. It is recommended that he take the appetizers, References 13 and 14, before he starts the full courses offered by References 2, 6, 10, or 15.

PROBLEMS

7-1: If a man submits to a diet of 2500 Cal/day, and expends energy in all forms to a total of 3000 Cal/day, what is the change in internal energy per day?

If the energy lost was stored as sucrose (390 Cal/100 g), how many days should it take to lose 1 lb? (Ignore water loss for this problem.)

7-2: (a) From the following heats of formation at 25°C, compute the heat of combustion (i.e., the "fuel value") of d-glucose. Give the answer in Cal/mole and Cal/gram.

	ΔH_f
All elements (Na, O_2, etc.)	0
CO_2	-94.4 Cal/mole
H_2O	-64.4
$C_6H_{12}O_6$ (d-glucose)	-279.8

(b) Given the heat of combustion of sucrose to CO_2 and H_2O to be 1349 Cal/mole, compute the heat of formation from the elements.

7-3: (a) From the values given for ΔH and ΔF for any two reactants tabulated in the text, calculate the entropy change per mole.

(b) For each of these two cases, calculate the standard emf of the reaction. Are these values for pH = 7?

7-4: Given the fact that the standard emf's for the redox systems methylene blue and maleate-succinate are respectively 0.05v and 0.1 v, at the physiological pH of 7, calculate the *standard* free energy of reaction (at pH = 0). (Note how important it is to define the pH, or alternatively that the living system keep its pH constant.)

7-5: (a) Using the Nernst equation, plot E as a *fn* of pH for:

(i) $1/2\,H_2 \rightarrow H^+ + e^-$	-0.42 v
(ii) succinate $\rightarrow$ fumarate $+ 2H^+ 2e^-$	-0.00 v
(iii) $4\,OH^- \rightarrow O_2 + 4e^- + 2\,H_2O$	$+0.80$ v
(iv) $Cu \rightarrow Cu^{++} + 2e^-$ at pH = 7.	$+0.36$ v

(b) If $E_0 = 0.50$ v and $n = 2$, plot E as *fn* of per cent oxidation from 0 to 100 per cent.

REFERENCES

1. Clark, W. M., "Topics in Physical Chemistry," 2nd ed., The Williams and Wilkins Co., Baltimore, Md., 1952.

2. Clark, W. M., "Oxidation-Reduction Potentials of Organic Systems," The Williams and Wilkins Co., Baltimore, Md., 1960.

3. Fruton, J. S., and Simmonds, S., "General Biochemistry," John Wiley & Sons, Inc., New York, N. Y., 1953.

4. Glasstone, S., "Thermodynamics for Chemists," D. Van Nostrand Co., Inc., New York, N. Y., 1947.

5. Kaplan, N. O., in "The Enzymes—Chemistry and Mechanism of Action," J. A. B. Sumner and K. Myrbäck, Eds., Vol. II, Part 1, Acad. Press Inc., New York, N. Y., 1951.

6. Sodeman, W. A., Ed., "Pathologic Physiology: Mechanisms of Disease," 2nd ed., W. B. Saunders Co., Philadelphia, Pa., 1956.

7. Szent-Györgyi, A., "Thermodynamics and Muscle," in "Modern Trends in Physiology and Biochemistry," E. S. G. Barron, Ed., Acad. Press Inc., New York, N. Y., 1952, p. 377.

8. Teilhand de Chardin, P., "The Phenomenon of Man," Harper & Bros., London, 1955.

9. Wilkie, D. R., "Thermodynamics and the Interpretation of Biological Heat Measurements," *Prog. in Biophys.*, **10**, 259 (1960).

10. Augenstine, L. G., Ed., "Bioenergetics," Acad. Press, New York, N. Y., 1960: dealing mainly with energy absorbed from radiations.

11. West, E. S., "Textbook of Biophysical Chemistry," The Macmillan Co., New York, N. Y., 1960: good discussion on energy of metabolism, with worked examples, p. 386, eg.

12. George, P. and Rutman, R. J., "The 'High Energy Phosphate Bond' Concept," *Prog. in Biophys.*, **10**, 1, 1960.

13. Szent-Györgyi, A., "Bioenergetics," Academic Press, New York, N. Y., 1958.

14. Lehninger, A., "How Cells Transform Energy," *Scientific American*, **205**, 62 (1961).

15. Oncley, J. L., *et al.*, Eds., "Biophysical Science—A Study Program," John Wiley & Sons, Inc., New York, N. Y., 1959: papers by Lehninger, Calvin, and others.

16. Lewis, G. N., and Randall, M., "Thermodynamics," revised by K. S. Pitzer and L. Brewer, McGraw-Hill Book Co., Inc., New York, N. Y., 1961.

CHAPTER 8

Speeds of Some Processes in Biological Systems

The ultimate goal of biophysical kinetics is the understanding of that remarkable integration of heat, mass, and work transfer by chemicals which maintains so reliably the steady-state condition in every spot in the living system.

INTRODUCTION

Biophysical kinetics is the study of the rate or speed at which chemical reactions or physical processes take place. Factors which influence the speed are elucidated in detail, when possible, by experimental methods, and are then analyzed in terms of the actions of the molecules which give the over-all result. It is the study of mechanism of reaction, and of molecular mechanism in particular.

Kinetics is formally defined as "that branch of dynamics which treats changes in motion produced by forces." It is the purpose of the subject to define and interpret these forces, which may be functions of temperature, pressure, molecular interactions, concentration gradients, electrical potential, etc.

Within the broad field of kinetics there are two main subjects which are of interest in biology:

(1) Kinetics of chemical reactions in solution.

(2) Kinetics of physical process such as diffusion, fluid flow, transport of electrical charge, and heat conduction.

The basic principles of the main subject are sketched, and then each of the subjects of particular interest is considered. Since chemical reactions are covered more or less comprehensively in textbooks in biochemistry, and since physical processes are very numerous in the living animal but usually receive very little attention from the kinetic point of view, most of the effort is put on the kinetics of physical processes. The presentation emphasizes the formal similarity of all these processes, and the fact that there are many common factors upon which the rates depend. Unfortunately we do not know enough at this time to achieve very much of the ultimate goal mentioned in the Foreword.

GENERAL PRINCIPLES

Rate-Controlling Step

If any physical or chemical process goes from initial state to final state through a series of intermediate steps, usually one of those steps is inherently slower than the others and controls the rate of the over-all process. For example, a bucket brigade passing pails of water hand to hand from the river to the burning house can transport water no faster than the little old lady who forms the slowest link. The principle is true for chemical and physical processes as well. In most processes in which we are interested, the over-all process involves physical transport as well as chemical reaction. One of the physical steps or one of the chemical steps may be rate-determining.

A measurement of the over-all rate or speed is always a measure of the speed of the slowest step. Consider the chain of events:

$$A \xrightarrow{k_1} B \xrightarrow{k_2} C \xrightarrow{k_3} D \xrightarrow{k_4} E$$

If the reaction $B \rightarrow C$ is the slowest, then the over-all rate is the rate of $B - C$. (As an exercise, apply this principle to the over-all event of free air becoming dissolved in the blood stream. What would you expect to be the slowest step?).

Equilibrium

If a process can proceed forward or backward, starting as either reactants or products and produce products or reactants, respectively, the process will move spontaneously (although perhaps slowly) in a direction toward minimum free energy for the over-all reaction materials: The reaction will "stop" when the concentrations are such that the work the reactants can do equals the work the products can do, and then apparently the reactions in both directions cease. The materials have then reached thermodynamic equilibrium.

The rate of the forward reaction will depend upon the inherent attraction the reactants have for each other, and upon the concentrations of the reactants. The same is true of the reverse reaction. Thus, if

$$aA + bB \underset{k_2}{\overset{k_1}{\rightleftharpoons}} cC + dD$$

where k_1 is the measure of inherent attraction A and B have for each other, the over-all rate of reaction in the forward direction of a moles of A with b moles of B (i.e., $v_1 = -d[A]/dt$, or $-d[B]/dt$, where [ ] denotes concentration), is:

$$v_1 = k_1[A][A] \cdots \times [B][B] \cdots = k_1[A]^a[B]^b$$

Similarly

$$v_2 = k_2[C]^c[D]^d$$

This first principle, that of mass action in reaction kinetics, was demonstrated quantitatively by Wilhelmy in 1850.

At equilibrium the over-all reaction ceases. Therefore $v_1 = v_2$ at equilibrium:

$$k_1[A]^a[B]^b = k_2[C]^c[D]^d$$

$$\frac{[C]^c[D]^d}{[A]^a[B]^b} = \frac{k_1}{k_2} = K_{eq}$$

where K_{eq} is the equilibrium constant. This form of the *Law of Mass Action* was stated thus by Guldberg and Waage in 1863. For any reaction $-\Delta F^0 = RT \ln K_{eq}$, which states that the free energy change per mole (eg., refer to sucrose oxidation) is a measure of the position of equilibrium.

Steady State

Consider again the consecutive process discussed above and consider specifically the case in which the supply of A is unlimited, so that the concentration of A, $[A]$, never changes. If $k_1 > k_2$, A will be converted into B faster than B will be removed into C, and B will accumulate. Since the rate of the reaction $B \rightarrow C$ is

$$v_2 = k_2[B]$$

as we saw above, as B accumulates, v_2 increases until it reaches the value of v_1. At this point B will have reached its steady-state concentration because the concentration B neither increases nor decreases further. The same is true of the other steps.

In the steady-state then

$$v_1 = v_2 = v_3 = v_4$$

or

$$k_1[A] = k_2[B] = k_3[C] = k_4[D]$$

Since the specific rates are all different, the steady-state concentrations are different; but if the process is in the steady-state condition, the concentrations are constant.

If the back reactions proceed at a measurable rate, the situation is more complicated, but the principles are the same.

When you hear the word "equilibrium" used, then think: Which is meant, true equilibrium or steady-state? In the latter case, continuous processing occurs; in the former no net reaction occurs. Figure 8-1 illustrates this difference.

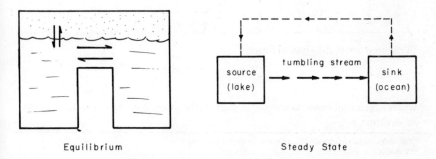

Equilibrium   Steady State

Figure 8-1. Equilibrium and Steady State.

ON CHEMICAL REACTION RATES; ENZYMES

Concentration and Temperature

The law of mass action has already been outlined under the discussion of the approach of a system toward true equilibrium. The rate is always proportional to some power of the concentration of reactants, and this index is called the "order" of a reaction.

There are really two orders obtainable from experiments, one with respect to *time*, and the other with respect to *concentration*. These will have the same value if the reaction is a simple one in which the slowest step is the first step, the one which involves reactant concentrations explicitly. If some other step than the primary one is rate-determining, or if products interfere with or inhibit the reaction, the power, a, of the concentration, $[A]$, which describes best the over-all rate may be different from that which describes the initial rate.

Complicated cases are not considered here. Some of the simpler cases are collected in Table 8-1, which shows the rate equation and the expression and dimensions of the proportionality constant, k, called *the specific rate constant*, when $a = 0, 1/2, 1$, and 2. In Table 8-2 are collected values of the specific rate constant for some first and second-order reactions.

TABLE 8-1.   Summary of Rate Equations for Some Chemical Reactions.

Order*	Rate** Equation	Expression of Specific Rate Constant	Units of Specific Rate Constant
0	$v = k$	$k = \dfrac{c}{t}$	moles/liter sec
1/2	$v = k(c_0 - c)^{\frac{1}{2}}$	$k = \dfrac{2}{t}[c_0^{\frac{1}{2}} - (c_0 - c)^{\frac{1}{2}}]$	moles$^{\frac{1}{2}}$/liter$^{\frac{1}{2}}$ sec
1	$v = k(c_0 - c)$	$k = \dfrac{1}{t}\ln\dfrac{c_0}{c_0 - c}$	sec^{-1}
2	$v = k(c_0 - c)^2$	$k = \dfrac{1}{t}\dfrac{c}{c_0(c_0 - c)}$	liters/mole sec

Reactions are of the general form:

$$aA \longrightarrow \text{Products}$$
$$(c_0 - c)$$

where c_0 is initial concentration of A, and c is the amount of some product formed at any time, t.

*The index of the concentration in the rate or velocity equation.
**Velocity $v = dc/dt$.

TABLE 8-2.   Table of Specific Rate Constants, k

Process	Order	Specific Rate Constant (25°C)
Mutorotation of glucose	1	1.03×10^{-4} sec^{-1}
Myosin-catalyzed hydrolysis of ATP	1	3.0×10^{-4} sec^{-1}
Decomposition of N_2O_5	1	3.4×10^{-5} sec^{-1}
Pepsin-catalyzed hydrolysis of a di-aminoacid substrate	1	2.0×10^{-7} sec^{-1}
Decay of Sr^{90}	1	8.9×10^{-10} sec^{-1}
Pyridine + ethyl iodate $\longrightarrow$ N$(C_2H_5)_4$I	2	1.25×10^{-4} liters mole^{-1} sec^{-1}
Thermal decomposition of HI (gas)	2	5×10^{-4} liters mole^{-1} sec^{-1}

The rate of every individual chemical reaction or physical process increases with increasing temperature, i.e., with increasing kinetic energy in the molecules. This is true without exception. However, in some physiological processes an increase in the temperature permits certain side reactions to occur, which so interfere with the chain of events that the rate of the over-all process decreases with increasing temperature.

For a great many chemical reactions it is found experimentally that the rate of reaction just about' doubles for every 10 Centigrade degrees of rise in temperature. For most physical processes involving mass transfer, the rate goes up from 1.1 to 1.4 times in a 10-degree rise. There are many exceptions to these rules of thumb, of course: for example, certain free radical recombinations have *no* temperature coefficient of rate; and by contrast the rate of inactivation of enzymes by heat, and of the denaturation of proteins, can increase by 1000 times over a 10-degree rise! The last column of Table 8-3 illustrates this point quantitatively.

TABLE 8-3. Dependence of Rates or Speeds of Various Processes on Temperature*

Process	Activation Energy, E^*	Rate at 37°/Rate at 27° C
Free radical combination	0	1.0
Free radical + molecule $\longrightarrow$ products	0 to 0.3	1.0 to 1.01
Transport in water solutions (diffusion, viscous flow, ion mobility)	1.0 to 5.0	1.06 to 1.28
Transport in fat and lipid (diffusion, osmosis)	8 to 15	1.5 to 2.2
Molecule + molecule $\longrightarrow$ products (hydrolyses, neutralizations, rearrangements and condensations)	10 to 30	1.8 to 5.0
(a) uncatalyzed	15 to 30	2.2 to 5.0
(b) catalyzed	10 to 20	1.8 to 3.0
Denaturation of proteins and inactivation of enzymes	30 to 150	3.0 to 3000

*Different processes of the same general type may have different activation energies. Therefore both E^* and the ratio of rates are given as a *range* of values. Units of E^* : kcal/mole.

In general this dependence upon temperature is understandable in terms of the postulates of the kinetic theory of matter. Molecules are presumed to be in a state of continuous motion and have a heat content (H) which depends upon the number of (degrees of freedom of) rotations, vibrations, etc. It is axiomatic that in such a case of random motion not all molecules will contain exactly the same kinetic energy at any one instant. In fact, it is inherent in the kinetic postulates that the energy distribution must be of the form shown in Figure 8-2.

The average heat energy, Q_{av}, per mole of material is $1/2\,RT$ (300 cal) for each translational degree of freedom, RT (600 cal) for each vibrational degree of freedom, and $1/2\,RT$ for each rotational degree of freedom. For a diatomic gas at 27°, then, with one degree of vibrational freedom, two of rotational, and three of translational, the average heat energy, Q_{av}, is 2100 cal per mole of gas.

In any collision of reactant molecules which is to result in reaction, a minimum or threshold energy must be involved in the collision, or else the molecules will simply bounce off each other. Let this threshold energy be E^*. A few molecules will have the excess energy sufficient to react; not every col-

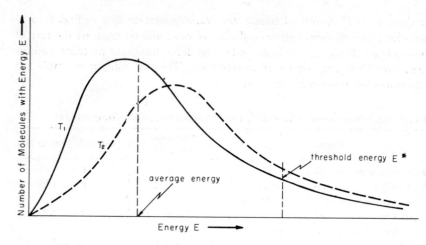

Figure 8-2. Maxwellian Distribution of Energies in Molecules.

lision need be a fruitful one. At a higher temperature, T_2, more molecules have the necessary threshold energy to react, and therefore the rate is faster.

Experimentally, Svante Arrhenius, about 1889, observed that the rate increased exponentially with the temperature. Since in solutions, the concentrations do not vary appreciably with the temperature, the temperature-dependence is practically all in the rate constant, k. Thus

$$k = Ae^{-E^*/RT}$$

where A is a constant in moles per liter per second, E^* is the threshold energy in calories per mole, R the gas constant (1.987 cal per degree per mole), T the temperature in degrees K, and "e" is 2.71828, the base of natural logarithms. Taking logarithms of both sides

$$\ln k = \ln A - E^*/RT$$

or, changing to the base 10, the more familiar system:

$$\log k = \log A - E^*/2.303\,RT$$

Hence a graphical plot of experimental results of rate measurements at different temperatures plotted as $\log v$ vs $1/T$ has a slope of $-E^*/2.303\,R$; and, since R is known, the value of the threshold energy, E^*, can be determined (see Figure 8-3).

Table 8-3 gives values of E^* for different kinds of processes. E^* is often called *energy of activation* as well as threshold energy, and the measured value can often aid in the characterization of the rate-determining step of a process.

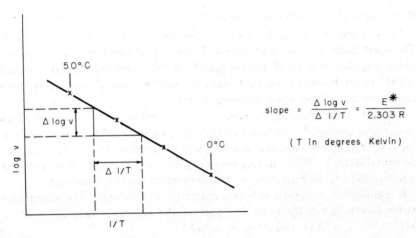

$$\text{slope} = \frac{\Delta \log v}{\Delta \, 1/T} = \frac{E^{\ast}}{2.303 \, R}$$

(T in degrees Kelvin)

Figure 8-3. Arrhenius Plot of Log Rate vs 1/T; Determination of Activation Energy.

Referring back to Figure 7-3 which describes a process proceeding from an initial state to a final state, we know now from the preceding discussion that it must be modified with the insertion of an activation "hump" or barrier (see Figure 8-4). Thus $E^{\ast}$ is related to the extra heat content, $\Delta H^{\ddagger}$, the heat content change between initial state and "activated" state.

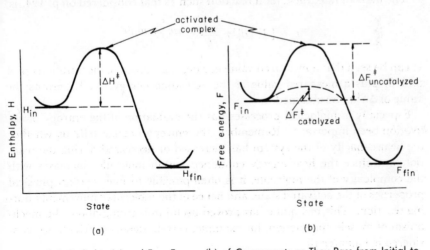

Figure 8-4. Enthalpy (a) and Free Energy (b) of Components as They Pass from Initial to Final State Over the Activation Energy Barrier. Note the position of the activated complex, and the energetically easier path of the catalyzed reaction.

More Factors of the Specific Rate Constant

Various interpretations have been given to the pre-exponential term, A. The most successful has come from the theory of absolute reaction rates, which was pioneered by H. Eyring mainly in 1935, and expounded in detail in 1941 in the famous book by Glasstone, Laidler, and Eyring[6], and since then in most books on physical biochemistry.

Essentially the reacting molecules are pictured (refer to Figure 8-4) as proceeding through a state in which they are in a metastable state called the "activated complex," which is more or less in equilibrium with reactants in the initial state, 1. While in this complex, the molecules can either proceed to form product, the final state, or return to reactants, the initial state.

If equilibrium can exist between reactants and complex, the thermodynamic functions can apply to this part of the reaction: thus $H^{\ddagger} - H_1 = \Delta H^{\ddagger}$; $S^{\ddagger} - S_1 = \Delta S^{\ddagger}$; and $F^{\ddagger} - F_1 = \Delta F^{\ddagger}$.

From statistical mechanical arguments the pre-exponential term by this theory reduces to·

$$\tau \; \frac{k_g T}{h} \; e^{\Delta S^{\ddagger}/R}$$

where τ is a "transmission coefficient," which expresses the fraction of complexes which proceed to products (often assumed to be 1.0); k_g is the ideal gas constant per molecule ($R/6 \times 10^{23} = 1.38 \times 10^{-16}$ erg per deg C per molecule), and h is Planck's constant (6.63×10^{-27} erg sec).

The over-all rate, then, for a reaction such as that considered on p. 194, is:

$$v = [A]^a [B]^b \tau \frac{k_g T}{h} e^{\Delta S^{\ddagger}/R} \; e^{-\Delta H^{\ddagger}/RT}$$

It can be seen that a measured value of rate, v, at known concentrations of A and B, plus a measured value of the activation energy, $\Delta H^{\ddagger}$, permits the value of $\Delta S^{\ddagger}$ to be obtained.

Especially in biological processes has the evaluation of the entropy of activation been important. Remember, the entropy change tells us whether the heat capacity of the system has increased or decreased during the reaction, and since the heat energy contained within molecules increases with the complexity of the molecule, it is often possible to infer certain physical properties of the activated state, and hence of the molecular movements during reaction. This technique has proved useful in learning about the mechanism of muscle contraction, for example, certain details of which are considered in Chapter 10.

In short, the rate of a process depends upon the concentrations and the temperature, and on the free energy change accompanying the formation of the activated complex from reactants.

The role of a catalyst is to provide an alternate path which is energetically easier. Thus the catalyst, because of the energetic advantages it offers, acts as a guide-post to direct the reaction through preferred channels or pathways (see Figure 8-4 (b)). This subject is now explored further.

Catalyzed Reactions; Enzymes

There are many chemical reactions and physical processes whose rate or pathway is controlled by one or more catalysts. Far surpassing all the rest in importance as biological catalysts are the enzymes. These are large protein molecules, which are often bound with metallic ions and are always heavily hydrated. They have the special property that at some site(s) on the surface both the kinds of atoms and their arrangement are such that more or less specific adsorption of a "substrate" molecule can occur. The substrate molecule is the one which is to undergo hydrolysis, hydrogenation, trans-ammination, or some other reaction.

In addition to the kind of atoms and their arrangement, a third essential requirement of the enzyme seems to be the presence, in the vicinity, of a large electric charge, usually in the form of a metallic ion such as Mg^{++}, or a charged chemical group, such as $-PO_4^{-2}$. The role of the charged group is to distort the electronic structure of the substrate molecule as it adsorbs on the enzyme, thus to make it energetically easier for the desired reaction to occur. The most easily measured manifestation of a catalyzed process is a lowered activation energy, E^*. Some values are collected in Table 8-4. Note especially the numbers for the decomposition of H_2O_2.

TABLE 8-4. Activation Energies for Some Catalyzed Biological Reactions.

Reaction	Catalyst	E^* (Cal/mole)
Inversion of sucrose	acid (H_3O^+)	20.6
	trypsin-kinase[a]	14.4
	malt invertase	13.0
	yeast invertase	11.5
Hydrolysis of ethyl butyrate	acid (H_3O^+)	13.2
	pancreatic lipase	4.2
Decomposition of hydrogen peroxide (H_2O_2)	no catalyst	17 to 18
	platinum	11.5
	Fe^{++}	10.1, 8.5
	liver catalase	5.5
Hydrolysis of urea	acid (H_3O^+)	24.5
	urease	12.5 to 6.5

[a] The suffix "ase" denotes enzyme.

A typical process can be illustrated as in Figure 8-5, and described as follows, a hydrolysis serving as the example: First the molecule to be hydrolyzed (the substrate molecule, S) bumps into the hydrated enzyme molecule, E; and if the collision occurs at the active site and is energetic enough, a slight bond will be made between the two, forming the enzyme-substrate complex, ES. The complex can then do one of two things: it can fall apart again (in which case we lose interest); or it can be "activated"—i.e., given excess energy by favorable collisions with its neighbors—and associate with a water molecule close by, to form the activated complex, $ES^{\ddagger}$. This in turn can either fall apart the way it was formed, or it can proceed on to split up in a new way—as reaction products—with the substrate molecule hydrolyzed and the enzyme ready to go again.

The process is sketched at the top of Figure 8-5, the energy of the reaction path at the bottom, and the formal equation in the middle. For the purpose of formulation of the rate equations, the reaction can be written:

$$E + S \underset{k_{-1}}{\overset{k_1}{\rightleftharpoons}} ES \text{ (formation of the Michaelis complex, } ES) \quad \ldots\ldots\ldots 1$$

$$ES \underset{ES\ddagger}{\overset{k_2}{\longrightarrow}} \text{ products (activation and reaction to products)} \ldots\ldots\ldots\ldots 2$$

where k_1, k_{-1}, and k_2 are the specific rate constants for the respective steps.

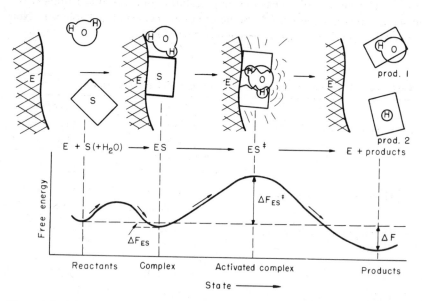

Figure 8-5. Schematic Representation of Catalyzed Hydrolysis Reaction, Showing Formation and Activation of the Intermediate Complex, ES.

Now this reaction can be very complicated, but for our purpose it will suffice to consider one (the simplest) set of conditions, and examine how the rate varies with changes in either enzyme or substrate concentration. First we assume that v_{-1} is much faster than v_2, and therefore that reaction 1 is essentially at equilibrium, or that $K_{eq} = k_1/k_{-1}$.

The rate is then given by

$$v_2 = k_2[ES]$$

where the square bracket again denotes concentration. Now the only problem remaining is to compute $[ES]$ from the equilibrium constant. If the initial concentrations of enzyme and substrate, respectively, are $[E]_0$ and $[S]_0$, the concentrations of free E and S are given by

$$[E] = [E]_0 - [ES]$$

and

$$[S] = [S]_0 - [ES]$$

and therefore the equilibrium constant is given by

$$K_{eq} = \frac{[ES]}{([E]_0 - [ES])\,([S]_0 - [ES])}$$

This becomes simpler if only the usual case is considered, namely that in which the substrate concentration is much higher than the enzyme concentration; for under this condition only a small fraction of the substrate molecules will ever be tied up as complexes ES because there are so few enzyme molecules with which the substrate can form a complex. Hence

$$[S]_0 - [ES] \approx [S]_0$$

Rearrangement gives

$$[ES] = \frac{K_{eq}[E]_0[S]_0}{1 + K_{eq}[S]_0} = \frac{[E]_0[S]_0}{K_m + [S]_0}$$

if K_m is defined as $1/K_{eq}$. This holds for *any* value of $[S]$ at any time.

Therefore the rate, v_2, of the enzyme-catalyzed reaction (proportional to the concentration of complexes) is:

$$v_2 = -d[S]/dt = \frac{k_2[E]_0[S]}{K_m + [S]}$$

This is the rather celebrated Michaelis-Menten Equation, and describes the rate as a function of initial substrate concentration under the particular conditions we assumed. A plot of v_2 vs $[S]_0$ is shown in Figure 8-6 for both high and low enzyme concentrations. The expression says that: (1) the rate is

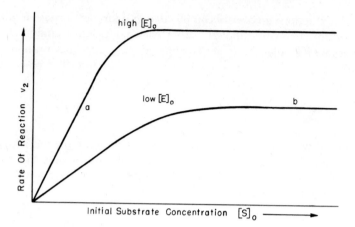

Figure 8-6. Rate of a Catalyzed Reaction as a Function of Substrate Concentration for Two Different Concentrations of Catalyst.

always proportional to the enzyme concentration if the substrate is much in excess; (2) the order, or the index of the substrate concentration, declines from unity down to zero as substrate concentration is increased. In other words, (note Figure 8-6, region a) if substrate is in great excess, $[S]_0 >> K_m$, and $K_m + [S]_0 \approx [S]_0$, and the rate expression reduces to

$$v_2 = k_2[E]_0$$

with rate independent of substrate concentration; but (note region b) if the substrate is in excess of enzyme, yet $[S]_0 << K_m$, and $K_m + [S]_0 \approx K_m$, the rate expression reduces to

$$v_2 = \frac{k_2}{K_m}[S]_0[E]_0$$

with rate increasing linearly with substrate concentration.

It is clear then that the nature and the extent of the binding of the enzyme-substrate complex, ES (i.e., the value of K_m) is all-important: the bigger the Michaelis constant the smaller the extent of binding; and the weaker the binding, the slower the rate of hydrolysis.

It is by good chance* that these E-S complexes generally absorb electro-magnetic radiation in the visible and near ultraviolet regions of the spectrum. Hence their existence, as well as their K_m, can be determined spectro-photometrically (by light absorption), and the value of K_m compared with

---

*This work was pioneered and developed to a highly specialized art by Britton Chance, of Yale University.

that obtained by measuring rates at various concentrations of substrate and enzyme.

The "catalyst law" (for enzymes, the Michaelis-Menten expression) rearranges to

$$\frac{v}{[S]_0} = k_2 K_{eq}[E]_0 - K_{eq} \cdot v$$

from which it is seen that the slope of a plot of $v/[S]_0$ vs v gives K_{eq} ($= 1/K_m$) directly as the negative of the slope. Figure 8-7 is such a plot for the hydrolysis of a particular dipeptide for which the stomach enzyme, pepsin, is a specific catalyst. The value of K_m obtained is 0.0014 moles liter^{-1}. This result is typical. The inverse, the value of K_{eq} at 25°, will usually be found to be between 100 and 600 liters/mole, which means that the substrate must be in excess 100- to 600-fold over the enzyme if the catalyst is to be more than 90 per cent complexed (i.e., "worked hard") at all times.

There are cases (certain chymotrypsin-catalyzed reactions, for example) in which the binding of the complex is much stronger. By contrast, the myosin-adenosine triphosphate complex, formed during muscle contraction is relatively a very weak complex.... The value of K_m is numerically equal to that value of the substrate concentration at which one-half the enzyme molecules are tied up as complexes. Electrical attractions and repulsions as well as the geometry of the molecules E and S determine the extent of

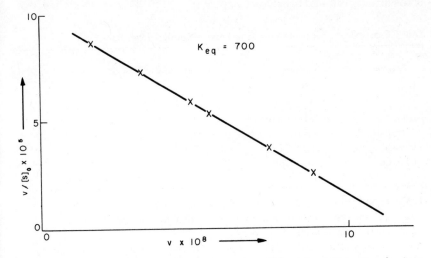

Figure 8-7. Determination of the Binding Constant of the Intermediate Complex in a Catalyzed Reaction (pepsin-catalyzed hydrolysis of carbobenzoxy-glutamyl-tyrosine ethyl ester, a dipeptide). Values plotted are those of initial rates found experimentally for six different initial concentrations of substrate.

binding and hence the specificity of a particular catalyst for a particular reaction.

Not all of the assumptions made nor the conditions assumed in the foregoing analysis are always met. Because equilibrium does not always exist in reaction 1, K_m can better be expressed as $(k_{-1} + k_2)/k_1$, which of course reduces to $1/K_{eq} = k_{-1}/k_1$ if $k_{-1} >> k_2$, the case we have studied already. There are further complications, such as competition by two or more reactants for the one active site, which introduce more terms in the expression for v. Although these are of pragmatic interest in biological chemistry, further discussion here is beyond our scope—our purpose is simply to illustrate complex formation and saturation of a catalyst.

It should be remembered that the rate constant, k_2, can be factored into

$$k_2 = \tau \frac{k_g T}{h} e^{-\Delta H\ddagger/RT} e^{\Delta S\ddagger/R}$$

Because the change in entropy $\Delta S^\ddagger$ accompanying activation gives an indication of the change in the freedom of motion within the complex $ES^\ddagger$, determinations of $\Delta S^\ddagger$ and $\Delta H^\ddagger$ have become very powerful tools for understanding the mechanism on a molecular scale. Some values are given in Table 8-5. A very interesting success story of this kind centers on myosin, the contractile substance in muscle and the catalyst for ATP hydrolysis. The "state of the art" is reviewed briefly in Chapter 10.

TABLE 8-5. Kinetic Parameters for Some Enzyme-Catalyzed Reactions.*

Enzyme	Substrate	T (deg C)	pH	$1/K_m$ (moles^{-1})	k_2 (sec^{-1})	E_2*	ΔS_2*
Pepsin	carbobenzoxy-l-glu-tamyl-l-tyrosine	32	4.0	560	0.0014	20.2	4.6
α-Chymo-trypsin	benzoyl-l-tyrosine ethyl ester	25	7.8	250	78	9.2	−21.4
Urease	urea [CO(NH₂)₂]	21	7.1	250	20,000	9.7	− 7.2
Myosin	adenosine triphosphate (ATP)	25	7.0	79,000	104	13.0	− 8.0

$1/K_m$: equilibrium constant for formation of ES complex (see Figure 8-5).

  k_2: specific rate constant for unimolecular breakdown of the ES complex.

  E_2*: energy of activation of ES complex.

ΔS_2*: entropy of activation of ES complex. Negative values are usually interpreted as evidence for the freeing of charged groups resulting in orientation of water molecules during activation.

Values in the last three columns were taken at high substrate concentration and therefore refer to the activation of ES complex into product.

*See the book by Laidler[15] for collections of data.

Generalization of Method

Enzymes are not the only catalysts in the living system, of course. Surfaces, acid (H^+), base (OH^-), and metallic ions are all important catalysts. The general principles outlined above apply to these equally as well as to enzymes. The factoring method of analyzing rates—that of extracting from the proportionality constant one after another the variables and universal constants upon which the rate of a process depends—in some ways has reached its highest state of development in chemical kinetics; and it is scoring rather remarkable successes with some very complicated biochemical reactions. Whether this method of analysis, which ultimately reduces to analysis of the intermolecular forces and molecular movements of a biological process, is properly termed "biophysical chemistry" or "chemical biophysics," is often uselessly debated. It is a matter of definition; and no definition has yet been generally accepted. We use this illustration of the factoring method not only to discuss the velocity of biochemical reactions in terms of molecular interactions, but also by analogy to discuss in the following sections the velocities of the physical processes of transport, namely diffusion, osmosis (a special case of diffusion), viscous flow, electrical conductivity of solutions and tissue, and heat conduction.

ON DIFFUSION; OSMOSIS

Diffusion may be defined as the movement, in a preferred direction, of one component relative to the other components, of a mixture or solution. The preferred direction is from the place of higher concentration to the place of lower concentration of diffusing substance. No flow of the whole fluid need occur—no turbulence, nor even convection; no gravitation, no electrical field is of importance to transport by pure diffusion.

The fact that diffusion occurs is not surprising when one remembers that all molecules are in a state of continuous motion. The more molecules of type P there are present in a particular volume of solution, the greater the likelihood that some of these will gain enough excess energy to find their way out of this volume. Consider two unit volumes with a common face, one with concentration P in Q higher than the other (Figure 8-8). Because all molecules are in continuous motion (i.e., have kinetic or thermal energy), on the average more P molecules from volume 1 pass into volume 2 than the reverse. In fact, the greater the concentration difference (actually the gradient dc/dx), the greater the speed at which they diffuse, other things being equal. Figure 7-7 was an earlier impression of this same idea.

If, however, some sort of barrier to diffusion is placed between volumes 1 and 2, the rate at which P diffuses is slowed down; and the greater the thickness of this barrier the lower the rate becomes. To a first approximation,

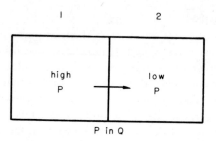

Figure 8-8. Illustration of Direction of Diffusion of P in a Mixture of P in Q.

therefore, it is the rate of change of concentration, c, with distance, x, which determines the rate of diffusion.

These intuitions were first set down and experimentally proven by the ingenious German anatomist, Adolf Fick, in 1855:

$$j = DA \frac{dc}{dx} \quad \text{(Fick's first law)}$$

where dc/dx is the instantaneous rate of change of concentration with distance, called the concentration gradient, in moles per liter per cm; "j" is the flux (i.e., the flow rate, v)—the number of moles passing through a particular area, A cm^2, in 1 sec; and D is the proportionality constant, which contains all the other factors—some of them still unknown—upon which the rate of diffusion depends. Self-diffusion of water across an erthythrocyte membrane is an example. Absorption of gaseous O_2 by the blood capillaries in the lung is another example: both the partial pressure of O_2 and the concentration in the circulating blood plasma are constant in time. Fick's first law is limited to the case in which concentrations do not change—the steady-state condition—and the source and the sink are infinite.

However, there are many specific cases, particularly in the gastrointestinal tract and associated with assimilation of the degraded products of foods, in which the concentration gradient is not constant, the state is not steady. Any periodic or sporadic phenomenon which makes a sudden change in the rate of supply of reactants to a certain part of the living thing, will cause a deviation from the steady state. Thus in the volume in which the change occurs, the rate of change of concentration, dc/dt, is given by

$$dc/dt = D\, d^2c/dx^2 \quad \text{(Fick's second law)}$$

Since d^2c/dx^2 can be written $\frac{d}{dx}\left(\frac{dc}{dx}\right)$, and since dc/dx is the concentration gradient, we see that the second law states that the rate at which the concentration changes within a volume is proportional to the rate of change of the concentration gradient at the boundaries of the volume.

One simple example will be used to illustrate the problem described by Fick's second law. This will be done only qualitatively, for the detailed description is too complicated to be practical here. Consider the red blood cell, with various components contained within, and separated from the medium by a membrane, the cell wall. There are fluids on both sides of the wall in osmotic equilibrium (see Chapter 2). This is a condition of no net change: potassium ion, at higher concentration inside the cell is being transported in *both* directions across the cell at equal rates; sodium ion, at higher concentration outside the cell, is being transported in by diffusion, out by "active transport," but both at the same rate so that there is no net change. Water moves across the membrane freely in both directions. (Recent radioactive tracer experiments using tritium have shown that complete exchange of water can occur in a few milliseconds.) If for some reason the "sodium pump," which provides the active transport, fails, then both K^+ and Na^+ will diffuse passively, each in the direction towards lower concentration (Figure 8-9). The rate of diffusion, expressed by the rate of change of concentration, dc/dt, is given by the second law as $D\,d^2c/dx^2$. Solution of the equation for c, gives c as a function of t; or $c = f(t)$. The form, f, can be worked out explicitly, provided certain other conditions are known. The result is approximately $c_{K^+} = c_1 + c_2/\sqrt{t + t_0}$ for the decay of the internal K^+ concentration and $c_{Na^+} = c_1' - c_2'/\sqrt{t + t_0}$ for the buildup of internal Na^+ concentration to the concentrations of K^+ and Na^+ in the plasma in

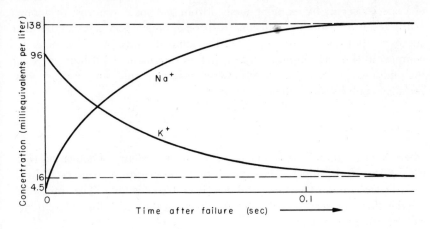

Figure 8-9. Readjustment of Concentration of Na^+ and K^+ Inside the Erythrocyte Following Failure of the Sodium Pump—A Diffusion-Controlled Process. Final values, 138 and 16, are those of the plasma.

which the cells are bathed. The inverse square root relationship occurs over and over again in diffusion-controlled processes.

In Figure 8-9 are shown the initial concentrations (milliequivalents per liter) of Na^+ and K^+ inside the cell (at $t = 0$), and their change toward the concentrations in the plasma (dotted lines) following failure of the sodium pump.

Diffusion Coefficient D, and Permeability Constant P.

Table 8-6 gives some representative values for the diffusion coefficient at $25°C$ in $cm^2 sec^{-1}$. The activation energy and the temperature coefficient of rate of diffusion in water solutions and in fat and lipid, were given in Table 8-3.

TABLE 8-6.   Some Diffusion Coefficients (D) $(cm^2 sec^{-1})$.

Substance into Water (at 12° C)	$D \times 10^5$
Glycerine	0.42
$MgSO_4$	0.35
KCl	1.59
NaCl	1.09
Sugar	0.29
Urea	1.12

Just as the specific rate constant of a chemical reaction can be broken down into the factors upon which it depends, so also can the diffusion coefficient be factored. Diffusion is a "jump process," in which the movement of a species occurs by its being pushed from one position of rest to another as the result of favorable collisions with neighbors. The distance between successive positions of rest is called the jump distance, λ. The activated complex in this case is pictured as being an intermediate position in which the jumping species is half way between rest sites and can go either way. Detailed analysis shows that

$$D = \tau \lambda^2 \frac{k_g T}{h} e^{-\Delta F\ddagger/RT}$$

where λ is the jump distance in cm, $\Delta F^\ddagger$ is the free energy of activation (Figure 8-4) for the "jumper," T is the absolute temperature (degrees Kelvin), k_g is the Boltzmann constant, and h is Planck's constant. The units of D are therefore $cm^2 sec^{-1}$. Table 8-6 gives some values of D for different species diffusing into water.

As in the case of chemical reactions, the term $k_g T/h$ is a constant at any temperature. The low diffusion constants (in molasses, in lipids, or in fats) and high values (in water or alcohol) are determined by the values of λ, and by $\Delta F^{\ddagger}$, the energy of binding within the shroud of neighboring molecules through which the jumping species must penetrate if it is to move successfully to the next position of rest.

Two innovations have been introduced into discussions of diffusion in recent years, one for theoretical reasons and the other for practical reasons. Firstly, it is more proper to consider activities (effective concentrations) than measured concentrations, and more proper still to consider as the "force," the gradient of the chemical potential which drives the diffusion process; and therefore dc/dx is replaced by $d\mu/dx$, in the more esoteric discussions, if not in practice.

Secondly, the thickness of the interface, at a cell wall for instance, is really a matter of definition rather than of position of chemicals. Who can say where the water phase stops and the heavily hydrated protein of the wall begins? Therefore dc/dx is hard to measure for living membranes, and recourse is made to a phenomenological trick: dx is taken *into* the diffusion constant, and the rate of flow is expressed as the difference between the flows in the two directions through the membrane. Thus

$$j = \mathcal{P}_1 A c_1 - \mathcal{P}_2 A c_2$$

where 1 and 2 represent diffusions in the forward and back reactions, and c_1 and c_2 represent concentrations on the two sides; the $\mathcal{P}$'s then have units cm sec^{-1} (velocity) and are called *permeability constants*. A few of these are collected in Table 8-7 for monovalent cations penetrating through living membranes. These permeability constants can be compared with values determined for synthetic interfaces also given in the table.

TABLE 8-7.   Some Permeability Constants ($\mathcal{P}$) for Synthetic and Biological Membranes.*

Interface Diffusion		Permeability Constant $\times 10^8$ (cm sec^{-1})
K$^+$ into erythrocyte of:	man	5.0
	dog	1.0
	rat	10
KCl, KBr, KI into nitrobenzene		0.007, 0.075, 1.4
Na$^+$ into erythrocyte of:	rabbit	3.0
	dog	0.5
Na$^+$ through frog skin		5.0
Na$^+$ (as iodide) into nitrobenzene		0.2
Alcohols into erythrocyte		10,000 to 100,000
Water into erythrocyte		~10,000

*Collected by J. T. Davies, *J. Phys. Coll. Chem.*, **54**, 185 (1950). See also Ref. 17.

For ionic flow the values in the table can be transformed very easily into electrical resistance units. Thus if the concentration of the salt at the membrane is 1 mole per liter, the values come out to 1000 to 50,000 ohms/cm^2, in general agreement with values found by direct measurement for living membranes. The values determined depend on the permeability, discussed later.

Osmosis

Following the foregoing discussion, very little needs to be said about osmosis. It is simply the diffusion of water from the place of higher water concentration to the place of lower water concentration. More properly, it is the diffusion of water down an activity (effective concentration) gradient. The speed of the process is described by Fick's laws—the first for the steady state of constant concentrations, and the second for the unsteady state of changing concentrations.

Osmotic pressure and water balance, both properties of the equilibrium state, were discussed in Chapter 2.

As an anatomist, Fick naturally had an interest in these important processes; but this interest must have been accompanied by a remarkable insight.

ON FLUID FLOW; BLOOD

Poiseuille's Law

Holding a special place among the kinetic processes of importance in biology is the transport of fluids, both gases and liquids, along tubes and in and out of storage chambers. One need mention only the circulation of blood and the respiration of air as examples.

The first striking fact is the flow itself: it takes place (almost) no matter how small the applied mechanical force; and the rate of flow increases linearly with increasing driving force. Flow is opposed by frictional forces or "internal barriers" which the moving fluid must surmount—the smaller the internal barriers the faster the flow resulting from a given applied force.

Ideally at least, as was first stated by the French physicist, J. L. Poiseuille, in 1884, a liquid moves in a tube by the sliding of one imaginary layer of liquid over another. The surface layer moves very slowly, if at all, relative to the speed of layers far removed from the surface. The presumed velocity distribution is indicated by the lengths of the arrows in Figure 8-10.

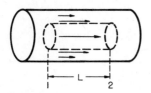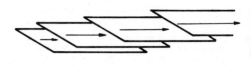

Figure 8-10. The Gliding Layers in Nonturbulent Fluid Flow. Length of the arrow is proportional to speed.

If P_1 and P_2 are the pressures measured at the points 1 and 2 in the tube, and R is the distance from the center bore of the tube, the driving force is given by

$$\pi R^2 (P_1 - P_2)$$

The frictional force on the layer at distance R from the center is proportional to the area of the layer $(2\pi Rl)$, and to the velocity difference between the layer we are considering and its nearest neighbors; in the limit this is dv/dR.

After the two forces have been equated, integration (or summing all velocities from that at the center of the tube to zero at the wall) gives

$$v = \phi \, \frac{P_1 - P_2}{4l} \, (r^2 - R^2)$$

where r is the radius of the tube. This expression gives the linear speed of the layer which is R cm from the center. ϕ is the proportionality constant, and is called the *fluidity* (the higher its value the higher the velocity).

The total volume of fluid flowing per second through the tube is calculated by summing all the elemental volumes, $2\pi R\, dR$, for which v is expressed. The result is the celebrated Poiseuille equation which expresses rate of flow (cc/sec) of liquid through a tube of radius r and length l under an applied pressure difference of $\Delta P = P_1 - P_2$:

$$dV/dt = \phi \, \frac{\pi r^4}{8l} \, \Delta P \quad \text{cc/sec}$$

If ΔP is given in dynes per cm^2, r and l in cm, and the speed of flow in cc per sec, the fluidity, ϕ, must be cm per sec for a force gradient of 1 dyne per cm; i.e., ϕ has the dimensions: $\dfrac{cm}{sec} \Big/ \dfrac{dyne}{cm}$. It is the velocity of flow of a fluid under a unit force gradient.

The case for gases is slightly more complicated because of the added fact that the volume depends strongly upon the pressure and the temperature. With the proper modifications the expression for rate of flow of gases approximates:

$$dV/dt = \phi \, \frac{\pi r^4}{16l} \cdot \frac{P_1^2 - P_2^2}{P_0}$$

if P_0 is the pressure at which the volume is measured.

Fluidity, ϕ, and Viscosity, η

Table 8-8 gives values of the fluidities of various substances at different temperatures. Of the liquids, ether is the most fluid one listed; glycerine at $0°C$ is the least fluid—indeed at $0°C$ it is almost a glass! The fluidity of

TABLE 8-8. Fluidities (ϕ) $\left(\text{poise}^{-1}, \text{or } \dfrac{cm}{sec}\bigg/\dfrac{dyne}{cm}\right)$

Temp (°C)	Hydrogen	Air	Ether	Benzene	Water	Butyric Acid	Castor Oil	Glycerine
−30	13040	6490						
0	11980	5850	352	110	56	44	0.00041	0.000083
10	11760	5680	392	132	78	50	0.0013	0.0011
25	11300	5410	450	164	112	71	0.0036	0.005
37	10990	5290	500	196	144	85	0.01	0.02
50		5150	552	227	182	105		
100		4440			352			

gases decreases as the temperature is raised (see Chapter 2); but that of all liquids increases with increasing temperature. In liquids the higher the temperature the greater the number of particles which have the energy to overcome the internal barriers to flow; or in other words, the higher the temperature the smaller the sticky frictional forces which must be overcome by the gliding laminae, and the faster the flow. The temperature coefficient of fluidity, factored as a specific rate constant, is given in the theory of rates as

$$\phi = \tau \,\frac{\overline{V}}{hN}\, e^{-\Delta F\ddagger/RT} = \tau\, \frac{\overline{V}}{hN}\, e^{\Delta S\ddagger/R}\, e^{-\Delta H\ddagger/RT}$$

where $\overline{V}$ is the volume of 1 mole of fluid, h is Planck's constant, N is number of molecules per mole, Avogadro's number, and $\Delta F\ddagger$, $\Delta S\ddagger$, and $\Delta H\ddagger$ refer to formation of 1 mole of activated complex in the glide plane as it slips from. one position of rest to the next .... The physical analogy between diffusion and flow thus is extended to the algebraic statement of the factors upon which they depend. The two processes can be directly compared in Tables 8-7 and 8-8. The experimental values of E^* (related to $\Delta H\ddagger$) are usually the same for diffusion and flow (Table 8-3). This indicates the inherent similarity of the two processes. Indeed in diffusion *the particles move individually at random* from one position of rest to the next. In flow *a plane of particles moves as a unit,* and no relative motion occurs between members of a plane; adjacent planes glide past each other. The intermolecular forces which oppose diffusion are the same as those which oppose laminar flow. That is, the barriers to flow are the same, and hence E^*'s are the same. The catalysts in this case are called surface-active agents. Washing detergents are good examples.

The inverse of the fluidity, i.e., $1/\phi$, is called the *viscosity,* usually expressed by the symbol η. Hence a high viscosity (cold molasses) means low fluidity. Viscosity can be considered as the frictional force opposing the flow. Its dimensions are $\dfrac{\text{dynes}}{\text{cm}} \Big/ \dfrac{\text{cm}}{\text{sec}}$, or dyne sec/cm^2; this unit is called the *poise*, after Poiseuille.

A very simple way to measure fluidity or viscosity is in the Ostwald viscometer. The capillary pipette is filled to a mark with fluid, and measurement made of the time it takes the fluid to run out of the pipette. This time is divided into the time taken by water, or some other fluid, to drain at the same temperature. The quotient is called the *relative viscosity*. A density correction is necessary if the driving force (gravitational) is to be equal in the two cases.

Solutions or suspensions (of molecules or particles respectively) in water usually increase the viscosity (decrease the fluidity). The fractional increase is $(\eta_s - \eta_0)/\eta_0$, where the subscripts s and 0 refer to solution and pure water, respectively. But this value, often called η', varies with the concentration. It is convenient, then, to measure the η' at several concentrations, and express each measurement in terms of unit concentration by dividing by the concentration at which the measurement was made. This number is called the *specific viscosity*. It is also concentration-dependent, because intermolecular interactions are higher at higher concentrations. It is useful, then, to extrapolate measurements of specific viscosity to infinite dilution (zero concentration), for this value is the value of that part of the viscosity due to the suspension only, and unaffected by interactions which solute particles could have on each other. This value is called *intrinsic viscosity*, usually symbolized $[\eta]$. Values range from .02 for small-molecular-weight solutes to 20 for macromolecules, and to much higher values for suspensions of living cells.

Turbulent Flow

Laminar flow will exist in most fluids at low rates of flow. When the flow rate becomes high, the glide planes get off-track, and turbulence sets in. Small whirlpools and eddy currents are initiated, and the fluidity drops abruptly; therefore, if the rate of flow is to be maintained, higher driving force must be applied and more energy must be expended. Unless some result of particular value is derived from the turbulence (more rapid mixing of chemical reactants at a reaction site, for example), it is obviously wasteful of energy. The circulatory system in man has certain features, such as flexible walls lined with hydrated protein "hairs," which help direct the fluid flow and damp out trends toward turbulence.

The Reynolds number, Re, a dimensionless parameter of fluid flow, is defined as

$$Re = 2\phi\rho\, vr$$

where ρ is the density of the flowing fluid, ϕ the fluidity, v the velocity of flow, and r the tube radius. For homogeneous liquids flowing at constant velocity, it is general experience that the flow is laminar and turbulence cannot be maintained if $Re \lesssim 2000$. For blood, Re has been found to be 970 ± 80 over the pertinent range of flow rates and tube sizes. Therefore, laminar flow probably occurs in the blood vessels at all times, although turbulence may set in momentarily at the valves during the pumping action of the heart.

Properties of Blood Plasma and Blood

Previous discussion has implied that the fluidity (velocity per unit force gradient) is independent of speed of flow, v. Liquids for which this is true are called *Newtonian liquids*. Pure water is a good example.

However, most real liquids are at least slightly "non-Newtonian"—that is, $\phi = f(v)$. One of the most complex examples of this behavior is blood—a suspension of cells in plasma, which itself is a water solution of salts and heavily hydrated macromolecules.

Figure 8-11 is taken from results which show that the ease of pushing the fluid through a tube—in this case a glass one—decreases rapidly with introduction of macromolecules and cells into water. Thus the ϕ for plasma is about half that for water $\left(144 \dfrac{\text{cm}}{\text{sec}} \middle/ \dfrac{\text{dyne}}{\text{cm}}\right)$; and increasing amounts of red blood cells reduce the fluidity still further. Yet, to a first approximation,

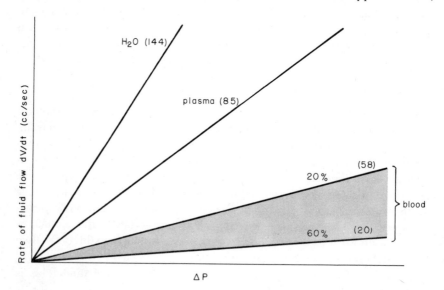

Figure 8-11. Rate of Flow of a Fluid Through a Tube as a Function of Driving Pressure. The slope is proportional to the fluidity, given in parentheses. The usual range of percentage of total fluid volume filled with cells is shaded in.

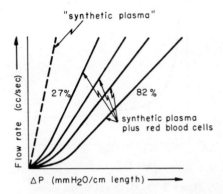

Figure 8-12. Fluidity (slope) of Synthetic Plasma to Which Different Volume Percentages of Cells Have Been Added.

within the physiological range of operation both plasma and whole blood are essentially Newtonian; that is, their curves are linear; Poiseuille's law of laminar flow is obeyed.

However, closer inspection of not only very low rates of flow but also very high rates reveals that the fluidities in these ranges are lower than in the intermediate range in Fig. 8-11: the fluidity is dependent upon flow rate in these regions. Thus at low flow rates an elasticity due to the formation of liquid crystals by hydrogen bonds makes flow more difficult and has to be broken down; at high flow rates turbulence sets in and makes flow more difficult.

Figure 8-12 illustrates the first point. Notice how the fluidity (slope) changes with flow rate, when flow is slow. On the other hand, turbulence can actually be *heard* (or its effects can be heard) over the heart where very high flow rates accompany the high pressure part of the beat.... The dependence of viscosity $(1/\phi)$ on tube radius (Figure 8-13), at first surprising, resolves to a question of the interruption of laminar flow when the diameter of the suspended particles (red blood cells) approaches the diameter of the tubes through which the suspension is flowing. This is the condition which exists in the blood capillaries—the process is more like an extrusion than a laminar flow. The velocity gradient across the tube is the cause of Bernoulli forces which not only make the cell *spin*, but also force it toward the center (the bore) of the tube. Further, the blood vessels are somewhat elastic and can increase their diameter under pressure. Thus the flow rate doubles for a 16 per cent increase in radius! This fact, plus the probably great difference between the surface of glass tubes and the molecular-hair-lined** blood

---

**These "molecular hairs" are hydrated protein molecules, partly detached from the wall, and jutting out into the tube.

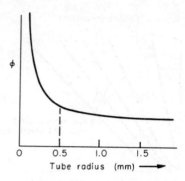

Figure 8-13. Fluidity of Whole Blood
vs Glass Tube Radius.

vessels, makes the whole study very complicated, easily subject to gross mis-interpretation, and certainly needing more careful experimental definition.

Circulation of Blood

Description of the circulatory system is not our objective here. This was done in 1628 by, at the time, the radical physician, Sir William Harvey, whose description of experiments proving the continuous circulation of the blood—from the heart through the systemic arterial and venous systems, back to the heart, thence through the pulmonary arterial and venous systems, and again back to the heart—is *still* one of the classics of clarity in medical literature.

The pressure difference between aorta and vena cava across the pump, the heart, is about 100 mm Hg, or 0.13 atm. Along the large arteries and veins and in the main arterial and venous branches, the pressure gradient is small; but because these vessels are of large radius, the flow rate is rapid. The pressure gradient is at its peak along the capillaries and the arterioles; because they have very small radii, the flow there is slowest—just where it should be the slowest—so that plenty of time exists for exchange to occur by diffusion through the walls of arterioles and capillaries. Figure 8-14 illus-

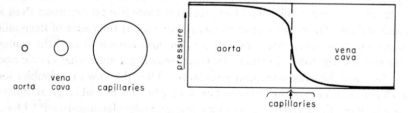

Figure 8-14. Relative Areas and Pressure Drops in Different Parts of the Human Circulatory System.

trates this point, showing the pressure changes and the relative *total* cross-sectional areas.

Two quantities can be measured, the flow rate (cc/sec), and the speed of flow (cm/sec). Measurements in the aorta show that enough blood flows past a flow-meter detector per second for one complete cycle to require 45 min. Insertion into the aorta of a bit of radioactive argon as an inert tracer, and measurement of how long it takes for the tracer to complete the ciruit, confirms this.

Speed is less easily measured. One method is by tracer. The ultrasonic method (see Chapter 3) introduces no pathological changes, but needs calibration.

ON ELECTRICAL CONDUCTANCE; EEG AND EKG

The next rate process to be considered in this chapter is the movement of ions under the influence of an electrical field—in other words, the conductance of solutions of salts in water. This subject is basic to an understanding of the gross current paths through the human body upon which are based the techniques of electrocardiography (EKG) and electroencepalography (EEG), and also basic to some of the transport processes driven by membrane potentials which are of importance in nerve conduction and electrical shock treatment.

Towards the latter part of the last century the big-three "solution" pioneers, Kohlrausch, Arrhenius, and Van't Hoff, showed that salts dissolve in water as ions. These are electrically charged and free to move about at random because of thermal energy, but subject to movement in a preferred direction under the force of an electrical voltage gradient. Positive ions are forced to the negative electrode, and negative ions to the positive electrode by the electrical field. The speed of movement, or mobility (centimeters per second under a voltage gradient of 1 v per cm) was understood quantitatively by 1923 (the work of Debye and Hückel, Onsager, and later others) as being determined by the ease with which a charged ion, complete with "hangers-on" such as electrically charged ions and water molecules, can slip from hole to hole in the liquid. The process is very similar to diffusion, which was described earlier. The difference is that *ions are charged and move under a voltage gradient*, whereas the *diffusing particle may or may not be charged and moves under a concentration gradient*. If a potential difference exists for any reason between two parts of an electrolyte, or is applied from the outside, ions move and current flows—in other words, charge is transferred. Hence this is just another transport process.

Ohm's Law Concerning Current

If n is the number of charge carriers per cc, w their average velocity under the impressed voltage, and q the electrical charge carried by each, then the amount of electrical charge passing per second through a plane of 1 cm² area, called the *current density*, I, is

$$I = nwq$$

If N is the number of molecules per mole: n/N is the concentration, c, in moles/cc; and qN is the charge per mole. The charge required to oxidize or reduce 1 mole of anything is $z\overline{F}$, where $\overline{F}$ is the charge (96,500 coulombs per equivalent weight) required to oxidize or reduce 1 g equivalent weight, and z is the number of equivalent weights per mole (i.e., the number of electrons transferred in the redox reaction). This is Faraday's law.

Summed (Σ) for all different ions, s, then

$$I = \overline{F} \sum_s c_s w_s z_s$$

Since c_s is moles/cc and w_s is cm/sec, the current density has the dimensions: coulombs per cm² per sec, or amperes per cm².

Note that the current increases linearly with the concentration of charged particles, with their speed, and with the charge they carry.

Specific Conductivity of a Solution, κ

This is defined as the current which passes for an impressed voltage gradient, $\mho$, of 1 v/cm. That is, $\kappa = I/\mho$. This is a form of Ohm's law. Now although the dissociation of ions of a salt is usually complete, sometimes there is association and always there is hydration, and hence often the effective "degree of dissociation," α, is less than 1. Introducing this concept gives

$$\kappa = \frac{\overline{F} \sum_s c_s w_s z_s}{\mho} \alpha \quad \frac{\text{amps}}{\text{volt/cm}} \quad \text{or ohm}^{-1}\text{cm}^{-1}$$

One more concept completes the picture. If the mobility, μ_s, which is the speed under an impressed voltage gradient of 1 v/cm, is defined as $w_s/\mho$, then

$$\kappa = \overline{F} \sum_s c_s \mu_s z_s \alpha$$

Note that this expression describes the rate of the electrical transport process. Thus κ *is the rate in amperes at which charge is transferred across 1-cm² area of electrolyte if the voltage gradient along the path is 1 v per cm.* The value is proportional to the concentration. The proportionality constant factors into three constants ($\alpha, z, \overline{F}$) and the mobility, μ; and μ is really the specific rate constant for the process. Therefore μ plays the same role for conductance as does k for chemical reactions, D for diffusion, and ϕ for fluid flow, respectively. The units of μ are $\dfrac{\text{cm}}{\text{sec}}\Big/\dfrac{\text{v}}{\text{cm}}$. Values of the mobilities of small ions average about 0.001 (see Table 8-9) for the ions of tissue fluids. The conductance, κ, then is easily computed from the above expression, since $\alpha \approx 1$ for salts in tissue fluids.

TABLE 8-9. Mobilities* (μ) of Selected Ions in Aqueous Solutions at 27° C.

H^+	362		OH^-	207
Na^+	52		Cl^-	79
K^+	77		I^-	80
NH_4^+	76		NO_3^-	74
$\frac{1}{2}Mg^{++}$	55		HCO_3^-	46
			$\frac{1}{2}SO_4^=$	83
			Benzoate$^-$	33

Blood Plasma Components:		
Albumins	5.7 to 6.2	
α-globulins	3.6 to 5.1	(buffered
β-globulins	2.5 to 3.2	at pH 8.6)
Fibrinogen	1.7 to 2.3	
γ-globulins	0.8 to 1.3	
Erythrocytes	13	

*Dimensions: $\dfrac{cm}{sec} \bigg/ \dfrac{v}{cm} \times 10^5$. For the small ions, the values refer to infinite dilution. From Ref. 20.

However, just as diffusion and fluid flow are concentration-dependent, so is electrical conductivity; and it is useful to express conductance per equivalent weight. It is called *equivalent conductance*, Λ, and is given by

$$\Lambda = \overline{F} \sum_s \mu_s \alpha \quad \frac{ohm^{-1}\ cm^{-1}}{equiv/l}$$

This is the most useful way to tabulate conductivity information; and values of Λ of importance in determining body currents are given in Table 8-10.

TABLE 8-10. Equivalent Conductances (Λ) for Selected Salts in Water.

Salt	Concentration, c (moles/l)		
	0.001	0.01	0.1
NaCl	124	119	107
KCl	147	141	129
KNO_3	142	133	120
$MgCl_2$	124	115	97
Na_2SO_4	124	112	90
$KHCO_3$	115	110	
NaI	124	119	109

The conductivity of a solution increases with increasing area and decreasing length of path. That is, it is given by

$$\kappa \, \frac{A}{L}$$

This, of course, is the inverse of resistance, which equals

$$(1/\kappa)\,(L/A) \;=\; \Re\,(L/A)$$

where $\Re$ is the specific resistance, or the *resistivity*.

Example: Calculate the electrical conductivity of a finger. A typical body solution contains about 100 meq of KCl per liter. The finger is about 10 cm long and 4 cm^2 in cross-sectional area.

$$Conductance \;=\; \kappa \, \frac{A}{L} \;=\; 129 \times 0.1 \times \frac{4}{10} \;=\; 5.2 \; ohms^{-1}$$

Resistance ($= 1/$conductance) $= 1/5.2 = 0.2$ ohms

Current driven through this column of solution by 110 v applied across the ends would be:

$$i \;=\; 110/0.2 \;=\; 550 \; amp$$

Hence body fluids are relatively good electrical conductors. By contrast, skin is relatively a very good insulating material, and provides a measure of protection against electrical shocks. It is estimated that 1 ma of total body current does irreparable internal damage. However, the calloused fingers of some electricians are legendary in this respect: some will span the contacts of a 110 v circuit with two fingers and allow the "tickle" to tell them whether or not the circuit is complete!

Difference in electrical mobility is the basis of electrophoretic separation of macromolecules, such as the globulins in solution. In Table 8-9 are some values which illustrate this. Characterization of the hemoglobins by this property was illustrated in Table 6-5. There it was called "l." Both l and μ are commonly used symbols for mobility.

The "Volume Conductor"

In a volume of electrolyte, the paths taken by the current depend upon the geometry (see Figure 8-15). Consider the two cases illustrated: (1) in a cylinder full of electrolyte, with glass walls and metal ends, the paths will be parallel; but (2) if the potential source is small relative to the electrolyte volume, the current paths diverge from the positive and converge back to the negative. Only two dimensions are represented in the figure, but the argument would be the same for three.

Analogy with metal electrical circuits is usefully drawn, for in metals the carrier is the electron cloud. Ohm's law is obeyed by electrolytic conductors

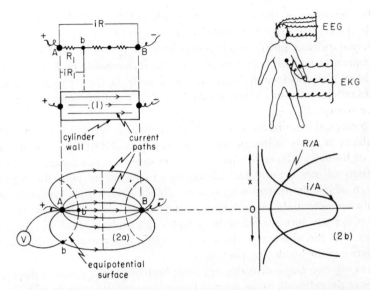

Figure 8-15. "Volume Conductors." *Top left*: Metallic. *Center and Bottom Left*: Electrolytic, with parallel (1) and diverging and converging (2) current paths. (2b) shows current density and resistance per unit area along current paths as a function of radial distance, x, from the straight line joining the sites (A and B) of potential difference. *Top right*: Positions of electrodes for electrocardiogram and electroencephalogram.

$(V = iR)$, and the voltage drop (iR_1) over any fraction of the resistor is proportional to the resistance, R_1, of the fraction in question. Thus (Figure 8-15) the total voltage drop across the resistor is iR, but is only iR_1 for the fraction A-b. The same arguments are true for the electrolytic case (1) above. However, if the current paths diverge (case (2)), certain paths are longer than others, and the resistance, per unit area, along the path is therefore higher. For a fixed voltage at the source, higher resistance means that smaller current will flow through the longer paths; in fact the current density (i.e., current per unit area along a path) will be high in the center, directly between the plates, lower as the radial distance, x, increases. The distributions of current density and of resistance, per unit area, along a path are shown in Figure 8-15, (2b). In the higher resistance paths on the outside of the volume conductor the total potential drop, V, between A and B has to be the same as in paths directly between the electrodes. In the outside paths, R is higher and the current density, i/A, is lower. Nevertheless, as in the metallic case, the voltage between two points, A and b, in the outside path, can be measured with a good voltmeter, and that value is numerically equal to the voltage between A and b' deep within the conductor.

The electrodes of the electrocardiograph (EKG) and electroencephalo-graph (EEG) are placed on the outside of such a volume conductor, the body, and measure potential differences between points in outside paths. If the concentrations of salts remain constant throughout the body, as they should in the steady-state, then any variations in the voltage measured should reflect variations in the internal currents resulting from variations in source voltage, E.

In biological systems the source of the potential difference between different places or spots is invariably a concentration difference, whether uni-ionic or bi-ionic. Concentration differences occur for two reasons: (1) ion selectivity of membranes, and (2) continuous exchange with the medium through which the distribution systems (blood and lymph systems) pass. Membrane potentials cancel out over the whole system, because the important ion selectors are cell walls, which completely enclose and isolate a volume. In the absence of disturbances then, concentration difference is the source of the bioelectric potentials.

However, two major disturbances exist, both of which "irritate" the membranes of the cell wall, cause them to become permeable, and thereby reduce the selectivity and permit mixing of otherwise separated salts. One is the *mechanical* pressure variations transmitted through the blood stream by the heart; the other is the *electrical* polarizing action of nerve. The former causes a concentration change by the application of a mechanical force, the latter by electrical interference with the membrane potentials of cells. Potential variations with time, between electrodes on the skull, above different lobes of the brain, give a precise record of the electrical action within the measured region; and electrodes placed on the torso and leg at spots where a major artery runs close to the surface, give a reliable record of the pumping action of the heart. Since any mechanical stimulus will cause momentary irritation (and therefore potential variations), the measurements are always made under controlled conditions when the electrical "noise" generated by the involuntary muscles of the organs (and always present) is at a minimum.

ON HEAT CONDUCTION; 98.6°F: A CONSTANT?

Heat Production

The human body has a heat capacity, as does any other, measured as the heat in calories required to raise 1 g 1°C. Also, the ambient (surrounding temperature may vary widely—for example, from 95°F (35°C) down to −20°F (−30°C). This lower value is 67 Centigrade degrees, or 119 Fahrenheit degrees, below body temperature, and yet the body is able to maintain within a small fraction of a degree the normal value of 37°C. Admittedly, insulation-aids such as skin, clothing, and hair play a large part; and the temperature in different parts of the body may vary. Especially on the outer part of the skin and in the extremities (fingers, toes), the temperature is lower than 37° C—i.e., at points farthest from the glycogen storehouse, the liver, and where the area to volume quotient is high.

As we saw in Chapter 7, heat is produced by oxidation of glycogens and by hydrolysis of fats and proteins. Under the reversible conditions of a perfect energy-converting machine, no heat energy would be given off as heat because ΔF is used for work and $T\Delta S$ is needed to establish the state conditions of the products of reaction. However, the body "machine" is not perfect, and in it conversions take place at efficiencies somewhat less than the maximum thermodynamic efficiency. Thus,

$$\Delta H = \Delta F' + q' + Q$$

where $\Delta F'$ is the work extracted, Q is the reversible, unavailable heat used to bring the products to the reaction temperature, and q' is that part of ΔF which could have been used to do work but which appears as heat because the "engine" could not extract the work reversibly. The degradation reactions of fats and proteins are especially inefficient from this point of view, and are thus good producers of "wasted" heat energy, q', which in fact is not wasted but serves to maintain body heat-content or temperature during cold weather. (Eskimos, for example, by design eat unprocessed animal fat for its heat-producing effects.)

Heat Loss; Fourier's Law

Heat energy is lost from the body by several mechanisms, all of which are simple physical transport processes or change-of-state processes. The basic method is by conduction, for which the rate of loss, v_1, is given by

$$v_1 = K_T A \frac{dT}{dx}$$

where A is the area exposed, T is temperature, and x is thickness of the insulation. If T is in degrees Fahrenheit, A in square feet, and thickness in inches, the rate of heat loss is given in BTU per hour; and the proportionality constant, K_T, is given in BTU per hr per sq ft of area per °F per in. of thickness. Common values of K_T for good insulating materials are: cork, 0.28; wood, 0.35; wool, 0.30; plaster, 0.48; fat, 0.33; skin, 0.30. Since

$$1 \frac{\text{BTU}}{\text{hr ft}^2 \,°\text{F/in.}} = 12 \frac{\text{Cal}}{\text{hr m}^2 \,°\text{C/cm}}$$

the conversion, if useful, is easy. Approximately 4 BTU = 1 Cal (or kcal). Usually engineers use the units on the left side of the conversion equality, and physiologists those on the right side.

The important effective-thickness term which determines dT/dx, depends upon the nature of the contact, whether skin-air, skin-water, skin-metal, etc., and also depends critically on the heat capacity and heat conductivity of the materials of the contact. Thus the rate of heat loss into cold water is greater than into cold air at the same temperature because of the higher heat capacity of the water; while the rate of heat loss to steel at the same temperature is greater because of the rate at which steel can conduct heat away.

Clothing increases the effective thickness and hence decreases the temperature gradient: so do hair, thickness of skin, and subcutaneous fat. One of the best insulators in the body is the dermis-epidermis combination, whose effective thickness changes with the ambient temperature by virtue of involuntary, lateral muscle movements which govern the depth of blood capillaries carrying the heat energy to be thrown away: in the cold these capillaries retract, thus increasing the effective thickness of the insulation.

Aides to Conduction

Conduction is aided—often exceeded—by convection, radiation and vaporization. A very brief account of these allied processes is now given, and then a comparison drawn among the relative methods of heat loss for man in different aspects.

For *convection* the rate is given by:

$$v_2 = K_2 \, dT/dx \, f(v) \qquad \text{Cal/hr}$$

where $f(v)$ is related to "wind chill" and increases with the velocity, v, of the air flowing over the surface. Convection losses are those of air circulation, and act primarily by removing the layers of semiwarmed air from above the surface of the skin, thus reducing the effective thickness of insulation.

The form of f is beyond the scope of this book, for it involves complex principles of eddy currents in the subject of aerodynamics. We shall content ourselves with the general observation that the stronger the breeze passing over the body, the greater the rate of cooling. In extreme cases this could be several hundred Cal/hr.

For *radiation* the rate, v_3, is given by

$$v_3 = \sigma A'(T_b^4 - T_a^4) \qquad \text{(the Stefan-Boltzmann law)}$$

where T_b is skin temperature, T_a is ambient temperature, A' is the body's *effective* radiating surface area (70 to 85 per cent of real area ($\sim$20 ft^2), depending upon posture and position, and correspondingly less if the area is clothed), and σ is the Stefan-Boltzmann constant. For the so-called blackbody, which the human body approximates in the sense that it absorbs and emits all wave lengths in the infrared (that is, those important at 37°C), the value of σ is about 0.045 Cal ft^{-2} deg^{-4} hr^{-1}. Thus if the surroundings are at $27°C$ ($T_a = 300°K$) and if the body is uncovered, up to 100 Cal/hr could be lost to the surroundings as infrared electromagnetic radiation alone.

For *vaporization*, the rate, v_4, is given by

$$v_4 = K_4 A_w f(v/d) \Delta P$$

where A_w is the *wetted* area of exposed skin; v is the velocity of the air; d is the effective thickness of the heated layer of air on the surface of the skin; $f(v/d)$ describes the convection which carries the moisture away; and ΔP is the driving "force," i.e., the difference in vapor pressure, P, of the liquid on the surface at skin temperature and that of water at the ambient temperature— the latter reduced by the relative humidity, RH. The important factor is the last one. Thus the liquid on the surface strives to set up an equilibrium pressure of vapor with the atmosphere which surrounds it, but never quite succeeds, since the atmosphere is nearly always undersaturated (RH < 100 per cent). For example, if the skin temperature is $34°C$ ($91°F$) and the RH = 60 per cent for an ambient of $20°C$ ($68°F$), quite common conditions,

$$\Delta P = P(34°) - 0.6P(20°) = 0.04 \text{ atm}$$

At very high temperatures ($T_a > 80°F$) this method is the body's escape valve for excess heat. Each gram of water lost by vaporization removes 0.58 Cal from the skin. In the lungs, inhaled air becomes saturated and then is

TABLE 8-11. Estimated Per Cent of Heat Loss, by Each of Four Principal Methods.

Activity	Body's Heat Loss (Cal/hr)	Per Cent of Skin Covered	Per Cent Heat Loss by			
			Conduction and Convection	Radiation	Water Loss from Skin	Respi- ration*
Studying, fully clothed, 70°F	150	85	68	20	10	2
Studying, lightly clothed, 70°F	200	15	20	58	20	2
Resting for BMR test, 70°F	70	15	20	70	8	2
Running mile race, 60°F	1500	25	20	20	50	10
Sunbathing on beach, 90°F	350	15	10	8	80	2
Walking, heavily clothed, 0°F	350	95	50	8	2	40

*Assume 50 per cent relative humidity. See Refs. 2 to 4, and 21.

TABLE 8-12. Formal Similarities Among Five Important Kinetic Processes.

Driving force and specific rate constant (left over after other experimentally extractable factors have been removed) are explicitly stated.

Process	Velocity Equation			Specific Rate Constant	
	Rate = Force factor	× Other Factors	× Specific Rate Constant	Name	Units
Chemical Reaction (Wilhelmy's law)	moles/sec = $dF/d\xi$	bV_C	k	sp. rate const.	$\dfrac{moles}{sec}\Big/dyne$
Diffusion (Fick's law)	moles/sec = dF/dx	$\dfrac{c}{RT}\cdot A$	D	diffusion coeff.	cm^2/sec
Fluid Flow Poiseuille's law	cc/sec = $\Delta P \cdot A$	$\dfrac{r^2}{8l}$	ϕ	fluidity	$\dfrac{cm^2}{sec}\Big/dyne$
Ion Transport (Ohm's law)	cou/sec = dE/dx	$A\overline{F}\;\alpha\sum_s c_s z_s$	μ_s	ionic mobility	$\dfrac{cm}{volt}\Big/\dfrac{sec}{cm}$
Heat Conduction (Fourier's law)	cal/sec = $S\,dT/dx$	$\dfrac{A}{S}$	K_T	thermal conductivity	$\dfrac{cal}{deg}\Big/\dfrac{sec}{cm}\,cm^2$

EXPLANATION:

b = a conversion factor, 4.18×10^{10} ergs = 1 Cal.

c = concentration (moles/cc); c_s = concentration of ion s.

α = ionized fraction of dissolved material.

$\sum_s c_s z_s \mu_s$ = sum of products of concentration, charge, and mobility of all ions present.

x = length (cm) along diffusion path or a conduction path; l = length (cm) along flowing fluid path.

r = tube radius (cm).

A = area (cm^2); V = volume (cm^3).

E = electrical potential (volts).

S = entropy (cal/deg. mole); TS = heat energy (cal/mole).

ξ = distance along a reaction path.

F = free energy (Cal/mole); $bF = 4.18 \times 10^{10} F$ ergs/mole (1 cal = 4.18 jou, and 1 jou = 10^7 ergs).

$dF/d\xi$ = force which drives a chemical reaction. Since $dF/d\xi$ cannot be measured, usually it is not factored from the rate constant, k, whose dimensions then become simply sec^{-1}.

$\phi = 1/\eta$: i.e., fluidity is the inverse of viscosity.

$(dF/dx \, c/RT) = dc/dx$, because $F = RT \ln c$. But dc/dx is not a force. If c/RT is replaced by b, then D has the units $\dfrac{\text{moles}^2}{\text{cm}^2 \text{ sec}}\Big/\text{dyne}$.

More rigorously, $\mu = RT \ln a$, where μ is chemical potential and a is (G. N. Lewis') activity, defined as effective mole fraction. From this, $d\mu/dx \cdot a/RT = da/dx$. Then D has units moles. cm^2/dyne because μ has units cal/mole^2, being $(\partial F/\partial n_i)_{T, P, \text{conc.}}$

Volts/cm and cal/cm have dimensions of force. With S taken into K_T, the rate constant for heat conduction has the units mole/sec cm.

(Note that the units of the rate constant depend entirely upon the units in which the velocity is expressed and upon what variables have been factored out and expressed elsewhere in the velocity equation.)

NOTE ON CONTINUOUS PROCESSES IN LIVING TISSUES:

Approached from the *systems* point of view, the five processes occurring in living tissue could, in principle, be linked quantitatively by a continuum theory, in which all five processes proceed at the same rate, and thereby maintain the steady-state. To describe and understand such a steady-state, and indeed to describe and understand the superimposed, temporary un-steady-states characteristic of different, specialized living tissues, is the ultimate goal of biophysical kinetics. Bird, Stewart, and Lightfoot have already gone part of the way, in their presentation[19] of a continuum theory of diffusion, heat conduction, and fluid flow. Hence, the direction of future development of biophysical kinetics is already clear. We need a more detailed understanding of the five processes on the molecular scale, and we need a workable, comprehensive theory of the macroscopic effects which exist as a result of the five processes.

exhaled, with the same loss of heat per gram of water. *Respiration* then becomes important, especially when the air is dry and/or cold.

Urine and feces contribute a small fraction to daily heat loss.

Heat Loss from the Body Under Various Conditions

Table 8-11 illustrates that the escape valve for excess heat may be any one of the several methods of heat loss and will vary for different activities. The very important role of the skin as a heat insulator and as a water supplier to the surface, and the role of cover and clothing now become clear.

To sum up: the maintenance of constant body temperature is a very remarkable example of the "steady state." In Chapter 7 we illustrated heat-producing reactions—chemical, physical, mechanical, etc. In this chapter we have discussed the rates of heat-producing reactions and the rate of heat loss. In the steady state there is continuous flow—and the rate of "waste" heat production is exactly balanced by the rate of heat loss, no matter what the ambient conditions. So it is with literally hundreds of processes in the living thing.

FORMAL SIMILARITY AND INTEGRATION OF THE FIVE PROCESSES

The method of presentation used in this chapter permits us to summarize in a table the factors upon which the rates of the five processes depend, and to note their similarities and differences. Since each of the processes was discussed individually, no comment on Table 8-12 and its extension, Table 8-13, will be made now, other than to ask the reader to note that the classical driving force and the role of the activated complex are both stated explicity. The reader should consider these tables to be a memory aide, which, if understood, will give him a powerful grasp of the nature of each of these important processes occurring within the living system.

In the living thing, these processes are not separate and distinct, isolated from one another. On the contrary, at every spot in the body probably three or more are simultaneously operative. For instance at some point each moment, a chemical reaction, requiring the transport in of reactants and the transport out of products, produces heat which must be removed if the steady state is to be maintained. As is the trend now in engineering kinetics[19], the future of biophysical kinetics lies in the study of the integration and control of rates of all the relevant processes proceeding in so orderly a manner within the framework of the steady state. Motivation for the ultimate mastery of biophysical kinetics is clear enough: deviations from the steady state are diseases, the most vicious of which today has the popular generic name "cancer." Some aspects of the all-important subject of control are discussed in Chapters 10 and 11, following (next) an important chapter on the biological effects of the ever-increasing ionizing radiation of our environment.

TABLE 8-13.   Components or Factors of the Specific Rate Constants for Chemical Reactions, Diffusion, Viscous Flow, and Electrical Conductivity.

$k = \tau \dfrac{k_g T}{h} e^{-\Delta F\ddagger/RT}$	τ = transmission coefficient (tau)
	k_g = Boltzmann's constant
	h = Planck's constant
$D = \tau \lambda^2 \dfrac{k_g T}{h} e^{-\Delta F\ddagger/RT}$	$\Delta F\ddagger$ = free energy of activation
	λ = "jump distance" (the distance between points of rest of the moving species)
$\phi = \tau \dfrac{\overline{V}}{h \mathcal{N}_m} e^{-\Delta F\ddagger/RT}$	$\overline{V}$ = volume of one mole of fluid
	$\mathcal{N}_m$ = no. of molecules per mole (6×10^{23})
$\mu = \tau \dfrac{\lambda^2}{E} \dfrac{k_g T}{h} e^{-\Delta F\ddagger/RT}$	E = applied voltage

NOTE: Heat conduction has not yet been studied from this point of view. If volume, voltage and jump distance terms are factored out of the above expressions, they all become the same: the pre-exponential term with dimensions sec^{-1}; and hence the specific rate would be dependent only upon the activation free energy for the process.

WEIGHTLESSNESS

In this era, on the threshold of space travel, it would be neglectful not to introduce into a chapter on speeds of processes occurring in the living system, the effects of gravitational force. Man must withstand a gravitational range from high-g conditions on through to the condition of weightlessness, or zero-g. So little has been published to date about those who have orbited the earth for any appreciable time that little can be written here. However, the general principle can be stated that the change in gravitational force on the human body from earth-bound to weightlessness is small relative to other forces. As a general rule, if the parts are fixed in position, they function normally. Solids and contained liquids, then, show no discernible changes in speeds of chemical or physical—and therefore, presumably, biological—processes.

With the gravitational restriction removed, blood circulation requires less expenditure of energy. Conversely the same expenditure of energy by the constant-pumping heart is able to accelerate the blood flow through the tissues, and provide exhilaration, just as would a slightly higher O_2 content in the respired air. The first astronaut, Juri Gagarin, reported that he "observed the earth and sang" during a $1\frac{1}{2}$-hr orbital flight. John Glenn had similar experiences during a busy $4\frac{1}{2}$-hr flight. Telemetered physiological data demonstrated normal biological functioning while he was weightless. However, after the 25-hr orbital trip of Gherman Titov, he reported that he felt depressed and nauseated during the flight. His successors, Nikolayev and Papov, flew weightless for several days without mishap or reported discomfort.

Perhaps the psychological effects of isolation, uncertainty, and frustration will prove to be far more important than the effects of weightlessness on the biophysics of the space traveler. The effects of ionizing radiation in free space, unfiltered by the atmosphere, are discussed in the next chapter.

PROBLEMS

8-1: The rate of denaturation of a protein or of inactivation of an enzyme by heat is dependent upon the concentration of the enzyme in a rather peculiar way, which can be represented as $v \propto [E]^n$, where $[E]$ is enzyme concentration and n is the order of the reaction, interpreted as the number of molecules of enzyme which come together to form a cluster in the inactivation process.

The temperature dependence is normal in that $v \propto e^{-E*/RT}$, where $E*$ is the energy of activation, R is the gas constant (2 cal per degree per mole), and T is the temperature *in degrees Kelvin*. For one case at low concentration, n was found to be independent of temperature, and $E*$ equal to 150,000 cal/mole.

  (a) Calculate the ratio of velocity at 104° F to that at 98.6° F.
  (b) Calculate the ratio for a 10° C rise in temperature.
  (c) Calculate the ratio for a 10° C rise in temperature for a hydrolysis reaction for which $E*$ is 20,000 cal/mole.
  (d) Calculate the ratio for a 10° C rise in temperature for a transport process for which $E*$ is 4000 cal/mole.

8-2: The basal metabolic rate of the "normal" man is about 0.1 hp. Express this in Cal/hr; in watts; in cal/sec.

8-3: Using Poiseuille's Equation, calculate the pressure which would have to be applied to a No. 17 hypodermic needle (2 cm long, 0.05 cm radius), if a water solution of viscosity 0.01 poises (dyne/cm. sec²) is to be forced, at a rate of 1 cc/sec, into an artery which is already 100 mm Hg average pressure above atmospheric.

8-4: Under low rates of flow, blood has a viscosity (∼0.02 poise) about twice that of water; but under high rates, such as in the capillaries, it flows more easily (∼0.012 poise). Calculate the flow rate through two parallel tubes 1 mm long, of radii 0.001 and 0.005 cm, if the pressure drop is 100 cm Hg.

8-5: One milliampere of total body current may be fatal. Estimate the path length and average cross-section from hand to hand; and given the fact that the specific conductivity (i.e., of a volume of soln. 1 cm² in area and 1 cm long) of a solution of 100 milliequivalents of KCl per liter (approx concentration of body fluids) is 0.015 ohm⁻¹ cm⁻¹ at 98° F, calculate the applied potential sufficient to force 1 ma of current from hand to hand.

REFERENCES

1. Newburg, L. H., "Physiology of Heat Regulation (and the Science of Clothing)," W. B. Saunders Co., Philadelphia, Pa., 1949.
2. Kuno, Y., "Human Perspiration," Charles C. Thomas Publ., Springfield, Ill., 1956.

3. Burton, A. C. and Edholm, O. G., "Man in a Cold Environment," Edw. Arnold Publ. Ltd., London, 1955.
4. Ruch, T. C. and Fulton, J. F., "Medical Physiology and Biophysics," 18th ed., W. B. Saunders Co., Philadelphia, Pa., 1960. (See the chapter by A. C. Burton on Hematolysis.)
5. Greisheimer, E. M., "Physiology and Anatomy," J. B. Lippincott Co., Philadelphia, Pa., 1955.
6. Glasstone, S., Laidler, K. F., and Eyring, H., "The Theory of Rate Processes," McGraw-Hill Book Co., New York, N. Y., 1941.
7. Gaebler, O. H., "Enzymes: Units of Biological Structure and Function," Academic Press, Inc., New York, N. Y., 1956.
8. Tyrrell, H. J. V., "Diffusion and Heat Flow in Liquids," Butterworths, London, 1961.
9. Baldwin, E., "Dynamic Aspects of Biochemistry," Cambridge Univ. Press, Cambridge, England, 1953.
10. West, E. S., "Textbook of Biophysical Chemistry," The Macmillan Co., New York, N. Y., 1956.
11. Szent-Györgyi, A., "Introduction to a Submolecular Biology," Academic Press, Inc., New York, N. Y., 1960.
12. Clarke, H. T., Ed., "Ion Transport Across Membranes," Academic Press, Inc., New York, N. Y., 1954.
13. Wintrobe, M. M., "Clinical Hematology," 4th ed., Lea and Febiger, Philadelphia, Pa., 1956.
14. Nikolaev, L. A., "Problems in Modelling of Biocatalysts," *Vestnik Akademii nauk SSSR*, 13 (1960); *LLU Translations Bulletin*, London, 1960.
15. Laidler, K. J., "The Chemistry of Enzyme Action," McGraw-Hill Book Co., New York, N. Y., 1958.
16. Dixon, M. and Webb, E. C., "Enzymes," Academic Press, New York, N. Y., 1958.
17. Davson, H. and Danielli, J. F., "The Permeability of Natural Membranes," Cambridge Univ. Press, Cambridge, England, 1952.
18. Höber, R., et al., "Physical Chemistry of Cells and Tissues," The Blakiston Co., Philadelphia, Pa., 1945.
19. Bird, R. B., Stewart, W. E., and Lightfoot, E. N., "Transport Phenomena," John Wiley & Sons, Inc., New York, N. Y., 1960.
20. Conway, B. E., "Electrochemical Data," Elsevier Publ. Co., Amsterdam, Holland, 1952; Parsons, R., "Handbook of Electrochemical Constants," Butterworths Scientific Publs., London, 1959.
21. Kleiber, M., "The Fire of Life," John Wiley & Sons, Inc., New York, N. Y., 1961.

CHAPTER 9

Biological Effects of Ionizing Radiations

The damage to living tissues caused by ionizing radiations was not always as well recognized as it is today, and many of the early investigators suffered painfully as a result. On a memorial unveiled in Hamburg, Germany, in 1936, in honor of the first 110 investigators and physicians who died directly as a result of X-irradiation, following W. K. Roentgen's discovery in 1895, we read the dedication:

"To the Roentgenologists and Radiologists of all Nations who have given their lives in the struggle against the diseases of mankind."

INTRODUCTION

This chapter could have been the longest in the book. Indeed, it could have been expanded to be the whole book, for such is the importance of biological effects of ionizing radiations, both for diagnosis and for therapy. However, we restrict ourselves here to the principles which are necessary to an *understanding* of the effects. Although some examples are given to illustrate the effects on humans, we carefully skirt the very complex and largely empirical subject of radiology, as compelling and as intrinsically interesting as the subject matter may be.

Within a few years after 1895, many effects of X rays on adult humans had been observed, and others imagined and foreseen. The early workers, and their patients, suffered from skin burns, some radiation sickness, warts, deformed fingers, loss of hair; and finally the onset of various forms of cancer (Figure 9-1).

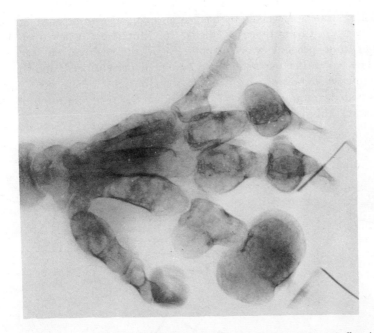

Figure 9-1. Abnormal Bone Growths in the Hand—Similar to those Suffered by the Early Radiologists. (Courtesy of A. F. Crook, Ottawa General Hospital.)

Recognition of these effects led to controls which by this time have completely removed, in medical use, the gross dangers described above, although there are still subtle possibilities, as we shall see, which may yet require that even further restrictions be instituted. Some dangers are not so subtle: this is the era of the megaton bomb.

Nonmedical applications of ionizing radiation are increasing rapidly, and render it important that safety measures and medical checks be more and more indicative of absorbed dose. For instance, the development of atomic power stations, irradiation-sterilization of food (potatoes, for example, to keep them from sprouting during long shipment) and of surgical and medical supplies, the production of new chemical polymers by irradiation, the detection of faults and flaws in metal castings and welds by X-ray fluoroscopy: all involve skilled and unskilled human labor. Furthermore, the increasing radioactivity "background" of the environment—even to the increasing tritium (two neutrons + one proton; a beta-emitter) content of our water supplies (blood is about 90 per cent water!)—makes it obvious, although perhaps distasteful, that man is being more and more heavily irradiated every day (Figure 9-2). Therefore the effects, especially the subtle ones, which may show up only after a few generations, must be understood and appreciated, especially by medical people. The three most important facts are: (1) Living tissue is killed. (2) Mutations, which may lead to cancer or to progeny which cannot live in the environment, can occur. (3) The central nervous system can become hypersensitized; and this could lead to a whole host of nervous and "somatopsychic" disorders. Radiologists understand much about (1); something, but really far too little, about (2); and at this date have only an inkling about (3).

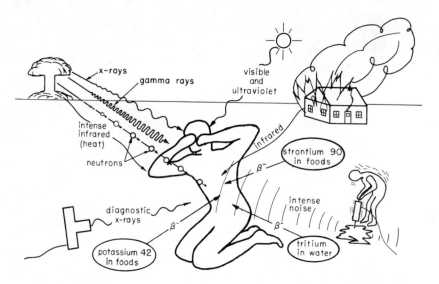

Figure 9-2. Man's Environment of Radiations. Normal background of ionizing radiations varies widely in the range 0.7 to 0.4 roentgens/yr, depending upon his location, natural shielding in his home, etc. Anything above 0.3 r/week is currently considered "dangerous."

DOSIMETRY

Dose Units

From the point of view of *effect*, the most important quantity is the rather empirical one—the rem (roentgen equivalent man). One rem is defined as that amount of damage to tissue caused by radiation of any type which produces the same biological effect as does 100 ergs absorbed per gram of tissue from incident X or gamma radiation. Since one rad (radiation absorbed dose) is defined as that amount of X or gamma radiation which, when absorbed, adds 100 ergs per gram (i.e., 6.24×10^{13} ev/g) to the energy of the tissue, one rem of damage is produced by 1 rad of absorbed X or gamma radiation.

Two other units are of importance. The roentgen (r), the earliest unit of dose, refers to absorption by dry air, and specifically is that amount of X or gamma radiation which, when absorbed, increases the energy of dry air at STP (0°C, 1 atm pressure) by 83 ergs/g. The rep (roentgen equivalent physical) was originally defined as the tissue-equivalent of the roentgen, but with conversion difficulties being as they are, it is best defined here as that amount of X or gamma radiation which, when absorbed, increases the energy of soft tissue by 83 to 93 ergs/g.

In Chapter 5 the density of ions produced along the paths of alpha, beta, gamma or X, and neutrons was described (refer to Figure 5-1). It is logical that the biological effectiveness of a unit of absorbed radiation should increase with increasing density of ionization. Density of ionization is expressed quantitatively as the linear energy transfer (LET). Therefore, the relative biological effectiveness of one unit (i.e., 1 rad) of absorbed radiation (of different kinds) should be proportional to the LET. For instance, slow alphas ($^4_2He^{++}$) do twenty times the damage of X rays of equivalent dose absorbed. Table 9-1 lists some average LET values for various energies of

TABLE 9-1. Linear Energy Transfer (LET) in Thousands (Kev) or Millions (Mev) of Electron-Volts Absorbed per Micron (10^{-4} cm) of Track for Some Atomic "Bullets." Accepted Values of Relative Biological Effectiveness (rbe).*

Type	Energy	Initial LET (Kev/micron)	rbe**
Co⁶⁰ gammas	1.1 Mev	0.2	1
X rays	250 Kev	1.0	⎫
	10 Kev	2.0	⎬ 1
	8 Kev	2.8	⎭
	250 kvp, usual distribution	3.5 average	1.0 (defined)
S³⁵ betas	46 Kev max	0.7	1 to 2
Electrons	1 to 2 Mev	0.2	1 to 2
Protons	0.9 Mev	30	8 to 10
	8.4 Mev	5.5	
Fast neutrons	0.1 to 10 Mev		10
Slow neutrons	less than 100 ev		2 to 5
Alphas	5.3 Mev	90	⎫
	12 Mev	50	⎬ 20 to 10
	38 Mev	20	⎭
Fission recoil	65 Mev	~7000	(200?)

*From Report of the International Commission on Radiological Units and Measurements (ICRU), Handbook 78, National Bureau of Standards, Washington, D.C., 1959, p. 50; and Ref. 19, p. 174.

** $\frac{rems}{dose} / \left(\frac{rems}{dose}\right)_{250\ kvp\ X\ rays}$

different radiations. One should bear in mind that the LET is not constant while the radiation energy is being absorbed by tissue because with every bit of energy lost there remains less to lose.

For several types of irradiation, approximate values of relative biological effectiveness (rbe)—i.e., damage per unit dose, relative to 250 kvp X rays—can be written down, and can be used if the reservation be kept in mind that they are rules-of-thumb, only approximate. Column 4 in Table 9-1 lists such values. In general, the higher the energy of the impinging radiation, the less energy it loses per unit length in tissue, and hence the longer it will take a source to deliver a unit of absorbed radiation. In summary, the biological damage is given as:

$$\text{rads} \times \text{rbe} = \text{rems} \cong \text{reps} \times \text{rbe}$$

Several ways of receiving 1 rem of damage are depicted in Figure 9-3. For workers, such as radiologists, who must necessarily be exposed, it is recommended (by international agreement) that the whole-body dose be kept to less than 0.3 rem per week in the blood-forming organs, the gonads, and the eyes; less than 0.6 rem per week for surface irradiation. Relaxation to 1.5 rem per week is permitted if the radiation is of low penetrating power or if only limited parts of the body are irradiated. Table 9-2 gives the number of rems received under different conditions.

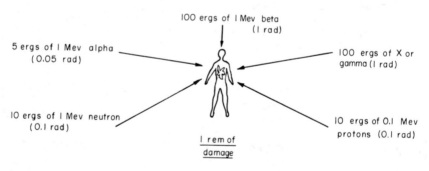

Figure 9-3. Some Ways of Receiving 1 rem of Damage.

Dose Measurement

In air the dose received is measured accurately by the ionization chamber and scintillation counters described in Chapter 5. However, in aqueous solutions or in tissue, the situation is quite different. Here the primary target is water, and it breaks up not into ions but into free radicals (H + OH); these react and produce new *chemicals*.

TABLE 9-2. Sources of Irradiation of Human Beings.

Source	Approx Dose or Dose Rate
Natural external background, including cosmic rays	0.073 rem/year (widely variable)
Increase in background due to nuclear testing 1945–1962 peak soon after test	0 to many thousand times natural background, depending upon location
Average increase	0.1% of natural
Internal exposure to Ra^{226} and K^{40} from foods	0.15 to 0.5 rem/yr
K^{40} alone	0.03 rem/yr
One chest X ray:	
best	0.006 rem
average	0.2 rem
fluoroscopic examination	$\sim$10 rem
Local dose during irradiation of tumors	3000 to 7000 rem
Median lethal dose, whole body	$\sim$400 rem
Maximum permissable* dose rate, whole body	15 rem/yr (0.3/wk)

*Recommended by the International Commission on Radiological Protection, 1958.

The celebrated Fricke dosimeter is based on this principle. It is an aqueous solution of 0.1 M-H_2SO_4 containing 10^{-3} M-$FeSO_4$ and a tracce of chloride. Upon irradiation, ferrous ($+2$) is oxidized to ferric ($+3$) iron, and the amount of ferric produced is easily estimated, as $FeCl_3$ from the extent of absorption of light of wave length 3040 Å. Thus 1 rad of hard X or gamma radiation has the chemical effect of converting 1.5×10^{-8} moles of Fe^{+2} to Fe^{+3} per liter of solution. The system is widely used, because it is simple, reproducible, accurate, and independent of dose rate (e.g., rads/hr). Its useful range is from about 500 to several thousands of rads. This dosimeter system—standard methodology, advantages and disadvantages—has been described in detail elsewhere.[18]

Since biological damage can occur at much lower doses than this, recent developments have been toward more sensitive aqueous dosimeters. In sealed vials, chlorinated hydrocarbons liberate chlorine and change color in crude field dosimeters—sensitive, but results are not too reproducible. Two other recent developments will now be described very briefly.

In the first, advantage is taken of the fact that certain molecules, such as hydroxybenzoic acid, in water will fluoresce. That is, if ultraviolet light impinges on them, they absorb it, turn some of the energy into heat energy, and re-emit the rest as light in the visible region. A sensitive photocell detects this re-emitted light, and the photoelectric current is amplified and recorded. The reduced form of the fluorescent material, benzoic acid, does not fluoresce. Irradiation causes oxidation. The intensity of the fluorescence is a function of dose. Of the order of 1 rad can be accurately measured.

In the second, advantage is taken of the fact that the electrochemical potential of an electrode, measured against some suitable reference electrode, is dependent upon the ratio of the concentrations of oxidized to reduced form present in the solution. For instance, Ag/Ag^+ in H_2SO_4 is one redox system which has been shown to be practical. Irradiation produces Ag^+ and the voltage of the cell (Ag in H_2SO_4 solution *vs* a mercury-mercurous sulfate reference electrode) decreases as the concentration of Ag^+ is increased by the radiation. Measurement of voltage *vs* time or irradiation thus gives a continuous measurement of absorbed dose. When done carefully, a fraction of a rad can be measured. This is the only continuous-recording and re-useable dose-measuring instrument known.

However, biological damage is not subject to such reliable, quantitative measurement. Measurement of biological damage, by its very nature, has so far had to be a quantity such as the LD_{50} (lethal dose$_{50}$). The LD_{50} is that dose in rads which will kill 50 per cent of the cells or organisms irradiated (see Fig. 9-4). Further, since irradiation damage is often not immediate, but may set in only after days or even years, in the case of mammals an arbitrary limit of 50 per cent killed within 30 days after exposure has been accepted by workers in this field as a further specification of the LD_{50}.

3 alive   3 dead

Figure 9-4. LD_{50}: 50 per cent Lethality, Measured at Some Constant but Arbitrarily Chosen Time After Exposure (30 days for man).

As a general rule, the LD_{50} (30 days) for mammals is 200 to 1000 rads; for man (whole-body irradiation), it is about 400 rads (equivalent to 400 rems if the radiation is X or gamma) (of course there are no good statistical data to support this number!). For lower animals it is higher: frog, 700; bacteria, 10,000; insects, 60,000; paramecia 300,000 rads.

The LD_{50} is a useful measure also of the effectiveness of partial-body irradiation. In some cases one simply makes a suspension and estimates the number of cells left living in the tissue irradiated.

As more is learned about effects of ionizing radiation on metabolic processes, physiological measurements of effects on rates of specific processes within cells and tissues will probably add much-needed refinements to the useful LD_{50} number.

Incidentally, one should realize that only a small *amount* of energy need be absorbed to cause damage. It is the *form* in which this energy enters the tissue that is critical. Thus the LD_{50} for man, 400 rads, is only 400×100 ergs/g. This is 0.001 cal/g, roughly enough energy, if in the form of heat, to raise the body temperature only 0.001 deg! Because the energy is concentrated in packets, so that when it is absorbed it tears apart the molecules of important biological structures, localized damage occurs at sensitive sites, enabling a small quantity of energy to promote death. Table 9-3 gives some useful irradiation data and conversion factors.

TABLE 9-3.   Some Useful Numbers.

---

1 rad $= 100$ ergs/gram $= 6.24 \times 10^{13}$ electron volts/gram.
1 roentgen of hard X or γ delivers 0.98 rad to water.
1 curie of radioactive substance delivers 3.7×10^{10} disintegrations/second.
1 curie of Co^{60} gives a dose rate of 1.35 roentgen/hour at 1 meter from the source.
1 curie of radium gives a dose rate of 0.83 roentgen/hour at 1 meter.
1 curie of cesium^{137} gives a dose rate of 0.33 roentgen/hour at 1 meter.

PRIMARY EFFECTS (on Chemical Composition)

Direct and Indirect Action

Two schools of thought have arisen on the question of how the primary effects occur. However, there are so many variables involved that it is unlikely that either will ever be proved to be unequivocally wrong.

The fact is that the solution after irradiation contains molecules (chemicals) which were not there before irradiation. One school maintains that this is because the solute dissolved in the water acted as a target, was blown apart by the incoming "bullets," and the fragments rearranged into a new molecule. The other school remembers that the whole target (tissue, for example) can be at least 80 per cent water, that eight out of ten potential targets are water molecules, and maintains that the primary act is the excitation of water, followed by its decomposition into the active chemicals hydrogen atom and hydroxyl radical. Enough energy is left over so that these are thrown violently apart. Hydrogen is a reducing agent, which can donate an electron to become H^+ in solution; OH is an oxidizing agent which can accept an electron to become OH^- in solution. From this view, then, these molecular fragments, H and OH, cause the formation of new molecules by their attack on dissolved solute. Figure 9-5 illustrates these two mechanisms.

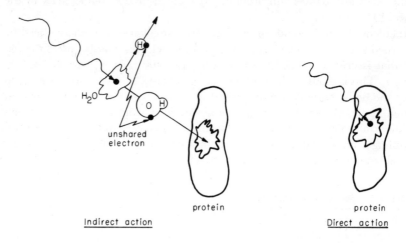

unshared
electron

protein   protein
Indirect action   Direct action

Figure 9-5. Indirect *versus* Target Action of Ionizing Radiations.

Effects on Some Biological Molecules

In his recent book, Swallow[11] has collected the known effects of X irradiation of hundreds of compounds of biological interest. For instance, the important generalization exists that reactive peroxides are formed from all the biologically active amino acids in solution. In addition, the molecular products of irradiated water solutions are H_2, H_2O_2 and O_2, each of which, and especially H_2O_2, can exert its chemistry on the solutes present.

The results are easy to state in general, difficult to state in detail, in all but the simplest cases. In general, new molecules can be produced from the old ones (plus water), and these new ones may exert catalytic, toxic, or no effect on the metabolic processes in the vicinity in which they are produced or to which they are carried by blood and lymph. In particular, the absorbed radiation is known to reduce the catalytic activity of many enzymes, and to alter their molecular weights and other physical properties. Large molecules (Figure 9-6) can be broken into many parts, or can be cross-linked through new hydrogen bonds or through the oxidation of two —SH groups by H_2O_2, for example, to form an —S—S— bond, with distortion of the molecule.

One of the most intensely studied molecules from this point of view is the nucleic acid, desoxyribonucleic acid (DNA). It is thought (the reasons were given in Chapter 6) to be the main carrier of hereditary information in the living system, and hence one that should not be tampered with in human beings without prior knowledge of the genetic result. Butler *et al* (1959) have partially clarified a rather confused picture, made not the least bit simple by the fact that the molecule is huge: as obtained from leucocytes it has a molecular weight of about five million. Two standard methods of determining molecular weight (also outlined in Chapter 6) were used. One, by measurement of the viscosity of DNA solutions and measurement of the speed with which the molecules settle out in a high-speed centrifuge, showed that the molecular weight falls during irradiation, as though the big molecule were being split into pieces. The other, however, by light-scattering techniques, gave a *constant* molecular weight during irradiation. The implication is that the molecule is broken all right, but the pieces do not completely uncoil. With such a loosened structure, easier degradation by heat should result, and that is just what has been found, not only for DNA but also for several enzymes as well.

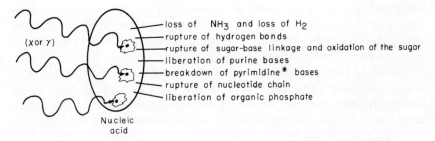

Figure 9-6. Things That Can Happen if a Macromolecule Such as DNA is Irradiated by Ionizing Radiation.

* Order of radioresistance: adenine > guanine ≫ cytosine > uracil > thymine (on isolated components).

Enzymes are known to have various sensitivities to radiations, at least in dilute solutions. The data on these are somewhat suspect because of the marked effect of impurities. However, one of the most sensitive enzymes seems to be carboxypeptidase; ribonuclease is ten times more resistant, and catalase ten times more resistant yet. Some enzymes are inactivated even when in the dry, crystalline state (this supports the target theorists). All enzymes studied are inactivated in aqueous solutions by ionizing radiations—this can mean direct target action or attack by radiation-produced free radicals, probably both.

Of the small molecules present in tissues, the most interesting from the medical point of view are cysteine and certain other molecules containing the sulfhydryl (—SH) group. These molecules are particularly sensitive to oxidation by radiation, and therefore are among the most effective *protectors* known. By one view they scavenge free radicals H, OH, HO_2, etc., produced in the radiolysis. By another view they attach themselves to enzymes or nucleic acids at just the spots most sensitive to radical attack (—SH groups) and thereby reduce the effects of irradiation on the big molecules. For example, even impure acetylcholinesterase, in a solution with much other protein, is only half as sensitive to irradiation damage in the presence of 10^{-3} M-cysteine as in its absence. In living cells the enzymes are well protected, and seem to be resistant to much larger doses of radiation than the same molecule *in vitro*.

The "Oxygen Effect"

The radiation sensitivity of most molecules is greater the higher the oxygen content of the solution. Thus, the rate of oxidation of Fe^{+2} to Fe^{+3} by X rays is twice as high in the presence, than in the absence, of oxygen. For small molecules like phenol and the amino acids the rate is often even more enhanced by O_2. This increased radiation sensitivity in the presence of oxygen is observed right on up the hierarchy of structures—viruses, bacteria, cells, tissues, to whole animals.

A striking practical demonstration of this effect has been shown with carcinoma tissue. Due to necrosis, many parts of a tumor can become anoxic. By increasing the pressure of the respired air this anoxia can be reduced, with a consequent increase in the radiosensitivity of the carcinoma cells.

Now, oxygen itself is known to accelerate many metabolic reactions, and the effect of oxygen in increasing radiation damage is thought by some to result from this fact. However, in other quarters the effect is thought to occur through the radical, HO_2. This radical is produced from the reaction

$$H + O_2 \rightarrow HO_2$$

after the radiolysis reaction has produced the hydrogen atoms as follows:

$$H_2O \rightsquigarrow H_2O^* \rightarrow H + OH$$

The radical HO_2 is a strong oxidizing agent, since it readily accepts an electron from any source to become the peroxide ion, HO_2^-. Hence, one can consider that the H atom simply puts O_2 into a form in which it can react faster. Since O_2 is used up in the reaction, it must be supplied continuously if advantage is to be continuously taken of enhanced rate of destruction. Conversely, of course, oxygen scavenger molecules increase the protection of macromolecules against ionizing radiations.

The mode of action of oxygen is one of the most intriguing practical problems of radiology. Once it is understood, it can be controlled and utilized more fully. Other species, such as NO and Co^{++} also enhance radiation effects.

BIOPHYSICAL EFFECTS

These can be considered as effects on molecular structure and type, with the resulting effects on the physical properties of agglutination and transport, and on the speeds of vital chemical processes.

Agglutination or Coagulation

Colloids—small particles, large molecules—are stabilized by electric charges on their surface. At any particular pH, the acidic and basic chemical groups on the surface are in equilibrium with the electrolyte, and the surface carries a net positive or negative charge.   Repulsion between like charges stabilizes the colloid. Further stabilization comes from water molecules adsorbed on the polar groups of the surface, so that, from the outside, the big colloid particle looks, to a particle in solution, just like a wall of ordinary water molecules.

Irradiation causes, first of all, chemical polymerization or cross-linking to occur between particles. It causes changes in the polar groups, and hence in the "water front" which the colloid presents to the solution.   Finally it causes rearrangement in acidic and basic groups such that the net surface charge changes. The colloid then precipitates, or agglutinates, and becomes semisolid.

On the other hand, the colloid may be split within by radiant energy, and the structure then rearranged to a form which is unstable, and it precipitates.

Modification of Transport Properties

Thermal Conductivity. This property is difficult to measure even under the most advantageous of circumstances, and nothing is known yet about how it is affected by radiation. Structural changes induced by radiation may turn out to be of importance to the structural lipoproteins and collagen of the skin, for example.

Diffusion. As it was shown in Chapter 8, the diffusion coefficient depends critically upon the molecular structure of the medium, with particular reference to the "jump distance" between rest sites in the medium and to the size and shape of the diffusing species. Naturally, if the diffusing molecule is broken up into small and free parts by the action of ionizing radiation, it will diffuse faster. Conversely, if it or the medium becomes cross-polymerized, diffusion will occur more slowly.

It is expected that, as more is learned about the diffusion of water, ions, and molecules through living membranes, the effects of irradiation on diffusion will become more evident. In the absence of definitive work on this subject, one can only say that the possibilities exist, and should be remembered during discussions of the physiological effects, which are currently receiving more attention.

Fluidity (Inverse of Viscosity). Most of the useful information on the effects of ionized radiations on fluidity (ease of flow in response to a physical force) has been done either on plastics or on aqueous solutions of big molecules.

From the former it has been learned that cross-linking of polythene by irradiation increases markedly its melting point and increases its elasticity. By contrast, irradiation of teflon (a fluorinated and inert organic) leads to hardening and embrittlement, and loss of elasticity. This might lead one to anticipate similar effects in elastomeric tissue in the walls of blood vessels, were it not for the fact that the effects are exhibited only after the absorption of a few million rads!

On the other hand, the fluidity of aqueous solutions of biologically active molecules has been intensively studied, especially as a technique of measuring the change in molecular weight effected by radiations. Like diffusion, many examples are known in which cross-polymerization is important, and many in which molecular rupture is to be inferred.

Electrical Conductivity. In body fluids the conductivity is high. Irradiation makes no detectable change.

It is in the inner, fatty-acid or lipid part of the living membrane (Figure 6-7) that we expect a change in conductivity. The lipid, an oil, has very low conductivity. Analogy with polythene or lucite may be useful as a guide. These materials break down internally under irradiation, such that electrons are knocked off one part of the molecule and caught or trapped elsewhere, leaving a positive site behind. The conductivity increases, because the charges are somewhat mobile, and a steady-state concentration, higher the higher the dose rate, is set up and maintained. Upon cessation of the radiation, the charges recombine slowly, and the conductivity drops to its original value. Although the κ for these substances is very, very small ($\sim 10^{-21}$ ohm^{-1} cm^{-1}), it is raised as much as fifty thousand times by an X-ray dose of only 8 roentgens (r) per min. By comparison, the conductivity of a resting nerve membrane is of the order of 10^{-12} ohm^{-1} cm^{-1}, due almost entirely to the lipid inner layer.

The "activation" of nerves by radiations, and some effects on the central nervous system, to be discussed in the next section, indicate that enhanced electrical conductivity may be one of the most important biophysical effects of ionizing radiations.

Chemical Reactivity

The effects of ionizing radiations on the rate of chemical reactions could be inferred from knowledge of the factors upon which rate depends. In general terms there are two methods by which the rate can be increased: through increase in local temperature (thermal energy of vibrations, etc.) in the vicinity of the ionized track, and through excited electronic states of reactant molecules (photochemical processes). The mechanisms have been discussed in Chapters 4 to 8. The synthesis of new isomers and of entirely new molecules was considered also in Chapter 6, as well as the nature of toxins, catalysts, and useful and destructive mutants.

PHYSIOLOGICAL EFFECTS

Outlined in this section are the effects of ionizing radiation on cells, organs and tissues.

Sensitivity of Cells

The sensitivity, σ (sigma), is the rate at which cells die because of irreversible damage suffered during irradiation. Since the unit of absorbed dose, D, is the rad, the fraction of cells lost per rad is the sensitivity. Thus

$$\sigma = - \frac{dN/dD}{N}$$

cells killed per unit dose per unit number of cells irradiated. If the dose rate, dD/dt rads/sec, is a constant, ρ, then the sensitivity can be expressed

$$\sigma = - \frac{dN/dt}{\rho \cdot N}$$

cells killed per sec per unit number of cells irradiated. Based on what is now known about factors affecting the radiosensitivity of cells, the early (1905) "law" of Bergonie and Tribondeau can be extended and rewritten:

$$\sigma = f\left(\frac{[dN/dt]_g \; \mathcal{W}, \alpha, dD/dt}{m} \right)$$

where f denotes a functional relationship between σ and the quantities in parentheses; $[dN/dt]_g$, the rate at which the cells reproduce themselves (i.e., the growth rate, or number produced per unit time); $\mathcal{W}$, the metabolic rate —energy used up per unit time; α, a number less than 1 which varies with the state of cell division—unity at the prophase of mitosis, much less at any other time; m, the degree of maturity—unity for old, well-developed, specialized cells, less for those newly formed; and dD/dt, the dose rate. In summary, the sensitivity increases with increasing rate of cell division, metabolic rate, and dose rate; increases sharply at prophase; and decreases as the cell becomes more mature. The exact functional relationships are not known.

The rule is generally obeyed, but there are exceptions. For instance, leucocytes (white blood cells) are quite mature, don't divide *in vitro*, divide only slowly in the body, and they have a low basal metabolic rate; but in spite of these facts, they are among the most radiation-sensitive cells known.

The relation between the number of surviving cells and the dose, D, absorbed, has had far better quantitative demonstration (Figure 9-7), especially for cells. If N is the number at any time, and N_0 is the number before irradiation started, then

$$N = N_0 e^{-\sigma D} \qquad \text{or} \qquad \log N/N_0 = -0.434\,\sigma\,D$$

This is simply the integrated form of the natural law (see Chapter 1) which says that the rate at which cells die from irradiation is proportional to the number of living or nondamaged cells which are being irradiated. This expression describes the case in which σ is constant during the whole irradiation.

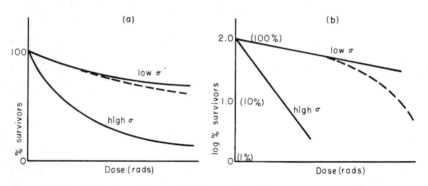

Figure 9-7. Radiation-Sensitivity, σ: The Slope of the Straight Line in the Logarithmic Plot (b) for Haploid Cells. Low slope means low σ. Broken curve is for multiploid cells: sensitivity increases as irradiation proceeds.

The radiation sensitivity constant, σ, is small for radio-resistant cells (e.g., nerve cells in adults), and large for radiosensitive cells (e.g., lymphocytes). It increases with increasing oxygen concentration ("the oxygen effect"), or increasing nitric oxide concentration. This is true also for whole animals. If the dose rate is raised, the value of σ increases, for the same reason it increases as the relative biological effectiveness of the impinging radiation is increased. It decreases with increasing concentration of certain protector chemicals, P, as we would infer from the discussion on protection of molecules earlier in this Chapter. Therefore we can incorporate all these effects into a modern version of the Law of Bergonie and Tribondeau, and write, as a memory aid:

$$\sigma = f\left(\frac{[dN/dt]_g, \tilde{W}, \alpha, dD/dt, [O_2], [NO], \text{rbe}}{m, [P]}\right)$$

Survival studies have been pursued vigorously in the past few years. The exponential decay law $N = N_0 e^{-\sigma D}$ is followed rigorously by irradiated haploid (simple-chromosome) yeast cells—linear portions on Figure 9-7. In this case σ has a value (Table 9-4) of 17.2×10^{-5} rads^{-1} at a dose rate of 425 rads/min, with the oxygen concentration equilibrated with air. The value of σ drops rapidly as the water of the medium (and hence in the cell) is partially replaced by such materials as glycerol. Furthermore, the sensitivity does not change down to $-10°$ C, but drops to 4.9×10^{-5} when the solution freezes. By way of contrast, bacterial cells are about 100 times less sensitive than human cells to irradiation (Table 9-4), but eventually show the membrane rupture and internal reorganizations of all others (Figure 9-8).

TABLE 9-4. Some Measured Fractions Killed per Rad (i.e., the Radiation Sensitivity, σ) and the Corresponding LD_{50}'s.

System	$10^5 \sigma$ (per rad)	LD_{50} (rads)
Human beings, whole body irradiation	about 170	about 400
Diploid human cells, generally	170 to 220	320 to 400
Aneuploid cells, from human cancer of cervix	220	320
Slowly multiplying cancer cells, estimated	170 to 200	340 to 400
Rapidly multiplying cancer cells, estimated	200 to 250	300 to 340
Haploid yeast cells		
normal suspension	17.2	4,000
frozen	4.9	14,000
in 1 molar glycerol	9.8	7,000
in 7 molar glycerol	4.9	14,000
E. coli bacteria		
parent	2.6 to 4.5	15,300 to 26,500
18th irradiated generation (less sensitive)	1.2	58,000
Spores	0.2 and down	350,000 and up

NOTE: $\sigma \cdot LD_{50} = 0.693; \sigma = -2.303 \dfrac{\partial \log N/N_0}{\partial D}$.

In contrast to this simple, first-order law, it has been found that if chromosomal material is present in quantities which are multiples of some basic unit (diploids, tetraploids, etc.), the rate of destruction of cells by irradiation is proportional to some power (of the number of cells, N) *different* from

Figure 9-8. Electron Micrographs of Normal and Gamma-irradiated *E. coli* Bacteria. *Left:* Parent, shadowed at an angle of 30° with evaporated chromium metal. Note the long flagellae still intact (10,000×). *Center:* A heavily irradiated (2 million rads), radiation-resistant strain, remarkably elongated, and with terminal budding (7,000×). *Right:* A stained, ultrathin section of a freeze-dried sample of the heavily irradiated strain, showing side budding (25,000×). (Courtesy of I. E. Erdman and B. Kronmueller, National Health and Welfare Laboratories, Ottawa.)

unity; the plot of log (survivors) *vs* dose is curved, not straight, σ varies, and the survival expression becomes more complicated.* Thus, the results of irradiation of multiploid yeast cells indicate very complicated kinetics—interesting enough, and of considerable significance because of what they will some day tell us about human multiploid cells under irradiation; but nevertheless not truly clear now, and therefore beyond our scope to discuss here. The general rule-of-thumb is that for multiploids the sensitivity, σ, becomes higher the longer the cells are irradiated. The numbers given in Table 9-4 for *E. coli*, for example, refer to linear portions of the log (survivors) *vs* dose curve, and therefore are only approximate. Higher up the animal heirarchy the deviations from this simply law are greater, and it is best then to rely on the LD_{50}, not the σ.

Arranged in decreasing order of sensitivity (σ) the following cells provide a broad spectrum of the general damage caused by whole-cell irradiation:

Lymphocytes > granulocytes > basal cells** > alveolar cells of lung > bile duct cells > cells of tubules of kidneys > endothelial cells > connective tissue cells > muscle cells > bone cells > nerve cells.

---

*One form, based on a multiple-hit theory, introduces a correction term:

$$N/N_0 = e^{-\sigma D} (1 - c/D)$$

where c is a constant.

**Producers of specialized cells of bone marrow, gonads, intestines, sometimes called stem cells.

Microirradiation of Cells

So far, the discussion has been on whole-cell irradiation. However, by microirradiation techniques, in which just a small volume within a single cell receives radiation, it has been found that not all parts of the cell are equally sensitive. In fact, σ is much higher if the nucleus (in particular the chromosomes within the nucleus), rather than any other part of the cytoplasm or cell membrane, is irradiated.

Microirradiation is not easy experimentally, but it has now been done with proton and alpha particles, and with X and far ultraviolet electromagnetic rays. Production of the micro beam is done by a colinear series of apertures in a number of absorbents (e.g., lead bricks). Sometimes it is done by passing the radiation through a glass or platinum capillary mounted in a lead shield. Thus any X rays falling on the wall of a Pt capillary at an angle of 0.6 deg or less to the axis of the capillary are completely reflected, and are propagated unchanged to the exit and thence to the target. The position of the target cells can be set by means of apparatus which is not essentially different from the traveling stage of a microscope: by means of a micromanipulator with worm gears the target can be moved into any desired position within a limited space.

Results with protons, alphas, X, and ultraviolet have all shown that the nucleus, and specifically the nucleolus which begins to become more prominent as mitosis begins, is far more radiation-sensitive than the rest of the cell. For example, in a specific case, irradiation through an area 2.5μ in diameter on a chromosome ($\sim 5\mu \times 30\mu$) with 36,000 rads of proton energy (60 protons, ~ 1.5 Mev) caused the chromosome to become sticky (to crosslink?) and the cell to die in the attempt to divide, while irradiation elsewhere in the cell with up to 1.7 million rads caused no change in speed or reliability of division, nor did it have any effect on the several observed succeeding generations.

However, indirect effects on the chromosomes by irradiation elsewhere in the cell have been demonstrated. Nor should one infer that irradiation elsewhere does no permanent damage to the cell or its progeny. For such spectacular things as blistering of the cell wall, and coagulation of cytoplasm and of the mitochondria, as well as death to all the progeny of cells irradiated generally elsewhere than the chromosomes, have been observed. Consideration of the cell as "a bag of enzymes," each subject to irradiation isomerization, gives one an idea of how complex this question can be.

Unfortunately the important microirradiation studies have not yet yielded any case in which irradiation of a certain part of the cell has caused an increased rate of reproduction of modified or cancerous cells. Hence, just how absorbed radiation induces cancer at the cell level remains unanswered. It is now generally assumed to be irradiation of the DNA of the chromosomes, but it could just as well be modification of one of the catalysts of the synthesis of DNA, or the membrane which contains them.

There is some direct information on DNA in solution, however. By viscosity and titration methods it has been found that the molecule is shattered by X and α rays, to an amount of about 1.5×10^{11} chain-breaks per gram of DNA per rad absorbed. The analogy with the effect of ultrasound on viruses is usefully drawn at this point, for ultrasound quite literally shakes the molecule to pieces.

There is also some semidirect information on DNA *in vivo*. Thus, T. T. Puck[4] and others have allowed irradiated human cells to culture, and have measured, not the LD_{50}, but the "reproductive death"—the irradiation dose which is just sufficient to cause the cells not to reproduce. These cells are not killed by the radiation, but often show abnormalities, such as growing to a huge size or showing a change in metabolic rates. Reproductive "death" is relatively very sensitive, its $L"D"_{50}$ being 25 to 40 rads in human cells. The corresponding sensitivity, σ, is about 2000 (compare with the values in Table 9-4).

Irradiation of Organs and Tissues

The histologic and pathologic changes in tissues resulting from irradiation are properly part of the subject matter of radiology, and will not be discussed here. However, as illustration, some of the results of whole- and partial-body irradiation are listed below, with no explanation, as simple statements.

Just as some parts of the cell are more radiation-sensitive than others, also some tissues and organs are more sensitive than others. The analogy goes further. Some parts of the human body can be irradiated relatively heavily without severe general damage; others are very radiation-sensitive. The following list includes the most sensitive.

(1) Red blood cell manufacture slows down in the bone marrow.

(2) Manufacture of lymphocytes in the spleen is drastically reduced and cannot replace fast enough those killed by irradiation of the general lymphatic circulation system.

(3) The skin shows reddening or blistering, after only 140 rem; larger doses can precipitate skin cancer.

(4) Impairment of secretion or of assimilation occurs in the alimentary canal, mostly as a result of membrane destruction. Sloughing off of the mucous lining of the canal is an early symptom of damage and often results in death due to infection.

(5) The critically important steady-states in the adrenal glands are upset. Because these are the source of certain rate-controlling molecules, the hor-

mones, greater body susceptibility to heat, cold, injury, and infection results from the damage.

(6) Decreased activity of the thyroid can result, causing lower basal metabolic rate.

(7) In the lungs, the membranes across which O_2 and CO_2 exchange between blood capillaries and air takes place are broken, and persistent oxygen deficiency and excess carbon dioxide in the blood result.

(8) Enough radiation can ruin the very selective membranes in the kidney.

(9) Similar damage in the liver results in hemorraging.

(10) Cataracts develop in the lens of the eye from coagulation of liquid crystals. The effects may be delayed, however.

(11) Large local doses ($\sim$400 rem) to the gonads can cause sterility by killing off the sensitive spermatogenic cells. The sperm themselves are relatively resistant. Much lower doses could cause mutations in the DNA-gene-chromosome structure of the germ cells, while large doses could simply break the chromosomes into pieces. Gonadal doses from various sources are collected in Table 9-5.

(12) Even low doses to some tissues can produce enough variation in the cell reproduction system so that the tissue becomes carcinogenic. (This is probably the most important, and still the least understood, physiological effect of irradiation. Unfortunately, the susceptibility may not become manifested for several generations of cells.)

(13) The rate of production of antibodies is lowered markedly, and the tissue is more subject to infection and disease. This effect is related to the rapid destruction of the lymphatic tissues.

TABLE 9-5. Gonadal Doses from Various Sources*

Source	Dose or Dose Rate
Background radiation	0.095–0.180 rem/yr
Maximum dose permitted to X ray workers	15 rem/yr (0.3 rem/wk)
Pelvic examinations, fluoroscopic	$\sim$1 rem
Salpingogram	$\sim$1.7 rem
Photographic X ray of kidney and ureters	0.9 rem
Photographic X ray of pelvis	0.7 rem
Photographic X ray of hip	0.5 rem

*Collected by C. Don.[22]

The following general principles are important to remember:

(1) The physiological effects are direct results of changes in the rates of chemical or transport processes.

(2) The long-term damage may prove to be greatest in the chromosomes, at mitosis, but such genetic effects may not appear for several generations.

(3) Damage to the fine network of molecular membranes and canals in the cell's substructure, where the enzyme-controlled protein and nucleic acid syntheses take place, can result in immediate physiological changes. Damage to cell walls and structural tissue is important at high dose or after some time at low dose.

EFFECTS OF WHOLE-BODY IRRADIATION

The Facts and the Complexity of the Problem

Three events, each horrible in its own way, provide the foundation of our knowledge about whole-body irradiation of normal humans. The first was the bombs at Hiroshima and Nagasaki; the second was an accident at Oak Ridge, and others, less publicized, later; and the third, unpredicted winds over Bikini and the Marshall Islands during H-bomb trials.

Three months after the publication by Roentgen of his experiments with X rays, puzzling radiation burns on the skin were observed. Within a few years, premature loss of hair and early ageing befell the early workers. From ten to forty years after intense exposure, some gruesome cancers appeared, and case histories showed they could be attributed to the exposures long before.

Careful analyses, now sixteen years in progress, of the results of the atom bombs over Japan, have yielded much modern clinical experience with radiation-induced epilation, premature ageing, and cancer. The effects resulted principally from gamma rays and neutrons given off by fission products. In the Marshalls it was principally betas from heavy hydrogen (tritium). At Oak Ridge two scientists died slowly from a 600-rad accidental exposure during a demonstration of thermonuclear fusion, and half a dozen more received severe, but sublethal, doses. All these cases were very carefully documented.

Studies on animals have mushroomed in the past decade. The guinea-pig, pig, mouse, dog, goat, monkey, rat, hamster, and rabbit: all have contributed their bit to the phenomenology. Various interesting things have been learned. For example, if any tissue is selectively protected by shielding, usually a substantial increase in the animal's LD_{50} occurs. In mice, protection of a hind leg, or the intestine, or the head, or the liver, but particularly the spleen, causes significant increase in the LD_{50}. In the larger animals, the results of protection (shielding) of the long bones, the site of red blood cell synthesis, have been spectacular. As a corollary, irradiation of specific tissues and organs in the larger animals has shown (1) the great sensitivity of erythrocyte synthesis (perhaps aided by reflection and strong absorptions of X rays within the long bones; and (2) the rather subtle, and perhaps more serious, sensitivity of the central nervous system itself. In the first case, changes in blood count have been measured. In the second, the appearance of new and changed peaks in the electroencephalogram have been observed. The meanings of these peaks in terms of effects on memory, judgement, irritability, etc., are only vaguely understood so far.

Accumulation of all this information—effects on both human beings and animals—has provided rough rules-of-thumb which are very useful. One can be sure, however, that they are by no means final. For instance, it is known from studies of persons connected with radiation therapy in hospitals that doses of less than 1 rem/wk produce definite symptoms of irradiation damage over several years. Yet a complete diagnostic X-ray examination of thorax and intestines, even when done under the responsibility of a very competent radiologist, delivers about 1 rem to the tissues being studied. Since long-term genetic effects are indicated by what information is available, and since the genetic results really are not yet known for humans, maximum permissable dose and dose rate have been arbitrarily chosen for radiologists, patients, and workers with ionizing radiations in industry and government. For X and gamma radiation, the current value is 0.3 rem/wk (or 0.3 rem individually to the blood-forming organs, to the gonads, to the lens of the eye, to other organs and tissues), and it may soon be revised downward. If the rate is 0.02 rem/hr the work is considered very hazardous. However, these tolerances, as well as the minimum shielding requirements, are now very carefully controlled by the governments of most countries, and the symptoms and necessary precautions are continuously being revised and published as new information bearing on these questions accumulates. However, background irradiation from rocks, cosmic rays, tritium in the water, etc., amounts to 0.15 to 0.4 r/yr, and because of long-term genetic effects which may result from even small doses to humans, physicians, especially, should be aware of the potential harm of needless and incompetent clinical exposure to diagnostic X rays, and aware of the possible effects which may result from an ever-increasing background. In these terms the probable effects of all-out or even limited nuclear war are distasteful to discuss. One could mention especially those effects from radioactive gases which could enter the lungs; and those from dust-carried "fallout" containing such isotopes as Sr^{90} which can enter the bones and teeth, and, having a low turnover rate there and being a hard beta-emitter (0.54 and 2.26 Mevs) with a long half-life (25 yrs), could irradiate the human body continuously from within—and nothing could be done about it, except to try to chelate it out by some chemical process.... However, one can provide for himself some protection (see Fig. 9-9).

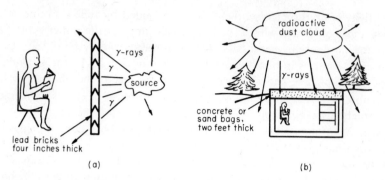

Figure 9-9. Protection against ionizing radiations is offered by relatively thin layers of heavy-atom absorbers (a), or by relatively thick layers of lighter-atom absorbers (b). Absorption follows approximately the Beer-Lambert Law (Chapter 4): intensity decays exponentially with thickness. Note protective chemicals in pill form!

The clinical symptoms of radiation sickness caused by the LD_{50} are fairly well known: diarrhoea, nausea and vomiting, followed by inflammation of the throat; loss of hair; loss of appetite; fever and pallor; rapid emaciation, and death—completed within 3 to 4 weeks of exposure. For less exposure, recovery begins after a period of time which is longer the greater the exposure. Repeated exposures with small doses precipitate the onset of leukemia or carcinogenesis, often years after the first exposure. Certain chemicals, mentioned earlier in the chapter, offer some protection against the chemical and physical effects which multiply into the biological effects. Further, experiments on the removal of Sr^{90} and other radioactive isotopes from the body after ingestion by complexing them away with the so-called chelating (complexing) agents, are showing limited promise.

Radiation Therapy

Because they are undergoing more rapid cell division and have certain instabilities which normal cells do not have, cancer cells are, as a general rule, more radiation-sensitive than normal cells. Further, by a continuous rotation of either target or radiation beam, it is a rather simple matter in principle for a radiologist to deliver a high accumulated or total dose to the cancerous volume and at the same time deliver only part of that dose to the noncancerous tissue which surrounds it. Radiation therapy is based on these two principles.

In many cases 2000 to 7000 rem of local irradiation will kill or sterilize a tumor so that it cannot grow. Machine-produced X rays, gamma rays such as those from the Co^{60} "bomb" (Figure 9-10), or radium needles inserted directly into the center of the tumor can be used to give local irradiation.

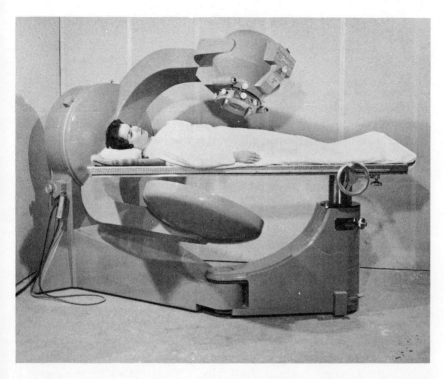

Figure 9-10. The "Theratron Junior," Typical of Co^{60} "Bombs" Used in Cancer Clinics in Many Countries. Source is contained in the lead head (above), and radiation is collimated by a tubular hole. Lead absorber and counterweight is below. Both source and patient can be moved so that the patient can be irradiated from several directions. Typical charge is 1000 curies of Co^{60}, which gives about 15 roentgens per minute at a spot 1 meter from the source (15 rmm). (Photograph courtesy of Atomic Energy of Canada Ltd.)

On the other hand, some atoms such as I^{131} will fit nicely into the biochemistry of the body, localize in the thyroid, and irradiate it with betas and gammas (refer to Table 5-7).

However, there is a basic difference between the two methods of application of irradiation. Machine-made X rays, or the gamma rays from a cobalt-60 bomb provide either a constant dose rate or one which can be varied at will by the radiologist. By contrast, radioactive isotopic therapy depends upon the biochemistry of the system to transport the injected isotope to the locale to be irradiated, and then to excrete it. If the application of the isotope is direct (see Figure 5-9), or if the induction time is short, the isotope has a biologically effective half-life, t_{eff}, which is the half-time of irradiation. In any case, the dose rate, dD/dt rads per sec, is proportional to the average energy*** of the emission and to the strength of the source, c microcuries. Thus

$$dD/dt = 5.92 \times 10^{-4} \overline{E}_\beta c$$

where the constant arises from the definitions of the curie (3.7×10^{10} disintegrations per sec) and the rad (100 ergs absorbed per gram), and the fact that 1 Mev = 1.6×10^{-6} ergs. In the case in which t_{eff} is shorter than the physical half-life of the isotope, the dose received integrates to

$$D_\beta(t) = 74 \, \overline{E}_\beta c_0 t_{eff} (1 - e^{-0.693t/t_{eff}})$$

for any time t; or

$$D_\beta(\infty) = 74 \, \overline{E}_\beta c_0 t_{eff}$$

for the total dose administered (by an initial concentration, c_0 microcuries, of a beta emitter with an average energy $\overline{E}_\beta$ Mevs and a biological half-life of t_{eff} days) up to the time the isotope has been practically completely excreted. Table 9-6 gives pertinent data for different isotopes and organs. In some cases t_{eff} is limited by rapid chemical turnover, in others by the decay half-life. Note that only a fraction of an isotope accumulates at a particular locale in the system. Therapy depends upon *preferential* uptake by an organ. The rest of the system gets irradiated too, but less.

P^{32} has been used successfully for the irradiation of excess white (leukemia) and red (polycythaemia) blood cells. Other isotopes are being used in ever-increasing numbers and amounts as new techniques (e.g., the insertion of radioactive colloidal material (Au^{198}, for example) into the tumor: it "floats," but it cannot get into the blood stream and be washed away), and as new methods of preparation and purification become known.

The technique of bone-marrow therapy is now in an advanced state, although its application is limited. The principle is the complete replacement of irradiation-damaged marrow with that from a donor. Transplants are normally limited to inbred strains or to isologous animals. However, if the natural immunity reactions of human beings are completely destroyed by large radiation doses first, then complete blood transplant *can* be successful. Even so, further complications often arise later, in terms of a secondary disease. Rare cases of transplant from one identical twin to another have been more successful.

An advanced technique, which may keep radiologists in business even

---

***Generally the average energy for gammas is about the same as the listed values, for gammas are monoenergetic; but for betas the average energy, $\overline{E}_\beta$, is approximately 1/3 the maximum (nominal) energy usually listed. For X rays the average energy is always well below the peak value listed—about 0.3 of the nominal kvp if the soft end has not been filtered out (by, say, 0.5 mm Al), and about 0.6 of the nominal kvp if it has.

TABLE 9-6. Data on Turnover of Some Isotopes in Humans.

Isotope	Organ Where Chiefly Concentrated	Organ Weight (kg)	Half-life (days, unless otherwise stated)		Per Cent of Ingested Activity Reaching Organ*
			Physical Decay	Effective in Tissue (t_{eff})	
H^3	total body	70	12.3 yrs	19	100
C_1^{14} {	fat	10	} 5600 yrs {	35	50
	bone	7		180	5
Na^{24}	total body	70	0.60	0.60	95
P^{32}	bone	7	14.2	14	20
S^{35}	skin	2	87	18	8
K^{42}	muscle	30	0.5	0.5	70
Ca^{45}	bone	7	164	151	25
Fe^{59}	blood	5.4	46	27	80
Co^{60} {	liver	1.7	} 5.2 yrs {	8.4	0.4
	spleen	0.15		9	0.005
Rb^{86}	muscle	30	18	7.8	42
Sr^{89}	bone	7	53	52	25
I^{131}	thyroid	0.02	8.0	7.5	20

*Rough and incomplete, but the best available information based on Recommendations of the International Commission on Radiological Protection, 1955.

though pressed hard by the radiomimetic (radiation-mocking) chemicals, involves the use of sensitizers. As we already have seen, certain chemicals protect molecules and cells against radiation damage; certain other chemicals can *sensitize*, or *increase* the damage which a dose of radiation will impart to molecules and cells. For example, excess O_2 and certain organic molecules such as synkavite have been used in selected tumor treatments.

The competition from radiomimetic chemicals is not just casual! The chemical action of the sulfur- and nitrogen-mustard gases is surprisingly like that of X rays on tissue: membrane destruction, some molecules broken, others polymerized, and the cell unable to reproduce. These agents can even cause genetic changes. The technique used is to stop the natural blood flow in the region to be treated, pump the dissolved mustard gas through the tissue for some minutes, and then to flush it out with a fresh blood transfusion before opening the stops again to full natural circulation.

This is the period of enthusiasm for the use of mustards in this new role (they originally saw service as war gases). As their limitations for therapy become better known, and if history repeats, both the new chemical therapy and ionizing radiation therapy will oscillate through periods of enthusiasm and reappraisal before ultimately finding their proper place in the medical arsenal.

．．．　　．．．　　．．．

The reader may now wish to pursue the subject matter of this chapter in more detail. The author suggests perusal of References 28 and 23, then of References 10, 1, and 2.

PROBLEMS

9-1: (a) From tabulated values of the sensitivity constant, σ, estimate the dose which would be expected to kill 20, 50 and 80 per cent of a tumor.

(b) Suppose this tumor were just under the skin. Discuss three different ways —ultrasonic, machine-made X-rays, and cobalt-60 gamma rays—in which you could apply the irradiation.

(c) How would you monitor the air dose? The tissue dose?

9-2: How do you rationalize the facts that X rays *induce* cancer, and that X rays are *used in the treatment of* cancer?

REFERENCES

1. Alexander, P., "Atomic Radiation and Life," Penguin Books, Inc., Baltimore, 1959: a "popular" introduction to the text, Ref. 2.

2. Bacq, Z. M. and Alexander, P., "Fundamentals of Radiobiology," Butterworths, London, 1955; 2nd ed., 1961.

3. Hollaender, A., Ed., "Radiation Biology," McGraw-Hill Book Co., Inc., New York, N. Y., 1954.

4. Oncley, J. L., *et al.*, "Biophysical Science—A Study Program," John Wiley & Sons, Inc., New York, N. Y., 1959; especially the contributions by R. E. Zirkle, W. Bloom, E. Pollard, T. H. Wood, C. A. Tobias and T. T. Puck on radiation effects.

5. Livshits, N. N., "Physiological Effects of Nuclear Radiations on the Central Nervous System," in *Adv. in Biol. and Med. Phys.*, **7**, 174–241 (1960): a review of the extensive Russian work, and that of others, on this important question.

6. Law, L. W., "Radiation Carcinogenesis," *ibid.*, **7**, 295–337 (1960): a penetrating survey of recent work, and a lucid account of the present position of knowledge on radiation-induced neoplasms.

7. Howard-Flanders, P., "Physical and Chemical Mechanisms in the Injury of Cells by Ionizing Radiations," *ibid.*, **6**, 554–596 (1958).

8. Kinsman, S., Ed., "Radiological Health Handbook," U. S. Dept. of Health, Education and Welfare, 1954.

9. International Conference, Geneva: "Peaceful Uses of Atomic Energy. II. Biological Effects of Radiation," United Nations, New York, N. Y., 1955.

10. Butler, J. A. V., "Inside the Living Cell," Methuen, London, 1960.

11. Swallow, A. J., "Radiation Chemistry of Organic Compounds," Pergamon Press, London, 1960.

12. Appleton, G. J. and Krishnamoorthy, P. N., "Safe Handling of Radioisotopes: Health Physics Addendum," Internat. Atomic Energy Agency, Vienna, 1960.

13. Hercik, F. and Jammet, H., "Safe Handling of Radioisotopes: Medical Addendum," Internat. Atomic Energy Agency, Vienna, 1960.

14. Glasser, O., "Medical Physics," Vol. III, Year Book Publ. Inc., Chicago, Ill., 1960: many contributed articles on radiation effects on living tissue.

15. Cronkite, E. P., Bond, V. P., and Dunham, C. L., "Some Effects of Ionizing Radiation on Human Beings," a Report by the U. S. Atomic Energy Commission, July, 1956.

16. Buchanan, A. R., Heim, H. C., Stilson, D. W., "Biomedical Effects of Exposure to Electromagnetic Radiation," a Report to Life Support Systems Lab., Wright Air Development Div., USAF, 1960.

17. Shchepot'yeva, E. S., et al., "Effect of Oxygen in Ionizing Radiation," publ. by State Publ. House for Medical Literature, Moscow, 1959 (U.S. A.E.C. Translation 4265, 1960).

18. "Report of the International Commission on Radiological Units and Measurements," U. S. National Bureau of Standards Handbook 78, 1959.

19. Burton, M., Kirby-Smith, J. S., and Magee, J. L., "Comparative Effects of Radiation," John Wiley & Sons, Inc., New York, N. Y., 1960.

20. Kuzin, A. M., Shapiro, N. I., Livshits, N. N., and Breslavets, L. P., "Reviews on Radiobiology," Inst. Biol. Physics, Publ. House Acad. Sci., SSSR, Moscow, 1956 (U. S. Atomic Energy Commission Translation 3353).

21. Peacocke, A. R., "The Structure and Physical Chemistry of Nucleic Acids and Nucleoproteins," Prog. in Biophys., 10, 55 (1960).

22. Don, C., "Radiation Hazards of Mass Miniature Radiography," Can. Med. Assn. Jour., 84, 5–7 (1961).

23. Lea, D. E., "Actions of Radiations on Living Cells," 2nd ed., Cambridge Univ. Press, 1955.

24. Henderson, I. H. S., "Electrochemical Radiation Dosimetry," Defence Research Chemical Laboratories, Canada, Report No. 352, 1961.

25. Hine, G. J. and Brownell, G. L., "Radiation Dosimetry," Academic Press, Inc., New York, N. Y., 1956.

26. Smith, D. E., Ed., "Proc. Internat. Cong. of Radiation Research," Radiation Research, Suppl. 1, Academic Press, Inc., New York, N. Y., 1959.

27. Augenstine, L. G., Ed., "Bioenergetics," Radiation Research, Suppl. 2, Academic Press, Inc., New York, N. Y., 1960.

28. Allen, A. O., "The Radiation Chemistry of Water and Aqueous Solutions," D. Van Nostrand Co., Inc., Princeton, N. J., 1961.

29. Haissinsky, M., Ed., "The Chemical and Biological Actions of Radiations," Vols. 1 to 5, Academic Press, Inc., New York, N. Y.; Vol. 5, 1961.

CHAPTER 10

Biophysical Studies on Nerve and Muscle

I had dissected a frog . . . and had placed it upon a table on which there was an electric machine . . . . I took up the scalpel and moved its point close to one or the other of the crural nerves of the frog, while at the same time one of my assistants elicited sparks from the electric machine . . . . Strong contractions took place in every muscle of the limb, and at the very moment when sparks appeared the animal was seized as it were with tetanus . . . . (Luigi Galvani, anatomist, surgeon, and obstetrician; 1781.)

This chapter presents an outline of some recent studies on nerve, and shows how these are related to motion effected beyond the nerve endings by excitable tissue in muscle. In the next chapter these facts are interpreted as part of the enveloping concept of the human physical system. Then some generalizations about this system are made which develop the framework introduced in Chapter 1 and upon which the various parts of this book are strung.

First, however: What is the nature of the physical apparatus—nerve and muscle?

TRANSIENT BIOELECTRICS IN NERVE

In Chapter 7 the rest-condition of tissue was shown to exhibit voltage differences in living membranes between the points at which solute activities differ—and even in normal bulk tissue (Chapter 8) if bioelectric currents are driven through it. Transient, or sudden, changes in voltages or currents are

262

common, however, throughout living tissue, and play a uniquely important role in nerve conduction. Here an electrical transient—the change in voltage across the nerve cell membrane—is propagated with great speed along the surface of the cell and along the nerve fiber formed by many axons in parallel. The voltage change is the unit of information. First we describe how this transmission takes place.

From Volta* to Hodgkin

It was in the late 1770's in Bologna that the Italian physician, Luigi Galvani, and his wife Lucia observed quite by accident that the leg of the frog with which they were experimenting could be made to twitch if certain parts of the animal were touched simultaneously with the ends of two different pieces of metal (iron and zinc, for example) joined together. Actually they had discovered two things: the electrical voltage of a Zn-Fe couple, and the electrochemical exictation of living tissue. In the succeeding two hundred years a great body of facts has accumulated; these have demonstrated quite conclusively the electrochemical nature of nerve conduction and the resulting stimulation of excitable tissue. The afferent and efferent nerve systems have been well tracked and catalogued—the job of the former being to conduct commands, despatched by the brain, out to muscles and other effector tissues. The so-called "all-or-none law," which says simply that the excitable tissue will not fire (act) unless the stimulus has some minimum power, and that the impulse moves down the nerve with constant amplitude and velocity,** is now an accepted working principle for the physiologist. Various chemical and physical methods have been developed to modify the sensitivity of the nerve to stimulating agents—chemical catalysts in the form of drugs; electrical pacemakers, etc.

However, even with all this great accumulation of useful knowledge on how to modify the operation of the nervous system, it has only been since the early 1930's that definitive examination could be made of several of the many theories of operation of the nerve fiber. About that time it was realized that the main nerve axon of the squid—in this respect unique among all others—is a tube large enough ($\sim$1 mm od and several centimeters long (see Figure 10-1)) to be examined both electrically and chemically, inside and out. The fact that its physical structure could be examined by both

---

*In *Phil. Trans.*, 1800, Alessandro Volta, Professor Natural Philosophy, University of Pavia, published a paper in which he not only described his new "artificial electric organ" (i.e., the first storage battery), but also discussed the effects which electric current from this invention "exercises on the different parts of our body," effects "which will open a very wide field for reflection, . . . particularly interesting to Medicine."

**In certain unnatural media (sodium-deficient, for example) decremental propagation occurs: both amplitude and velocity decrease as the impulse moves along the nerve.

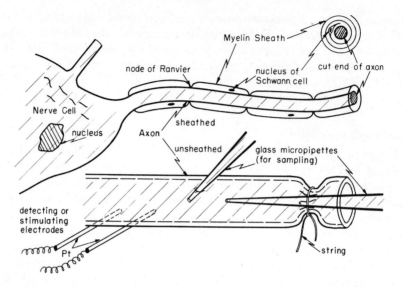

Figure 10-1. Nerve Cell and Axons. The length of the axon is sometimes as much as 100,000 times the length of the cell. Insertion of Micropipets and Micro-electrodes. Stimulating (or detecting) electrodes touching myelin sheath.

optical and electron-microscopic methods made it all the more attractive as a subject for study.

In the next section some of the pertinent information which has been obtained from the lowly squid is summarized. This information has formed the basis of a better understanding of the biophysics of nerve conduction. Nerve is similar enough from one species to another that some generalities can be assumed on the basis of information gained from the squid axon.

The Era of the Squid

Curtis and Cole by 1936 had placed metal electrodes inside and outside the squid's tube-shaped axon; and with a conventional Wheatstone bridge, had made measurements of the electrical resistance (20,000 ohms/cm^2) and electrical capacitance (1 microfarad (μf) per cm^2) of the membrane. Further, they showed that the resistance is much lower when the nerve is actively transmitting impulses.

With the development of electronic dc amplifiers and oscilloscopes, it became possible to display the passage of the nerve impulse as detected by thin platinum-wire contacts (electrodes) touching the nerve (see bottom of Figure 10-1, for example). The impulse turned out to be a band of negative charge passing down the outside surface of the axon, from the point of stimulation to the far end. The insert in Figure 10-2 shows the electrical shape of the impulse. Further, the use of two pickup electrodes placed a few centimeters apart, each feeding an oscilloscope, permitted measurement of the time it takes the impulse to cover the distance between them. The speed of transmission was thus shown to be about 100 m/sec (about 200 miles/hr), less if the nerve were bathed in media of low electrical conductivity. Since an excised squid axon bathed in seawater would live and reliably transmit for about 1 hr, one can well imagine the exciting days for Hodgkin and Huxley of Cambridge University, working at Plymouth, England; and for Curtis and Cole at the famed Marine Biological Institute at Wood's Hole, Massachusetts—but hard times for the squid population in the waters close by.

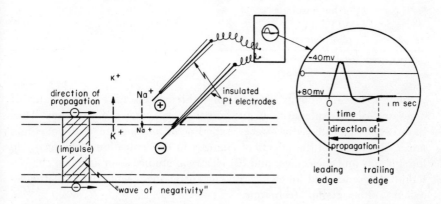

Figure 10-2. Potential Changes as the Impulse Passes Detector Electrodes, One Inside and One Outside the Axon. Normally the axon is negative to the outside electrolyte, but as the impulse passes, the potential is momentarily reversed.

By 1939 researchers had micropipets inside the axons (see Figure 10-1, bottom) to sample the fluids during stimulation (Table 10-1); and microelectrodes, too, to record the change in voltage across the membrane. J. Bernstein's hypothesis (1902), that the potential difference across the resting membrane is due to a difference in salt concentration, was fully confirmed.

However, as the impulse passed any point on the nerve, the nerve membrane's voltage-difference from inside to outside at that point was found not only to drop to zero, but actually to reverse—the inside to become positive some 40 mv (the so-called "spike"), before it started its recovery to the normal state! There the puzzle had to stand during World War II. Figure 10-2 shows how the potential difference between inside and outside the axon at a point on the surface changes as the wave of negativity passes.

TABLE 10-1.   Natural Content of the Solution Within the Giant Axon of the Squid*

Substance	Concentration (millimoles/1000 g H_2O)
K	400
Na	50
Cl	40
Ca	0.4
Mg	10
isothionate	270
aspartate	75
glutamate	12
succinate-fumarate	17
orthophosphate	2.5 to 9
ATP	0.7 to 1.7
phosphagen	1.8 to 5.7

*Data collected by Hodgkin.[14] Compare with ionic content of erythrocytes (Table 2-1):

Since 1947 experiments of essentially three kinds have added valuable clues toward the explanation of just how the nerve carries information. They have been: (1) radioactive tracer experiments on sodium and potassium ions; (2) studies of the effects of changes in concentration of natural and foreign ions and molecules; and (3) electrical studies such as fixing the potential difference and following the current changes which result—the so-called "voltage clamp" technique.

In short, these three techniques have established the facts that the impulse is associated with: (a) a rapid increase in the membrane's permeability to Na^+, an increase which lasts only about one msec; and concurrently, (b), a smaller and later increase in the K^+ permeability, which has a slower recovery lasting over several msec.

(1) *Tracers:* Hodgkin, Huxley, and Katz were the first to use effectively the radioactive beta and gamma emitters, Na^{24} and K^{40}, to follow sodium- and potassium-ion permeabilities across the axon wall. If the active Na^+ salt is placed in the external solution, samples of the internal fluid can be withdrawn via the micropipet and checked periodically for radioactivity. Alternatively, small amounts of radioactive K^+ salt can be inserted into the axon, and samples of the external fluid measured periodically for radioactivity. The rate of permeation of these ions through the axon wall when it is passive is much smaller than the rate of permeation when the axon is repeatedly stimulated and is carrying impulses. This difference in rate of penetration is greater the greater the number of pulses being passed along the axon per second.

(2) *Concentration Ratio:* Table 7-12 gave data which show that the resting potential measured across living membranes is in substantial agreement with the value calculated from the ratio of the two concentrations of salt, outside and inside the membrane. Calculation is done via the Nernst equation, suitably modified to express the voltage of a concentration cell:

$$E = 60/n \log (a_1/a_2) \quad \text{mv}$$

where n is the number of charges carried on the ions of the salt, and a_1 and a_2 are the effective concentrations (activities) on opposite sides of the membrane.

However, such a relationship as that shown above between the potential of a concentration cell and the ratio of the activities of the salt on the two sides of the membrane is actually a special simplified case, used here for introductory purposes. More generally, when two such salt solutions with activities (effective concentrations) a_1 and a_2 abut each other, and if diffusion is restricted so that salt cannot flow,

$$E = 2 \frac{RT}{n\overline{F}} \ln a_1/a_2$$

or

$$E = 2 \times 60 \log a_1/a_2$$

The 2 comes from the fact that work is potentially available from the concentration ratios of *both* the positive and negative ions.

If salt *can* diffuse, a new factor, t_-, the transference number of the anions, enters (for reasons which will not be developed here) so that

$$E = 2 t_- \times 60 \log a_1/a_2$$

Here $t_- = \mu_-/(\mu_+ + \mu_-)$, where the μ's are the mobilities, or speeds, of the ions in centimeters per second when the voltage gradient is 1 v/cm. Introduction of the expression for t_-, and rearrangement, gives

$$E = 60 \log a_1/a_2 - 60 \frac{\mu_+ - \mu_-}{\mu_+ + \mu_-} \log a_1/a_2$$

This expression gives the potential if cations and anions are *not restricted* in their motion. When both move with the same speed (KCl in water, for example) $\mu_+ = \mu_-$ (or $t_- = 1/2$), and the second term drops out. If the motion of one is completely restricted, there can be no motion of the other if micro-neutrality is to be maintained, and the potential is given by the first term only. In such a case—charged protein ions plus salt in water, the Donnan case, for example—the values of a_1 and a_2 are the activities of the *unrestricted* ion.

When the membrane is like that of nerve (Figure 10-3)—partially permeable to several ions—the potential across it can be related to the permeability constants, $\mathcal{P}$ (Chapter 8). The deduction gives

$$E = \frac{RT}{F} \ln \left(\sum_i \mathcal{P}_i{}^{out} c_i{}^{out} \Big/ \sum_i \mathcal{P}_i{}^{in} c_i{}^{in} \right)$$

where the summations are of the products of permeability ($\mathcal{P}$) and concentration (c) for all the ions (i), and the superscripts refer to outside (out) and inside (in) the cell. In other words the permeability constants express as a number the contributions which the different ions make to the potential difference across the membrane. Thus a membrane which is selective can pass one ion more quickly than another, so that the $\mathcal{P}$'s are not equal. In the case of resting nerve, $\mathcal{P}_{K^+} \gg \mathcal{P}_{Na^+}$ or $\mathcal{P}_{Cl^-}$. The rapid potential changes which occur while the impulse is passing by are now generally believed to result from rapid changes in the permeabilities. The reader is invited to follow the fascinating efforts of our contemporaries, Ussing, Teorell, Sollner, Schlögl, and other membrane researchers.

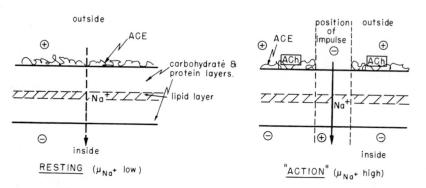

Figure 10-3. Illustration of Construction and Ionic Penetration (μ's) of the Nerve Membrane. During rest the mobilities of Na^+ and K^+ are low, but during action they become momentarily very high. (Refer back to Fig. 6-8.)

Sodium deficiency in the external electrolyte slows down the speed of conduction. Further, it leads to a spike height which decreases as the impulse passes down the nerve—"decremental conduction," it is called. Sodium is pumped out of the axon through the membrane by a yet unknown mechanism, and this requires energy. It has been found that, during treatment with metabolic inhibitors, adenosine triphosphate (ATP), the mobile power supply, disappears at about the same rate at which the sodium pump slows down and stops. It is therefore inferred that reactions involving the hydrolysis of ATP are probably the source of energy for this process, as they are for many other biological processes.

(3) *Voltage Clamp:* This is a technique, rather simple in principle, in common use in solid-state research and in electrochemical research. In short, electric current is passed between two electrodes maintained at some constant potential difference, or voltage. A steady current is a measure of the rate of the steady-state which is operating within the system. Suddenly the voltage is changed to another value, and "clamped" there; and the current is followed closely as it changes toward a new steady-state value. The shape of the current versus time curve (Figure 10-4; top right) is diagnostic. Illustrated in the figure is evidence that the first part of the action spike is due to rapid sodium ion transport through the membrane: the inward current disappears if the electrolyte in which the axon is bathed contains no sodium. Of course, propagation of the impulse disappears under the same conditions also.

Theories: Quantitative descriptions of the electrical phenomena have been attempted, it being variously assumed that deviations from the Nernst equation (see Table 7-12) are due to (a) poor knowledge of the activity at the

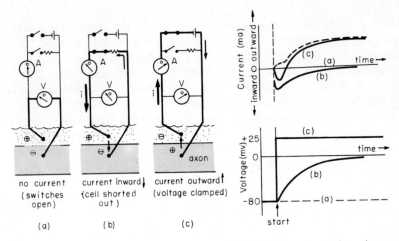

Figure 10-4. Voltage Clamp Technique. Two reversible electrodes, one inside and one outside the axon are used. (a) Natural voltage (50–100 millivolts) measured across axon. Current (top, right) is zero; voltage (bottom, right) is steady. (b) Membrane voltage is short-circuited through external resistive load. Positive current (due to Na⁺) flows *inward*. Voltage and current both decay toward zero as energy is dissipated as heat in external load. (c) Voltage is "clamped" at unnatural value by connection to a potentiostat, a source of constant voltage. *After* the first millisecond, positive current (due to K⁺) flows *outward*. Within the first millisecond, inward current (due to Na⁺) flows because the membrane's permeability to K⁺ is still small. The inward current is completely absent if external fluid has no sodium in it (top, right; broken curve).

given concentrations; (b) leaky membranes, through which the Na^+ and K^+ permeate, or diffuse down their respective gradients; (c) electrical charges permanently fixed within the hundred angstroms or so of effective thickness of membrane; or (d) changes in shape of acetylcholinesterase (ACE), an enzyme located on the surface of nerve (Figure 10-3 illustrates) and thought by some to be the cover whose shape determines whether or not Na^+, or K^+, or both, can enter the slip through the pores in the membrane.

Two quantitative theories permeate the literature on nerve transmission: the use of the electrical cable theory to describe the spread of a localized electrical disturbance; and the description of ionic currents through the membrane as a function of permeability.

Early in the century electrical engineers had worked out the effect of a break, or a series of breaks, in the insulation of an electric cable having a metallic conductor inside and salt water outside. By 1938 Curtis and Cole had used this application of Ohm's law to describe how a localized disturbance in a nerve membrane can spread on down the nerve. The key expression is:

$$\frac{\partial^2 V}{\partial x^2} = -\frac{r_1 + r_2}{r}\left[E - V - rC_m\frac{\partial V}{\partial t}\right]$$

where E is the concentration-cell voltage across the membrane in the absence of a disturbance, i.e., when the membrane is resting; V is the "action" voltage at any time, t, at a distance, x, along the surface from the site of the disturbance, O; r_1 and r_2 are the electrolytic resistances (ohms), between O and x, in the outside conductor and the inside conductor, respectively; r is the resistivity of the membrane (fixed, unknown thickness) in ohm cm^2; and C_m is the capacitance of the membrane, which is being depolarized (discharged) at a rate dV/dt. The expression teaches that the depolarization occurs at a rate which increases as the divergence (spread) of voltage along the surface increases, and decreases as the resistances to ion flow (r_1, r_2, and r) increase.

By 1952 Hodgkin and Huxley had described measured changes in membrane conductance of the giant axon of the squid in terms of change in the permeabilities of the simple ions of the external and internal media. The principle ideas of this theory will now be given.

Currents through the membrane are considered to charge (or discharge) the membrane capacitance and to leak Na^+, K^+, and other ions as well. Thus:

$$I = C_m \, dV/dt + I_{Na^+} + I_{K^+} + I_i$$

where I is total current, and the I_i's are the currents due to the different ions. Then each I_i is expressed as being the product of the membrane conductance (g_i) and the driving voltage for that ion. Thus: $I_i = g_i \, \Delta V$

Each g_i was then related by a phenomenological trick to time and voltage in such a way as to fit the experimental results. Thus, for potassium ion,

$$g_{K+} = g_{K+}{}^{max} n^4.$$

and

$$\frac{dn}{dt} = \alpha_n n (1 - n) - \beta_n n$$

where n is a dimensionless parameter which has a value between 0 and 1; it is time-dependent and is related to voltage-dependent penetration constants, α_n and β_n. The first, α_n, expresses the rate of K^+ movement into the cell, and β_n expresses its rate out. Similar expressions have been devised for Na^+ and the other ions of the system. From these expressions the total current (I) can be expressed in terms of time-dependent and voltage-dependent parameters related to permeability. With proper choice of the values of the different parameters, the experimental values of conductance as a function of time and voltage can be completely described.

These two theories have been bright lights in the quantitative description of nerve propagation. The interested reader is referred to the analytical and summary papers[21,22] for the detailed arguments. The papers are difficult, but rewarding.

The charged-pore theory of membrane potential differences has been successful with synthetic membranes of collodion, ion-exchanger resins, and other synthetic polymers. It will not be developed here, although it has been put into elegant quantitative form by Meyer and Siever and, more recently, by Teorell.

This is a very active and important part of biophysics today, and, as was stated in Chapter 6, probably there is no part of the research in the subject which will be more rewarding. Hodgkin's Croonian Lecture[14] is an excellent statement of the state of the art, and Nachmansohn's recent, short review,[18] more from the biochemical viewpoint, will nicely balance the further development of the reader's concepts.

Is Semiconductivity Important?

It may be. We saw in Chapter 4 that the π electrons of many organic compounds have a certain freedom and can move under the influence of an electric field. Most vertebrate nerve is sheathed in myelin, the protein-and-fat wrapping formed by the doubled membrane of the Schwann cells. This is illustrated schematically in Figure 10-1, top right, and shown very dramatically by the electron micrograph, Figure 10-5. The myelin sheath offers physical protection to the fine nerve fibers of vertebrates. But it has further roles. For instance, since it completely covers the nerve fiber except at certain interruptions about 1 mm apart, called the nodes of Ranvier (Fig-

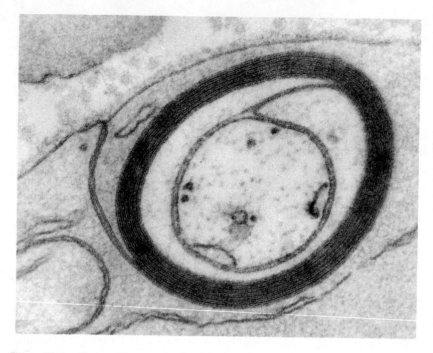

Figure 10-5.   Electron Micrograph of an Ultrathin Section of Nerve Axon which is Myelin-
ated by the Spiral Wrap of the Double-Membraned Schwann Cell. Magnification 90,000 ×.
(Courtesy of J. D. Robertson, Harvard Medical School, and of *Scientific American*.)

ure 10-1) the impulse is forced to skip from node to node, perhaps via semi-
conductivity, although it may be by proton transfer ("protochemical" cells
have been demonstrated in the laboratory) *through* the myelin. In any case
the skipping mechanism is very fast, and therefore a sheathed nerve normally conducts an impulse somewhat faster than an unsheathed one.

The Trigger

To fire the nerve and incite the transmission of an impulse, a stimulus is
required. Stimuli are essentially of five kinds:
(1) *Electrical:* voltage changes applied directly to the cells of the nerve—
in the brain for example.
(2) *Mechanical:* pressure changes causing distortion at nerve endings—
ear, and mechanoreceptors associated with the sense of touch.
(3) *Electromagnetic:* incident radiation absorbed by pigment molecules in
cells sensitive to visible light, and by other transducer molecules
sensitive to warming (infrared) radiations—eye, and a multitide of
closely spaced detectors all over the body's surface.

(4) *Chemical:* foreign chemicals applied, or changes in concentration of natural chemicals—taste buds, dehydrated tissue cells, etc.

(5) *Gravitational:* continuous attraction to earth, occasionally varied by superposition of various accelerations—balance-detectors in middle ear, for example. (These are essentially of type (2).)

Deserving special mention as a trigger is the "pacemaker" of the heart, which in man repetitively stimulates the pump to compress and relax once about every 1.3 sec 24 hr a day for life. Recordings from microelectrodes inserted into pacemaker cells show that they are self-contained oscillators. Very recently D. Noble has shown[19] that if certain limiting conditions are imposed on the cable-and-changing-permeability theory described above, the theory can describe the condition of oscillating permeability and oscillating potential of the membrane of the pacemaker cell.

When and if the pacemaker fails, it has been shown to be possible to stimulate the heart artificially. With small transistor circuitry and small zinc-mercuric oxide batteries, it has been demonstrated recently that an artificial pacemaker can be buried, by surgery, in the abdominal cavity under the skin and stimulate a weak heart regularly for at least a year before the battery has to be changed (again by surgery). This device has brought a normal life to many people.

Recent advances in microelectrode preparation have permitted glass tubes to be drawn down to an outer diameter of 0.0005 cm, filled with electrolyte, and the ends inserted carefully right into the individual muscle cells in the animal's beating heart. Thus the electrical measurements on cells working *in situ* are now being made. Great care has to be taken that the electrical measurements are not affected by the huge electrical resistance of these micrelectrodes (try Problem 10-5). For steady potentials an electrometer with a high impedance is usually used; but for rapidly-varying potentials, such an instrument is too slow to follow the potential changes without inducing distortion. There this problem of measurement presently rests. Once it is solved, although the cross-correlation of electrical and chemical information may still not be possible in these small cells because of the size of the object under study, pharmacological problems should receive much attention with this technique. Indeed the neuromuscular junction is already being so explored.

Studies on the Central Nervous System

By contrast with the normally resting peripheral nerve tissue, which is activated upon demand, the brain is a mass of spontaneously pulsating neural networks, seemingly continuously energized and active. It is usually assumed that the basic processes are electrochemical, like those just outlined as being proper to nerve conduction. However, biophysical knowledge of this organ is meager. Thus, while neuroanatomy, which deals with the geography of the brain and the relation of various parts of the brain to certain functions of the whole system, is well advanced, and its daughter, neurosurgery, is in a rapid state of development, physiological studies are necessarily phenomenological because of the complexity of the system under study; and biophysical studies, mainly electrical because of the fast electrical responses of the system, tend to be either empirical or theoretical— and hence do not assure a *correct understanding* of the phenomena under study.

As a result of this complexity, the most important advances of the past decade have not been biophysical at all. Three different kinds of study will now be briefly noted: (a) the recording and analysis of gross electrical signals of the brain; (b) the transmission across synapses in the spinal cord; and (c) the electrical behavior of single neurons in the cortex.

The method of electroencephalography (EEG) is as follows:

Small pellets of solder, or other metal-contact electrodes, preferably nonpolarizable,*** are placed on symmetrical points of the scalp and fastened

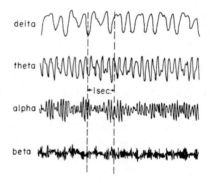

Figure 10-6. Components of an Electroencephalogram.

there with a binder such as collodion. Twelve to twenty-six leads cover the scalp in localization experiments, overlying each important lobe of the brain, and even different portions of each lobe. Voltages between these and some reference position, such as a lead to the ear lobe, are fed into standard high-gain amplifiers, and traced by pen recorders. Five or six seconds of recording gives patterns (Figure 10-6) which, quite empirically, have been cata-

---

***A nonpolarizable electrode is one in which the voltage with respect to some reference remains unchanged when current is passed through the electrode. A silver disk coated with a thin layer of AgCl, which makes contact with the chloride-containing body salts, is nonpolarizable in EEG work where the currents are very small ($<10^{-6}$ amp).

logued as coming from normal or diseased tissue. Patterns taken on an individual vary with the emotional state. A creative man is said to have patterns quite different from one who lacks new ideas. However, the fine structure of these waves is not well understood. Recorded spikes are only about 150 μv high. Characteristic spikes of different shapes and frequencies have been named alpha, theta, delta, etc. These are depicted in Figure 10-6.

Location of tumors, via predominance of the delta waves (see Table 10-2), has been particularly successful, with 73 to 90 per cent accuracy claimed. Bagchi has reported 84 per cent in 333 tries. Other abnormalities, such as epilepsy, have been studied by this technique.

TABLE 10-2.   Classification of Electroencephalograph Waves.

Names of Waves	Frequency (cps)	Association
delta	0.5 to 3.5	"disease, degeneration, death; defence"*
theta	6 to 7	
alpha	8 to 13	a scanning mechanism?
beta	14 to 30	alertness; active response

*Walter, W. Gray, "The Living Brain," Penguin Books, Baltimore, 1960, p. 81.

While the all-encompassing phenomenological techniques of EEG have been making useful contributions to life, studies of individual neurons, via microelectrodes in the cortex, and studies of the properties of synapses and ganglia in the spinal cord have demonstrated interesting phenomena such as: inhibition of transmission across nerve endings (strong signals passed through one nerve ending reduce the effectiveness of one close by); post-tetanic potentiation (faster and more energetic transmission through a particular nerve path following a rapid succession of pulses through that path); and the promotion of epileptic-like seizures and peculiar mental images in man by electrical stimulation of particular spots in the cortex via microelectrodes.

Transfer of an impulse across a synapse (Figure 10-7) is currently thought to be by means of "chemical" transfer rather than by "electrical," for two reasons: the observed salt concentration changes associated with a single impulse are very small; and there is fairly good evidence that acetylcholine (ACh) accumulates *in the gap* during transmission across the gap. A theory is that ACh is contained in the many little vesicles in the pre-synaptic ending: that, during "activity," ACh is expelled through the membrane and diffuses to the post-synaptic membrane and locally depolarizes it. The details of this mechanism are still unknown.

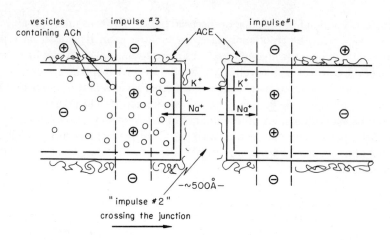

Figure 10-7. The Synapse or Junction Between Two Nerve Endings (conceptual and schematic). As the impulse reaches the end of the nerve, acetylcholine (ACh) is released in quantity from the little (∼300 Å) vesicles contained in the presynaptic nerve ending. This ACh depolarizes the membrane, and free flow of K^+ out and Na^+ in, on the presynaptic ending, and of ACh across the gap, occurs.

The neuro-muscular junction, shown and described later, is similar to the neuron-neuron junction in many ways.

Synapses are apparently very sensitive to ionizing radiations, for Livshits and others in the Russian school have observed changes in the EEG pattern during even very weak (1 r/hr) X- or γ-irradiation, although peripheral nerve is relatively quite insensitive. The subtle psychological effects which result from such interference with, or modification of, the normal pulsating activity of the brain can therefore be considered as due to electrochemical noise generating by radiations from *outside*. Noise in our reckoning system, produced by such stresses from without, is considered a bit more fully in the next chapter. Noise from within—disordered inputs from crossed neural circuits, from the physical apparatus of memory, and from the metaphysical parts of mind, intelligence, and will—is the basis for further psychological stresses and disorders. Memory-stimulation by electric shocks applied to the interpretive cortex of the brain seems to be another experimental avenue by which man can apply biophysical methods to the study of this wonderful organ. The uninitiated but interested reader is referred to the well-illustrated review by Penfield.[8]

Entering the brain are several trunk lines, each main line being many-stranded, and every strand insulated electrically from every other so that many signals may pass simultaneously down the trunk line. In the case of the two optic nerve trunks, a nerve-ending from each fiber carries an impulse from a rod or cone to a bipolar cell, thence to the brain. There is evidence now that insulation among these strands is not complete, and that parallel signals from two may trigger a third, and so on. This is a mechanism which seems to be operative in color vision, as was inferred in the discussion on that subject in Chapter 4. Cross-stimulation seems to be very generally operable, for there is a great deal of psychological evidence that saturation of one sensing organ will have a marked effect on the sensitivity of another. Mentioned earlier was the dentist's new trick of flooding the ear with noise of a suitable frequency so that the pain of drilling cannot be felt!

The physical network which accommodates, sorts, and retains certain impulses and rejects others is a topic for future study. Furthermore, memory is still a very mysterious phenomenon. One recent proposal about the physical mechanism of memory deserves mention: the "training" of the neural network to store information is done by means of the synthesis of certain ("different") protein molecules. These result from a *change in shape* of the ribonucleic acid (RNA) *effected by a passing stimulus*—i.e., the RNA within nerve and neighboring glial (Schwann) cells. Although this does not sound very convincing at first glance, it seems to be the best model yet put forward in the baffling question of what is the physical apparatus of memory; and it certainly is consistent with the known fact that the rate of protein synthesis is very high in active nerve cells. One cannot help thinking that these "different" proteins may be imbedded right *in* the membrane, and exert their effect as "permanent" changes in its permeability. In conclusion, one could say that, from the biophysical point of view, the study of the central nervous system is becoming more and more a study in applied electrochemistry, a study of membrane biophysics.

THE MOLECULAR BASIS OF MUSCLE CONTRACTION

By means of nerve, the brain exercises control over both chemical and physical processes in the body. There are good examples of each: for the former, the endocrine gland system; and for the latter, muscle. Of the two, the latter is in many ways inherently less complicated, and only it will be discussed in this attempt to illustrate how control is achieved in a particular case of a physical action. For this we need to know some relevant physical properties of muscle tissue; and, more important still from the biophysical point of view, we need to know the molecular behavior which is at the root of this physical behavior. Fortunately, both electron microscopic examination of muscle-tissue slices, and kinetic methods of analysis of rate data seem to be succeeding with this problem of providing an understanding of muscular contraction. On the other hand, a review of muscular contraction from the molecular viewpoint has the added advantage of illustrating the powerful methods of kinetics in displaying the physical movements of molecules. First, however, comes a discussion of the fact that activated muscle tissue often behaves like a critically damped helical spring. The model is illustrated in Figure 10-8.

The Helical-Spring Analogy

The activated muscle has several physical properties in common with a stretched spring. The latter obeys certain well-known physical laws, for example that of Hooke: viz, the restoring force, F, is proportional to the displacement, Δs, during stretching, or

$$F = k_1 \Delta s$$
$$= k_1(s - s_f)$$

where s is length at any time, t, and s_f is the final (fully contracted) length (see Figure 10-8).

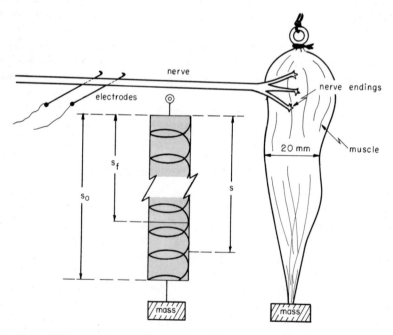

Figure 10-8. Stretched-Spring Model of Muscle. Defined are: s, the length at any time during shortening; s_0, the initial (resting) length before contraction starts; and s_f, the length at complete contraction.

Now if speed, v, of shortening is always proportional to restoring force (this is equivalent to assuming the spring is embedded in a plastic or highly viscous mass, and that the spring is critically damped) then:

$$v = k(s - s_f)$$

Integration gives

$$s = s_f + (s_0 - s_f)e^{-kt}$$

where s_0 is the initial, or starting, length. From this the shortening speed can be expressed as a function of time by finding the derivative. It is

$$v = k(s_0 - s_f)e^{-kt}$$

The *fraction* shortened, f, defined as $(s_0 - s)/(s_0 - s_f)$, at any time reduces to

$$f = 1 - e^{-kt}$$

and k becomes known as the *shortening constant*. This expression is illustrated in Figure 10-9, in which the fraction shortened during shortening is plotted for both the case discussed and for muscle. Elasticity in the muscle, which lowers the initial rate of shortening (df/dt), and recovery following full contraction are the chief differences. Note that the S-shaped curve in the case of muscle *can* appear to be linear, especially if sensitivity of measurement is not high enough; and hence the shortening rate $(-ds/dt)$ is often considered to be constant.

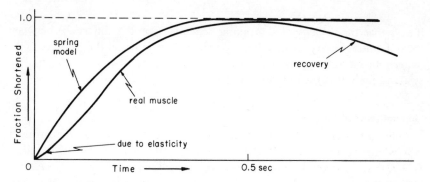

Figure 10-9. Fraction Shortened as Function of Time During Shortening.

The larger the load, m, the smaller is the shortening constant, k. This is to say that the muscle can contract quickly if the load is light, and only slowly if the load is heavy. It is found that k varies with m in such a way that momentum, mv, is conserved (remains constant):

$$\left(\frac{v - v_0}{v_{max}}\right)\left(\frac{m - m_0}{m_{max}}\right) = \text{constant}$$

where v_{max} is the maximum speed of shortening (no load), and m_{max} is the largest weight which can be lifted. Here v_0 and m_0 are constants. This result is often written as a product of velocity and force, when the acceleration is that due to gravity—a constant; it then becomes the "force-velocity relationship." Thus for two masses, m_1 and m_2, momentum conservation is expressed

$$\left(\frac{v_1 - v_0}{v_{max}}\right)\left(\frac{m_1 - m_0}{m_{max}}\right) = \left(\frac{v_2 - v_0}{v_{max}}\right)\left(\frac{m_2 - m_0}{m_{max}}\right)$$

The denominators cancel out. Then if mass 2 is chosen to be just big enough that the muscle can sustain it but not lift it, $v_2 = 0$, and $m_2 = m_{max}$. Multiplication through by g, the acceleration due to gravity, converts masses to forces ($F = mg$), and then rearrangement gives

$$(F + a)(v + b) = (F_{max} + a)b,$$

the force-velocity relationship, first stated in 1938 by A. V. Hill (a and b are his constants, equal to $-gm_0$ and $-v_0$ respectively). Figure 10-10 illustrates this equation, and says simply that the greater the force to be overcome by the contracting muscle the less the speed at which it can contract. Rearranged in the form

$$v = (F_{max} - F)b/(F + a)$$

it says that the velocity of shortening depends upon the difference between the maximum force it can develop and the actual force on the muscle. This hyperbolic relationship is obeyed by a wide variety of muscle and muscle systems, including the human arm.[16]

On Energetics of Muscle

The work done by the muscle in lifting a weight is given by the product mgh, where g is the acceleration due to gravity (and therefore mg is *force*, since $F = ma$) and h is height to which the weight is lifted. We saw in Chapter 7 that part ($\Delta\mathfrak{F}'$) of hydrolysis of ATP—a reaction catalyzed by the contractile enzyme, myosin—could appear as work of contraction. Thus:

$$\Delta\mathfrak{F}' = mgh$$

and the rest of the total free energy of reaction ($\Delta\mathfrak{F}$) is wasted because of irreversibility or inefficiency in the process, and thrown away as heat, $T\Delta\mathfrak{S}'$.

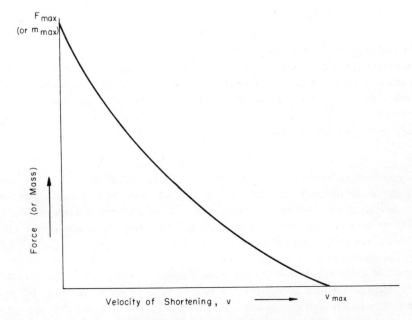

Figure 10-10. Force-Velocity Relationship (see text).

In review of the discussion in Chapter 7, we recall that the physical process derives its energy from chemical reactions, and that the heat of reaction, $\Delta \mathcal{H}$, can appear in several forms:

$$\Delta \mathcal{H} = \Delta \mathcal{F}' + q' + T\Delta \mathcal{S}$$

$$= \Delta \mathcal{F}' + \Delta \mathcal{F}'_{int} + q'_{irr} + T\Delta \mathcal{S}$$

where $\Delta \mathcal{F}'$ is the external work; $\Delta \mathcal{F}'_{int}$ is the internal work, degraded into heat and given off by the system as heat; $T\Delta \mathcal{S}$ is the reversible entropic heat, unavailable for work; and q'_{irr} is the extra heat produced because of the nonreversibility (inefficiency) of the process. It was also shown that q' can be expressed as $q'_{bm} + q'_{ex}$, so that

$$\Delta \mathcal{H} = \Delta \mathcal{F}' + q'_{bm} + q'_{ex} + T\Delta \mathcal{S}$$

where q'_{bm} is the basal metabolic heat given off, and q'_{ex} is the excess heat given off during exertion. (These q's are irreversible heats, can be factored into $T\Delta \mathcal{S}''$'s, and are sometimes called entropic heats.)

Now although $\Delta \mathcal{H}$ and $T\Delta \mathcal{S}$ depend only upon the amount of material reacting, and q'_{bm} is substantially constant since it refers to a particular physiological state, values of $\Delta \mathcal{F}'$ and q'_{ex} generally depend markedly upon the *rate* at which the physical process occurs. Thus the faster the process the less efficient it is: i.e., the greater the fraction $q'_{ex}/(\Delta\mathcal{F}' + q'_{ex})$ which is lost as heat, and the less is the fraction $\Delta\mathcal{F}'/(\Delta\mathcal{F}' + q'_{ex})$ which is realized as external work. However, whether the work is done fast or slowly, numerically the same *amount* of work is done; and therefore, because $\Delta\mathcal{F}'$ is independent of speed, so must q'_{ex} be, provided the same amount of fuel is consumed. It is a well-established experimental finding that the total heat, $\mathcal{Q}'_t$, given out during a shortening (the "contraction heat")

$$\mathcal{Q}'_t = q'_{bm} + q'_{ex} + T\Delta\mathcal{S}$$

is constant, independent of speed of shortening. However, $\mathcal{Q}'_t$, is proportional to the distance (x) shortened; i.e., $\propto a\,x$; and the constant a has the same dimensions (energy/distance, or force) *and* numerical value ($\sim$400 g wt/cm^2 area of cross section) as the a in the force-velocity relationship. The significance of this coincidence is not yet clear.

Careful measurements, with small thermocouples imbedded in the muscle and fast galvanometers to record small electrical currents, have shown that the contraction heat is composed of two parts: a rapid initial surge following stimulation, and completed before contraction starts; and then the contraction heat proper. The first has been called the heat of activation, A, by analogy with the terminology of the threshold in chemical kinetics. Therefore q'_{ex} can be written as

$$q'_{ex} = A + ax$$

in Hill's terminology, the first term being the activation heat and the second the contraction heat proper.[†]

Discussion of the production of enthalpy, $\mathcal{H}$, by biochemical reactions in muscle is beyond our scope in this book. A few notes suffice. Muscle glycogen is the primary fuel, being oxidized to lactic acid with $-\Delta H = 16.2$ Cal/mole of lactic acid produced. This energy is used in the synthesis of creatine phosphate (CP) which acts as a secondary fuel. Both glycogen and creatine phosphate supply free energy for the synthesis of adenosine triphosphate (ATP), the hydrolysis of which is the immediate source of free energy for the physical work of contraction. Regeneration of the hydrolysis product, the diphosphate (ADP) is effected by reaction of ADP with CP— the famous Lohmann reaction. The enzyme myosin, which has the contractile property, adsorbs ATP and catalyses its hydrolysis.

[†] In Hill's terms (Ref. 23, for example) the extra metabolic energy involved in contraction is composed of three parts: the work done $(\Delta\mathcal{F}')$, the activation heat (A), and the heat of shortening (ax). The *total* energy will include q'_{bm} and $T\Delta\mathcal{S}$.

Power of Contraction

The power—the rate of energy release, or "energy flux," as some people call it—is given by

$$P = d(\Delta \mathcal{F}')/dt + d\mathcal{Q}'_t/dt$$

$$= P_w + P_{\mathcal{Q}'_t}$$

the first term being the rate at which work is done, and the second the rate at which heat is liberated during shortening. Resting muscle in the steady-state condition at 20°C has a basal metabolic rate (bmr) of heat loss, dq'_{bm}/dt, of about 2 cal per kg of muscle per minute. The rate is 2.5 times higher at 30°, 2.5 times lower at 10°C. Extrapolated to man (the example is Hill's[16])—30 kg of muscle at 37°C—the value of that part of the bmr due to muscle alone is about 18 Cal/hr, about 25 per cent of man's total bmr. During action, i.e., during a single twitch, the muscle gives out a contraction heat of about 3 cal/kg of muscle. For a fast muscle which twitches in 0.1 to 1.0 sec, therefore, the rate of heat loss, $P_{\mathcal{Q}'_t}$, would be 180 to 1800 cal per kg per min—up to many times the bmr ($\sim$14 cal per kg per min).

Because the contraction heat is independent of rate of shortening, the rate of heat loss, $P_{\mathcal{Q}'_t}$, increases linearly with increasing speed of shortening. But the power expended to do work, (i.e., P_w) is zero if no load is lifted ($v = v_{max}$); it is also zero if the load is so heavy that the muscle can just sustain but not lift it ($v = 0$); and it goes through a maximum value for intermediate loads. Figure 10-11 illustrates this behavior of P_w and $P_{\mathcal{Q}'_t}$. The top curve gives the total power expended by the muscle.

The key to all this activity in muscle is the molecule myosin. But before discussing myosin itself, we must first understand the structure of muscle

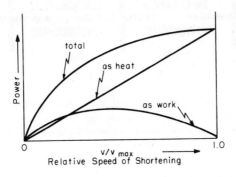

Figure 10-11. Power as a Function of Fraction Shortened (after Podolsky, 1961).

tissue, as revealed by the light and electron microscopes, and a bit about the chemistry of muscle proteins, to see where myosin fits in.

Structure of Muscle Tissue

Figure 10-12 illustrates what is seen by means of higher- and higher-resolution microscopic examination of muscle. A muscle is made up of fibers, which appear striated under the light microscope. Phase contrast and interference attachments reveal that a fiber is composed of myofibrils, along the side of which lie mitochondria and nuclei (not shown). The electron microscope reveals that a myofibril appears segmented because of a repeating pattern of light and dark bands throughout. Repeating patterns, bounded by the end- or "Z"-lines contain a faint "M"-line in the middle, bounded first by narrow H-zones and then the wider "A"- (for anisotropic) bands which span the middle. Isotropic "I"-bands span the "Z"-lines (see Figure 10-12).

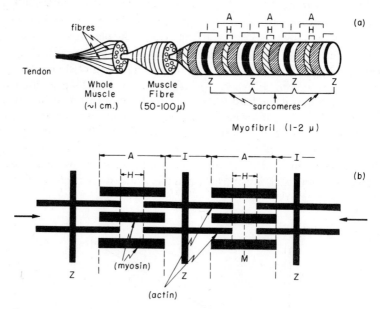

Figure 10-12. Schematic Drawings of Muscle Under Higher and Higher Resolution Microscopy. (a) Light microscope; (b) Electron microscope. During shortening the horizontal thick and thin filaments slide farther into each other, so that only the H and I bands shorten.

Under great magnification ($\sim$300,000 ×) a rather comical contraption is disclosed: an array of overlapping thick and thin filaments, which run parallel to the myofibril, and which apparently slide back and forth over each other as the muscle contracts and relaxes. Partial overlap of the thick and thin filaments gives rise to density gradients which appear to us through the light microscope as the bands (Figure 10-12 (b) and Figure 10-13).

The motive power is provided by the inherently contractile molecular actomyosin complex, a complicated protein condensation product of two complex units, actin and myosin—the former apparently primarily a structural support and the latter an enzyme which catalyzes the hydrolysis of ATP. There is evidence that myosin is contained principally in the thick

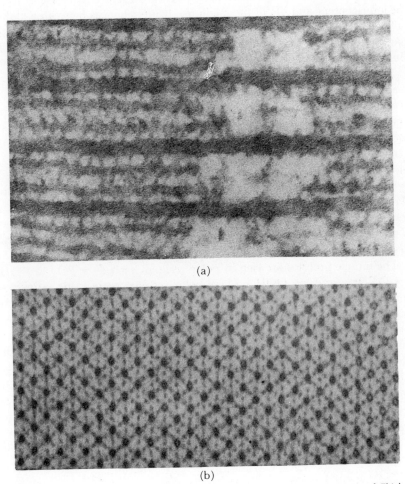

(a)

(b)

Figure 10-13. Huxley's Famous Electron Micrographs of Intermeshing Arrays of Thick and Thin Filaments of Striated Muscle Fibers. (a) Side view (longitudinal section). Note how the light H-band is formed by a discontinuity in the thin filaments. Note also the direct evidence for cross-bonds between thick and thin filaments (300,000×). (b) End view (cross-section) (170,000×). (Courtesy of H. E. Huxley, Laboratory of Molecular Biology, Cambridge University.)

filaments, actin in the thin ones. The Z-lines are the outer edges of areas which bisect the myofibril, and have been shown to be the medium through which the stimulus, or order to contract, is carried from the surface membrane of the fiber (the sarcolemma) *into* the myofibril. The sarcolemma carries it electrochemically (like nerve) *along* the fiber.

Muscle consists of 18 to 20 per cent protein, by weight. About 60 per cent of this protein is a condensation product of several "myosins" with actin, a very complex molecule whose complete physical structure is very sensitive to the ionic content and pH of the medium. It interchanges between a globular, almost spherical, hard G-actin, to a fibrous, stiff F-actin. Only myosin has the ATPase activity and can accept the free energy of hydrolysis of ATP. But the myosin of muscle is itself made up of smaller parts:

Rapidly extractable from minced muscle in salt solutions is *myosin-A* (called "myosin" or "*l*-myosin" in some books). Electrophoresis causes separation of myosin-A into three fractions: one heavy (H) meromyosin, and two light (L) meromyosins. Only the H-meromyosin retains the ATPase activity, Extractable only slowly, or in other media, are myosin-B ("natural actomyosin" or "*s*-myosin") and tropomyosin, which differ in physical properties from myosin-A. Rejected by the extraction procedures is the globular G-actin, which, in the presence of ATP and dilute salts, slowly converts to the much more viscous, fibrous F-actin. The chemical composition is not simple. Thus there is some evidence that tropomyosin + G-actin + another protein constitute myosin-A. Some physical characteristics of myosin and actin are gathered in Table 10-3.

The muscle proteins are rich in polar residues such as $-PO_3^{-3}$, $-OH$, $-CONH-$, and $-COOH$. These polar residues seem to be intimately connected with the process of contraction. Myosin's partner in the contractile reaction is ATP. To ATP, the fact that the catalytic enzyme, myosin, contracts during the hydrolysis, or splitting of ATP into ADP + P, is quite incidental. To the living system, however, the fact is vital! Dephosphorylation occurs during or immediately after the contraction process.

Hydrolysis of ATP as a free energy-producing reaction is not confined to myosin as a catalyst, as we saw in Chapter 7. It provides the energy which drives many living processes. The following scheme represents the splitting reaction and its auxiliary reactions:

$$H_2O + ATP^{-4} \overset{L}{\rightleftharpoons} ADP^{-2} + HPO_4^{-2}$$

$$+ \qquad K_2 \updownarrow \qquad +$$
$$H^+ \qquad H^+ \qquad H^+$$
$$K_1 \updownarrow \qquad + \qquad K_3 \updownarrow$$
$$ATP^{-3} \qquad ADP^{-3} \qquad H_2PO_4^{-}$$

The L-step is the splitting reaction proper. In the vicinity of pH = 7, the values of the equilibrium constants, K_1, K_2 and K_3, are such that most of the adenosine is in the form of either ATP^{-4} or ADP^{-2}; and hence the measured values of ΔH and ΔF refer mainly to the hydrolysis itself—the horizontal reaction. The reaction is both exothermic and exergonic, a source of heat and a source of free energy for work. Respectable values (see comments in Table 7-3) are:

$$\Delta F = -10.5 \text{ kcal/mole}$$

$$\Delta H = -9.2 \text{ kcal/mole}$$

However, as is obvious from the reaction scheme, a shift in pH can shift the position of equilibrium of reactions 1, 2, and 3, and therefore shift the free energy of the splitting reaction. In a similar manner to the effect of hydrogen ions, metallic cations—principally Mg^{++} and Ca^{++}—can and do form complexes with the highly charged phosphate groups; each complex with its own equilibrium to affect the reaction scheme, and thereby to affect the values of ΔF and ΔH.

TABLE 10-3.   Sedimentation Constant (s), Diffusion Coefficient (D), Molecular Weight (M), Intrinsic Viscosity ($[\eta_0]$), Length (l) and Thickness (d) of the Muscle Proteins.

Protein	$s \times 10^{13}$	$D \times 10^7$	M	$[\eta_0]$	$l(\text{Å})$	$d(\text{Å})$
Tropomyosin	2.6	2.4	53,000	0.523	400	15
H-meromyosin	6.96	2.91	232,000	0.32	435	15
L-meromyosin	2.86	2.87	96,000	1.0	550	25
Myosin	5 to 8.2	1.0	420,000*	2.0	1700+	~25
G-actin	3.2	2.5	70,000*	0.21	290	25

*Dimers can be formed.
+Unfolded.
(From data collected by K. Bailey.[16])

The source of the free energy in the hydrolysis reaction is the breaking of the intrinsically unstable, mutually repelling polyphosphates (as typified by ATP) and the formation of products with strong electronic resonance. When one remembers that during the splitting reaction both ATP and ADP are bound more or less tightly to the protein, one can understand why with different proteins the energy available for doing useful work, ΔF, can vary.

Although the free energy of the hydrolysis of ATP catalyzed by the enzyme myosin is certainly associated with the work done by the enzyme as it shortens, there is evidence that this relationship is somewhat indirect. This can be seen in the important facts which follow.

To a fairly good first approximation, the Michaelis-Menten Law, which relates the rate, v, of hydrolysis to catalyst (myosin) and substrate (ATP) concentrations,

$$v = \frac{k_2[E]_0[S]_0}{[S]_0 + K_m}$$

(see Chapter 8 for symbols), is well obeyed. Measurement of rate as a function of temperature and substrate concentration permits evaluation of $\Delta H^\ddagger$, $\Delta F^\ddagger$ and $\Delta S^\ddagger$, the thermodynamic quantities associated with formation of the activated state. Since $\Delta S^\ddagger$ is usually (for various conditions) found to be positive, it is inferred that a change in configuration of the enzyme (and/or the release of adsorbed water molecules) occurs during the binding step in which an ATP molecule sits down on the myosin molecule. This step is then followed by the splitting reaction proper. In the terminology discussed in Chapter 8 and illustrated in Figure 8-5:

$$E + S \underset{k_{-1}}{\overset{k_1}{\rightleftharpoons}} ES^\ddagger \overset{k_2}{\longrightarrow} \text{product}$$

in which process 1 is adsorption and shortening; and process 2 is the hydrolysis step.

When experimental conditions are such that the kinetic results are amenable to analysis without ambiguity of mechanism, analysis shows that the binding of the (enzyme) myosin molecule to the (substrate) ATP molecule occurs spontaneously with release of 6.6 kcal/mole. That is,

$$\Delta F_{\text{binding}} = -6.6 \text{ kcal/mole}$$

and

$$\Delta H_{\text{binding}} = -8.0 \text{ kcal/mole}$$

Thus the free energy released in the *binding* process is a sizable fraction of that for the whole process (-10.5). This indicates that the structural change (shortening) of the myosin molecule may occur *at the time of binding of ATP, before ATP is split* by hydrolysis. The inference is, then, that the resting muscle is very much like a stretched molecular spring, ready to contract when released from the forces which hold it extended. Indeed X-ray diffraction patterns suggest that the famous alpha helix, discussed in Chapter 6, is the basic structure in myosin, as well as in so many other proteins.

Studies of effects of pressure and of dielectric constant on the rate have given values of the entropy of complex formation (i.e., of enzyme-substrate binding) to be $\Delta S_{\text{binding}} \approx 48$ cal/deg. mole, with half of this value purely electrostatic, due to the charged groups on ATP and myosin.

Under certain experimental conditions the rate of desorption of the hydrolytic fragments is slow, causing inhibition by the products. Activators and inhibitors can complicate the picture much further. However, enough has been shown to illustrate the fact that the kinetic methods, although very specialized in detail, provide a general mechanistic description of the physical actions of the key molecules which play the vital roles.

A Theory of Contraction

One simplified working hypothesis about the physical activity of the contractile molecule will now be outlined. It is as though the myosin were a coiled molecule (like other proteins whose structures are known from X-ray diffraction) which, at rest, is held in a stretched condition by virtue of a series of mutually repelling, charged ionic groups along its length, $-COOMg^+$ or $-NH_3^+$, for example. Adsorption of ATP^{-4} to form the Michaelis-Menten complex, discharges the myosin network, permitting the interatomic restoring forces, which exist because of bent bonds, to relax the molecule to its neutralized (contracted) length. After hydrolysis, ADP^{-2} and P^{-2} desorb, because they are bound less tightly than ATP^{-4} and are perhaps aided by other molecular species in the vicinity. After the products have desorbed, the positive charges along the molecule lengthen the coil again, and the molecule is ready to repeat the cycle.

What is the nature of the trigger which starts ATP^{-4} adsorbing? The answer is not known, but the hypothesis, based on indirect (but nevertheless substantial) evidence, is that a covering molecule, the "blanket," weakly adsorbs on and protects the charged network of the stretched myosin. Its shape is thought to be determined partly by Mg^{++} ions, without which the contractile power of myosin ceases. Distortion of the shape of the blanket by the more strongly chelating (complexing) Ca^{++} is supposed to bare the myosin to attack by ATP^{-4}: thus injection of Ca^{++} causes contraction. Nerve endings, which run almost to the membranous sheath (sarcolemma) which covers the muscle fibers, are thought by some to be capable of releasing Ca^{++} at the myosin sites via electrochemical stimuli propagated down nerve axons to the nerve ending, and thence down the sheath and in the Z-bands to the myosin sites.

The connectors between filaments, shown so beautifully in the electron microscope pictures of sliced muscle tissue (Figure 10-13), in this theory take on a very positive character, composition, and role: viz., the ends and particular side groups of stretched myosin molecules, attached at one end to a thin actin filament, but lying within and forming part of an adjacent thick one so that shortening of the myosin molecule itself causes filaments to slide over each other, and the whole tissue to contract. The concept is illustrated in Figure 10-14. Approximate obedience of the whole muscle to Hooke's Law would qualitatively result from behavior on the molecular level. Both the chemistry of the contraction process and the physical sliding of the fibers complement the model.

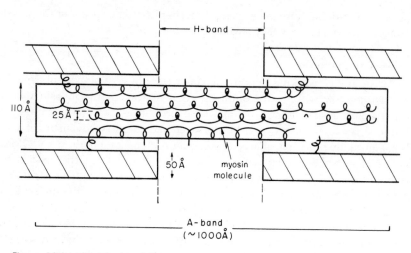

Figure 10-14. Stretched and Contracting Muscle—Molecular Model. Myosin molecules in the thick filaments contract and expand depending upon the ionic character of the medium. Ends stick out and join to actin molecules contained in thin filament.

It is a bit ironic that, after carrying about 60 lb of these little machines, and using them himself, day and night, for many thousands of years, *homo sapiens* still does not know exactly how they work.

EFFECTS OF ENVIRONMENT ON CONTROL

Both nerve and muscle are pretty complicated molecular machines. The statement is also very true for the neuromuscular junction or synapse. The neuron-neuron synapse was depicted schematically in Figure 10-7. Figure 10-15 is a beautiful display of the substructure of a neuromuscular junction in which the nerve ending, the synaptic gap, the continuous, infolded sarcolemma, and substantial portions of two myofibrils with their thick and thin filaments and the black Z-line perpendicular to them, are all clearly visible. Repeated study of this and of Figures 10-5 and 10-13 discloses the fine, detailed design.

Although the neuromuscular system is inherently subject to disturbances of even molecular dimensions, it is remarkably well protected, and can adapt to many environmental conditions. Both the nerve fiber and the contractile molecule are buried deep within tough tissue, well fed by capillaries of the blood and lymphatic systems. Response to environmental changes is directive, and remedial action usually is swift and accurate.

However, response to the environment of radiations—both matter waves and electromagnetic—is a matter of increasing concern as our environ-

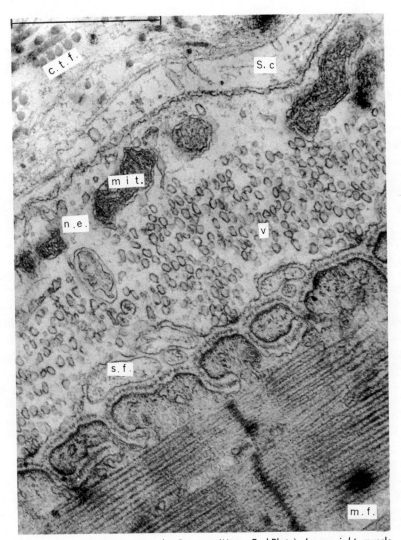

Figure 10-15. The Neuro-Muscular Synapse (Motor End Plate). *Lower right*: muscle myofibrils (mf) bounded at their top edge by a continuous folded membrane. Across the gap (~500Å) is the nerve-cell membrane, touched in places by fingers (sf) from the Schwann cell (Sc). Note the many little (~100Å diameter) vesicles (v). The theory is that these contain acetylcholine which is released during the passage of an impulse; and that in their thermal motion they bounce against the membrane and locally depolarize it, thus to give rise to the micro end-plate potentials which occur even when the nerve is at rest. Also marked: nerve ending (n.e.), mitochondrion (mit.), and connective tissue fibers (c.t.f.). *Scale at top left*: 1 micron. (Courtesy of B. Katz, Department of Biophysics, University College, London, and of *J. Physiol.*)

ment becomes "noisier." In Chapter 2, the effects of shock, blast, sound, and ultrasound were reviewed; and in Chapter 4 the effects of the warming, visible, ultraviolet, and ionizing regions of the electromagnetic spectrum were discussed. In Chapter 7 heat production, and in Chapter 8 heat loss were discussed, as also were changes in our chemical environment (poisons and catalysts—competitors) as they affect the metabolism of the system and its control. Although the details of the complicated processes of control are beyond our means in this book, enough has been introduced to illustrate the mechanisms and the A-B-C's of environmental effects—atomic, biological, and chemical, at least in general terms.

One further point will be made on the effects of ionizing radiations on the physical apparatus of control—of increasing importance, especially to medical people, in this atomic age. Nerve itself is relatively insensitive to X rays (Chapter 9). Muscle shows good resistance too: it takes thousands of rads to cause detectable damage. The neuromuscular junction, however, is much more sensitive. For instance, consider a nerve-muscle system such as the sciatic nerve-gastrocnemius muscle freshly dissected from a frog, mounted in such a fashion that the nerve can be stimulated electrically by short, square pulses of voltage applied by the platinum wire contacts refer to (Figure 10-8). If the stimulus repetition rate is chosen at about 1 pulse per sec, the muscle will respond faithfully. If now the whole is irradiated, the muscle soon stops, although the nerve continues to transmit, and the muscle will respond to a stimulus given directly to it.

Further, the neural network in the brain is now known to be affected by only a few rads; and although this radiation does not affect the motor ability of a man, there is reason to believe that short-circuiting in the network and psychological effects accrue. Since it is not likely to be the nerve cells themselves, it is probably the synapse, or "junction box" which is implicated as radiation-sensitive.

The parallelism is clear. The neuromuscular junction and the synapse are the most sensitive parts of man's physical control system. Both of these junctions involve production of a chemical or chemicals at one spot in the junction, transport across the junction, and utilization of the chemical(s) at the other end of the junction. With the background of knowledge of the pertinent chemical and physical effects of ionizing radiations discussed in the previous Chapter, and that of the physical apparatus of control given in this Chapter, what do you think is likely to be the first molecular process to fail during irradiation of the control apparatus?

PROBLEMS

10-1: If one side of a concentration cell has KCl at 0.002 equivalents per liter, what must be the opposing concentration so that the "membrane" potential reaches 90 millivolts? Assume restricted diffusion.

10-2: Two platinum electrodes placed 3.0 cm apart on a nerve fiber detect the "wave of negativity" of a transmitted impulse 0.37 milliseconds apart. Calculate the speed of transmission in meters/sec, yards/sec, and miles per hour. Compare this with the speed of sound in air (1090 feet/sec); of light through a vacuum (186,000 miles/sec); of a signal along a telephone cable (1000 miles/sec); of the fastest thrown baseball (88 miles/hr); of the fastest sprinter (100 yds/10 sec).

10-3: During the testing of a reflex at the sole of the foot, the signal must travel up the leg to the spinal column and an order be transmitted back before the response can occur. If the distance is 3 ft each way, how long should the interval between stimulus and response be?

10-4: Good rules-of-thumb to remember are: (a) the speed of shortening of a striated muscle can reach a maximum value v_{max} of about ten times its length per second; and (b) it can exert a force which can reach a maximum F_{max} of about 42 lb per sq in. of cross-sectional area of the muscle.

Assuming the model of Figure 10-5, the force-velocity curve of Figure 10-10, and the above data, calculate values of velocity with which three different weight forces can be lifted, at v/v_{max} equal to 0.1, 0.5, and 0.9.

REFERENCES

1. Keynes, R. D., "The Nerve Impulse and the Squid," *Scientific American*, **199,** No. 6, p. 83 (1958).

2. Podolsky, R. D., "The Mechanism of Muscular Contraction," *Amer. J. Medicine,* **30,** 708 (1961).

3. Huxley, H. E., "The Contraction of Muscle," *Scientific Amer.*, **199,** No. 5, p. 66 (1958).

4. Szent-Györgyi, A., "Mechanochemical Contraction in Muscle," *in* "Enzymes: Units of Biological Structure and Function," O. H. Gaebler, Ed., Academic Press, New York, N. Y., 1956.

5. Morales, M. F., *et al.*, "The Mechanism of Muscle Contraction," *Physiol. Rev.*, **35,** 475 (1955).

6. Hodgkin, A. L. and Keynes, R. D., "Active Transport of Cations in Giant Axons from Sepia and Loligo," *J. Physiol.*, **128,** 28 (1955).

7. Nachmansohn, D., "Chemical Factors Controlling Movements during Nerve Activity, from The Method of Isotopic Tracers Applied to the Study of Active Ion Transport," Pergamon Press, New York, N. Y., 1959.

8. Penfield, W., "The Interpretive Cortex," *Science,* **129,** 1719 (1959).

9. Walter, W. G., "The Living Brain," Penguin Books, Harmondsworth, England, 1961.

10. Shedlovsky, T., Ed., "Electrochemistry in Biology and Medicine," John Wiley & Sons, Inc., New York, N, Y., 1955: review papers by B. K. Bagchi, H. H. Jasper, K. S. Cole, and others.

11. Hodgkin, A. L.; "Ionic Movements and Electrical Activity in Giant Nerve Fibers," *Proc. Roy. Soc.*, B., **148,** 1 (1958); a fine review lecture.

12. Szent-Györgyi, A., "Chemistry of Muscular Contraction," 3rd ed., Academic Press, Inc,, New York, N. Y., 1960.

13. Wilkie, D. R., "Facts and Theories about Muscle," *Prog. in Biophysics and Biophysical Chem.*, **4**, 288 (1954).
14. Hodgkin, A. L., "Ionic Movements and Electrical Activity in Giant Nerve Fibers," *Proc. Roy. Soc., B.*, **148**, 1 (1958).
15. Hill, A. V., "Chemical Change and Mechanical Response in Stimulated Muscle," *Proc. Roy. Soc., B*, 314 (1953).
16. Paton, W. D. M., Ed. of special issue: "Physiology of Voluntary Muscle," *British Med. Bull.*, **12**, 161–236 (1956); see especially the papers by A. V. Hill, A. F. Huxley, D. R. Wilkie, and R. G. Bannister.
17. Bourne, G. H., Ed., "Structure and Function of Muscle," Vol. I, Academic Press Inc., New York, N. Y., 1960; contributions by H. E. Huxley, J. Hanson, and A. Csapo.
18. Nachmansohn, D., "Basic Aspects of Nerve Activity Explained by Biochemical Analysis," *J. Amer. Med. Assoc.*, **179**, 145 (1962).
19. Hodgkin, A. L., and Huxley, A. F., "A Quantitative Description of Membrane Current and its Application to Conduction and Excitation in Nerves," *J. Physiol.*, **117**, 500 (1952).
20. Cole, K. S., and Curtis, H. J., "Electric Impedance of the Squid Giant Axon during Activity," *J. Gen. Physiol.*, **22**, 649 (1939).
21. Suckling, E. E., "Bioelectricity," McGraw-Hill Book Company, Inc., New York, N. Y., 1961.
22. Noble, D., "A Modification of the Hodgkin-Huxley Equations Applicable to Purkinje Fibre Action and Pace-Maker Potentials," *J. Physiol.*, **160**, 317 (1962).
23. Three short papers on contraction of muscle, *Nature*, **167** (1951): by A. V. Hill, p. 377; by A. Szent-Györgyi, p. 380; and by H. H. Weber, p. 381.
24. Stacy, R. W., Williams, D. T., Worden, R. E., and McMorris, R. O., "Essentials of Biological and Medical Physics," McGraw-Hill Book Company, Inc., New York, N. Y., 1955: Chapters 32 to 34.
25. Brazier, M. A. B., "The Analysis of Brain Waves," *Scientific American*, **206**, 142 (1962).

CHAPTER 11

The Language and Concepts of Control

The natural systems are of enormous complexity, and it is clearly necessary to subdivide the problem . . . .

The first part of the problem [is] the structure and functioning of such elementary units individually. The second part of the problem consists of understanding how these elements are organized into a whole, and how the functioning of the whole is expressed in terms of these elements . . . .

The number of cells in the human body is somewhere in the general order of 10^{15} or 10^{16}. The number of neurons in the central nervous system is somewhere in the order of 10^{10} . . . . All artificial automata ["thinking machines"] made by man have numbers of parts which, by any comparably schematic count, are of the order of 10^3 to 10^6 . . . . The prototypes for these [living] systems are the modern computing machines . . . .

[However], whereas I can conceive of a machine which could reproduce itself, I cannot imagine a machine which could create itself! (John von Neumann, Vanuxem Lectures, Princeton, 1952.)

INTRODUCTION

In the very first chapter of this book we introduced rather superficially the concept of man as an integrated system operating in continuous exchange with his environment. During the next few chapters we dwelt on the forces, momenta, and energy which comprise this exchange, and showed what these are, their properties, and their effects on the living system. Through the middle of the book we dwelt on the workings of individual parts of the human being, discussions proceeding from first principles of physics and physical chemistry. Then, to introduce control biophysics, in Chapter 10 we considered some of the physical aspects of control of the system. All this was in mechanistic terms, based on the movements of atoms and molecules.

In Chapter 8 we saw what happens if the speeds of biological processes are not regulated and intermeshed. To illustrate the molecular mechanics of control, we chose nerve and muscle, and discussed how commands are passed down the nerve, across synapses, and then across the neuromuscular junction to cause contraction. Probably the stimulation of the endocrine gland system to chemical activity would have served equally well, although to use that example would have required a rather bold and risky step into biochemistry, which probably has the most prolific scientific literature of our time, whereas there are plenty of problems yet in biophysics which warrant attention.

The principles and the language of the engineering concepts of control are universal, however. They refer equally well to the monitoring of a chemical processing plant, to the guidance of an intercontinental ballistic missile, to the control of a large telephone exchange, or to a human being. There are persons working in the computer technology who now believe that there is a critical complexity to control systems above which they will have enough versatility to be completely self-determining, like man, in many situations: "ultrastability," Ashby calls it. The clever English logician, A. M. Turing, was one of those persons; he predicted, slightly before his death in 1954, that by the year 2000 a computer will be built which will confound its interrogator with its ability at intellectual repartee! Most others are much more conservative. In any case, as von Neumann indicated in the introductory quotation, the Turing computer would need a prodigious 10^9 (one thousand million) parts and cost one or two orders of magnitude more in dollars! With these possibilities, however, it should not be necessary, in view of the lessons of history, to recall that careful definitions of general terms such as "intelligence," "learning," etc., should precede philosophical and scientific discussions of these questions. Here we confine ourselves to subject matter which is *experimentally* testable (at least in principle), and therefore we are able to leave the philosophical discussion of these terms to others.

THE SYSTEMS CONCEPT REDEFINED

Man In His Environment

Life is a continuum of events, with no isolation. A *system* is a collection of things or events contained within some specified boundary. Man is such a system, or more properly a subsystem operating within a larger system—the environment. *To* man there are inputs, and *from* man there are outputs. Inputs are information, or noise, and energy. Outputs are information, work, or losses. (One would hope that only **some** of his output is noise.)

Figure 11-1 illustrates this concept. Note the directions indicated by the arrows. For example, information enters through the sensory organs which are responsive to chemical, electrical, gravitational, electromagnetic, and mechanical stimuli. It enters raw, essentially unsorted, except for the fact that only part of the information available from the environment is able to enter through the five senses. For example only those electromagnetic radiations of wave length 4000 to 7000 Å are recorded through the eyes, and some in the infrared region is detected by mechanoreceptors just below the surface of the skin. Otherwise the whole spectrum of electromagnetic radiations in the environment so far as we known goes undetected.*

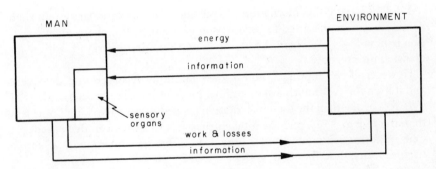

Figure 11-1. The Human Being as a "Black Box" in His Environment.

Some of the inputs are ordered, sorted, and organized (lectures to students presumably are). This is true *information*. Some inputs are not ordered, nor are they even useful; this is noninformation, or *noise*.

Work and losses, as well as thermodynamic and practical efficiencies, were discussed in Chapter 7, and the reader should recall again the principles of available and unavailable energy, and of efficient and nonefficient operation of machines.

---

*This raises the irrelevant but interesting question of how the still-controversial extrasensory perception (ESP) might occur, with its manifestations of telepathy, clairvoyance, etc. Supposing we accept the psychological evidence in favor of ESP, the job in biophysics is to try to understand how ESP *could* occur. Speculations can take three directions. Thus information reaches our central nervous system directly (i.e., not via the senses) as: (a) electromagnetic radiations of wave lengths out of the range of the senses; (b) matter waves of wave lengths out of the range of the senses; or (c) some new, yet undiscovered radiation.

Information and Entropy

The broad use of the term "entropy" as a quantitative measure of the amount of disorder in a system, or subsystem, was introduced in Chapter 7. Now we carry the concept one step further. For communication, which requires a description of a system in words or codings, the simpler the system the simpler the information needed to describe it. Four sticks standing fixed in a row (||||) is a very simple system, A, easily described; but the same four sticks comprise an infinitely complex system, B, if the four sticks are thrown off a roof-top and each stick allowed to assume any position and degree of rotation during fall. The information required to describe A unambiguously is small; likewise its entropy or disorder is low. By contrast the information required to describe B unambiguously is relatively very large; its entropy or disorder is high.

Therefore, a *measure of the quantity of information* needed to describe something *is the entropy* of the system being described.

It follows that if the information, S, put into a computational system such as man becomes distorted for one reason or another, the changed information is now $S + \Delta S$, where ΔS is the distortion. It is always positive, increasing the entropy.

However, if two inputs, S_1 and S_2, are faithfully recorded and analyzed, and if from the two informations a third piece of information, a synthesis of the two, occurs, then the total information needed to describe S_1 and S_2 is less than the sum $S_1 + S_2$, and the total entropy has thereby been decreased.... One's information is now better organized. One remembers now a simple *principle* which describes both systems 1 and 2.

Measurement

Measurement implies a reference. What is measured is a difference between two quantities, one of which is taken as the reference, against which many similar quantities are measured. The fact that no two physical beings are in all respects identical implies variation. Variation in turn introduces uncertainty.

There is an inherent uncertainty in all measurement, a principle first propounded by Heisenberg. The formal statement of this is known as his "uncertainty principle." It takes various forms, a simple statement of which is the following: To make a physical measurement, energy must be transferred between the object and the measuring device; otherwise there is nothing to detect; this transfer introduces uncertainty, because the object is not now the same as it was before the energy was transferred: the smaller the object the more difficult it is to measure its properties.

However, in the macroscopic physical world, objects are big enough so that this uncertainty is far smaller than are gross errors in measurement, be they random or constant errors. No measurement is likely to be perfect. We are always faced with this probability of error, and of (biological) variation in the thing being measured.

The human machine is subject to error in measurement, just as is any other machine. It is no accident that athletic competitions, especially by professional athletes, are described as "games of inches," the differentiating factor being the ability to estimate distance under great psychological stress.

In summary, it is a **measurement** which is fed back into a computer to guide it in making corrections to its actions. This measurement is of the difference, Δ, between where one is and where one wants to be—that is, of the error. The error is increased by noise.

Noise

The subject of the detection of a signal of information (energy) over background was discussed in Chapter 3 in the discussion of sensitivity of a detector and the Weber-Fechner Law. The principles introduced there apply also to the detection of information to be fed to a computer. If the source provides a strong signal over background, the detector will feed a correspondingly strong signal to the computer. If the background noise is high (i.e., the signal-to-noise ratio is low) the signal sent to the computer may not be intelligible (discernible from the background). Strength of the signal, background noise, and degradation of the information by noise introduced in the detector determine what the computer receives as input.

Unfortunately there usually are many strong signals entering a detector, only some of which are useful. Those which are not useful are also noise, like the background. The machine must be able to classify signals: to accept the information and by-pass the rest. One of the most useful systems yet built to separate information from noise is the EEG analyzer, a machine which scans the information and sorts the rather complex total waves into their three or four main components.

Continuously confusing the control circuits of a human being is an unremitting input of noise—disordered, and perhaps not even useful information. Noise can take several forms. First of all it may be of either external or internal origin. External noise comes in from the environment through the senses. It is probably better to call it incomplete rather than disordered, for there is order and regularity reaching our senses from everywhere about us in nature. The trouble arises because we have only a limited capacity or interest—subject to, or determined by our freely-chosen goals in life. In other words, what is useful, interesting information to one man is noise to another; and for one man, what is noise at 9 P. M. may not be so at 9 A. M. (traffic information, for example). This is unfortunate, but nevertheless true. It is unfortunate because it means that two men with a common interest in

some narrow field may each have rejected as noise some information border-
ing on the subject which would be more pertinent to their discussions than
either realizes. This is one of the reasons for disputes, sometimes very
heated ones, between logicians who are specialized in different fields. Then
of course there are man's errors in logic—and they are a fact too. Over even
an hour's test, the adding machine will demonstrate man's errors in logic
very vividly.

We have seen that there is variation in nature. There is also order. There
is variation in the physical structure of man's sensory organs. Therefore
the nonverbal impressions which two men have of the same object may be
quite different. The verbal impression each would give—thanks to training,
experience, and definition—would, however, be about the same. It is generally accepted that the essentials can be abstracted by one and com-
municated to another by words. The variations can be described also, if
they can be observed. Further, McCulloch and Pitts showed in a famous
deduction that if anything can be described fully in words, the description
can be programmed accurately into a man-made computer, provided the
computer is comprehensive enough. Therefore our own "built-in" computer, as well as the man-made one, should have the physical capability to
receive (as well as give) a complete description. Yet language has a drift in
meaning over a course of time. Does the concept also drift?

Feedback

Control of a system by its computer is accomplished by feeding back into
the controller the result of the measurement of difference or error (Figure
11-2). The computer can then dispatch the corrective order, the order which
when carried out will reduce or eliminate the error. This is accomplished
in mechanical and electrical machines through what is called a *control amplifier*, a device which takes the determined error, amplifies it, and inverts
it as the corrective "order" to the process. In the living thing this is accomplished either by the conditioned reflex of the autonomic nervous system, or the voluntary control by the central nervous system.

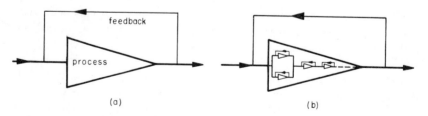

Figure 11-2. The System Diagram, I.   (a) General feedback only; (b) General plus
particular feedbacks.

Since the corrective order must operate in a direction opposite to the measurement of error, the principle is one of *negative* feedback. For instance, if a factory's production occurs at a rate larger than the rate of sale, product soon piles up: the amount of product, measured against some economically sound inventory, increases. The difference, Δ, increases. Fed back into the production line, this information (Δ) is used to cause a decrease in the rate of production, so that the excess inventory will decrease toward zero. Again, in cholesterol synthesis, the rate is controlled by enzyme-catalyzed processes in which there exists inhibition by a reaction product. Thus, as the cholesterol concentration gets larger, more of it absorbs on the enzyme, and the over-all rate of synthesis slows down because of the inhibition. Hence there can be general feedback to control the over-all process, or there can be particular feedbacks to control small parts of it (Figure 11-2 (b)).

As a whole, the human body obtains feedback from the five sensory organs plus a number of other internal detectors such as the organ of balance in the inner ear and the temperature controller at the base of the brain. Man's thermostat, in the hypothalamus at the base of the brain, was recently appreciated for the first time. The trimmer, or fine controller, is the cerebellum.

The human body has the physical properties of a zero-seeking servo-mechanism—a device which sets for itself a goal, attempts to achieve that goal, then measures the error in the achievement before it feeds this information back negatively through a control amplifier so that the error is cancelled. The system diagram in its barest essentials of *general* feedback is given in (a) of Figure 11-2, while (b) illustrates the case of *particular* feedbacks.

The feedback and the amplification of the error by the control amplifier, are both critical if satisfactory control is to be achieved—as we can see from Figure 11-3. The broken line denotes the task and the solid lines the

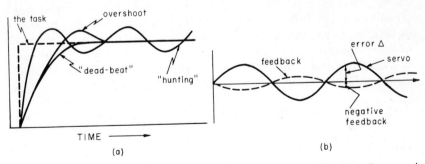

Figure 11-3. The System Diagram, II. (a) Hunting, overshoot, and "dead-beat" approach to the task; (b) Operating process and *negative* feedback.

achievement for an elementary process such as heating a house. More sensitive detectors provide more accurate feedback and reduce the oscillation about the task. The loss of fine control in a man's attempt to walk along a straight line under the effects of drugs, disease, or alcohol is well known.

A recent innovation into the heating systems which the human body has had for thousands of years is the facility for *anticipation*. This takes two physical forms in the human being, only one form in the heating system. The one which is common to both, is the early-warning system: the external thermostat in the heating system, which predicts a change inside as soon as the weather changes; the kinematic (or kinesthetic) sense, for example, in the human which tells him where his hands are even when his eyes are closed. In addition, the human has a memory, which helps his anticipation by extrapolating from the present situation into the future along a path suggested by previous experience. Modern computers have the memory circuits and the extrapolation circuits too.** Whether man will eventually be able to make computers which can abstract and then extrapolate with abstractions, as man can do, remains for the future to answer.

The sensory detectors are so sensitive in the human, and the cerebellum such an effective trimmer on the control apparatus, that man is the ideal example of a "dead-beat servo," with no cycling at all about the task . . . . This is true only as a first approximation, however. Thus the physical trim of a trained athlete or of a practiced surgeon is far more precise than that of his neighbor. Similarly, those who are afflicted with Parkinsonism or alcoholism are less precise in their physical and chemical process control. *Precise control* of the biological chemistry and physics is at the very root of the prevention and cure of disease, and of life itself.

Memory, Concept and Implementation

The mind stores information. Physical machines can be made to do this by (a) magnetic tapes or magnetic cores, (b) on-or-off relays, (c) slow penetration processes in which electric or sonic signals bounce around inside crystals for a time before escaping, and (d) electrochemical devices such as capacitors. In fact the machine can be programmed to collect information while it is operating and use it thereafter, thus closely simulating man's memory. A recent postulate about the physical nature of neural memory apparatus is that the repeated, passing electrical signal distorts the RNA

** Perhaps the earliest popularly recognized and amusing example of machine out-anticipating man came during the counting of the U. S. Presidential election returns in 1948. The computer, UNIVAC, on the job seriously for the first time, started predicting a Truman victory at about 8:15 P.M., much to the derision of the human political pundits. By 11 P.M. the pundits were beginning to waver, remarking that the pollsters *could* possibly be wrong. Meanwhile UNIVAC was pounding out a 99 per cent certainty for Truman. Dewey finally conceded to Truman at 2 A.M!

molecule for a time sufficiently long to give the oddly-shaped protein molecules an opportunity to synthesize. These then slip into the chemistry of the cell and perhaps later affect the rate of a reaction which guides the neural switching pattern which is characteristic of the fact so "memorized." The machine can be taught a rudimentary classification, and can thereafter classify appropriate inputs. That a machine could be made which can take random information and develop a classification, as Farley says,[17] "is not impossible; it is just excruciatingly difficult."

However, the question of whether a machine can be made which will be able to develop a concept or abstract idea is destined to remain unanswered for the foreseeable future, for it is subject to only one experimental test: a machine must be built capable of developing a concept, and then it must be able to tell us about it! As a first step a machine must be developed which can do abstract mathematics. Already the groundwork is being laid. In the meantime, concepts *as such* are probably better analyzed from within the framework of epistemology, in which, like mathematics, logical self-consistency is the final criterion of certainty.

Physically very real, however, is the *implementation* of a concept through the action of physical things. An artisan produces with his hands, in real materials, a structure in conformity with the concept in his mind. Having made one, he can make others. Having been *told* of an object in great enough detail (i.e., having been *given* a concept), he can make the object. Thus the surgeon fashions a heart valve in conformity with a concept in his mind; but he modifies in detail as he goes along if he finds odd shapes or formations which need correction.

Control Biophysics

The discussion in the proceeding sections has defined terms for comparison of the modern computer with man's brain as units of control. Both can accept, store, and redeliver information, and in this sense can learn. Both can do logical arguments, (i.e., decide on the basis of premises), do arithmetic and solve equations. Both can issue commands which result from logical arguments, and can receive feedback which tells whether or not the commands are being successfully carried out.

There are major differences. The brain is usually able to find another route to accomplish a task if the direct route is physically damaged. Generally, malfunction of one component of a machine will stop its operation, although Ashby's machine was said to have sufficient parallel circuitry that he could rip out a wire at random and the machine still function. Machines are generally much more accurate and much faster than humans at computation. Machines have not yet been made which can do abstract mathematics, or do pattern recognition other than rudimentary classification, although the best informed opinion today is that it will be possible, but difficult, to construct a machine to do such work. On the interesting subject of self-control or self-determination, which implies judgment of what is good and bad, and free choice to do either, nothing can be said about what a machine of the future will be able to do. Today's machines are completely deterministic—as are many of man's acts.

The question of whether creativity and the emotional, psychic, and religious experience of man can be contained within the *physical* structure of the human brain is unanswerable from the framework of science, because the extrapolation from experimental test is simply too far to be reliable. This will be especially evident to those doing experimental work even in heavily experimented subject matter: the results are, even there, always full of surprises! To assume an answer to this question, then, would be unscientific, since experimental verification is not yet possible.

A more useful question for control biophysics is: "How far can physical equipment be made to go toward reproducing the functions and behavior of man's brain and mind? How does the brain actually do the job of controlling so finely the human body? The answer seems to lie in models or representations.

This is the interest of biophysics in Samuel's checker-playing machine; Shannon's chess-playing proposal; the U. S. Naval Research Laboratory's self-replicating machine; psychologist Ashby's homeostat, which adapts itself into compatibility with a new environment; Walter's *Machina Speculatrix* and MIT's mechanical hand—robots which have component parts which give them many of the response characteristics of animals; and other machines, some much more complex.

Within the past few years there has been considerable effort expended in making models of the nervous system. The work falls roughly into two forms. In one, man attempts to represent or reproduce the biological phenomena as closely as possible. In the other he explores the behavior of simulators—electronic elements, for example, whose electrical behavior is similar to that of the nervous system. For example, M. L. Babcock, F. Rosenblatt, B. G. Farley and L. D. Harmon have all done intriguing pioneer work. Farley *et al.* have simulated the firing pattern of a two-dimensional array of neurons (Figure 11-4) by programming their TX-2 computer with correlative information on 256 circuits, each of which can do several of the tricks that a single nerve cell can do. An input (stimulus) at some point causes a firing pattern to occur throughout the network; and, if properly displayed on a television screen, this firing pattern can be watched as it progresses. With such an apparatus a study can be made of the characteristics which lead to different firing patterns. There and elsewhere the following have been simulated: the all-or-none firing pattern of the axon, the slow

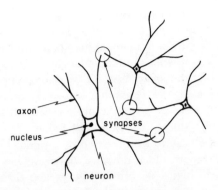

axon

nucleus

synapses

neuron

Figure 11-4. A Neural Network.

chemical step of the crossing of the synapse, and the smaller, graded, attenuating potential induced at the far side of the synapse. Because other properties such as a slow wave of electrical activity on the neuron itself, variable spike amplitude, varying wave form and overshoot of the spike, and shifting baseline potentials are ignored, the simulations are still approximate. Replicated by such simulation have been: (a) intensity of electrical activity as a function of time; (b) burst firing; (c) repetitive firing; (d) accommodation, and change in excitability. Further, the simulated circuits have disclosed certain conditions under which the firing *frequency* of the network will shift. This is a clue from the machine about a phenomenon which has not yet been observed experimentally by neurophysiologists. Thus workers in the field hopefully look forward to advances in man's understanding of his brain through its simulation by machines. The reader is encouraged to study the papers by Bullock,[18] and of Harmon,[19] and to treat himself to the optimism of Reiss,[17] and the careful analysis of Farley,[17] thereby to prepare for himself a proper perspective of this exciting new aspect of biophysics.

We turn now to an outline of the principles upon which are based the two great classes of computers, digital and analog.

ANALOGIES

The Digital Nature of Nervous Propagation

The electrochemical burst arising at the point of stimulation and moving rapidly along the nerve, and called the impulse, was discussed in Chapter 10. To a first approximation, the nerve is either stimulated into action or it is not. This is the "all-or-none" property. The stimulation must be above some critical minimum strength,*** otherwise the nerve will not fire. That the threshold is not really as critical as is often claimed, and that the spike, or "wave of negativity," modifies its shape under certain circumstances, are useful facts to know and are thought by some physiologists to be more important that the spike itself. The main point for the moment, however, is that the passage of a stimulus is a binary process, to a first approximation always the same. Only the pulse-repetition frequency (pulses per second) can change; this is frequency modulation.

For example, in the case of transmission of a signal from the pressure-sensing device which reports blood pressure, the nerve encodes the information as a frequency: the higher the pressure the greater the number of pulses per second (e.g., 125 pulses per sec for high pressure, 70 for low). There is an inherent accuracy in the counting, or digital, method of transmitting information—more so than in the decimal-expansion method. The accuracy comes from repetition, or redundancy.

The Digital Computer

Information can be fed into a machine in either of two ways: intermittently or continuously. If done intermittently, it takes the form of pulses of energy. The *number* of pulses then becomes the important thing, for in the number is contained the information in question. Thus five pulses means one thing, three another, and so on. (The Morse code was an early example of this idea.) Since number is important, counting and recording of number are necessary. Therefore, the performing of operations on the information becomes simply a matter of arithmetic, nothing more. Since it is numbers, or digits with which the arithmetic is done, a machine which processes information in the form of numbers is known as a *digital computer*. An adding machine is a primitive example; IBM's "650" has intermediate complexity; and IBM's 7090 (see Figure 11-5) is a 20,000-component, complicated example. It has 32,000 words of high-speed memory and can add two 10-digit decimal numbers in 4.5 microseconds—facts to be compared with 2000 words for the 650 and an addition time of 800 microseconds.

In computation with digits we normally use the decimal system, with units of ten. This system was chosen quite arbitrarily by our ancestors during a process of arithmetical evolution in which they counted in twos (hands), tens (fingers), twenties (fingers and toes), etc. Other systems could have been chosen equally well. For instance the binary system (units of two), it is now realized, more closely represents many naturally occurring phenomena than does the decimal system. Thus only two digits are needed

---

*** That is, a minimum *energy* must pass through the nerve membrane—most simply stated: a current, at some voltage, for some length of time (amps × volts × sec = joules).

to describe the switch on your reading lamp because there are only two positions, "off" and "on." The former is recorded by the digit zero (0) and the latter by the digit one (1).

Figure 11-5. IBM's 7090 Digital Computer—A typical installation. A big, fast, transistorized machine, it can be used to simulate neural networks. To the right of the operator's console are the card reader and printer; to the far left are the magnetic tape units. (Courtesy of International Business Machines, Inc.).

At the same time, the binary system of two digits can nicely represent information which is transmitted as pulses, because the information-carrying equipment *either is or is not* delivering a pulse of energy at any particular instant. If it is, it is described by the digit 1; if it is not, by 0. Remember now that information is carried along the nerve in the form of electrochemical explosions. The nerve is either firing (1) or it isn't (0). Therefore, the all-or-none law is basically a physical manifestation of the binary number system.

In summary, digital computers built of mechanical or electric binary elements (e.g., relays) not only compute, but also provide a prototype or model for the study of nerve transmission and neural switching.

The Analog Computer

This second general class of computational machines is built around the fact that useful electrical or mechanical analogies can often be made of physical phenomena, analogies which can be used to enable a continuously varying measurement to be recorded, amplified, analyzed or operated upon, and the results used as an immediate control on the process. Analogies can be very simple. A small-scale drawing can be used in the solution of a geometrical problem of finding the height of a tree from the length of its shadow. The sliderule is an analogue of logarithm tables. The addition of two continuously varying numbers can be done by superposing two electrical currents, each in a separate circuit and proportional to one of the numbers, and measuring the total current through a common part of the circuit.

This principle has been built into *analog computers*. Much of the analog computer is electrical, but mechanical wheels, gears, cams, and levers, and magnetic and electromagnetic devices are used wherever they can provide a closer analogue to the real process being represented. Such computers are ideal instruments for solving simultaneous and differential equations, as will be shown in an example in a later section.

Many continuously varying systems are suited to analogies of this sort. Generally speaking there are continuous processes in the living thing, the most easily recognizable ones being at the molecular level, continuous expression of which was detailed in Chapter 8. The general control of the system is a result of control of each process at the molecular level. Thus the speeds of the parts control the general health of the whole, and the general health of the whole in turn adds the fine adjustment to the speeds of the parts.

However, on a larger scale analog control is not so easy to recognize, partly because the physiological basis for digital control by the pulsating nervous system is easier to study experimentally than the continuous variation which are superimposed on the pulses; and partly because this language of control has not yet been successfully used to describe chemical regulatory systems such as the endocrine glands.[†] One can find many examples of analogies used as *parts* of a controlling system in the living thing, but one is hard put to it to describe clearly at this time a full analog computer which is in *complete* control of part of the living system. Many neurophysiologists now feel that the digital computation may be only a small part of the complete story of control, even in the central nervous system.

New Dimensions

In summary, then, the human being, and indeed every living organism, has control operations which might be described in the same terms used to describe digital and analog computers. How fruitful this description will

---

[†] See Schueler's recent book[22] for examples of pharmacological control.

be in man's understanding of his control biophysics is hard to predict; but today it is an exciting avenue by which people are approaching the subject.

Quantitative description of these ideas is developing rapidly, as an integral part of missile and space technology, in which man has control of the characteristics of the components, through design. The neuronal circuit, with switches (synapses) (Figure 11-4), is about a billion times smaller than the vacuum tube circuit, and perhaps about a million times smaller than the transistor circuit, and a thousand times smaller than thin-film, solid-state circuits now in the research stage. The neuron operates on the movements of ions rather than electrons, and much has yet to be learned about its operation. Further, the number of "components" in the brain is about a million times the number in the largest of today's computers. Therefore it is certain that **quantitative** description of the control circuitry of the central nervous system is a long way off!

Inherent in all these systems is an error, or noise, or background, above which the information, the signal, must be distinguished. It is easy to build an analog computer with a precision of about 1/1000; harder to build one with 1/10,000: and impossible to build one with 1/100,000 or less because machining of parts and electrical measurements cannot be made with greater precision. By contrast, simply increasing the number of components can increase the precision of the digital machine to 1/10,000,000,000, if it is desirable and practicable.

Since the central nervous system operates with about 10,000,000,000 components, or neurons, and since it has both digital and analog facility, the problem of understanding this system is obviously not an easy one. Although the *normal* operation of this system is wondrous enough, errors in "switching" can give rise to a whole host of disorders—problems not only for the neurologist but also some that are likely to keep the psychologist and psychiatrist in business for a long time to come.

THE COMPUTER IN BIOLOGICAL RESEARCH

As a tool in medical research, the computer can do many useful things. The day may not be too far off, for instance, when medical clinics will be equipped with general diagnostic machines which, when properly fed with factual information on symptoms, will not only punch out a statement of what the possible diseases are but also arrange them in order (with the most probable one at the top) and state what further examinations can most profitably be done to save the time of the physician and the money of the patient. The machine-processing of records and accounts in clinics and hospitals is closer still. With us now is the use of computational machinery to help the researcher in studies of those biophysical problems in which reasonably precise quantitative measurement is possible. Rapidly maturing as an aid in diagnoses is the determination of rates of specific steps within an over-all process from measurements of those variables which are susceptible to measurement. It will be recalled that in Chapter 8, in the discussion on the steady-state, we emphasized how necessary it is that *all* the small steps of a process should proceed at some well-defined rate if the over-all steady-state is to be maintained. Further, we discussed at length the factors upon which rates depend. The use of radioactive tracers to examine the steady-state was described in Chapter 5.

The topical and interesting, if not classical, study of the biochemical kinetics of iron metabolism in the red blood cells, work which was reported by Huff and Judd[1] in 1956, ties many of these ends together. It is a very instructive work because (a) measurements were made of iron turnover rate by a radioactive tracer technique, using the hard gamma emitter, Fe^{59}; (b) they were analyzed by means of an analog computer programmed to a model based on known and suspected biochemical kinetics of iron; (c) the comparison was made between normal human beings at atmospheric and at reduced pressure; and those with polycythemia vera, aplastic anemia, and other blood diseases; (d) both the factual information and the results of the analyses have unquestioned clinical importance; and (e) the report is written clearly and concisely, and is an excellent source of the detail which cannot be given here.

Kinetics of Iron Metabolism

The study by Huff and Judd was on the kinetics (rates and mechanism) of iron in human blood plasma, as followed by measuring turnover rates of Fe^{59}. The iron exchanges with various "pools" (Figure 11-6), which are not precisely specified because they are not precisely known. Two possibilities are shown in the figure; but many other pools of iron-containing pigments, such as peroxidase, catalase, cytochrome, and myoglobin are ignored. Also the iron may exchange with that from the intestine as well as that recirculated from the bile. Therefore this work must not be considered complete.

A microcurie dose of tagged iron was administered intravenously in the chemical form in which it naturally occurs in the blood. From time to time after injection, blood samples were taken and the plasma's radioactivity measured. At the same time the body was surveyed outside with a highly collimated Geiger counter which would pick up the flow pattern by detecting Fe^{59}'s hard gamma rays.

For the first few hours the loss follows the "natural" law that the rate is proportional to the amount present, or

$$-\frac{da}{dt} = ka$$

where a is activity in per cent of initial value, and k the specific rate of loss or iron, in hours^{-1}. Values of k for different subjects are given in Table 11-1.

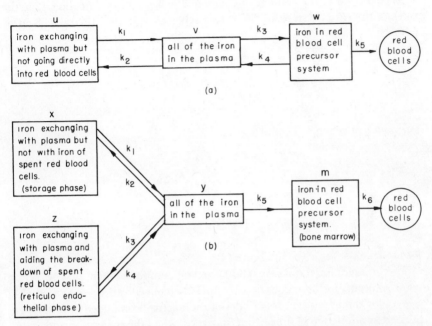

Figure 11-6. Schematic Flow Sheet for Production of Red Blood Cells, Showing Two Models or Theories, (a) and (b), of the Metabolism of Iron. The k's are specific rate constants, assumed to be for first-order reactions.

If this law were obeyed rigorously, the story would now be complete. However, this law is seen to be badly broken if measurements are continued for a few days instead of a few hours: the rate constant diminishes as the

TABLE 11-1. Values of the Turnover Rate Constant* for Iron in Blood Plasma.

Subjects	$k\,(hr^{-1})$
Normal subjects	0.18 to 0.21
Polycythemia vera	0.9 to 1.1 (very fast turnover)
Aplastic anemia	~0.05 (very slow turnover)
Normal subjects taken to 15,000 ft above sea level	0.3 to 0.4
Normal subjects living at 15,000 ft above sea level	0.25 to 0.30

*For the first few hours only.

fraction of injected Fe^{59} diminishes in the plasma. The analysis was intended to suggest why.

Recollection of the content of Chapter 8 will permit verification that the rates of the various steps in these two schemes (Figure 11-6) are given as follows:

$$du/dt = -k_1u + k_2v$$
$$dv/dt = +k_1u - (k_2 + k_3)v + k_4w$$
$$dw/dt = +k_3v - (k_4 + k_5)w$$

for model, or scheme (a), and

$$dx/dt = -k_1x + k_2y$$
$$dy/dt = +k_1x - (k_2 + k_3 + k_5)y + k_4z$$
$$dz/dt = +k_3y - k_4z$$
$$dm/dt = +k_5y - k_6m$$

for model, or scheme (b) in Figure 11-6.

The problem for the REAC C-302 analog computer, then, was to find a set of solutions to these equations so that the concentrations u, v, w, and x, y, z, and m (all in per cent remainder of radioactive iron added) could be expressed as a function of time, from time zero, when the tracer was added, out to about ten days, the last of the measurements. More specifically stated, the problem was: For what values of the rate constants, k, would the concentrations v and y, for example, have values which corresponded most closely with the concentrations measured by sampling? If the k's could be so found, then some knowledge would exist about the relative rates of the various metabolic processes into which this added iron enters from the plasma.

We shall not discuss how the computer was programmed, for this is involved and would serve no useful purpose here. Suffice it to say that the values of k could be adjusted as voltages on control potentiometers, much like the volume control on a radio. They could be adjusted and readjusted until the best fit of the experimental data was obtained. Some final, best-fit values are given in Table 11-2, from which it can be seen that the rates of the processes defined by Figure 11-6 do indeed change markedly from normal to diseased patients. Note, for instance that the slow step in the aplastic anemia case is the synthesis of bone marrow (k_5), while this is just the process that runs amok in polycythemia vera.

This is only a first approach to this problem, and is described here primarily to illustrate the method, and the power, of machine-aided analysis. As the authors state, in future runs certain other experimentally measurable

TABLE 11-2. Table of Rate Constants and Steady-State Concentrations Evaluated by Analog Computer and Giving Best Fit to Experimental Results.

	Normal Humans	Polycythemia Vera	Aplastic Anemia
k_1	12	34	1.2
k_2	80	495	150
k_3	200	960	120
k_4	62	280	108
k_5	395	2000	50
k_6	40	44	40
x	29.5	27.5	1480
y	4.42	1.89	11.1
z	14.3	6.5	12.4
m	43.7	85.9	13.8

quantities will be fed into the analysis: red cell turnover rate, iron turnover in the percursor step, the side reactions in the reticulo-endothelial phase and in the iron pigments, for example, plus better pre-experimental clinical data.

REFERENCES

1. Huff, R. L. and Judd, O. J., "Kinetics of Iron Metabolism," *Adv. in Biol. and Med. Phys.*, **4**, 223 (1956).
2. von Neumann, J., "The General and Logical Theory of Automata," in "The World of Mathematics," J. R. Newman, Ed., Simon & Schuster, Inc., New York, N. Y., 1956, p. 2070.
3. Hutley, A. M., "The Engineering Approach to the Problem of Neural Organization," *Prog. in Biophysics and Biophysical Chem.*, **11**, 26 (1961).
4. Walter, W. G., "The Living Brain," Penguin Books, Ltd., Harmondsworth, England, 1961.
5. Ashby, R., "Design for a Brain," Chapman and Hall, Ltd., London, 1952.
6. Rothstein, J., "Communication, Organization and Science," The Falcon's Wing Press, Indian Hills, Colorado, 1958.
7. Stacy, R. W., "Biological and Medical Electronics," McGraw-Hill Book Co., Inc., New York, N. Y., 1960.
8. Abrams, Sir Adolphe, "The Human Machine," Penguin Books Inc., Baltimore, Md., 1958.
9. "The Language and Symbology of Digital Computer Systems," R.C.A. Institutes, Princeton, N. J., 1961.
10. Wiener, N., "Cybernetics," John Wiley & Sons, Inc., New York, N. Y., rev. edn., 1961.
11. Cherry, C., "On Human Communication," John Wiley & Sons, Inc., New York, N. Y., 1957.

12. von Neumann, J., "The Computer and the Brain," Yale University Press, New Haven, Conn., 1958.
13. Adrian, E. D., Bremer, F., and Jasper, H. H., Eds., "Brain Mechanisms and Consciousness," Blackwell Scientific Publications, Oxford, 1954.
14. Shannon, C. E., "Mathematical Theory of Communication," University of Illinois Press, Urbana, Ill., 1949.
15. Thomson, Sir G., "The Two Aspects of Science," *Science*, **132,** 996 (1960).
16. Teilhard de Chardin, P., "The Phenomenon of Man," Harper & Bros., London, 1955.
17. Barnard, G. A., Chairman, "Proc. 1962 Spring Joint Computer Conference," The National Press, Palo Alto, California, 1962: see papers by Ernst, Reiss, Farley, Harmon and Tiffany.
18. Bullock, T. H., "Neuron Doctrine and Electrophysiology," *Science*, **129,** 997 (1959).
19. Harmon, L. D., "Artificial Neuron," *Science*, **129,** 962 (1959); see ref. 17 for summary of more recent work.
20. Rosenblatt, F., "Perceptron Simulation Elements," *Proc. Institute of Radio Engineers*, **48,** 301 (1960).
21. Minsky, M., "Steps toward Artificial Intelligence," *Proc. IRE*, **49,** 8 (1961); see also his bibliography on artificial intelligence, *IRE Trans. on Human Factors in Electronics*, March 1961.
21. Davis, M., "Computability and Unsolvability," McGraw-Hill Book Co., Inc., New York, N. Y., 1958 (interpreting Godel's incompleteness theorem as applied to computers).
22. Scheuler, F. W., "Chemobiodynamics and Drug Design," McGraw-Hill Book Co., Inc., New York, N. Y., 1961.
23. Donaldson, P. E. K., "Electronic Apparatus for Biological Research," Butterworth's Scientific Publications, Ltd., London, 1958.
24. *Proceedings of the Institute of Radio Engineers*, **50,** Issue No. 5, May, 1962: a review of the progress of the last 50 years, and prognostications for the next—with special emphasis on informational science and control. Many contributors.

Epilogue—A Perspective

It is useful to have a perspective of a subject such as biophysics. In the Introduction we located the subject nestled in among other pure and bio sciences. However, the questions raised about information and control in the last chapter—about man's brain and the computers which he is fashioning—make us wonder where biophysics fits in among those disciplines which are *not* physical sciences. In other words, Where does the biophysics of man fit into the framework of *all* knowledge about man?

F. O. Schmitt has introduced the thought very nicely:*

"Biophysics, like biochemistry, has to reckon with hierarchies of organization and with the properties that are characteristic of systems no less complex than those provided by living organisms at each particular level of organizational complexity: viz., molecular, macromolecular, subcellular, cellular, supercellular, organismic, and superorganismic...theoretical biology must deal not only with the properties of cellular constituents but also with the properties of the organism as a whole."

Interpreting man as an organism, complete with his esthetic, emotional, and religious experiences, and as part of a superorganism complete with social, cultural, and religious activities, we *can* view man's knowledge of himself, his history, and his destiny, in a very broad and intriguing perspective. However, within the framework of the logical disciplines as they now exist, we know: that logic and experiment are the tools of the scientist; that logical *self*-consistency is the final test for philosophers and mathematicians; and that the theologion has logic, the results of natural science, and revelation in his workshop.

Man's intellectual destiny is to know the *truth*—about the Creator, about Man, and about Nature—even though "man's body is but a fleeting thing."** He has the right to know, the ability to find out, and the responsibility to try. Ultimately there is no substitute for the truth in any intellectual disciplines.

Classification of inputs into "information" and "noise" (in the sense in which these terms are used in the last chapter) is man's greatest obstacle to knowing all about man, for such classification is highly subjective.

---

*Biophysical Science—A Study Program," J. L. Oncley, *et al.*, Eds., John Wiley & Sons, Inc., New York, N.Y., 1959, pp. 5 and 6.
**Ecclesiasticus, 41, 11.

Man's problem is to find the truth, in spite of the noise which plagues him from *without* and *within*. There are many pitfalls. Will he find truth by rejecting *a priori*, or subjectively, part of the input? Or by rejecting logic's prime tenet of the excluded middle, as some now suggest? . . . . I think not.

Tables of Common Logarithms and Exponential Functions

Abbreviated Table of Common Logarithms*

N	log N	N	log N	N	log N	N	log N
10	000	34	532	58	763	82	914
12	079	36	556	60	778	84	924
14	146	38	580	62	792	86	935
16	204	40	602	64	806	88	945
18	255	42	623	66	820	90	954
20	301	44	644	68	832	92	964
22	342	46	663	70	845	94	973
24	380	48	681	72	857	96	982
26	415	50	699	74	869	98	991
28	447	52	716	76	881	100	1000
30	477	54	732	78	892		
32	505	56	748	80	903		

* Examples: $\log 1.6 = 0.204$; $\log 72 = 1.857$; $\log 0.5 = \overline{1}.699$, or $= 9.699-10$.

Abbreviated Table of Exponential Functions

e^{-x}	x	e^x	e^{-x}	x	e^x	e^{-x}	x	e^x
1.000	0	1.000	0.549	0.6	1.822	0.050	3.0	20.1
0.951	0.05	1.051	0.497	0.7	2.014	0.030	3.5	33.1
0.905	0.10	1.105	0.449	0.8	2.226	0.018	4.0	55
0.861	0.15	1.162	0.407	0.9	2.460	0.011	4.5	90
0.819	0.20	1.221	0.368	1.0	2.718	0.0067	5.0	148
0.779	0.25	1.284	0.287	1.25	3.490	0.00055	7.5	1808
0.741	0.30	1.350	0.223	1.50	4.482	0.000045	10	22,026
0.705	0.35	1.419	0.174	1.75	5.755			
0.670	0.40	1.492	0.135	2.00	7.389			
0.638	0.45	1.568	0.106	2.25	9.488			
0.607	0.50	1.649	0.082	2.50	12.182			

List of Symbols

GREEK LETTERS USED AS SYMBOLS

α—alpha—a radiated particle (Ch. 4, 5, 9); degree of ionization (Ch. 8); state of cell division (Ch. 9); membrane penetration rate *in* (Ch. 10).

β—beta—a radiated particle (Ch. 4, 5, and 9); membrane penetration rate *out* (Ch. 10).

γ—gamma—ratio of specific heats measured under constant pressure and constant volume (Ch. 3); radiated electromagnetic radiation (Ch. 4, 5, and 9).

δ—small delta—a small, measureable length (Ch. 1).

Δ—capital delta—"a little bit of" (Δx, Δy, ΔS, ΔH, ΔF, etc.).

ϵ—epsilon—dielectric constant (Ch. 2); incremental energy (Ch. 4).

η—eta—viscosity (Ch. 8); the neutrino (Ch. 5).

η_0—eta subscript zero—viscosity of solvent (Ch. 8).

$[\eta]$—eta in square brackets—intrinsic viscosity (Ch. 8).

θ—small theta—scattering angle (Ch. 4).

K—capital kappa—specific conductivity of a solution (Ch. 8).

λ—small lambda—usually a decay constant (Ch. 5); a wavelength (Ch. 3); jump distance (Ch. 8).

Λ—capital lambda—equivalent conductance (Ch. 8).

Λ_0—equivalent conductance at infinite dilution (Ch. 8); a nuclear particle (Ch. 4).

μ—small mu—mesons (Ch. 4); free energy per mole ("chemical potential") (Ch. 7).

ν—small nu—frequency (Ch. 4).

π—small pi—the constant circumference/diameter of a circle; osmotic pressure (Ch. 2 and Ch. 6); pion (Ch. 4).

ρ—small rho—density (Ch. 2).

$\bar{\rho}$—small rho overscored—ratio of densities of solvent to solute (Ch. 6).

σ—small sigma—standard deviation (Ch. 1); Stefan's constant (Ch. 8); specific radiation sensitivity (Ch. 9).

Σ—capital sigma—a fermion (Ch. 4); a type of bond (Ch. 4); see also below.

τ—small tau—transmission coefficient.

ϕ—small phi—fluidity (Ch. 8); a dependent variable.

ψ—small psi—an independent variable; pressure or amplitude (Ch. 3).

Ψ—capital psi—potential.

ω—small omega—unit of resistance, ohms; angular velocity of centrifuge (Ch. 6).

ξ—small xi—reaction path length (Ch. 7).

Ω—capital omega—the number of ways a system can be arranged (Ch. 7).

MATHEMATICAL SYMBOLS

$\int$—elongated S to represent elongated sum—the sum of an infinite number of infinitely small parts: the integral sign.

∞ —the "infinity" sign.

$\propto$ —the proportionality sign.

$\sqrt{}$—the root sign; if no number appears in the hook, *a square root* sign.

$\sum$—capital sigma—to denote the summation of a finite number of small but finite parts.

∂—rounded "dee"—the partial differential symbol.

$\equiv$ —identically equal to.

$\ddagger$—as superscript—refers to activated complex.

Index